THE AFTERMATH

THE
AFTERMATH

THE LAST DAYS OF THE BABY BOOM AND THE FUTURE OF POWER IN AMERICA

PHILIP BUMP

VIKING

VIKING
An imprint of Penguin Random House LLC
penguinrandomhouse.com

Charts by the author.

LIBRARY OF CONGRESS CATALOGING-IN-PUBLICATION DATA
Names: Bump, Philip, author.
Title: The aftermath : the last days of the baby boom
and the future of power in America / Philip Bump.
Description: New York : Viking, [2023] |
Includes bibliographical references and index.
Identifiers: LCCN 2022029991 | ISBN 9780593489697 (hardcover) |
ISBN 9780593489703 (ebook)
Subjects: LCSH: Baby boom generation—United States. |
Population aging—Political aspects—United States. | United States—
Social conditions—2020– | United States—Economic conditions—2009– |
United States—Politics and government—2021–
Classification: LCC HN59.3 .B86 2023 | DDC 305.20973—dc23/eng/20220923
LC record available at https://lccn.loc.gov/2022029991

Printed in the United States of America
1st Printing

Book design by Daniel Lagin

For Thomas and Henry,

as is everything

Contents

Introduction

There aren't many people left in the United States who experienced a time in which the baby boom had never existed. For most Americans, including members of the baby boom itself, it was just there—the world they entered into, one in which there was this large group of people in the same general age range who were regularly carved out in the public conversation as something to be dealt with, credited, or blamed.

For some small portion of the current population, maybe 2 percent, there's memory of a time before Americans started having more babies than at any point prior. A time when a person could watch the entire country scramble to try to accommodate this sudden massive shift in the population.

For everyone else, the America shaped by the baby boom is simply America, in the same way that a child born today just lives in a world with the internet and with airplanes. It takes a conscious awareness of the baby boom's existence and uniqueness to understand the grip that it held and still holds on our national conversation. And that takes putting it in context—if not overhauling our understanding of the boom more dramatically.

In 1945, the year before the boom began, the population of the United States was about 140 million.[1] Over the next 19 years, 76 million babies were born.[2] If America experienced a proportionately equivalent boom beginning in 2021, it would mean 186 million babies being born between then and 2040—nearly 10 million new kids annually compared to the 3.6 million born in 2020. For every birth recorded that year,[3] add another three babies or so[4] and you get close to the mark.

Quickly, things would start to break. The government projected that there would be about 3.8 million kids in public kindergartens in 2022, with that figure expected to increase slightly by 2026.[5] If we'd had 9.5 million babies born in 2021, though, where would we put them? Who would pay for it? The problems would show well before that, of course, with strains on daycare programs and fierce competition for baby products of all kinds. There would be huge shifts in a number of industries as this massive market blossomed. The country would suddenly become focused on those kids, on meeting their needs year after year as they got old enough for elementary school, high school, driving, jobs, college.

This is exactly what happened with the baby boom. They opened their eyes and everyone around them was working to meet their exceptional needs.

"They are a generational tyranny," Landon Jones wrote in one of the first serious examinations of the baby boom.[6] This wasn't meant accusatorially— at least not entirely. The boom was demanding in the way that an unshoveled driveway is demanding: it's not the snow's fault. Eventually, baby boomers came to recognize their own power, the power the generation was granted by marketers and by dint of sheer volume—volume in numbers, volume at times in decibels. Jones's book is called *Great Expectations*, which he frames as a descriptor of the hopeful investment that the country made in the members of the baby boom. But it has an inverse interpretation, too: the boomers themselves expected a lot.

"A woman born in 1946 once remarked to me that for most of her youth she thought that *all* new generations were afforded such attention," Jones writes. "Only much later did she realize, 'This wasn't the way it always was; we were the ones who were different.'"[7]

Over time, the baby boomers became the norm. Rather than reshaping the country in specific ways, they instead redefined it entirely. Those tropes about midcentury Americana are largely boomer tropes, the rock and roll and the blue jeans and the ads for Barbies and Chevys on TV. These are the Cold War kids who grew up to take over government and business and entertainment. They went from invaders to administrators. And, of course, they had their own kids.

By the turn of the twenty-first century, the baby boom wasn't the dominant force it had been, demographically or culturally. The number of living people born in America during the boom years, 1946 to 1964, was declining. But the number of boomers had been increasing, thanks to immigration— immigration that was rapidly diversifying the population. Meanwhile, many of the boomers' kids were members of a new, huge generation that was seizing attention and resources: the millennials.

Suddenly, members of the baby boom generation see something they've never seen before, a group of people competing with them for power and cultural heft. Not only was the center of gravity shifting, it was shifting to a group that didn't look much like the baby boom, often literally. These young Americans are more diverse, more likely to come from an immigrant family, better educated, less religious, more liberal. America was visibly changing, as it had visibly changed when the boomers were kids. But this time, the changes were away from the boom, not toward it.

About 15 years ago, there began a cascade of events that sharpened this tension. The recession destabilized economic security, shifting upward the age when older Americans expected to be able to retire—just before the first boomers started turning 65. Barack Obama's election sparked both optimism and a furious backlash centered heavily among older Americans. White Christians, for the first time, constituted less than half of the country's population. And then the Census Bureau announced that the same demographic fate awaited Whites overall, sooner rather than later.

All of this fed into an energy that first broke into national politics with the selection of Sarah Palin—that real American, that stalwart conservative— to join John McCain's 2008 Republican ticket for the presidency. It was a dynamic (and a selection) powered by an interlocking conservative media ecosystem that spanned from radio to the web to television. In the first months of the Obama administration, it coalesced into the right-wing Tea Party movement, participants in which were mostly older, mostly White, and worried about things like government spending on noncitizens and the fact that their kids and grandkids had been duped by this Democratic president of dubious origins.

That organization and that energy proved useful to the man who succeeded Obama. As the Republican Party fretted about losing the 2012 election thanks to an increasingly diverse electorate, Donald Trump amplified the themes and furies bouncing around in right-wing media. The emergence of Black Lives Matter and an influx of child migrants at the border increased the salience of issues of race and immigration, to Trump's direct benefit. In 2015, he became the guy who would say what the too-timid establishment wouldn't—and he packaged his pitch with precision: Make America great again. Bring back the America we used to have, the one the boomers grew up with. In 2016, the only age group he won were those aged 50 and up—that is, the baby boomers and those older.[8] Luckily for him, they made up 56 percent of the electorate.

These are, of course, generalizations, the first in a book necessarily rife with them—as well as the evidence that undermines and contradicts them. In a group as populous as the members of the baby boom generation, there arise myriad facets of diversity. The organized backlash against Trump's presidency, for example, was itself centered among older Americans, primarily college-educated women. It was a fight for dominance within the boom itself.

During the past few years, pressure below has also increased. Younger Americans now dominate a cultural conversation that often depends on the sorts of technologies that have emerged only relatively recently. Those technologies, in fact, amplify individual voices in an unprecedented way, so that a smattering of mocking videos targeting older Americans can blossom into a phenomenon. OK, boomer? But they also facilitate shared grievances, like frustrations about homeownership and college debt and the country's boomer-choked leadership. As older Americans were pushing against the changes driven by younger Americans, younger Americans were banding together and pushing back, shouting through newly invented megaphones.

It is the thesis of this book that all of this—the fears of the boom, the downward shift of the population's center of gravity, the political fevers, the frustrations of younger Americans—overlaps and explains many of the country's fissures. A generation used to accruing and defending its power through sheer scale is watching that power crumble. We've seen generational tensions before, as when the boom emerged, but we're now living through something exceptional, a decline not of the Spartan civilization but of the Roman one. We are living through a historic disruption of the American empire.

So the question becomes what we might expect next. Where does this go? To consider this, we'll look at three conduits for power: culture, economics, and politics.

As mentioned, the cultural shift is all but over. The generation that established the primacy of the teenaged consumer is now watching its teenaged kids and grandchildren getting that attention. No one over the age of 30 can recognize Grammy winners and no one under the age of 30 watches the Grammys on television. Heavily centered on youth, American culture tends to preview the country's future, and American culture now largely reflects a younger, more diverse, less conservative country.

How economic power disseminates remains unresolved and depends on a few factors. Some are macabre: how long baby boomers live and how much it costs them to do so affects when and how much they might bequeath to younger generations. Others are practical, like uncertainty about how the housing market might be affected by a steady (and at times sudden) increase in available supply. Then there are economic questions centered on younger Americans: How rapidly is the generation's unusually large student debt resolved—not to mention the student debt held by older Americans? How does the generational shift affect wealth inequality? Perhaps most important, how does a country that's aging quickly fill newly vacant jobs and generate enough tax revenue to ensure that older Americans are cared for? We can't answer all of these questions, but we'll explore what we know and what statistics and indicators are the most important to watch.

Then there's the future of American politics, the transition on which the future of the United States as a cohesive entity depends. Electorally, there are two central questions: to what extent will young Americans retain their sharply leftist politics and to what extent will Black and Hispanic voters stay loyal to the Democratic Party? Each of these is a complex issue that depends on a surprisingly shallow pool of historic data. Of course, the political future will also be guided by the structures and organizations that hold power, including the political parties themselves. It depends on the ability of the voice of the majority to be heard in fair elections and on the minority to understand that losing is only temporary. Whether the country retains social institutions that aren't overtly political and sees neighborhoods in which political and racial diversity thrive will help determine the extent to which the fractious politics of this moment endure.

The target I kept in sight as I sought to answer these questions was the year 2060, the year to which the Census Bureau's estimates of the country's population and demography extends. This is . . . ambitious, as should be readily apparent if you imagine trying to forecast the present back in 1980. So I also stepped back and considered the things we know we don't yet know and that will influence how the nation shifts. Climate change, for example, which will affect the economy in dramatic ways and people's lives in unpredictable ones. There's also the more nuanced question of how stable those demographic projections will be. The bureau's expectation for when Whites will no longer be the majority depends heavily on fixed racial identities that fail to capture how people actually evaluate their own race and the ways in which that understanding can change. I also spend some time considering a more fundamental question for the future of the country: whether there will be a constituted United States in 40 years' time. I try to be optimistic.

Any such optimism is, in part, a function of having spoken with scores of political scientists, researchers, sociologists, economists, journalists, data scientists, political party officials, college professors, doctors, marketers, Americans of every political and generational persuasion, and, for good measure, one guy who runs a cemetery. From these conversations emerged a great deal of pessimism, certainly, and a number of points of caution—but also some useful thinking on how we might avoid paths toward more dire fates. This is the benefit to looking into the future. It is what we make it.

The past is set in stone until, eventually, it crumbles. Perhaps you're left with a Roman Colosseum, a testament to a great civilization that's been cleaned of any lingering bloodstains. Perhaps you're left with two vast and trunkless legs surrounded by open desert and a snippet of pithy cockiness. Which you get depends a little on construction and a lot on who's left to care for it. On the amount of time, energy, and interest those caretakers can or wish to invest in maintaining the monument. How's that for a metaphor?

As we consider the crumbling of the baby boom's influence on the United States, it's fitting to begin where author Landon Jones began: with the birth of the first baby in the first seconds of the boom's first year. Where the boom itself began.

I

THE BOOM

A Baby Tsunami

Had Kathleen Casey Kirschling been born a few seconds earlier, she would never have been a celebrity. She would never have been the subject of multiple magazine articles, been the first name mentioned in an era-defining nonfiction book, or been asked by the United States government to persuade millions of Americans to sign up for essential federal programs. For the first four decades of her life, though, Kirschling was just another member of the generation that America had started to call the baby boom.

The way she tells it, she was 39 when she was discovered. Her father called to let her know that some magazine was trying to get in touch with her and that he'd passed along her number. The magazine kept calling, she says, but she assumed that they were just trying to get her to subscribe. Finally, they wore her down, informing her that she played a prominent role in a new book from their managing editor, Landon Jones. That 1980 book, *Great Expectations*, focused on the members of the baby boom generation and, thanks to that fluke of circumstance at her birth—any one of a thousand things could have caused her to arrive an instant earlier than she did—Kirschling was born just after midnight on January 1, 1946, the year the baby boom began. So Jones bestowed upon her the distinction she's carried since: Kirschling is America's first baby boomer.

Jones and *Money* magazine sent a crew down to interview her and do a photo shoot. From there, she told me when we spoke in 2021, "it snowballed."

She was invited to the Time & Life Building in Manhattan for a fortieth birthday party. She was on *Good Morning America*. She was on the *Today* show with Jane Pauley. It was a dramatic and discombobulating shift for a woman going through a divorce and juggling the demands of both night school and two young daughters. "I wasn't used to the publicity," she told me. "I started breaking out in hives."

But she settled into the role. Jones checked in with her every ten years as she got older. Reporters would call and use her to take the temperature of her generation. The Social Security Administration asked her to enroll in their program in front of news cameras to encourage others of her age to do the same. She got a boat and named it *First Boomer*.

All of this depends on the alignment of a number of small, important factors in those first seconds of 1946. That the clock was accurate, of course, and that the nursing staff had the presence of mind to mark the moment with precision. And assuming that no kid was born a few instants after midnight, beating Kirschling to the mark—which, given the haziness of the recording process, certainly might have happened, particularly in a year when babies were being born every nine seconds. This coronation also depends on our privileging the East Coast; some poor kid born in Sacramento at a micro-second past midnight is excluded simply due to the vagaries of the sun's movement.

And then there's another niggling point: the baby boom didn't actually start on January 1, 1946, according to demographers. Instead, it started in the middle of the year—which makes sense just given logistics. World War II ended in August 1945; GIs would have had to hustle back to the States pretty quickly and defy a few biological barriers to start churning out babies less than four months later. But, then, the genesis and progression of the boom is more complicated than the typical horny-soldier theory of things. The boom lasted until 1964. Upon consideration, that's a long time to be working out frustrations pent up over the course of a four-year war. But someone had to be the first baby boomer, and Jones unilaterally decided it was Kathleen Casey Kirschling. So that's who she became.

To a large degree, the things we think we understand about the baby boom—how it is bounded, what it looks like, the role it plays and has played in shaping the United States—are arbitrary, misguided, or incomplete. The assumptions we make about the generation serve the same role that Kirschling does for its members: encapsulating something big and complex and intricate in a way that makes it tangible, even if only through an approximation.

What we can report about the generation without qualification is that the baby boom was big: eruption of Krakatoa big. Blot out the Sun big. And everything else follows from that.

THE PYTHON SWALLOWS THE PIG

The biggest population shift in the history of the United States had a modest debut. Buried on the opinion page of *The New York Times* on December 14, 1946, came a brief notice. Commuters on the Third Avenue Elevated with sufficiently long journeys would eventually have gotten to page 14 and the headline "More Babies in New York."[1]

"While such statistics must be interpreted with caution as to the future, we may at least take satisfaction for the present in the birth rate in New York State," it began. "Thirty thousand births were recorded in October, or 24.9 per 1,000 population, a rate not equaled in any month since 1918." This, the paper reported, was the seventh successive month in which there had been more births in 1946 than in 1945. And 1945 was already a barn burner, with the number of births nationally in the five years of World War II among the highest in American history.

"This is a cheerful condition," the story concluded, "provided, of course, that these children are well-behaved."

This was not the pattern that had been expected. Instead, demographers anticipated that the number of births (and, therefore, the country's population) would decline. A 1938 report from the National Resources Committee warned that the country was entering a "transition from an era of rapid growth to a period of stationary or decreasing numbers," with a decline in the number of births expected after 1950 unless "present trends in fertility are reversed or unless the population is augmented by heavy immigration."[2] *Life* magazine reported in late 1945 that the United States was following a pattern displayed in Europe prior to the war, with a projected drop in the country's "youth base" of 8 percent from 1940 to 1970 and population growth flattening out.[3] The *Times* itself invited sociologist William Ogburn in 1948 to inform its readers that "the birth rate will decline from the peak of 1946" though it might remain fairly high if "there are several years of prosperity and continued preparation for another war."[4] (Covering his bases, Ogburn noted that the birth rate "fell during the very prosperous Nineteen Twenties.")

An observer in 1946 might have assumed the United States was seeing the *end* of a boom, not the beginning. The country's population expanded by more than 1 percent[5] in 1945 to nearly 140 million, thanks to immigration and relatively modest American fatalities in the war, a 1948 Census Bureau report explained.[6] "But the major part" of the increase, it continued, "was due to the so-called 'baby boom'"—referring to babies born *by* 1945, not those soon to come. The population that year landed 1.5 million people above the highest projection; the number of babies born during the war was by itself 1 million above the highest forecast.

This boom before the boom rippled into the economy. In February 1949, the Census Bureau reported that baby-buggy manufacturers were making 450 percent as much gross income in 1947 as they had in 1939.[7] The country saw an increase from 44 manufacturers in 1939 to 120 in 1947. The Manhattan phone book reflects a similar change. In 1940, it listed 14 baby-related businesses whose names began with the word "baby" or some variation thereof.[8] By 1946, there were more than 40.[9]

The pre-boom also quickly appeared in governance. The Office of Education, then part of the Department of the Interior, warned in 1947 that all of those kids—what the *Times* dubbed "war babies"—would soon strain the schools. The office's commissioner estimated that the country might need as many as 1 million new teachers over the following 10 years and perhaps 350,000 new classrooms.[10]

Those figures must have seemed outlandish. They were not. From 1947 to 1957, the number of teachers in the United States increased from 861,000 to 1.2 million. By 1967, the figure was 1.8 million. Ten years after that, it was 2.2 million.[11] Because, of course, the "baby boom" under discussion in 1947 wasn't anywhere close to the actual boom that occurred.

From 1941 to 1945, the country averaged 2.9 million births a year,[12] up from 2.4 million over the prior decade.[13] From 1946 to 1964—the baby boom—the annual average was just shy of 4 million.[14] The number of kids born during the baby boom was equal to more than half of the entire population of the United States in 1945. For every two Americans alive at the end of World War II, another was born over the next 19 years, and then some.

The pattern that emerged was not unlike a tsunami. After years of slow

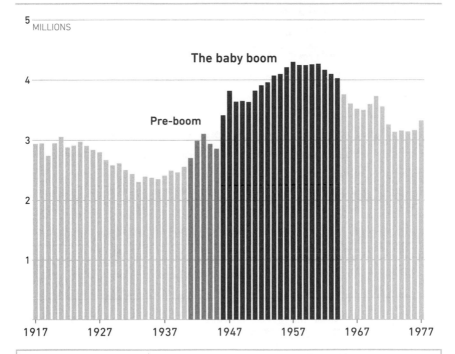

CHART 1
Births per Year in the United States

5 MILLIONS

The baby boom

4

Pre-boom

3

2

1

1917   1927   1937   1947   1957   1967   1977

 **HOW TO READ THIS CHART** Over the course of this book, there will be a number of graphs showing data related to the subject. Some, like the column graph above, will be straightforward. But it's worth a quick delineation of its components anyway. Each column above represents the number of births in a year as measured by the Centers for Disease Control and Prevention. The higher the column, the more births. The World War II period from 1941 to 1945 is indicated in slightly darker gray. The baby boom itself is indicated with black columns.

population growth—the tide pulling out—there was suddenly a slowly rising flood of babies that kept coming and coming and coming. For those at the very front end of the wave, there was no warning. Businesses and organizations focused on children were deluged and then overrun. For some, it was fortuitous. For others, a struggle.

In June 1958, *Life* magazine dedicated its cover to kids, the "built-in recession cure." A multipage spread documented the capitalist bonanza that had followed close on the heels of the boom. A $5 million market for bronzing baby shoes; $50 million for diaper services. In total, children were generating $33 billion in retail sales annually. And starting early. "In its first year as a consumer," the magazine reported, "baby is a potential market for $800 worth of products"—more than $7,300 in today's dollars.[15]

Places that earned money from kids were booming. Places where kids *cost* money were not. Schools, Landon Jones reported in *Great Expectations,* became "the first of our institutions to feel the strains brought by the baby boom."

"In 1952, some 50,000 new classrooms were built, but they were hardly enough," Jones wrote. "That next fall, some 2 million more students headed for school. California was opening one school a week in the fifties, and Los Angeles was spending $1 million a week on new schools by the mid-sixties, opening 62 elementary schools, 26 junior highs, and 10 senior highs in less than a decade."[16] A 1972 report by the Los Angeles Unified School District indicates that, during the years of the baby boom, the district opened an average of one elementary, middle, or high school a month.[17]

This gives some sense of the sudden scramble the boom prompted. The analogy Jones and others have used for its impact on the country is that of a python swallowing a pig. It's not an appealing analogy, but it is an apt one: America unhinged its jaw, for better and worse, and the pig began to move through the system.

BOOMERS TAKE OVER

By 1960, the bulge had entered its teen years.

At the time, the idea of the teenager as a possessor of a unique consumer status was novel, a creature that *The New Yorker* in 1958 described as having "been on the scene for only about fifteen years."[18] The occasion the magazine had for discussing the group was a profile of Eugene Gilbert, a former teenager who'd come to understand that the independent sensibilities and well-stocked pockets of his peers provided a unique business opportunity. At 19, Gilbert created a marketing firm that eventually hired hundreds of part-time employees selected from the teenaged ranks, each of whom was tasked with quizzing his or her peers about whether they might "have any influence on your friends' purchase of a particular brand of gasoline" (for the Esso corporation) or if they knew that the Coast Guard Academy was located "across the street from the Connecticut College for Women" (for the academy as it struggled to boost enrollment).

Gilbert was ahead of the curve in understanding that there was a unique market emerging. He tracked the group's disposable income, measuring an average allowance in 1944 of about $2.50 that, by 1958, had swelled to $10 a week—more than $90 in current dollars. This was money that was almost entirely unobligated. Adults made more each week, but they had bills and mortgages. Teenagers had only themselves and, in Gilbert's phrasing, had "never known a non-prosperous world."

"These figures indicate why businessmen find the teenage market so fascinating," *The New Yorker*'s Dwight Macdonald wrote, adding a bit later that "merchants eye teenagers the way stockmen eye cattle, thinking in terms of how much the creatures will cut up for."

In fact, Gilbert told his clients, teenagers were not only spending their own money, they were spending their parents'. "An advertiser who touches a responsive chord in youth can generally count on the parent to finally succumb," he wrote. A survey he conducted for a newspaper industry group found that 80 percent of young people believed that they had "all or most of the say" in where their parents bought their clothes. A third believed they'd been the deciding factor in identifying their family's vacation plans.

More broadly, "the teenager is important in the marketplace as an innovator and style-setter for older people," Macdonald wrote, pointing to the American "cult of youth"—like that idolization of baseball players that remains so common—as a reason why. It's this insight, perhaps more than any other, that resonates. This was 1958, when the number of teenagers was starting to spike (thanks to the pre-boom boom) but before the tsunami had arrived.

Here, too, is another important overlap. In 1946, the first year of the boom, an estimated 8,000 households in the United States had television sets, according to Census Bureau data.[19] By 1964, 51.6 million did—92 percent of the households in the country. Not only was there a massive emerging market with money to spend, there was a new way to reach it.

Ann Larabee is a Michigan State University professor with an unusual combination of expertises. When we spoke in 2021, she was both co-editor of the *Journal for the Study of Radicalism*, a scholarly publication analyzing radical social movements, and the editor of *The Journal of Popular Culture*, the

CHART 2
The Number of Teenagers in the United States Each Year

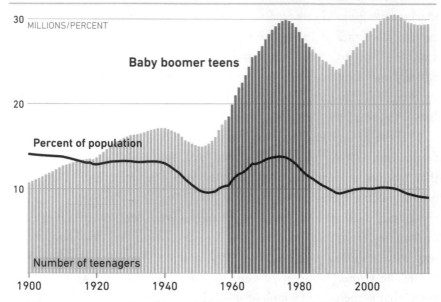

HOW TO READ THIS CHART In this graph, we've overlaid two sets of data. The columns represent the number of teenagers in the population in millions, using Census Bureau data. The line is the percentage of teenagers in the population overall.

Two things stand out. The first is that the absolute number of teenagers at the boomer height was nearly the same as seen in the early 2000s, despite the U.S. population being far larger in the later period. That overall larger population is in part a function of Americans living longer, which is why the density of teenagers—the percentage of the population—is so much lower in the 2000s. It's also why the density of teenagers prior to 1940 was about the same as at the boomer peak: the country was less populous but much younger.

official publication of the Popular Culture Association. That latter organization is centered on "honoring the experience of the everyday," Larabee explained, citing the group's founder.

The everyday life of many boomers included not a little bit of television. A 1977 National Science Foundation study cited research indicating that the average high school graduate at that time—the tail end of the boom—would have "spent some 22,000 hours in front of the set and may have been exposed to as many as 350,000 commercial messages."[20]

"They have spending power, they're getting allowances," Larabee said when we spoke. "So the entertainment industry and other culture producers start to think of youth as this kind of marketing group. They're interested in what young people think about and what attracts them.

"As they become teenagers," she added, the boomers understood "that they have a certain amount of cultural power, that they can influence culture. And that becomes more pronounced as they reach adulthood."

The influence barely needs articulation. Music, clothing, art: everything shifted as the boom arrived and then aged. To honor the boom's fortieth anniversary, the *Wisconsin State Journal* in 1986 documented 40 things associated with the boom, from plastic to designer jeans to marijuana to highways.[21] Thirty years after the 1957 peak in births, a new television show called *Thirtysomething* debuted. That's dominance.

The warping influence of the baby boom was so strong that it changed the meaning of age itself—in a sense. In Macdonald's 1958 *New Yorker* article, he focused heavily on the magazine *Seventeen.* Despite its name, he wrote, the periodical was focused on what "concerns, excites, annoys, pleases and perplexes the girl between thirteen and nineteen," a group that included the front end of the boom. By the late 1970s, Landon Jones reported, the magazine's motto had changed: "Today, she's really 18–34."

What being 17 meant depended on where the market for being 17 was. The pig was moving on and the magazine was moving along with it and its money.

THERE IS NO GENERATION BUT
THE BOOMER GENERATION

One refreshing aspect to the baby boom generation is the solidity of the whole thing. The generation is definable, its members obvious. Born between 1946 and 1964 and you're in. Pedants will dispute the inclusion of people born early in 1946 or late in 1964, given the Census Bureau's boundaries, but this is what pedants do and we've all learned to tune them out by now.

For everyone else, things are murky. You might have noticed that people born in 1980, for example, are often unclear on whether that slots them into Generation X, the first generation after the baby boom, or if they are instead millennials. Those born in the late 1990s have similar uncertainty: What is their generation? What do we call it? What's the boundary?

The answer is an unsatisfying one: the lines blur because most generational identities and boundaries are contrived. In part because of the cultural weight granted to the baby boom generation, other groups of other ages—what demographers refer to as cohorts—seek out a similar overarching generational identifier. Marketers, eager to promote that shared identity, stoke the urge. Those cohorts, though, lack an obvious demographic fingerprint like annual birth totals that allow the definition of boundaries. "Unlike the baby boom generation," the Census Bureau's chief demographer told me in 2015, "the birth years and characteristics for other generations are not as distinguishable and there are varying definitions used by the public."[22] It's like the world before we standardized clocks: everyone's sense of what constitutes noon is generally aligned but there may be some significant variations depending on whom you're talking to.

However muddy the boundaries over time, there's a consistent pattern that plays out every 10 years or so, one that admittedly may have more to do with individual aging than cultural disruptions. The people who were ignorable teenagers a few years ago become car buyers and opinion havers, prompting a brief branding tumult. There's an increasing self-awareness to it, as *USA Today* noted in 2012: whoever's lucky enough to name the next generation "could walk off with fame, fortune—and way cool bragging rights."[23]

Like Douglas Coupland. Coupland's had a remarkable career even independent of his first novel, but it's clear that it will be that book—*Generation X: Tales for an Accelerated Culture*—that leads his obituaries. Through some ineluctable process, Coupland's description of the generation that followed the boom caught on. He didn't set out to describe it demographically or to identify the generation specifically through his anonymized descriptor. It just . . . fit. His novel captured a sense of rootless resentment that the nondescript "X" embodied. So it stuck.

Well, eventually. The book came out in 1991, nearly thirty years after the baby boom ended, but it didn't affirm the new descriptor immediately. In 1992, writing for *The Atlantic,* the demographers Neil Howe and William Strauss included Coupland's name among a number of other options for the generation. There was "baby busters," which carries some grim undertones. Someone else had offered the cerealesque "posties," a reference to the generation following the boom. Their own offering, cemented in their book *Generations,* which had been published a few months earlier, was "thirteeners," because the generation was the country's thirteenth (by their count) and because the generation, like the number 13, was "a gauntlet, an obstacle to be overcome."[24] This didn't catch on, but Strauss and Howe would later end up with way cool bragging rights for naming the fourteenth generation: the millennials.

People love these discussions. *The Atlantic* piece was part of a volley of debate in that period about the name for the generation, including entries by *Businessweek* ("Move Over, Boomers") and the *Times* ("The Boomlet Generation"). That latter essay sought to carve out an even younger group from Gen X ("we're not the younger Grunge Kids," its authors moped[25]), which gets to that other feature of these fights, that no one is even sure where the generational lines should be.

So we get little blips, like *60 Minutes* in 2004 identifying the post–Gen-X generation as the "echo boomers," given that its members were mostly boomers' kids.[26] This spanned the period from 1982 to 1995, the television program stated with authority—a period that was also called Gen Y but later subsumed into the millennials. The result is not only a lack of clarity but the presence of the internet's favorite commodity, disagreement.

Most people who care about such things tend to defer to the Pew Research Center generational delineations,[27] in part because Pew is deliberate about where it draws its lines, and in part because these debates tend to approach general agreement over time. Pew's director of social trends research, Kim Parker, explained to me in 2021 that its decisions about where generations began and ended depended to a large extent on cohort analysis, an assessment of the group looking not just at age but shared experiences. There's nuance to those determinations, except, of course, for the boomers. "That," Parker explained, "was a purely demographic phenomenon." Or as Columbia University sociology professor Tom DiPrete put it when we spoke in 2014, "History isn't always so punctuated."[28]

DiPrete sees the wars over generational designations as being "drawn to some extent by the media," a group that "wants definitions, identities." The media also likes the reader interest that accompanies generational debates, so it encourages them with aggrieved essays about generational stereotypes and by presenting new generational theories to their customers. Pew itself held a

CHART 3
The Messy Effort to Catalog Generations

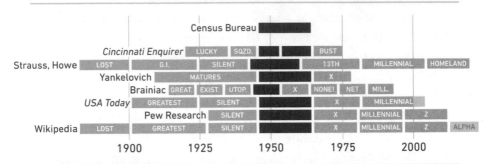

I gathered a series of published generational definitions simply to illustrate the confusion and how it tends to resolve. The period identified as that encompassing the baby boom in each definition is shown in black. Definitions that lack clear boundaries are in gray.

Included are a *Cincinnati Enquirer* column from 1985, in which the period before the boom is broken into first- and last-wave segments called "lucky" and "squeezed." Strauss and Howe's 1992 book, *Generations*, includes a number of familiar terms, though the boundaries vary, including from the Census Bureau's boomer endpoints. A 1997 report from Yankelovich Partners, a firm credited with popularizing "baby boomer" in the late 1960s, broke out three generational groups. In 2007, the Brainiac column in *The Boston Globe*, trying to figure out where Barack Obama landed, invented its own bespoke groupings—a reflection of the appeal and marketing utility of doing so. Wikipedia's 2021 delineations largely mirror both *USA Today*'s from 2012 and Pew Research Center's 2019 boundaries.

contest in 2014 asking for names for the post–millennial generation; the initial suggestions from Pew's staff—the TwoKays, @generation—suggested strongly that they were better at demography and analysis than marketing.[29]

By now, we've settled on the name for the post-post-boomer generation anyway. It's iGen, according to a 2017 book from Jean Twenge.[30] Or it's the homeland generation, as the White House of Barack Obama offered.[31] Or it's the founders, as attempted by MTV.[32] Mostly, we tend to call them Gen Z, following Gen Y, which is what we used to call millennials, who followed Gen X, who used to be called the busters. The important point is that almost everyone has a generation that they can wear around like a comfortable jacket.

Or, a bit more aptly, like the fine-if-surprisingly-translucent garments created for an emperor. As DiPrete argued, these identifiers tend to be age-related branding exercises, at a minimum an easier way of referring to groups as they age than saying "people who were 20 in 2010" and, more typically, as a way of conveying a neat package of stereotypes about someone.

Barbara Kahn, a professor of marketing at Wharton, described the mechanics of generational identity very much in those terms when we spoke in 2021. What's more, she pointed out how adopting these descriptors might reinforce those stereotypes.

"It's going to be a little bit iterative, right?" she said. "If I call you Generation X and say you do these kinds of things, then you'll start to do those things more. So to the degree that anything's labeled, it may start to generate groupthink. And if you believe that there's something to what I'm saying and a lot of the advertising and marketing tends to go in that direction and then people respond to that—you can see how it would kind of be a little bit of cause and effect."

Think of it another way: generations are horoscopes. Based on when someone was born, we derive and apply a broad range of generalizations, both facetiously and earnestly. You know the stereotypes that accompany someone who's in Generation X. You've probably subconsciously attributed some behavior or comment to the speaker's being a millennial. That there isn't yet a robust market for delineating the purported psychological overlap of generations and zodiac signs is a failure of capitalism.

But there's a utility in these distinctions, which is why they exist. Over the course of this book, I'll refer to them with some regularity specifically because they provide an easy way to affix a cohort in time. While the primary generation I'll consider is the baby boom, I'll draw contrasts between them and the silent generation (born from 1928 to 1945 using Pew's definition) and the millennials (1981 to 1996). When you see those terms, remember the asterisk that accompanies them, some form of "or thereabouts."

I'll note that the generalizations about our ad hoc delineations begin with the name of the generations themselves. The descriptors we use are often qualitative, meant to capture something about the group, like its insouciance or about when and how it appeared. The boomers were just . . . part of a boom. There were a lot of them and, more than those who came before or after, they warped the world into which they were born. The boom started and the boom ended and we've been dealing with the shock wave ever since.

In his novel *Cat's Cradle,* Kurt Vonnegut imagines a religion called Bokononism. It held that some people were cosmically linked into groups of significance, which were called *karasses.* Others imagined that groups to which they belonged were significant though they weren't, as when a character assigns cosmic import to being a Hoosier. Such groups the Bokononists called a *granfalloon*—other examples of which included "any nation, anytime, anywhere."[33]

At the risk of offending Bokonon and Gen X, Gen X is a *granfalloon.* Boomers are a *karass.*

THE BOOM HAS PEAKED

But not like it used to be. Time has done what it always does. The number of residents of the United States born during the baby boom has declined over the past 20 years, dropping by nearly 10 percent since 2000.

This is what happens to generations, necessarily. Because the number of people born in a certain period is fixed, we would expect the total population in a generation to decline from a peak at the end of that period over time: members can only leave the group (by dying) and no new members can be born into it. However, because the United States is home to so many immigrants, the number of boomers didn't peak in 1964—it increased until the 2000 census. People born from 1946 to 1964 moved to the United States and indirectly became part of the American baby boom.

As we'll explore in greater detail later, this was not the immigration that the boomers' parents had seen. Then, immigration was largely from Europe. The immigration boom that began in the late 1960s was, instead, heavily from Latin America and Asia. In 1990, 1 in 5 immigrants to the United States came from Mexico, a percentage that rose to 30 percent 10 years later.[34] The increased density of immigrants among the baby boomers shifted its demography. In 1970, about 5 million of the 72 million boomers identified as Hispanic, around 7 percent. By 2000, 9.7 million of the 77 million boomers did, a bit more than 1 in 10. Put another way, the number of Hispanic boomers nearly doubled.

The year 2000 was the peak. But a contraction in the size of the most dominant generation in American history does not mean that the generation is not still dominant.

CHART 4
The Size of the Boomer-Aged Population

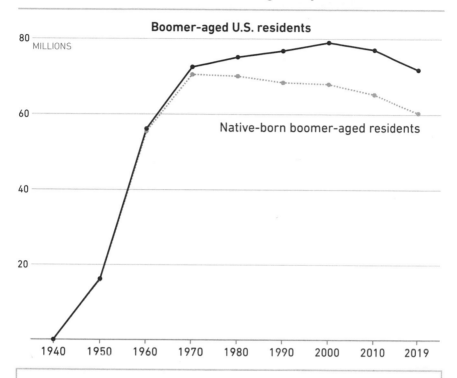

Boomer-aged U.S. residents

Native-born boomer-aged residents

80 MILLIONS

60

40

20

1940   1950   1960   1970   1980   1990   2000   2010   2019

HOW TO READ THIS CHART A line graph comparing two trends: the number of residents of the United States—a Census Bureau category including both citizens and foreign-born residents—born between 1946 and 1964 and the subset of that group born in the United States.[35]

Over the course of this book, I'll use the word "density" as a way of talking about the size of a group relative to a total population. For example, the density of 56- to 74-year-olds—the age range of the baby boom in 2020—is much higher relative to the total population now than it was three decades ago, back when the members of the baby boom were roughly the same age as millennials are now.[36]

It's easier to depict the shifts in density that accompanied the baby boom visually. We'll assess density among three generational groups (the silent generation, the boomers, and the millennials) using as our benchmarks the years 1968, 1986, and 2020—about when the first members of those groups turned 40. (Skipping over Generation X, the generation of which I'm a member, is not meant as disrespect, of course, but our generation is used to such slights anyway.) Comparing where boomers stood when they were aged 20 to 40 with where the millennials are now that they're in that age range

CHART 5
The Change in the Density of Age Groups

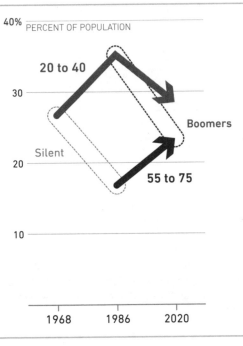

HOW TO READ THIS CHART This graph shows the difference between an age cohort and a generation. Arrows indicate the percent of the total population for each age group, 20- to 40-year-olds or 55- to 75-year-olds. Outlined ovals indicate the change in population density for members of the silent and baby boom generations as they age from the younger age cohort to the older one. Perhaps the most useful shorthand for these charts is to compare the relative positions of the silent and boomer ovals.

In 1968, 20- to 40-year-olds—the silent generation—made up about 27 percent of the population. By 1986, when the boomers first started turning 40, 20- to 40-year-olds made up 35 percent of the population. In 2020, when millennials first started turning 40, that age group was back down to 29 percent. That's in part because, in 2020, the boomers (or at least those aged 55 to 75) still made up 23 percent of the population. In 1986, the 55- to 75-year-old silent generation members had been only 17 percent of the population.

will give a sense both for how the baby boom was exceptional and for the power it still retains.

For all of the preceding dissection of the decline in the size of the boomer population, it's worth noting that it is actually declining less rapidly than past generations. A central reason that boomers still make up more than a quarter of the population is that Americans are living longer than they used to. But more on that later.

THE POWER OF THE BOOMERS MAY NOT HAVE PEAKED YET

The continued density of boomers in the population is central to the continued strength of the generation in both politics and economics. In other words, to its power.

We often use that word in a know-it-if-you-see-it sense, but it's worth being a bit more specific here. What "power" do the boomers manifest? Well, what makes someone powerful? Some examples are obvious. A president is powerful because he commands the military and can sign legislation; a billionaire is powerful because she can buy anything or employ hundreds of people. As we refine the idea, though, the line becomes less sharp. How much more power does a president have than one member of a Senate split along party lines? How much more power does a member of the House of Representatives have than a major political donor who has relationships with multiple members of Congress? Who is more powerful, someone who owns a million-dollar home or someone with $100,000 in the bank? Less clear still is aggregated power. The Senate, sure. But a generation?

Our examples offer an answer. Power manifests in the ability to apply power. It's about being able to do things or to *not* do things—to, for example, not have to move when your lease is up. That it's situational helps explain why, despite the ways in which members of the baby boom generation have collective power attributed to them, many of them often feel powerless or even resentful at the idea that they're powerful. Baby boomer Bill Gates's wealth doesn't make all boomers rich.

Few have spent as much time considering power as G. William Domhoff, distinguished professor emeritus at the University of California, Santa Cruz. Domhoff is a member of the staff of the university's psychology department, which is an interesting bit of context when considering that he focuses heavily on manifestations and measurements of power. (It's also interesting to consider how it overlaps with another specific area of interest he holds: dreams. His UC Santa Cruz bio still points to an online dream repository, DreamBank, that he helps run.)

When we spoke in 2021, Domhoff was cautious about any attempts to delineate power with precision. "I think you have to look at outcomes," he told me. "The basic point is you can't look at the process, in the sense that you can do a study and watch people do power to each other."[37] Call it the behavioristic approach to identifying the powerful.

In his 1967 book, *Who Rules America?*, Domhoff offered some insights into appropriate methods for tracking those behaviors. Power can be differentiated between collective power—the power of the state—and distributive power, which Domhoff succinctly describes as "the ability of a group or social class within a community or nation to be successful in conflicts with its rivals on issues of concern to it." The ability to do things.

"Most social scientists think of distributive power in the sense of great or preponderant influence," Domhoff wrote, "not in the sense of complete and absolute control. More specifically, a powerful group or class is one that can realize its goals even if some other group or class is opposed."[38]

This is professor-speak, certainly. He's saying power is relative, not universal. That's why there might be senators who can outmaneuver presidents or why labor unions can force concessions from massive corporations. But this also makes it trickier to assess power, since it's often contextual. Domhoff offers a system for estimating power, including evaluations of who benefits in society (meaning in a material or economic sense) and who governs in it.

Assessing that first metric is fairly uncomplicated, even if parsing what you learn might be. Income and wealth (measured in things like owning stock and real estate) aren't inherently measures of power, he writes, but instead "are visible signs that a class has power in relation to other classes." Having a lot of money doesn't necessarily mean you're powerful, but it's a pretty good indicator that you might be.

The assessment of governmental power is more direct. "If a group or class is highly overrepresented or underrepresented in relation to its proportion of the population," Domhoff writes, "it can be inferred that the group or class is relatively powerful or powerless." If, say, the state of Wyoming was to have one senator for every 288,000 residents while the state of California had one for every 19.8 million, one might safely assume that Wyomingites are relatively more powerful in the Senate than Californians.

With that loose framework established, we can begin to measure my stipulated assertion about the relative economic and political power of the boomers. We'll begin with the governance benchmark.

An obvious measure of political power is representation in Congress. Again looking at our three key generational years, we see that in 1968 only about 12 percent of Congress was aged 20 to 40. By 1986, when the first boomers turned 40, 15 percent of Congress (including both representatives and senators) were in that age group. In 2020, the density of the age group had declined to about 7 percent of legislators.[39]

CHART 6

The Age Composition of Congress over Time

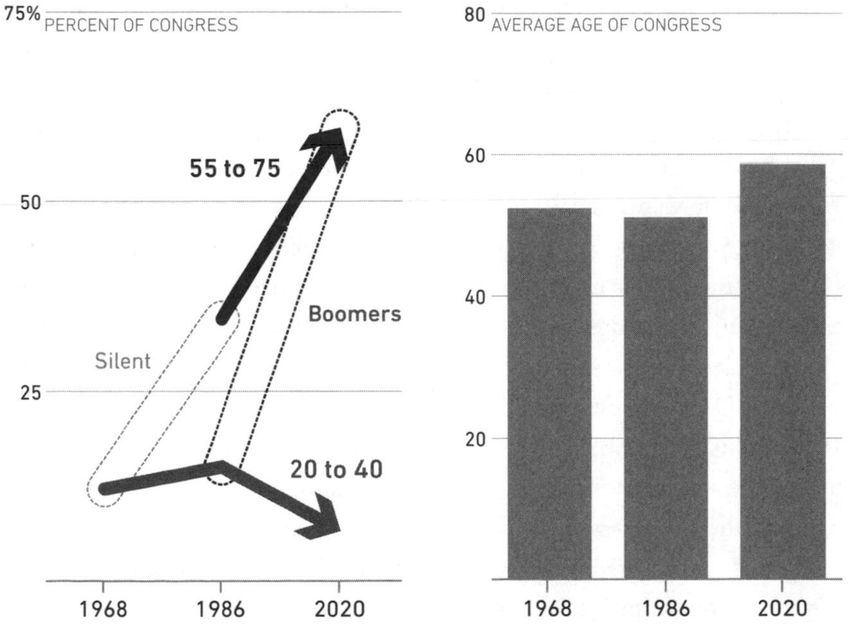

HOW TO READ THIS CHART In the graph at left, age groups are delineated by arrows and generations by ovals. At right, a simple column graph.

Why was that the case in 2020? In part because so many members of Congress by that point were boomers. In 1986, about 35 percent of legislators were aged 55 to 75. By 2020, nearly 60 percent were.

The effect of the boomers' arrival in Congress is visible in the shift in the average age of members. In 1968, members of Congress were 52.4 years old, on average. That had dropped to 51.1 by 1986, with boomers beginning to be represented on Capitol Hill. By 2020, the average age had risen to 58.6 years.[40] Remember that boomers constitute only about 29 percent of the population. Their representation in Congress, then, is about twice their density in the country.

There's an important qualifier to this: you have to be at least 25 to serve in Congress, meaning that the lower quartile of the 20-to-40 group couldn't be in Congress if it wanted to. (It's likely that William C. C. Claiborne was elected to the House at age 23 in 1797, but it's safe to say that was unlikely to occur in 1986.[41])

Regardless, you can already see the python-pig action here. But this isn't some run-of-the-mill muckery like the number of students in a classroom; this is the United States Congress, that most estimable and respected of institutions. And, of course, one of the country's most powerful.

A similar pattern happens for state governors. In 1986, 34 percent of governors were aged 55 to 75. By 2020, 62 percent of governors were, a density of boomers about the same as the density in Congress. While two governors in 1986 were aged 20 to 40, in 2020 none were.

One reason that boomers were winning election to Congress in 1986 is that boomers made up more of the electorate. Since there are turnout differences between midterm and presidential elections, let's consider the three midterm elections closest to the years we've been looking at: 1966, 1986, and 2018. Census Bureau tallies of turnout in each election show that 20- to 40-year-olds outnumbered 55- to 75-year-olds in 1986, when boomers first turned 40—and that 55- to 75-year-olds outnumbered 20- to 40-year-olds in 2018, when boomers had moved into that upper age group.

How much has federal power been centralized in the boomers? For the 28-year stretch from 1993 to 2020, the country was led by a boomer president. There's only been one president from the silent generation: Joe Biden, who took office in 2021.

By Domhoff's governance standard, it's clear that the boomers manifest

CHART 7
Age Groups in Midterm Electorates

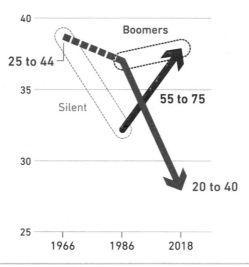

45% ─────────────────────────
    PERCENT OF VOTERS

40
                    Boomers
25 to 44
                                    55 to 75
35
        Silent

30

                            20 to 40

25 ─────┬────────┬────────┬──────
      1966   1986   2018

HOW TO READ THIS CHART This graph is broadly similar to the prior one, but with an important caveat. Again, the ovals represent different generations. On this graph, though, the number of 20- to 40-year-olds in 1966 is not available—nor is it commensurate: it wasn't until 1970 that most people under the age of 21 could vote in federal elections. So the identified 25-to-44 group makes up a higher percentage of the population in part because older Americans are more likely to vote than younger ones and because there are no 18- to 20-year-olds to include in the overall total.

Less important, the value for the 55-to-75 group in 1986 is an estimate, because the Census Bureau data for that year included 75-year-olds in a "75 and older" category.[42] And one last note: the y-axis begins at 25 percent instead of zero.

---

outsized power. For all of the focus on the generation's demonstrated economic power, though, boomers are there more modestly advantaged.

When you speak with young people, they repeatedly identify two economic hurdles that they face: debt (often from college) and diminished homeownership. Ask economic experts, they say the same.

We'll start with housing. In 1986, about a third of homeowners were in

CHART 8
Differences in Housing Between Generations

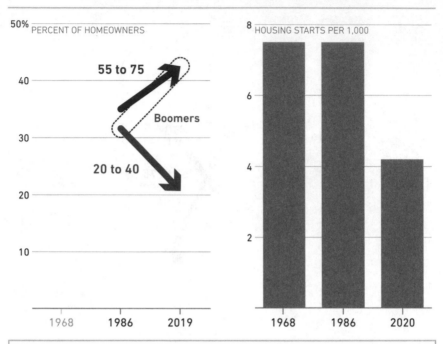

HOW TO READ THIS CHART   At left, the percentage of members of each age group in the
pool of all homeowners. At right, the relative level of new home construction.

the 55-to-75 age group and another third were aged 20 to 40. (These data are
Census Bureau figures for which 1968 numbers weren't comparable.)[43] In
2019—selected because of questions about data collection during the pandemic year of 2020—twice as many homeowners fell into the older age group
as the younger.

We'll get into this in more detail later, but one reason for the discrepancy
is that the United States dramatically slowed down its home building. In
1968 and 1986, there were 7.5 new houses being built for every 1,000 Americans. In 2020, that figure was 4.2 houses.[44] Relatedly, prices are rising. A
house that cost $100,000 in 1980 cost $136,000 in 1986 and $462,000 in
2020—significantly more than the rate of inflation.[45]

Homeownership is a central component of household wealth; in 2020,
real estate made up more than a quarter of total wealth in the United States.[46]

So, given the lopsidedness of homeownership, it's not surprising that the boomers hold a disproportionate amount of the country's wealth.

That's despite boomers making up relatively little of the country's *income* in 2020, as opposed to aggregated wealth. This is an easy distinction to blur, so it's worth highlighting briefly. Income is what you earn from your job or your investments; wealth is what you own and your savings.

The divide also shouldn't be surprising, given that there are fewer boomers working. In 2019, about 23 percent of the workforce was boomer aged—an

CHART 9
Wealth and Income by Generation

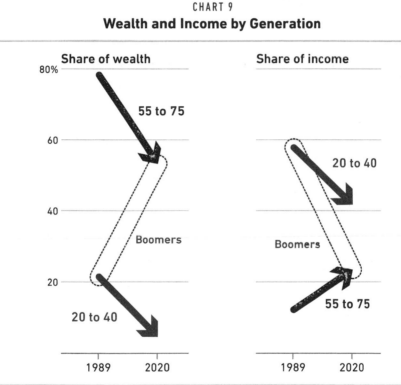

HOW TO READ THIS CHART We've eliminated the 1968 column for these graphs because the data from which it is derived[47] only go back to 1989, the year at which this begins. It's also important to note that the wealth distribution, which is from the Federal Reserve, breaks out households by generation explicitly. Members of the silent generation are here combined with members of earlier generations, helping to explain why the 1989 55-to-75 figure is so high. The income data come from an analysis of Economic Policy Institute figures.[48]

increase over the density of 55- to 75-year-olds in 1986 but still well below
the 45 percent of the workforce that was aged 20 to 40. There's nothing
magical about this: half of the 55-to-75 age range falls within retirement age,
though, as we'll see, that doesn't mean that they're retiring.

In 1989, nearly everyone who wasn't a boomer was older than that generation, making it more remarkable that boomers nonetheless controlled 20
percent of the country's wealth. Again, that was a function of the size of the
generation, which we can see skewing the wealth numbers even now. Since
1989, those aged 55 and older have always controlled at least 54 percent of
the wealth in the country. By 2019, that figure was over 70 percent—with
the youngest boomers already at the age of 55.

CHART 10
As the Baby Boom Aged, It Held More of the Country's Wealth

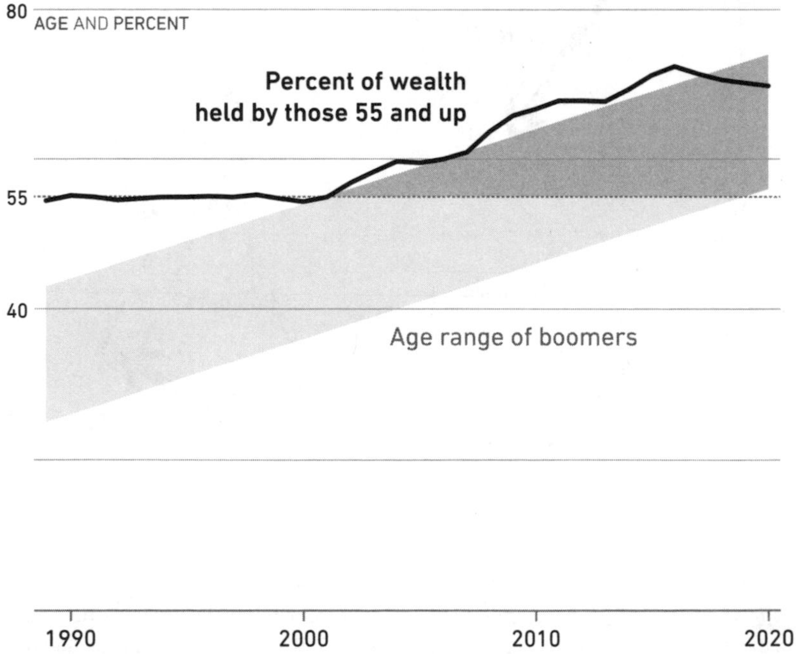

| HOW TO READ THIS CHART | Another graph where the vertical axis is serving two roles. Reading from left to right, you see years. From top to bottom, the black line indicates the percent of wealth held by those at or over the age of 55. The shaded area is the age range of the boomers in each year, with the darker shading indicating those in the 55-and-up age group.

It's an artifact of how the graph was made, but there's some symbolism on display: as the boomers turned 55, it was as though they steadily pushed the amount of wealth held by those in that age group higher.

Debt is more complicated and more intertwined with age. By the end of 2020, 70 percent of the $1.5 trillion in student debt was held by those aged 25 to 50, with the ratio balanced slightly more heavily toward the upper end of that age range.[49] But millennials held only about 27 percent of all liabilities tracked by the Federal Reserve, well under the 58 percent held by boomers at the end of 1989.[50]

That is admittedly a lot of numbers. So allow me to summarize. Boomers made up about 23 percent of the population in 2019 and 2020 but constituted 43 percent of homeowners, held 50 percent of wealth, and owned 55 percent of corporate equities and mutual fund shares. They made up 25 percent of registered voters, 38 percent of the vote in 2018, and 58 percent of Congress. As a sardonic member of Gen X like myself might say, that does seem a bit imbalanced.

HOWEVER

But there are two important qualifications. The first, once again, is the generation's initial and ongoing size. The second is our Bill Gates example: in part because of that size, the generation has never been uniform.

Population size matters when discussing wealth, as Monique Morrissey, an economist with the Economic Policy Institute, explained to me. I asked her the question at the heart of the data above: Are the boomers disproportionately wealthy and powerful? Her answer was a blizzard of context.

"Any older generation is going to have to have a greater share of wealth than any younger generation because people accumulate savings over time. So that's normal," Morrissey said. "So the real question is, if you compare the boomers to millennials to Gen Z to Gen X at the same point in time, are the boomers hogging more than their share? And the answer, surprisingly, is no"—because there are so many boomers.

Morrissey pointed to the Federal Reserve data. "Basically, the share for people seventy and over—the wealth share or the net worth share—has been flat since 1989, which is as far back as it goes. And for people fifty-five to sixty-nine it has actually declined in the last decade, and was flat before then." In fact, if we adjust the wealth held by each generation to the generation's population, we can see how boomer wealth tracks with younger generations at the same age on a per capita basis.

"The simple story," Morrissey summarized, "is the boomers in the aggregate are not holding a greater share of wealth than previous generations did, as far as we can tell from existing conventional sources and adjusting for the size of these different generations."

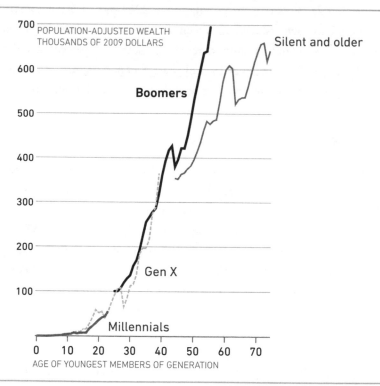

CHART 11
Wealth by Age, Adjusted for Population Size

HOW TO READ THIS CHART The visualization is straightforward, even if the numbers aren't. Here we're using Federal Reserve data from the fourth quarter of each year between 1989 and 2019. For each year, we figured out the population of each generation and compared that to the wealth held by the generation, adjusted to 2009 dollars. That value was then plotted according to the youngest age of the generation in that year—25 years for the boomers in 1989, for example. The useful pattern? How the curves for boomers, Gen X, and millennials all line up. (As with the other Federal Reserve data, the silent generation data include everything pre-boomer.)

But there is a reason it might *feel* that way: wealth inequality. The more uneven the distribution of wealth, the more people whose wealth is below the average. Because wealth inequality has increased in recent decades, that means that more millennials are below the average than was the case when boomers were their age.

Here, too, a simplified visual will help. Imagine that we depict the distribution of wealth among the millennials with either relatively even or relatively uneven distribution and compare it to where the boomers were at the same age. In the even scenario, depicted at left, the five least-wealthy deciles—that is, tenths—have less wealth than did the boomers at that age. The five wealthiest deciles (the top half) have more. The difference isn't dramatic, though.

If there's a wider gap between the wealthiest and least-wealthy deciles,

---

CHART 12
Demonstrating How Inequality Can Affect Perceptions

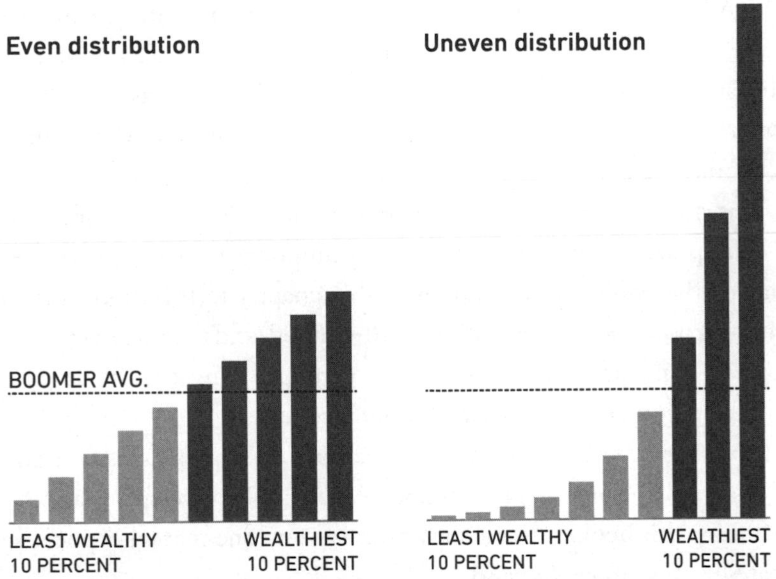

Even distribution

Uneven distribution

BOOMER AVG.

LEAST WEALTHY 10 PERCENT   WEALTHIEST 10 PERCENT

LEAST WEALTHY 10 PERCENT   WEALTHIEST 10 PERCENT

HOW TO READ THIS CHART The graphs here don't represent real data, just two scenarios. In each case, we're divvying up 110 imaginary units of wealth among chunks of the millennial generation representing one-tenth of the total population of the generation. The "boomer average" is also invented, included to show how the perception of relative wealth would likely be more skewed in a more unevenly distributed wealth scenario.

only the upper end of millennial wealth holders exceeds the boomers. In the graph at right, the seven less-wealthy deciles are all under the standard enjoyed collectively by the boomers. The more unequal the distribution, the more millennials trail where their parents or grandparents might have been.

That we're talking about *perceptions* of boomer wealth as opposed to *actual* boomer wealth is important. Most individual boomers won't feel particularly wealthy or powerful and would likely resent the implication that they are uniquely privileged by virtue of their membership in the generation. But they are nonetheless part of a large, wealthy, powerful generation.

Which brings us back to the second qualifier for our assessment of boomer power: no generation is homogeneous. This is obvious when considering wealth. Jeff Bezos is one of the wealthiest people in the world; he was born at the very tail end of the baby boom. Clearly not every boomer is as wealthy as Jeff Bezos. But it's also apparent when considering the generation's political power. Yes, most members of Congress in 2020 were boomers, but since the group included both Democrats and Republicans, they were not likely to leverage that power toward an agreed-upon political outcome. In 2018, Pew Research Center estimated that boomers themselves were about evenly split between the two parties.[51] For as much tension as exists between boomers and other generations, there's no dearth of tension within the massive boomer generation itself.

This is an obvious point but it's one that is often lost, given our rhetorical and conceptual tendency to extrapolate assumptions from groups we treat as uniform. The two great hypocrisies of this chapter to this point have been dismissing non-boomer generations as ill-defined (and then referring to them repeatedly) and promoting boomers as demonstrating consistent patterns (and then pointing out the scale of differences).

"Arguing in terms of broad demographic categories takes you only so far," Harvard sociologist Theda Skocpol put it when we spoke as I began researching this book. It was a fair warning—and one that will appear again repeatedly as we move forward.

THE BOOM BEGINS ITS WHIMPER

What I haven't addressed is how economic and political power reinforce each other. It's not simply that boomers control more wealth and more seats in

Congress; wealth strengthens the ability to hold seats in Congress and holding seats can help build wealth.

We'll explore the latter point in more detail, but it's immediately obvious
that legislative action has repeatedly helped bolster the wealth of those who
already have wealth. From laws aimed at protecting homeowners to tax cuts
skewed for the wealthy, politics is a central tool for the wealthy to maintain
their positions. Less recognized, though readily articulated, are the subtle
ways wealth can influence political power beyond the (often overstated!) factor of campaign contributions. Consider, for example, the usefulness of being
a retired homeowner in being able to vote. In 2020, the Census Bureau estimates that about two-thirds of people living in owner-occupied residences—
people who own homes or live with the homeowners—cast a ballot. Less
than half of those who lived in renter-occupied units did.[52] Renter turnout
was not unusually low in 2020. In fact, it was fairly *high*. In the 2014 midterms, just shy of half of those living in owner-occupied residences voted. Just
over a quarter of renters did.[53] If there's a low-turnout local election proposing to raise property taxes to fund schools, how likely do you think that is to
pass? Now consider that today there are a lot more retired homeowners, thanks
to birth rates 70 years ago.

Voting, income, homeownership, and age all blend together in influenc-
ing voter turnout. Renters vote less in part because they may not have updated
their voter registrations from the last time they moved. They're also more
likely to have jobs that make it hard to get to the polls. They tend to be
younger, a group for whom voting has not yet become a habit. In 2020, 18
percent of those under the age of 25 who didn't vote told the Census Bureau
that it was due to schedule conflicts. Among those aged 65 and older, only
2 percent cited that reason.[54]

Consider the catch-22 made clear to me in a conversation with Amanda
Litman, who in 2017—on the day Donald Trump was inaugurated, in fact—
cofounded an organization aimed at getting more young people to run for
office.

"There's a big conversation to be had about when most of your governing
is happening by homeowners, the conversation around affordable housing
really prioritizes homeownership, which is not how most twenty- and thirtysomethings are participating in the housing market right now," Litman
said. "We also have worked with a bunch of candidates who are still living

in their parents' basement or in their parents' homes, which creates an interesting dynamic. And the structural reality is that it's often harder to run for office if you don't own a home, because you're less tied and maybe seen as less committed to a place when it's in fact reflective of a broader generational wealth situation."

An example she gave was Alex Lee, a member of the California State Assembly elected in 2020. When we spoke, Lee, representing a district in the hyper-expensive San Francisco Bay region, was still living at his mother's house. He told me that his political opponents at times mocked him for that, but he saw it as legitimizing.

"That's just part of my life, and it's something I freely talk about because it's the reality for a lot of my constituents," he explained, "and it's not always by choice—but that's the way to have to live, to be able to be able to live in the community that they grew up in or have been building for many, many decades. That's the reality."

Lee ran for the assembly during the coronavirus pandemic, earning income by delivering groceries through an app-based retailer. He is also Asian American, bisexual, and in his twenties—a divergence from the boomers in nearly every imaginable way.

He looks the way a lot of young Americans do. And as the python's meal is nearly completed, that generational difference will reshape the United States.

All Things Must Pass

When you begin to think about how the baby boom has affected America, it's impossible not to contemplate its natural conclusion.

There was a sudden, unexpected surge in births—and within a decade, diaper services went from a novelty to the equivalent in 2021 dollars of a nearly half-billion-dollar industry.[1] Cities rushed to build more schools. Then a bit later America had millions of teenagers, so businesses and industries reorganized around them.

Over and over, age-dependent systems struggled to accommodate the encroaching boomers. To use a boom-appropriate analogy, America has been a nation of Lucille Balls scrambling to handle the conveyor belt of chocolates.[2] And now, more than 75 years into the boom, you might be able to predict which systems will be overrun.

FLORIDA BOOMS

Harold Schwartz made just such a prediction back in the early 1980s.

Schwartz had been selling tracts of Florida real estate by mail until the practice was banned in 1968. After a brief foray into mobile-home parks, Schwartz brought in his son Gary Morse, an advertising executive from Chicago, to overhaul the sales strategy. Morse shifted the focus to houses, including offering prospective retirees a half-hour "video tape tour" of the concept by mail. The pitch went from shoddy to showbiz.[3]

The eventual result was the Villages, a series of interconnected housing developments—the "villages" themselves—marketed as an all-inclusive life-style that redirected retirement from senior community centers to senior-centered communities. Year after year over the past decade, the Villages landed among the fastest growing regions in the United States. In 2010, the Census Bureau estimated that about 86,000 people lived in the area.[4] By 2020, the population neared 130,000.[5] More than 7 in 10 of those residents are aged 55 or over, the largely inflexible minimum age required to own a home in one of the villages. Most of the Villages is contained within Sumter County, where, in 2003, 21.3 percent of its population were baby boomers. In 2019, 42.8 percent were, the third-highest percentage of any county in the United States.[6] The Villages grew so fast that, in the past two censuses, it helped Florida's center of population stop moving toward Miami and start moving back toward Sumter County.[7]

When I visited the Villages in May 2021, a board listing new residents, broken out by state, had dozens of names. Those were the people who had moved in in less than a week. Ryan Erisman, a writer focused on Florida's retirement communities, estimated that 2,000 homes are sold in the Villages a year. Other estimates have that figure in a matter of months.[8] The develop-ments, often distinguished with vaguely elegant or Spanish-ish names, line two major thoroughfares. The homes themselves are generally small ranch houses that differ little from one to the next. It's simple to get lost within or between the developments because of the similarity from one street to the next and because everything's shifted off-kilter by dozens of golf courses.

The villages serve the Villages like a congregation singing in a church: a lot of shaky individual performances that fuses into something with a bit more energy and appeal. People come not for the homes but the amenities—and for the community within and between the developments.

There's an insistence to that community; the Villages cannot be an easy place for an introvert. The ubiquitous golf carts often have the names of the passengers emblazoned in script on their hoods, man in the driver's seat, woman on the passenger side: Dennis and Sally; John and Beth. Signs outside of houses often offer the same information. There's no excuse for not know-ing your neighbor in the Villages.

While homes are often subjected to strict constraints on displays and decorations, there are clearly no rules for the golf carts. What Myspace was to the expressiveness of young millennials, these golf carts are for their parents and grandparents. They range from standard Yamaha models to custom-built jobs that look like actual automobiles. The machines are littered with political stickers and mentions of families and countless expressions of support for various sports teams, with the Big Ten clearly overrepresented. In 2019, *The New York Times* wrote a feature about the golf carts themselves, reporting that some residents spent north of $20,000 for customized rides.[9]

I rented a golf cart during my visit, paying $25 for a day of puttering around. It was mid-May, so already fairly hot. Presumably due to the combination of age and weather, there weren't many people out. On the main cart thoroughfares, golfers would whiz past my speed-regulated rental, prompting me to offer repeated apologetic waves. There are wide-open gates at the entrances to the various villages, policed by local residents who nod everyone through. Most residential streets that morning were empty, treeless under a cloudless blue sky. Driveways were occasionally ornate and, to a house, clean, but nearly every house was shut up tight. People were watching, though; one woman with whom I spoke as she was watering plants assured me that she would receive multiple calls after I left to inquire about who I was and why I was there.

The network of neighborhoods is anchored by three manufactured town centers. The first and northernmost is Spanish Springs, built across the highway from Schwartz's first big development in the area. It resembles what a southern border town would look like if nearly everyone was White. (As 97 percent of Villages residents are.[10]) Farther south is Lake Sumter Landing, focused on the eponymous lake and its canal, which extends south for a few hundred feet, complete with locks, and then turns into a stream that runs for a few hundred more feet before ending. At the southern end of the complex— as of this writing—is the unappealingly named Brownwood Paddock Square. Built in 2012, its theme is cattle ranching; the road leading to the square from the outside world includes cattle guards for livestock that never walked the decade-old streets. Nonetheless, Paddock Square is probably the most authentic downtown area if only because there are actual cattle ranches on the outskirts of the Villages.

This is the most important thing to understand about the Villages. Spanish Springs was built in 1994, by the same company that designed the nearby Universal Studios theme park. Speaking to the *Sun-Sentinel* in 1994, Morse celebrated that they had "the luxury of doing this backward," creating the downtown after the suburbs already existed. In each town center, plaques describe the history of significant buildings with the aim of making the town seem more cohesive—but of course it isn't, so the presented history has simply been invented from thin air.

People commonly refer to the Villages as "Disney World for adults," an analogy that likely stems in part from its proximity to the amusement park. But here, too, reality is submerged in fantasy. There are never-used trolley tracks embedded in sidewalks and faded paint on buildings suggesting what they "used" to be. It's a lot more charming to imagine that a building was the Acme Taxidermy and Trophy shop than it is to recognize that it was built in the past few decades to be what it is now: a comfortable footwear emporium. It's nice to think that the row of buildings lining one street used to house early settlers of Central Florida instead of having been stood up to house a string of financial firms and mortgage companies. It's more fun to think that the region's history was a mesh of idiosyncratic characters and wacky happenings than to remember that less than 40 years before Spanish Springs was constructed, a Black man in the nearby town of Wildwood was arrested for talking to a White woman in a grocery store before being kidnapped from the jail and beaten nearly to death.[11]

"We decided to bring the baby boomers to a home that they were familiar with when they were young," Richard Schwartz, son of Howard, explains in the film *Some Kind of Heaven,* a look at the Villages and its residents. (Richard speaks while standing in a fountain next to a statue of his father.) But there was no hometown with an entirely noncontroversial history, much less any that, like the Villages now, were primarily centered on letting older people grab a cocktail and manage their assets. So the Villages pretends it's about something else.

The idyllic consistency in the Villages is maintained through the control of the holding company that owns it. The Villages has its own daily newspaper, its own cable channel, and its own radio station—all managed through the company. That means that a rash of sinkholes alarming residents went mostly unreported by the newspaper,[12] save one located near a busy street that the paper claimed without explanation was likely not a sinkhole.[13] ("You won't read anything negative about the Villages at all," Erisman said of *The Villages Daily Sun*.)

The radio station, WVLG, is piped into the downtowns, offering a steady stream of boomer-friendly oldies mixed in with a bit of syndicated Fox News Radio programming. It's probably useful to have a locally centered station since the complex isn't really near much except the small town of Lady Lake; even Orlando is an hour away. Interaction with the outside world is possible in the way that extravehicular activity is possible in space: with some preparation and a recognition that something unusual was underway.

The Villages is a bubble, one created specifically to make boomers in particular feel comfortable and happy. Relatedly, it is a densely conservative area both socially and politically, something that would be hard to avoid in a place specifically predicated on rejecting the modern world in favor of a place "familiar to boomers when they were young," as Schwartz had it. America was already made great again at the Villages, if you will, which is likely why Donald Trump was received warmly during stops there in both his 2016 and 2020 campaigns. As president in 2019 (and with an eye toward reelection), he visited the complex to sign an executive order focused on Medicare. He told the audience then that he'd thought about moving to the Villages but "got stuck at Mar-a-Lago."[14]

No one in the complex's administrative offices (located in one of those pseudo-historic houses) was interested in talking to me about how the Villages was positioning itself for the future, and the residents with whom I spoke understandably didn't know any details.

Erisman's been tracking it, though. He explained that, even when I was there and although no one mentioned it, there was a fourth town square, Sawgrass Grove, nearing completion past the southern boundary of the existing complex. This was unexpected to those who'd been reading the tea leaves; the plan for years had been to stop after Brownwood. But the Villages kept pressing, with company officials explaining that they expected the size of the complex to double with the next two decades or so.

If so, the population would hit a quarter million. The size of Winston-Salem, North Carolina.

What's more, Erisman explained, they were planning on building out more housing for people younger than 55. There was already some tsking from those I spoke with about the younger crowd moving into Brownwood, a function of its being newer and therefore more likely to have homes available for those just hitting retirement age. But the need for workers also means a need for building capacity for the people cashing paychecks as part of the Villages micro-economy.

"I do think that they'll always keep—whether it's six town squares or five or seven—I think they'll always keep pace with the growth," Erisman explained. Meaning more houses for more retirees and more amenities for those houses and more staff for those amenities.

But the market for senior housing keeps ballooning. With more than 10,000 people a day turning 65 in 2020, this is not a bad bet for an investment. And other developers of housing for seniors are salivating. "We've been waiting for this moment for a long time," Beth Mace, the chief economist for the National Investment Center for Seniors Housing and Care (NIC) explained to me with pleasant frankness.

In the context of that industry, boomers are still relatively young. Senior housing typically kicks in at 82, Mace said; the first boomers won't get there until 2028. A boomer who turned 56 in 2020 was as close to her thirtieth birthday—last century—as her eighty-second. But even before reaching that point, boomers still play a significant role in the industry—one that would sound familiar to Eugene Gilbert, the enterprising market researcher who was helping businesses prepare for the onslaught of boomers when they first reached their teens in the late 1950s. His advice then still echoes: the boomers are guiding where their parents spend money.

"What we've found," Mace explained, "is the baby boomers influence their parents and where their parents live and what type of housing and care options the parents have." Boomers now generally have parents in that 82-and-up age group and may recognize needs that their parents ignore or overlook. But they influence in other ways, like spurring their parents to move to particular communities where they can be near their grandkids.

Even before the boom arrives, Mace said that the senior housing market had been expanding at a rate of 2.5 percent per year over the preceding 10 years. But she expected that it would be revamped once boomers began needing some level of care.

"I think it's true that the baby boomers are quite different than the generations that have been in seniors' housing," she predicted. "The baby boomers are looking more for purpose and meaning in life. They want a third act. They had a career, maybe they had children and now they're ready to do something new. And so I think that's going to shift the types of services and the types of real estate physical structures of what we're talking about for housing."

Imagine a household where a younger person pays less rent in exchange for doing more chores and casework. Imagine what Mace described as "Golden Girls" housing, a shared space for several older people akin to the 1980s sitcom. Or imagine entire neighborhoods, what she called a "naturally occurring retirement community" that's skewed older and self-supportive, an informal Villages.

One advantage of these alternative scenarios is that they can be less expensive. While boomers hold a lot of wealth, the size and diversity of the generation means an enormous number of people who have too much income to be eligible for government programs but too little to afford private-sector assistance. Research conducted by NORC in 2019 and funded by NIC found that by 2029, half of those aged 75 and over would fall into that gap.[15] Seven in 10 of the members of that age group at that point will be boomers.[16]

Polling data reflect this. In the early 2000s, the boomers ranged in age from about 40 to 60 and about 2 in 5 thought they could retire before they turned 65, according to polling data from Gallup. Fifteen years later, when they ranged in age from about 50 to 75—and after the recession of the late aughts—half thought they *wouldn't* be able to retire at the traditional retirement age.[17] That was twice the figure recorded previously. Some of this was probably a function of overconfidence when they were younger but part was certainly a function of simply not having the expected resources.

The specific instabilities woven through the generation are an important part of the story. But it is the case that, as the boomers get older, the country is again warping to accommodate them.

We see this in jobs data. The Bureau of Labor Statistics tracks employment by industry, including those jobs in what it clumsily refers to as "continuing care retirement communities and assisted living facilities for the elderly." Between May 2002 and May 2020—the months in which these data are calculated—the number of people working in the United States overall increased by 6 percent. The number of people working in retirement care increased by *75 percent*, jumping from about 537,000 to 941,000. In 2002, 42 out of every 10,000 people working in the United States worked within that broad employment category. By 2020, that had increased to 68 out of every 10,000 workers.[18]

As you might expect, much of that work is being done by members of younger generations. This points to another looming problem hidden within the retirement boom.

"Today there are seven adult children for every senior," Mace explained. "An adult child here is the forty-five- to sixty-four-year-old relative to those over eighty. By 2030, that shrinks to four to one. And by 2050, it shrinks to three to one."

The genesis for those numbers is projections from the Census Bureau, which we'll get into in a moment. For now, though, it is time to acknowledge where any discussion of the baby boom must inevitably terminate.

In every conversation I had about the baby boom, death was an undercurrent. That was particularly the case when speaking with residents in the Villages: that the house across the street was up for sale after a death, that the man with whom I was speaking had lost his wife the prior year. That's part of the community, too, that broadly shared understanding. Those most committed to the Villages call themselves frogs, as Erisman's website explains, because they're there until they croak. The immortality of youth bonds; so does the proximity of death.

THE BOOMERS' LAST DISRUPTION

One thing I quickly discovered in my conversations is that there isn't a natural way to refer to the inevitable deaths of tens of millions of Americans. I usually resorted to apologetic terms like "fading." But, perhaps predictably, boomers themselves are more sanguine about their inevitable future. No one is less fazed by the subject than the experts on the "death-care industry," as it's known, or on life expectancy broadly. It's the difference between talking about *an* embarrassing moment and talking about *your* embarrassing moment. The latter can be much easier to approach breezily.

To a death-care expert, death is just death. So I had more than a few chirpy conversations about life expectancies and terminal disease and projected death totals with all of the emotional hesitation of doctors swapping stories about their most nauseating operations.

What I assumed was that, like so many other aspects of American life, the, uh, fading of the boomers would spur a sudden crunch for those businesses that cater to the dead and dying. That, for example, the surge in deaths would overwhelm cemeteries or spur as many new funeral homes as the boomers once spurred new baby-carriage companies. It won't.

It's obviously the case that more older Americans means that more people will die each year. A Census Bureau projection released in 2017 estimated that the United States would hit 3.1 million deaths a year by 2030, an increase over the 2.7 million predicted for 2020. Due to the coronavirus pandemic, though, we exceeded the 2030 mark a decade early.

Assuming that the pandemic years are an outlier, the boom will fade more slowly than it arose. There were about 74 million boomers in 2020, meaning that, if *only* boomers died each year, it would take 23 years for every

CHART 13
The Lives and Deaths of Pre-Boom Americans

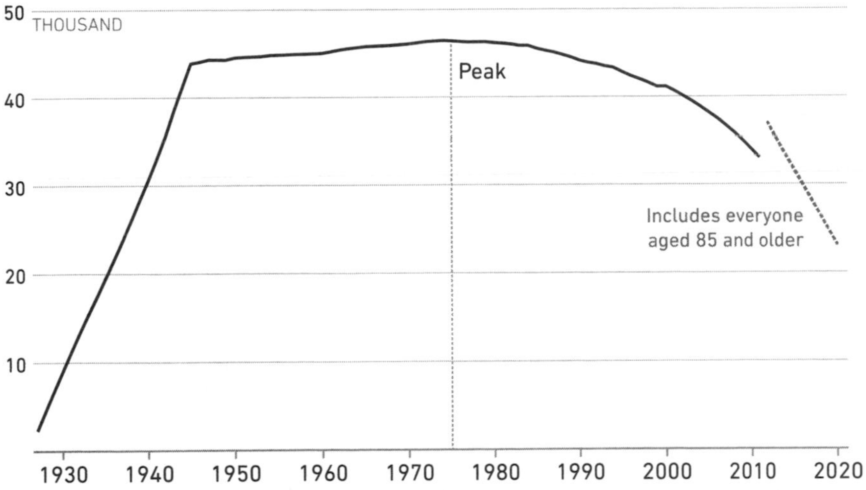

HOW TO READ THIS CHART   The curve above shows the size of the population of U.S. residents (including immigrants) born from 1927 to 1945. In 2012, the oldest members of that group turned 85—the year at which Census Bureau single-year-of-age data start grouping everyone into an 85-and-older bucket. So the dashed line at right includes everyone even older than those born in 1927. The line has fallen quickly, but not as quickly even now as it rose at the beginning.

boomer to die even at the exceptional rate seen in the first year of the pandemic. Consider the trajectory of the 19-year period prior to the boom, those born between 1927 and 1945. That population was at its largest in 1975 and then began to taper downward. Over time, the tapering has sped up, but the group grew much faster at the front end than it has been shrinking at the back.

There's a slowly-then-all-at-once quality to this, an accelerating decline in population groups. But, mirroring the generation before, we can expect that the baby boom will end not with a bang but a fizzle.

That said, its scale is already changing the profile of death in the United States. Over the past two decades—prior to the pandemic—the percentage

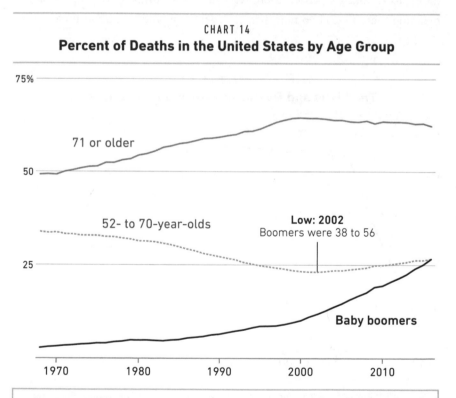

CHART 14
Percent of Deaths in the United States by Age Group

HOW TO READ THIS CHART Each line shows the percentage of deaths in the United States each year that occurred among the age group, according to my analysis of Centers for Disease Control and Prevention data.[19] The most recent age-distribution data as of this writing were for 2016.

of deaths among those aged 52 to 70 began to increase, a function of the sheer number of people joining that age category.

As we saw occur with wealth in the same period in the last chapter, boomers reshaped the death curve. They hit their fifties and suddenly more people in their fifties were dying relative to the total population. So we come back to our original question: How much will this shake up the death-care industry? Will there be as robust a surge in demand for cemetery space as there was for kindergarten classrooms in the 1950s?

We can do a bit of grim back-of-the-envelope math. If the average coffin is about 84 inches long by 28 inches wide[20] and there are 74 million boomers in the United States, burying all of them would require about 43 square miles of space, not accounting for any space between interments. In other words, we could simply take all of the land that's part of the Walt Disney World complex and convert it into the most densely packed cemetery in North America.[21] The Grievingest Place on Earth™.

But that's not the pattern that we see. In contrast to the growth in employment in the retirement industry, the number of people working in death care fell by 6 percent from 2002 to 2020—again, even as the number of people employed overall in the United States increased by 9 percent. In 2002 about 140,000 people worked in death care. By 2020, that had dropped to 130,000.[22]

The concern that America will run out of cemetery space is—with few exceptions—not actually a significant one as we know, because Iowa State University's Carlton Basmajian has researched this question. Not because he's particularly morbid, mind you (though he did cop to being a Tim Burton fan when we spoke on the phone), but simply because it was a niche (ahem) that had gone unfilled in academic research.

For example, it's not even clear how many cemeteries there are in the United States. In response to my question on that point, Basmajian cited research from Wilbur Zelinsky that identified about 100,000 named cemeteries, only a fraction of which are active, and perhaps as many anonymous ones: family plots, cemeteries from the Civil War era, etc.[23]

Basmajian and his frequent research partner Christopher Coutts created an algorithm meant to address the space issue more concretely than our quick calculations above. They found that the issue isn't space but proximity.

"There's probably not a space problem at all, at least in the gross sense of the term," Basmajian told me—then adding the key qualifier. "The United States has plenty of space to bury bodies, especially in places like Iowa. We don't in metropolitan areas where people live. And if people are assuming they're going to be near where they live after they're alive, in death, then we do have an issue."

Consider Brooklyn's Green-Wood Cemetery. Now located in the second-most densely populated county in the United States, it was created in 1838 as a rural cemetery to help alleviate overcrowding in New York City itself.[24] (Brooklyn didn't join the city until sixty years later.) Now, though, it is the final resting place of 570,000 people—more than lived in New York City at the time of Green-Wood's founding.

Though the cemetery is over 180 years old, its president, Richard Moylan, has worked there for one out of every four days it has existed. He started half a century ago with a gig mowing the facility's lawns and, slowly, moved up. One of the things he enjoys about his job, he told me, was being able to be part of "reinventing" the cemetery as its ability to inter new bodies decreased.

"We are planning for that day when we run out of space," Moylan said. The cemetery already stacks caskets three high, more than in most places, though common for New York City. Still, though, he didn't anticipate being able to accommodate more people for long. "I've said we have about five years left," he told me when we spoke in 2021. But, then, "we keep finding spots."

It's sort of like drilling for oil. Past projections that every field had been discovered and many deposits emptied are proven wrong as new findings and new technologies keep the industry going. (This analogy collapses given the negative side effects of fossil-fuel consumption, but you get the point.) At Green-Wood, they find some small amounts of additional space or, when possible, move infrastructure in order to create it.

Green-Wood is particularly instructive, though, because it's an outlier: an old, full cemetery in a densely populated area. Most cemeteries aren't that. What's more, boomers are actually slightly less likely to live in densely populated places like Brooklyn than Americans overall.

But then we get to another reason that Green-Wood keeps being able to find space: dead people aren't using as much cemetery space as they used to. That's because, as of 2016, more than half of those who die in the United States had chosen to be cremated.[25]

"A lot of people who were cremated don't end up in cemeteries anymore," Basmajian told me. "They end up on mantels and bedside tables and scattered in places. Whether there will ever need to be a public memorial space for those folks is a good question."

For Moylan, this was a mixed blessing. More cremations mean less space required for interment ("We can put a lot more in a lot less space," he said), but also less interment altogether. He estimated that only about 1 in 10 cremations led to a memorialization.

Crucial to our broader point is that growth in cremation. CDC data tell

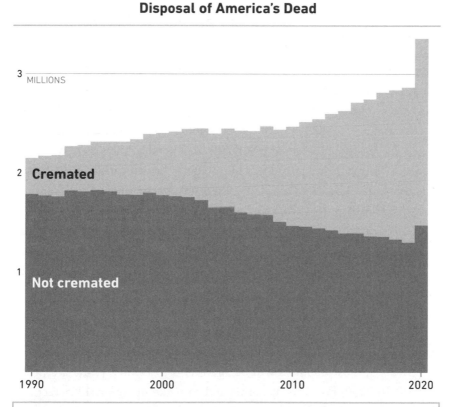

CHART 15
Disposal of America's Dead

HOW TO READ THIS CHART This stacked column graph shows the total number of deaths (the total height of the columns for a year) as well as the portion of those deaths that result in cremation. As you can see, the number of deaths in total has increased as the number of non-cremated bodies has declined.

us how many people die in a year. By applying cremation rates calculated by the evocatively named Cremation Association of North America, we see that even as the number of annual deaths has increased over the past 30 years, the number of full bodies that might be interred in a cemetery dropped: the rate of cremations is increasing faster than the number of deaths. Until we hit 2020, that is; that first pandemic year again disrupts the pattern. CANA data indicate that, in that year, more than 56 percent of those who died were cremated.[26]

In short, then, there will be no rush to build new cemeteries as there was to build new elementary schools. That's in part because the boom will end more slowly than it began—leaving decades more to reshape the country.

THE DECLINE OF THE BOOM IS ONLY THE START OF A CHANGING AMERICA

No American has ever lived longer than 119 years. That record was held by Sarah Knauss, born in 1880 and died in 1999—a life that spanned a period from the gunfight at the O.K. Corral to the impeachment of Bill Clinton. Knauss was alive at the same time as both Jefferson Davis and Kamala Harris. As *The Washington Post* put it at the time of her death, Knauss "was older than the Brooklyn Bridge and was born before the dedication of the Statue of Liberty. She was 28 when Henry Ford introduced the Model T and 88 when Neil Armstrong walked on the moon in July 1969."[27]

I mention Knauss because it suggests that final, ultimate endpoint of the baby boom will probably come no later than the year 2083. Most boomers, of course, won't make it that far. As of its 2017 estimate, the Census Bureau expected there to be only about 2.5 million boomers alive in the United States by 2060, less than 1 percent of the country's population.[28]

Those projections allow us to visualize our now-tedious analogy, the passage of the boomers through the population overall.

By 2025, most boomers will be aged 65 or over; five years later, they all will. In 2030, boomers are projected to make up about 17 percent of the population, the lowest density since 1955. And, of course, it descends from there.

What's particularly interesting is what happens to the 65-and-up category as the years pass. The baby boom comes and goes—but the percentage

CHART 16
The Pig Wends Its Way Through

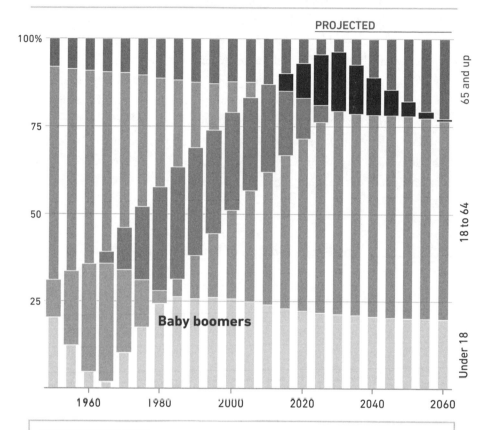

PROJECTED

65 and up

18 to 64

Baby boomers

Under 18

1960   1980   2000   2020   2040   2060

HOW TO READ THIS CHART The graph depicts 110 years of the U.S. population, from the first census in which boomers were included to the latest projection of the 2017 census estimates. The boomers are depicted as a percentage of the country's total population over time, showing how much of each age group—children, adults, those of retirement age—they constitute.

(and number) of Americans of retirement age continues to increase. When the first boomers reached age 65, in 2011, those aged 65 and over made up 13.3 percent of the population. When the last boomers reach that age in 2029, they'll make up 20.3 percent of the population. But in 2060, when less than 1 in 100 Americans is a boomer, those aged 65 and up are expected to be more than 23 percent of the population.

(Technically, the Census Bureau measures not the number of Americans, as such, but instead the number of United States residents, a group that includes noncitizens. It is, however, clunky to repeatedly refer to portions or tallies of "residents of the United States," particularly in a book throughout which that phrase would need to appear frequently. So your patience with my using the briefer but slightly less accurate "Americans" phrasing is appreciated.)

We can visualize the shift in age groupings a bit differently. There are two ways in which the population will change over the course of the next 40 years or so: in raw numbers and in percentages. The number of people aged 65 and up will increase in raw terms, from about 56 million in 2020 to nearly 95 million in 2060. (Any concerns about overbuilding to accommodate the elder-care needs of the aging baby boom should therefore be somewhat mol-

CHART 17
The Projected Age of the Population

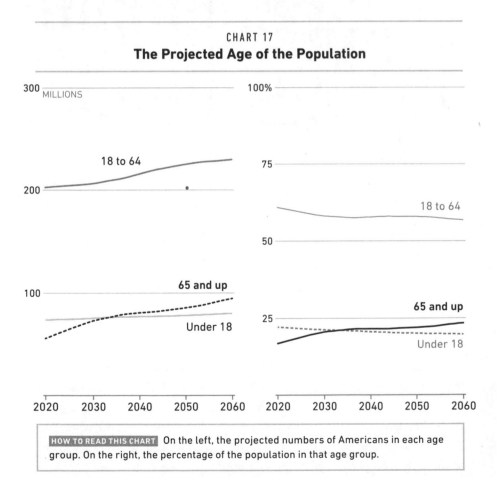

HOW TO READ THIS CHART On the left, the projected numbers of Americans in each age group. On the right, the percentage of the population in that age group.

lified.) But the population overall will also grow, so the increase in the *density* of those aged 65 and over in the population will grow more modestly.

There's the increase in the density of those aged 65 and over. But notice that the number of people under the age of 18 is essentially flat. In 1900, there were about 10 times as many people under 18 as aged 65 and over. A century later, the ratio was a bit over 3 to 1. By the mid-2030s, the two groups will be about the same size, and, 25 years later, there will be almost 1.2 people over the age of 64 for every one under 18.

Again, this isn't a function of the boomers. Instead, it is a function of Americans living longer and having fewer children. The number of Americans aged 85 or older will more than double over the period from 2020 to 2060, for example. The number of Americans aged 75 to 84 is expected to

CHART 18
The Number of Elderly Americans in Future Years

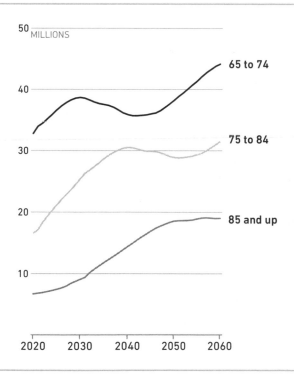

HOW TO READ THIS CHART A simple line graph.

increase by 90 percent, all while the population overall increases by about a fifth.

The short version of all of this is that America will be getting older. Grayer. At the same time, the data suggest, it will be getting less densely White—the change that creates the most significant ripples throughout the rest of this discussion.

Before we explore this aspect of things, though, we should explain how and why the Census Bureau measures the number of people of a particular race or ethnicity in the country. Since the first census in 1790, conducted soon after the Constitution was ratified by enough states to bring the United States into existence, the government has counted the country's residents using groupings that align with how we now recognize race. Then, the categories were "White" and "slave," with no further articulation of the race of the latter group required. Each decade, the census evolved, measuring different categories of interest to the government, from complicated combinations of racial history—"octoroon" was an 1890 category meant to identify a person with one Black great-grandparent and therefore track perceived racial shortcomings[29]— to specific places of origin like Filipinos and "Hindus" on the 1930 form.[30] By that census, anyone with any Black ancestor was categorized as Black, "no matter how small the percentage of Negro blood."[31] We'll explore these changes and the shifts in how Americans consider race in chapter 8.

Over time, the collection of this data was formalized across the government. In 1997, the White House Office of Management and Budget published revised standards for collecting racial data, establishing five categories: American Indian or Alaska Native; Asian; Black or African American; Native Hawaiian or Other Pacific Islander; and White. It's important to remember that racial categorization is done by the respondent; that is, people get to pick their own racial identities. Notice that there's no categorization for "Hispanic." That's because the OMB standard includes a second question focused not on race but on *ethnicity*, and that question is centered on whether a respondent is Hispanic or Latino. This distinction is the subject of robust debate and we'll get into it a bit later. But for now, it's important to understand that data on race (White, Black) are collected separately from data on Hispanic ethnicity.

You can see how things get complicated. People who are racially Black in the census, for example, may also be Hispanic. It's not hard to come up with examples of this group: immigrants from the Dominican Republic, for example, or some people from Colombia. What's more, since these are self-identified categories, they do not necessarily follow from skin color. In the Dominican Republic, adults are less likely to identify as White and more likely to identify as mixed race than are adults in other Latin American countries, suggesting likely differences in census self-reporting.[32] More on these distinctions later as well.

This division of race and ethnicity makes the government's race data a bit clunky in the way that government analyses can be. You have a count for Whites and a count for Hispanic Whites (broadly the group that we think of when we think of Hispanic Americans). There are Hispanic Asians (though not very many) and non-Hispanic Hawaiians (most of them). Making things *more* complicated, the bureau has found in recent years that respondents don't find the existing race categories to be sufficiently descriptive.[33] If you're Middle Eastern, for example, what race would you choose? There is a category for "some other race," and that, in both the 2000 and 2010 censuses, was the third most commonly selected race group.[34] By 2020, it was the second most common.[35]

As part of a federal working group, the bureau conducted experiments aimed at improving how racial data are collected. There was a recommendation that the bureau use a refined tool for collecting racial data in the 2020 census, a single-question option that included "Hispanic" and "Middle East ern or North African." This was not implemented by the OMB during Donald Trump's presidency for reasons that were not articulated publicly. But it's not hard to make some guesses. You'll recall that the administration was actively working to use the 2020 census to tally the number of undocumented immigrants in the country, an effort that the Brennan Center for Justice at NYU Law described aptly as an effort to "exert extreme partisan influence" over the count.[36] There were political benefits to maintaining the status quo, like that including Hispanic among the delineated races would almost certainly decrease the number of people who identified as both White and Hispanic, shrinking the perceived size of America's White population. It would also create the new MENA racial group, which conservative writer Mike Gonzalez argued in *The Wall Street Journal* was one of "the building blocks of the progressive plan to transform America."[37]

So we come back to the bureau's 2017 projections of how the racial

CHART 19
America's Projected Racial and Ethnic Composition

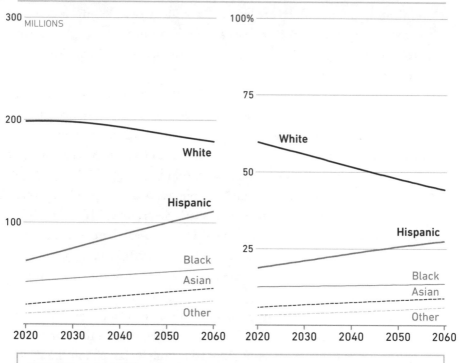

> **HOW TO READ THIS CHART** As before, the graph at left shows the composition in absolute terms and, at right, in relative ones.

composition of America is likely to evolve over the next few decades. By the mid-2040s, America will be less than half White—or, more accurately, the Census Bureau expects that, by the mid-2040s, less than half of Americans will describe themselves as both White and non-Hispanic.

There are two reasons for that, as there were two reasons for older Americans surpassing younger ones in the projections above. The first reason is that the number of White Americans will decline. The second is that the number of non-White Americans will increase (including an expected dramatic increase among Hispanics).

Largely because of the baby boom, White Americans tend to be older than Hispanics. (Until further notice, I'll use "White" to describe non-Hispanic Whites.) In 2018, Census Bureau data indicated that the most

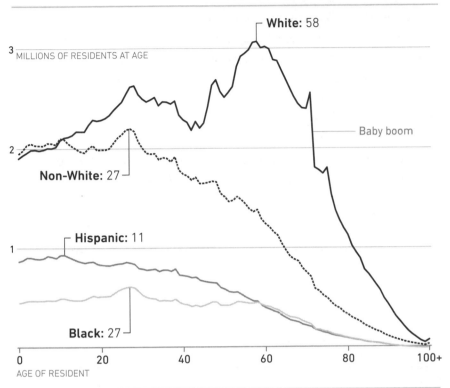

CHART 20
Most Common Ages Among Racial Groups in 2018

White: 58

3 MILLIONS OF RESIDENTS AT AGE

Baby boom

2

Non-White: 27

Hispanic: 11

1

Black: 27

0   20   40   60   80   100+
AGE OF RESIDENT

> **HOW TO READ THIS CHART** Using data from 2018, the graph shows the number of people of each racial/ethnic group at a specific age. The ages at which there are the most people in the group are indicated; for example, the most common age for Whites was 58 that year—meaning they were born in 1960, near the tail end of the baby boom.

common age for Whites was more than five times the most common age for Hispanics and twice the most common age for non-Whites overall.

In other words, there's a strong correlation between White Americans and older Americans, an overlap that is a pretty central part of the rest of this book.

Forgive the lack of drama surrounding that revelation.

While more than two-thirds of 58-year-old Americans were White in 2018, Whites made up fewer than half of 8-year-olds. That weighting is the flip side to the White majority in America—and it has the side effect that

Whites are going to make up far more of the country's deaths over the next 40 years or so. In 2030, nearly three-quarters of deaths are expected to be among Whites. Thirty years later, even as the number of Whites dying each year declines, 3 in 5 deaths will be among Whites.

One of the things that will contribute to the composition of the population over the long term, including its racial makeup, is new immigration. The density of foreign-born people in the United States has surged since immigration laws were relaxed in the 1960s. Over the next several decades, the percent of U.S. residents born elsewhere is projected to rise to about 17 percent and then hold steady.

By 2060, the Census Bureau estimates that nearly 70 million people in the United States will have been born in other countries—more than the

CHART 21
The Projected Density of Immigrants in the Population

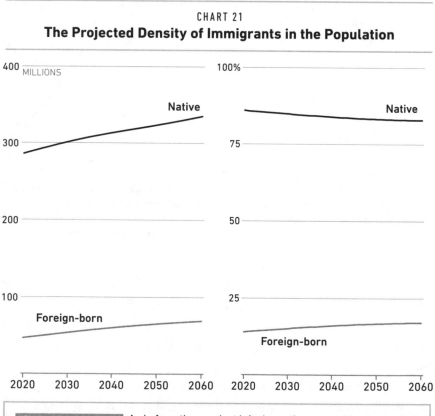

HOW TO READ THIS CHART As before, the graph at left shows the composition in absolute terms and, at right, in relative ones.

entire population of the United States in any year prior to 1895. Of course, the population overall is projected by then to exceed 400 million.

That assumes the country meets the predicted level of immigration. If the Census Bureau's 2017 estimates of migration to the United States are accurate, the country passes the 400 million mark in 2058. If immigration is lower than expected, some 27 million fewer people are projected to live here. And there's certainly reason to think that the bureau's estimates of immigration might have been higher a few months into Donald Trump's presidency than were warranted. After all, immigration is not a natural force, but one that's been shaped primarily by politics and policy for more than a century. Lower immigration means a smaller population—and an older and less diverse one.[38]

That has secondary implications that become obvious when we consider Mace's warnings about the imbalance in age groups. In the normal projection scenario, there will be 2.4 people of working age for every person aged 65 or older, 230 million versus 95 million. In the low immigration scenario, the number of elderly people falls by about 3 percent to 91.4 million. The number of working-age people, though, falls by nearly 8 percent to 212 million. The result is that there would be 2.3 working-age people for every person of retirement age—increasing the strain on both government programs and the ability of the economy to meet labor demands. Using Mace's age ranges, the difference is between 3 adults per senior and only 2.8 adults in the low immigration scenario. This is a central question for how the economy looks in the future, and one we'll return to.

Regardless of which scenario is more accurate, though, we can say that the country will be reshaped over the next several decades, becoming grayer and less White. Assuming either scenario is terribly accurate at all.

THE CLARITY OF THE CRYSTAL BALL

Predicting the future is rather famously tricky. Fortune-tellers aren't known for offering useful, unfailing insights unavailable elsewhere.

The Census Bureau has the advantage of being able to deploy statistical modeling and historical data to improve its forecasting, but, even then, things change. As it prepared the 2010 census, the bureau could not have predicted that 2020 would arrive in the midst of a global pandemic at the tail end of an administration that actively tamped down immigration to the United States. These are things that are difficult to predict.

At the time of a report published by the Roosevelt-era National Resources Committee in 1938 called *Population Problems*, for example, it seemed nearly certain that "[u]nless large numbers of immigrants are admitted or unexpected increases in the birth rate occur, the rate of growth will continue to slow down."[39]

"Even on the most conservative estimates of the population experts the population of the United States in 1980 would be equal to that of today," the report argued, before deviating into a little reassuring xenophobia. "The idea that great numbers of men are needed to protect the Nation against the mighty hordes of more prolific foreigners, is based on ancient history and has little support from present military experience."

In his history of the baby boom, Landon Jones walks through a litany of similar assertions. Even as the boom arrived—certainly an "unexpected increase in the birth rate"—it was waved off as aberrant, a blip, a function of those returning soldiers and pent-up demand. But the population in 1980 was not equivalent to that of 1938. It was 74 percent larger.

The bureau's projections even in the 1980s were, as expected, not perfect. The population trends from 1990 to 2020 tracked closely with the bureau's highest-population series of estimates published in 1986.[40] The density of the population of people over 65 trailed a bit behind. The density of non-Hispanic Whites was well below even what the high-population estimate projected.[41] A mixed bag.

You can look at this in a variety of ways. One is that the projections weren't bad, which is fair. Another is that the central trend we currently see—an older, less White America—was underestimated in both regards.

That's puzzling until you realize that the projections in 1986, like those in 2017, were heavily dependent on immigration expectations. The highest population series included among its assumptions that 750,000 more people would immigrate to the United States each year than emigrate out. For the lowest series, the assumption was one-third as large. And, in fact, immigration often exceeded the larger number. From 1990 to 2000, the United States averaged a net immigration of about 823,000 people a year.[42] That explains not only the high population but also the lower density of older people and the more rapid decrease in the percentage of the non-Hispanic White population.

CHART 22
How the Census Bureau's 1986 Projections Held Up

— Actual/current projection   *1986 projection series:* ··· Lowest   — Middle   -- Highest

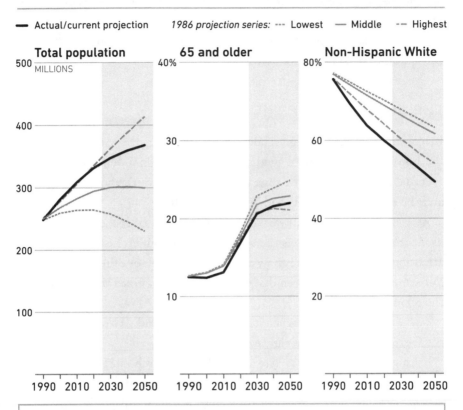

HOW TO READ THIS CHART   Here we compare three series of projections from 1986 with both what happened and what's projected to happen moving forward. The darkest-colored line represents the actual values and the current projections, extending into the future, which is indicated with a gray background.

This is why the question of how immigration has shifted or may shift is so important. If the United States suddenly curtails migration from Mexico and Central America, it has significant implications for population size, the labor force, and the density of the population by age.

It also has significant implications for race. These projections are necessarily dependent on how Americans describe themselves and how the Census Bureau allows them to do so. So they hinge on an increasingly urgent question that spent centuries as something of an undercurrent: What makes an American White, and how does someone qualify for that categorization? America is riven by the idea that Whites are in decline, a debate muddied by our lack of a common understanding of who is granted inclusion in that group.

The last days of the baby boom may end up being the moment at which this question must be confronted.

THE SKELETONS OF THE BOOM

Benjamin Keys went to high school near Chicago. In the early 1970s, when the boom was high school aged, more than 4,000 students attended his eventual alma mater. By the time he arrived, though, the boom had passed and the number of students had dropped by half.

"There were these hallways that were just full of lockers that weren't used," Keys told me. This is the sort of thing to which he pays particular attention at this point: he is now an associate professor of real estate at the Wharton School. And, given that expertise, he recognized the inefficiencies the boom had created.

"It's a very hard thing when it's in cement," he said. "How do you shrink the footprint? How do you rightsize this?"

Auburn, Massachusetts, had an answer. In March 2021, the town held a virtual groundbreaking ceremony on a project to "rightsize" two old schools. Elected officials from the lieutenant governor down praised the innovative plan: transform the Mary D. Stone and Julia Bancroft schools into senior housing.

Each building is being overhauled to provide 55 units of housing for people aged 55 and older. During the groundbreaking ceremony officials praised the neatness of the plan.[43] It gives older residents a place to live and some assistance while freeing up housing for younger residents. Multiple birds slain.

It's hard not to appreciate the parallels. Places to educate being converted into places for the elderly, tracking the baby boom? Nor is this the only such example. In recent years, schools have been converted to senior housing in Fulton, New York,[44] Glassport, Pennsylvania,[45] Macomb County, Michigan,[46] and Portland, Maine,[47] among others. In 2005, well ahead of the curve, the *Pittsburgh Post-Gazette* reported on the conversion of schools to senior facilities as a trend.[48] That it's particularly common in places where the population shrank, like the Rust Belt, is not a coincidence. There, that ratio of old to young is already skewed in the way that the Census Bureau projects the rest of the country will in future decades approach or match. In Pittsburgh's Allegheny County, there were more people over the age of 65 in 2019 than there were people under the age of 18.

While the effort to repurpose excess educational infrastructure is interesting, the shift the country will undergo as the baby boom ages is much broader and more complicated than simply dealing with the stretch marks the boom caused. What the Census Bureau projections show is a country changing in obvious ways. What it doesn't show is the nonobvious shifts that will occur as the boom ages and changes in politics, in education, and in religion.

And that transition, not the cleanup from the boom, is going to reshape the country.

3

How to Spot a Boomer

So the way he tells it, Peter Kuli was waiting to pick up a prescription at CVS when he noticed that a bunch of people he knew were remixing a jokey track by his friend Jonathan Williams. This is how it works sometimes in a certain segment of the online music community: people create a song and then share the pieces to be remixed and reused. Kuli, not to be left out of the goofiness he saw on his phone, went back to his dorm room at Champlain College in Vermont and quickly created his own iteration.

He saw its potential. "I messaged Jonathan on Twitter and I said, you should totally put your song on TikTok," Kuli recalled to me. "I think tweens would really get a kick out of it." But Miller shrugged, encouraging Kuli to put up his remix instead. And Kuli did. "The rest is kind of history there," Kuli said, with little exaggeration.

If you're reading this book, it's fairly likely that you may not spend an inordinate amount of time on TikTok. It's the evolution of a music-specific app called Musical.ly that encouraged users to sing along with existing tracks, pushing people to offer their own interpretations of popular or featured music. When Kuli put his song on TikTok, a few of his friends made videos to accompany it. Then, within a week, its popularity exploded.

"Eventually, it just got this kind of snowball effect," he told me. "It got a little out of hand—it got out of hand very quickly."

"What does 'getting out of hand' look like?" I asked.

"Well," he told me, "the *New York Times* article."

That article did, in fact, get somewhat out of hand. It was centered not on the song itself but on the song's title, which had picked up on an increasingly popular online meme: dismissing baby boomers as out of touch or embarrassing. The song was called "OK Boomer."

> You're all old and racist, all about the fakeness / I'm tryna pay my bills, but I'm all on the wait list . . . Cremated to ashes, disappear like magic / When you wear that MAGA hat, lookin' like a fascist.

"'OK Boomer' Marks the End of Friendly Generational Relations," Taylor Lorenz's *Times* article was titled, without much overstatement.[1] Within days, maybe hours, the phrase and the culture it spawned drew an enormous amount of attention.

"The article blew up," Lorenz told me. "It immediately became one of the most read articles at *The New York Times*. It popped off, getting tons of traffic and millions of views." That rippled out from the paper to merchandisers Lorenz mentioned in the article and to Kuli's song, which by now has been heard millions of times and earned him a first-look deal with Warner Music.

Part of that was because the reactions that people had to the article were the same reactions that people were having on TikTok: either amusement or blind fury. "It became a thing where the older people online were really mad about it," Lorenz said. "The cable-news people all talked about it."

I sincerely wasn't clear whether she meant "cable-news hosts and personalities" or "people who watch cable news," a group that overlaps neatly with "older people." She clarified that it was the former, who invited her on to harangue her about what kids are doing today.

That's a fitting response, given the genesis of the song in the first place. Musical.ly folded into TikTok in August 2018. By the autumn of 2019, when Jonathan Williams first built the bones of the "OK Boomer" song, older people were just starting to use the app. In the early days of the internet, when its user base was centered on university campuses, there would be a flurry of tension each September as freshmen arrived and began puttering around, failing to understand the rules and norms by which longer-term users abided. In September 2019, the freshmen were boomers and the norms were those of TikTok.

Combine that influx of older people posting about selling real estate or opining on politics with TikTok's emphasis on responding to videos with videos and a phenomenon is born. Instead of rolling their eyes at the new posts, young users could respond not just with text but with Kuli's staticky, aggressive track. Thousands had, even before Lorenz's article was published. As a troll, an effort to provoke irritation, the song proved enormously effective.

"If they do take it personally, it just further proves that they take

CHART 23
Google Searches for "What Generation Am I" by Month

MORE SEARCH INTEREST →

November 2019

2015   2016   2017   2018   2019   2020

HOW TO READ THIS CHART Google is a bit coy about the data it makes public. Instead of sharing precisely the number of times a term was searched in a certain period, it instead offers relative values through its Trends tool, comparing the number of searches in a period with the maximum value found in any period. So if in a year the term "Congress" was searched 400 times in every month except May, when it was searched 500 times, the value for May would be 100 and every other month 80—because 400 is 80 percent of 500.

Luckily, that suits us fine for the comparison above. In November 2019, there were more searches for "what generation am I" than in any other month between January 2015 and December 2020.[2] As you can see, the number of searches that month was significantly higher than the other months, even if we don't know exactly how many times it was searched.

everything we do as offensive," one 17-year-old said of annoyed boomers for Lorenz's original article. "It's just funnier."

All of a sudden, a generational tension that had been present for some time was distilled into a punchy phrase. And all of a sudden an ancillary weirdness emerged: people suddenly wondered what generation they belonged to.

Generally, the number of Americans searching "what generation am I" on Google tracks about evenly with "how big is the Earth," though that latter search is seasonal, rising and falling with the school year. That November, after Lorenz's article was published, searches for "what generation am I" spiked.

People have always been curious about their generation. But suddenly they were *really* curious. Were the tweens complaining about *me*?

CHART 24
How Often Americans Correctly Identify Their Own Generation

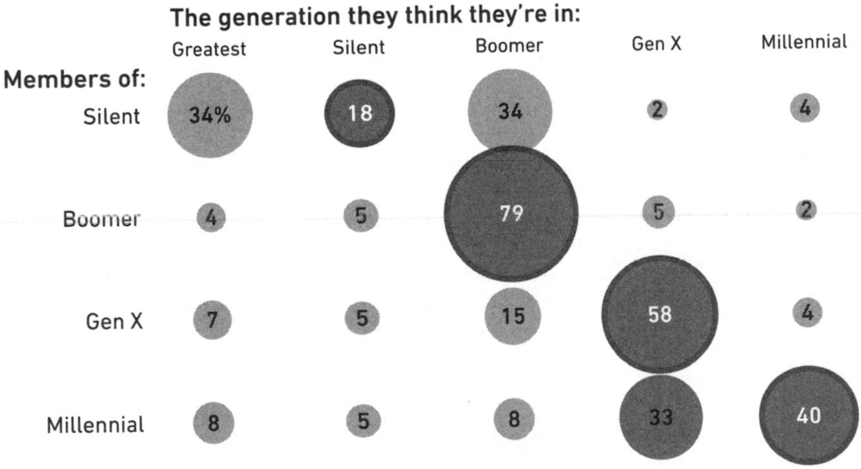

The generation they think they're in:

Members of:	Greatest	Silent	Boomer	Gen X	Millennial
Silent	34%	18	34	2	4
Boomer	4	5	79	5	2
Gen X	7	5	15	58	4
Millennial	8	5	8	33	40

HOW TO READ THIS CHART This is an exploration of how members of a given generation, listed at left, perceive the generation to which they belong among those listed along the top. The circles are scaled to the percentage of each generation that picked any of the five offered generations. The circles outlined in black are the actual generations to which the respondents belonged—according to Pew's boundaries, which are, of course, subjective. (Too few members of the Greatest generation were polled to be able to show their responses.)

You'll remember that there are good reasons for generational uncertainty. Because the boundaries are, for the most part, after-the-fact constructs meant to facilitate how we (and, particularly, marketers) refer to different age groups, the edges can be a bit blurry. So it's not surprising that a 2015 Pew Research Center poll found that only 4 in 10 millennials identified themselves as such.[3]

Some of this may be a function of self-deception; that 1 in 12 millennials identified as members of the greatest generation, the youngest members of which were born in 1928, is probably more about the adjective than about accuracy. That a third of millennials called themselves Gen X suggests a broad familiarity with the category, if not the specific years by which Pew bounds it.

It's nonetheless hard not to escape the extent to which boomers identify as boomers. Maybe some of those Google searches were boomers eager to reassure themselves that the kids weren't making fun of them. The Pew research, though, suggests that most knew exactly who they were.

This is made easier by the fact that the boomer generation is cohesive in ways that later generations weren't. There is a boomer *type* in a different way than there is a millennial type, and much (though not all) of it has to do with the same demographics that are projected to shift in the United States in future generations.

There are at least seven characteristics in which boomers (and older generations) are distinguishable from millennials (and younger ones). Some are obvious. Others less so. But, in the aggregate, these distinctions by themselves do a lot to illuminate common divisions in American culture—ones interwoven into Kuli's song.

1. BOOMERS ARE OLDER

Not the most incisive observation, certainly, but the central and defining difference between older and younger generations is that they are older and younger. Fully 100 percent of boomers are at least in their fifties. No millennial joins them there, by agreed-upon definition. What this means, though, is that cultural and political aspects of being young manifest for one group and not the other.

Political leadership provides a concrete example. The Constitution requires that candidates for Congress be of a certain age; in the case of the House of Representatives, that's 25. But in early 2022, the average age was well above that: 58 years. People who turned 58 in 2022, incidentally, are baby boomers.

CHART 25
Median Age of Congressional Districts vs. Ages of Representatives in the House

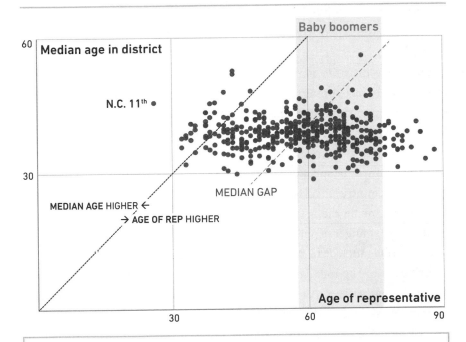

HOW TO READ THIS CHART This is a scatter plot, comparing the median age in congressional districts in 2019 (from 0 to 60 on the vertical axis) to the age of those districts' representatives in the U.S. House in 2022 (from 0 to 90 on the horizontal axis). Each dot represents one of the districts for which both sets of data were available. At far left, for example, is North Carolina's Eleventh District, represented at the time by Madison Cawthorn. He turned 27 in 2022, putting him well under his district median—and, therefore, to the left of the longer diagonal line. A dot on that line indicates a district in which the representative is precisely the same age as the district median. The median gap in age between district and representative is shown with the shorter dashed line.

The median age in the country, meanwhile, is about 20 years younger than that. Only about 30 members of the House were younger in 2022 than the median age of their districts; the same number of representatives were at least 43 years older than their district medians. One generation holding federal legislative power over another.

Another example of how that age difference emerges: When hundreds of thousands of Americans protested racial injustice throughout the United States in the summer of 2020, they did not perfectly reflect the country's composition. Instead, Pew Research Center analysis indicates, 4 in 10 of the adults who participated were under the age of 30, twice the density of that age group in the adult population overall at that point. Only about a fifth of participants were aged 50 or over, a group that made up half of the country's adults.[4]

This age disparity is not unique to those particular protests. Analysis from Orb Media of protest participants in nearly 100 countries during 2016 and 2017 found that those under the age of 40 were 9 to 17 percent more likely to participate in protests and demonstrations than those aged 40 and over.[5] That was an increase; in 2000, Orb found a gap of about 3 percent globally. Younger people were more likely to participate in protests in three-quarters of countries, including the United States.

One reason for the age divide on protests in the United States is certainly availability; younger people are less likely to have typical employment hours or family obligations. (In 2020, the ongoing coronavirus pandemic probably contributed to the imbalance.) Part of it is also likely cultural. Since the boomers, really, there's been an association between American youth and protest, an association that overlaps with college and the intimate socialization of higher education. Importantly, though, the divide isn't simply on participation. In September 2020, a *Washington Post*–ABC News poll asked Americans whether they supported those racial justice protests. Among those aged 40 and younger, 64 percent said they did. Among those aged 65 and older, 52 percent said they didn't.[6]

This example is useful as an exploration of how views differ by age—but it's not as though you didn't know that. It also points to the difference in political engagement, an important question later in the book. It's mostly useful to consider those 2020 protests, though, because they were confounded by another key difference between baby boomers and younger Americans.

2. BOOMERS ARE WHITER

A central point of this chapter—and, really, this book—is that those age divides overlap with other demographic splits. We began this chapter talking about the age gap in use of TikTok. As it turns out, about 3 in 10 Black and Hispanic Americans said they used TikTok, compared to 2 in 10 Whites.[7] This is in no small part because younger Americans are also less likely to *be* White. Disentangling one demographic trait from another is often complicated, including on that question of protests.

Race is a consistent factor in the distinction between older and younger Americans. Consider just the difference between the boomers and millennials, whom we'll define using the Pew boundaries as those born between 1981 and 1996.[8] More than 70 percent of boomers are non-Hispanic White, compared to 55 percent of millennials.[9] Thanks to recent immigration and differences in birth rates by race and ethnicity, millennials are nearly twice as likely to be Hispanic as boomers and more likely to be Black, Asian, or fall into one of the Census Bureau's other, smaller racial categories.

This is simply picking two points out of a continuum. If we overlap racial density with the density of age groups in 2021 (using Census Bureau projections[10]), we see how the composition of the country shifts by age. Those younger than millennials are about half non-White. Those older than boomers are about three-quarters White.

I'll put it less abstractly. If you were to pluck a White American out of a crowd, there's a 1 in 3 chance they'd be a boomer or older and about a 1 in 2 chance they'd be a millennial or younger. If these were coin flips, every other flip would come up "young" and every third "old" (to put it inelegantly). If you plucked a non-White American out of that crowd, though, they're three times as likely to be in that younger group as the older one. Three flips coming up "young" for every "old."

The present also tells us about the future. A fifth of the population in the United States in 2021 was White people of boomer age or older. A quarter of the population was non-White people of millennial age or younger. Because the demographic composition of generations doesn't change very much over time—the members of a generation age consistently and the racial density tends to remain relatively steady—this gives us a sense of how the country

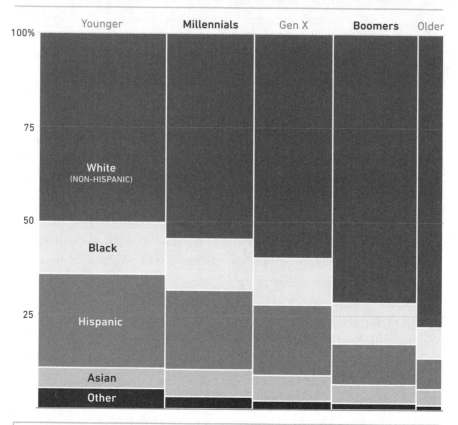

CHART 26
The Distribution of the Population by Race and Age

HOW TO READ THIS CHART   Americans are broken out into five age groups: millennials, boomers, the members of Gen X in between, and those older and younger. Each of those five columns shows the distribution of the group by race. Each column is scaled horizontally to represent its portion of the overall population. That group of Whites who are too young to be millennials makes up about 16 percent of the total graph area—because that group is about 16 percent of the total population.

itself will evolve. So, in 2060, after the older, Whiter group has faded some-what, the Census Bureau estimates that 16 percent of the country will be White people aged 60 and over (a group that will then include all of the mil-lennials) while about 29 percent of the country will be non-Whites under the

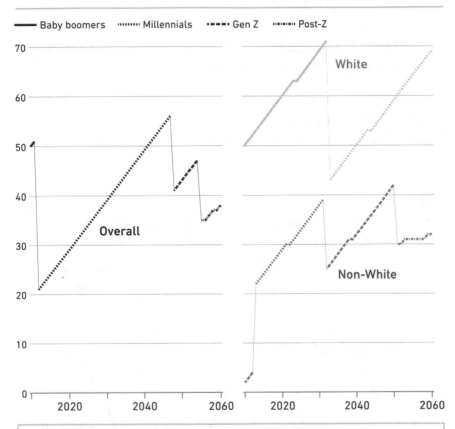

CHART 27

The Projected Most Common Age for Americans Each Year

— Baby boomers   ·········· Millennials   ·—·—· Gen Z   ·—··—·· Post-Z

White

Overall

Non-White

2020   2040   2060   2020   2040   2060

HOW TO READ THIS CHART The two graphs above show the same thing, the projected most common age in the identified population from 2010 to 2050. So in 2010, for example, there were more 50-year-olds—born in 1960 and therefore late boomers—than any other age. But while that was also true of the subset of White Americans, the most common age for non-White Americans in 2010 was two.

age of 40. That's a shift of about 4 percentage points for each group—subtle, but measurable.

Census Bureau projections allow us to see how the prominence of different generations emerges over time, as above, and the ongoing gap in age between racial groups.

For at least the next decade, the most common age for non-White Americans will place them in the millennial generation. The most common age for Whites will land in the baby boom.

3. BOOMERS ARE LESS LIKELY TO BE IMMIGRANTS OR HAVE IMMIGRANT PARENTS

Part of the reason that the baby boom generation is so densely White is that it occurred at an anomalous moment in American history.

In 1924, the xenophobic Johnson-Reed Act became law, instituting firm

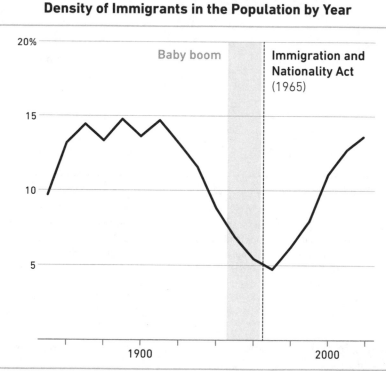

CHART 28
Density of Immigrants in the Population by Year

HOW TO READ THIS CHART A simple line graph showing the percentage of foreign-born residents in the population of the United States by decade.[11] The years of the baby boom are indicated, as is the 1965 passage of the Immigration and Nationality Act.

limits on immigration aimed at restricting arrivals from outside western Europe—meaning not only those who today would not generally identify as White but also the eastern and southern Europeans who were at the time often seen as sitting outside that category. As a result of these restrictions and the advent of World War II, immigration plunged from more than 700,000

CHART 29
Immigration Status of U.S. Residents

■ Immigrant ▨ Native-born, two immigrant parents   ▢ Native-born, one immigrant parent
▨ Native-born, native-born parents

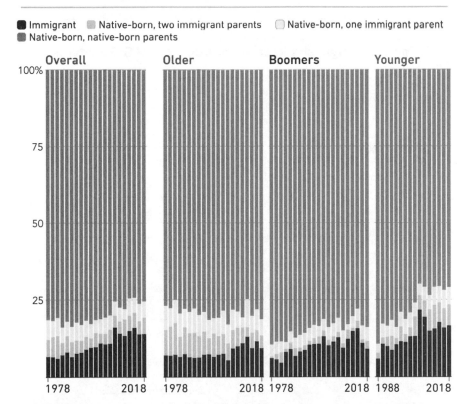

HOW TO READ THIS CHART This graph uses biennial data from the General Social Survey, displayed in stacked columns.[12] (Data for 1992 are averages of the values for 1991 and 1993.) Each vertical column shows 100 percent of a population group in a year and is broken out into the composition of nativity and parentage indicated by the key at top. Since people born after 1964 have only been included in GSS polling for a shorter period of time, the graph for those younger than the boomers is more narrow.

in 1940 (equivalent to one-half of 1 percent of the population) to 38,000 in 1945.[13] And then the boom began.

"The baby boom grew up in the Whitest, most native-origin population in U.S. history," Princeton University sociology professor Douglas Massey explained to me. "In 1970, the percentage of foreign born fell to its lowest point ever in American history, 4.7 percent. The average immigrant in 1970 was somebody's grandparent."

This lull was reversed just as the boom was ending. The years following the assassination of John F. Kennedy were ones in which the country was

CHART 30
Points of Origin and Race of Foreign-Born U.S. Residents

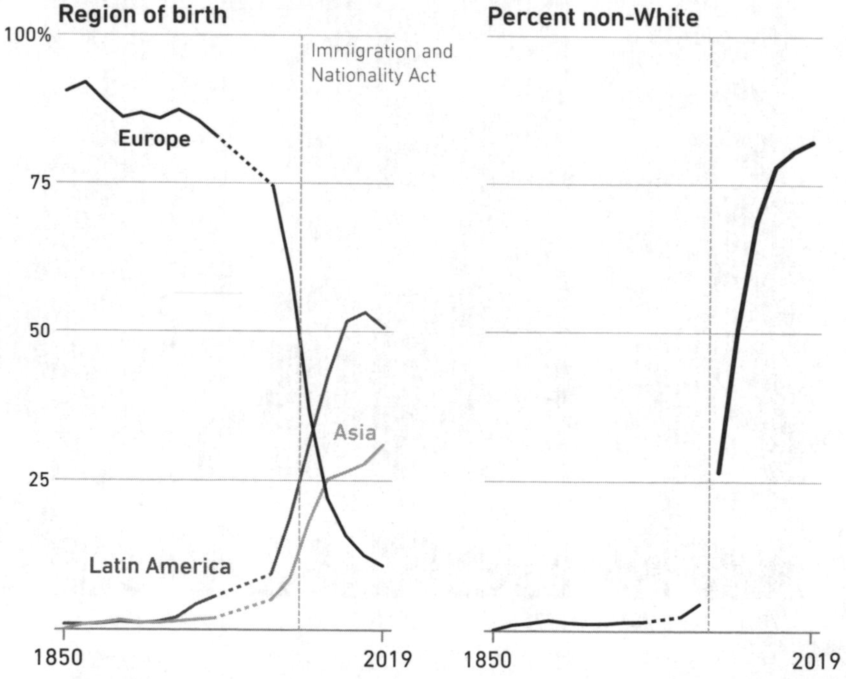

HOW TO READ THIS CHART Twin line graphs showing the evolution of the foreign-born population in the United States. At left, the place of origin of the foreign born, though data for 1940 and 1950 aren't available because, in those years, data on the foreign born were "limited almost entirely to the White population," according to the Census Bureau. At right, the density of non-Whites in the foreign-born population. Prior to 1970, the available data don't exclude Hispanics from the White population.

revisiting its past approach to race and migration. Kennedy's book *A Nation of Immigrants* was published posthumously in 1964. At President Lyndon Johnson's urging, the existing limits on immigration by country were lifted in 1965 and a more liberal policy created.

Between 1970 and 2000, the number of baby boomers increased by 9 million thanks to immigration. But in 2018 the General Social Survey (GSS), a nationally conducted poll that originated in 1972 and that is now conducted every two years, determined that both older and younger respondents had stronger ties to immigrants: the older group was still much more likely to have a foreign-born parent and the younger group more likely to be immigrants themselves.

That 1924 law aimed in part at preserving the racial homogeneity of immigrants. Prior to 1970, most immigrants came from Europe.[14] After the law was reversed, Europe fell behind Asia and Latin America as point of origin for foreign-born residents of the country. Population diversity increased rapidly. That was particularly the case after passage of the Immigration Reform and Control Act of 1986, which (among other things) created a path to citizenship for people in the country without documentation, many of whom were from Latin America.

That one post–1965 shift—more Hispanic immigrants—is a central reason for the racial divide between the boomers and those who came after. There are about 10 million more White boomers than White millennials and about 13 million more non-White millennials than boomers. Sixty percent of those non-White millennials are Hispanic.

4. BOOMERS ARE LESS LIKELY TO HAVE A COLLEGE DEGREE

In 1961, the year before the first baby boomer turned 16—Kathleen Casey Kirschling, as you'll recall[15]—there were for the first time more than 22 million people aged 16 to 24. By 1968, there were more than 30 million, in a year when a group the size of 1 percent of that figure was drafted into the military.[16] In 1979 there were more than 38.5 million people aged 16 to 24, nearly double the low seen in 1956.

In the abstract, this is simply an interesting, predictable trend. Sure: baby boom, more people in their twenties 20 years later, not very complicated math. But this isn't just an academic assessment of population growth. This is a sudden spike in adults who are graduating from high school or otherwise entering the workforce.

Between 1954 and 1978, the number of 16- to 24-year-olds working in the United States increased by 160 percent, while the number of those aged 25 and over increased by less than 50 percent. Despite that substantial rise in the number of working people under the age of 25, the number of people in that age group that *weren't* working also increased by nearly 50 percent. Not only did the country need to find 14 million jobs over that period, it also needed to figure out what to do with the millions more 16- to 24-year-olds who *weren't* going to work.

In his history of the baby boom, *Great Expectations*, Landon Jones frames this glut of young people in not-very-complimentary terms. "If the young people attempted to find jobs at the same rate their parents had, then the job market would be flooded. Then unemployment would surely rise and, with it, crime," Jones wrote. He noted that the military could offer additional employment to some but not all of those young people—which it did, often by force of law, right as the oldest boomers were reaching their late teens.

"In the end," Jones continues, "we decided in effect that the economy was not prepared to absorb the baby boomers after they left high school. All we could do was to delay their arrival. . . . [T]he educational system, which had borne the brunt of handling the boom generation in the fifties, would have to make room for it again in the sixties. Only now the front line had moved from the schools to the colleges."

As a non-boomer, my sense of the generation is colored heavily by its cultural presentation, and that presentation often revolves around college. My associations are centered on things like Woodstock or *The Graduate* or Kent State or young men conscripted into combat—associations born of having grown up in an era when the boomers were documenting their generation's to-that-point tumultuous history. But it isn't simply a matter of my being blinkered by popular movies. As the baby boom moved from high school to adulthood, enrollment in college had begun to climb. In 1950, there were about 2.3 million Americans enrolled in college ("degree-granting postsecondary institutions," to use the specific descriptor preferred by the National Center for Education Statistics). By 1964, when the first boomers were turning 18, enrollment was over 5.2 million. By 1988, when the youngest

CHART 31
College Enrollment

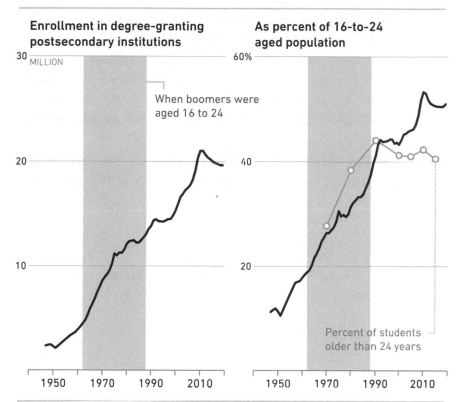

Enrollment in degree-granting postsecondary institutions

As percent of 16-to-24 aged population

When boomers were aged 16 to 24

Percent of students older than 24 years

HOW TO READ THIS CHART The black lines on these graphs show the same data in two different ways, first as a raw count in millions of Americans, and second, that figure as a percentage of the country's 16- to 24-year-old population. Because the second graph is showing percentages, we can use the same axes to show a related data point: the percentage of college attendees over the age of 24, data useful a bit later in this chapter.

boomers were turning 24, enrollment was over 13 million—a total equal to 38 percent of the entire population of 16- to 24-year-olds.[17]

When *Time* magazine named "the twenty-five and under generation" its "man of the year" in 1966, it declared that "today's youth is most accurately viewed through the campus window."[18]

The robust postwar economy and swelling worker pool contributed to seeing college as a competitive advantage. In 1962, *The New York Times* described a meeting of school superintendents in New York where administrators wrung their hands about the new pressures they were seeing from parents.

"Dr. Francis Bower, a school psychiatrist for the Third Supervisory District in Suffolk County, said that since money and the use of goods had become accessible to all, they had lost their value as status symbols," the paper's Leonard Buder reported in 1962. "'To satisfy their competitive needs,' he continued, 'parents seem to have turned their attention to the only things left to manipulate—their children.'"[19] The new status symbol, according to those school officials, was getting kids into the "right college."

As with high schools and elementary schools before them, the surge in new students spurred a massive investment in colleges. In 1950, there were a bit under 1,900 postsecondary schools in the United States. From 1951 to

CHART 32
16- to 19-Year-Olds in the United States

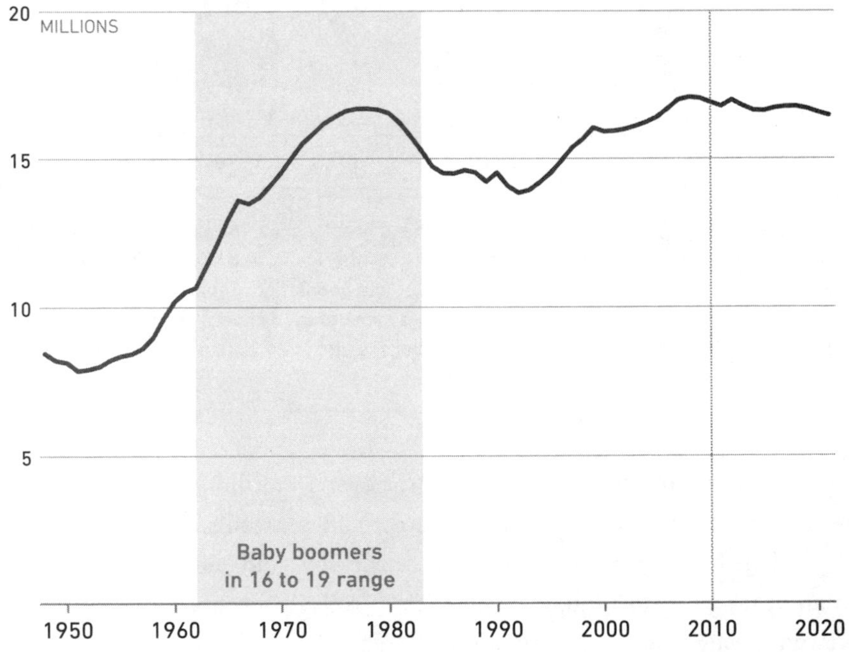

Baby boomers
in 16 to 19 range

HOW TO READ THIS CHART A simple line graph, but notice that the year 2010 is indicated.

1961, the number of enrolled students nearly doubled; from 1961 to 1971, it more than doubled.[20]

Around 2010, the upward trend began to slow, in part because the economy was beginning to improve after the recession, providing more immediate employment opportunities to young people. But there were also fewer college-aged Americans. By 2008 or so, the number of 16- to 19-year-olds in the United States flattened, helping to stall and even reverse growth in college enrollment.

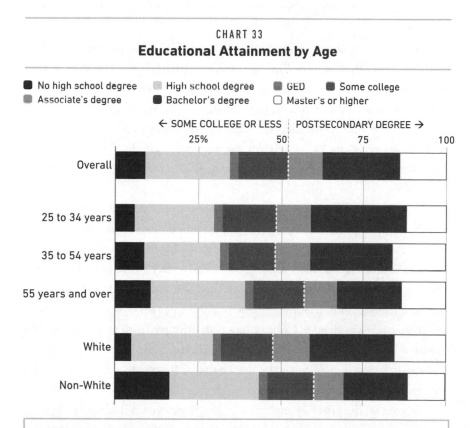

CHART 33
Educational Attainment by Age

- No high school degree
- High school degree
- GED
- Some college
- Associate's degree
- Bachelor's degree
- Master's or higher

← SOME COLLEGE OR LESS ┆ POSTSECONDARY DEGREE →

HOW TO READ THIS CHART This is a stacked bar graph, showing percentages of demographic groups in a different way. Each bar represents 100 percent of the indicated group (like 25- to 34-year-olds) with the percentages who've achieved each educational milestone represented by the corresponding percentage of the bar. So among 25- to 34-year-olds, for example, just under half have gotten some college education or less, as shown by the dashed line appearing just to the left of the 50 percent mark. The age group that's most likely to have a master's degree or higher is 35- to 54-year-olds.

Colleges are now again worried about what one person I spoke with referred to as an "enrollment cliff." The National Center for Education Statistics projects that the number of high school graduates each year will decline from a rate of 11,000 per million in 2020 to just over 10,000 per million 10 years later.

That the rate of enrollment continued to climb for so long, though, means that while boomers began the pattern of using college education as a social differentiator, members of later generations were more likely to obtain degrees. Therefore, a younger American is more likely to have a degree than an older one.

There's an interesting divide, though. While younger people are less likely to be White and more likely to have a degree, it is nonetheless the case that White Americans are much more likely to have a degree than non-Whites. This is thanks to the age divide within the White population itself. Of the nearly 62 million degrees held by White Americans in 2020, 55 percent were held by Whites under the age of 55. Of the 7 million White Americans without a high school diploma, nearly two-thirds were over the age of 65.

What was once an exception has become more of a norm. The density of college graduates in the working-age population doubled from 1980 to 2020 as the baseline education for many occupations shifted up from a high school diploma to a collegiate one.[21] Georgetown University's Center on Education and the Workforce estimates that more than 70 percent of jobs in 1973 required a high school diploma or less. In 2020, nearly two-thirds required a diploma from college.[22] College has transitioned from status symbol to required checkbox, even as the strategic investment it represented was increasingly intermingled with the drawback of lingering debt. No wonder the frustrations of recent graduates.

Of course, the grinding malaise of the college aged is itself not new, even in the context of college itself. Consider Benjamin Braddock, the character at the center of *The Graduate*. After receiving his diploma, he moped back home, where his father berated him for his lack of motivation.

"Would you mind telling me then, what were those four years of college for?" his father asks. "What was the point of all that hard work?"

"You got me," Ben replies.

The movie came out in 1967. If he graduated at 21, he would have been one of the first boomers.

5. BOOMERS ARE MORE LIKELY TO BE RELIGIOUS

By the mid-1970s, the boomers had attained self-awareness.

It's not clear when exactly boomers were aware of themselves as "boomers"—that is, as members of a massive generation of exceptional if not always deliberate power. But by the mid-1970s members of the generation were clearly aware of *themselves*, aware of being individuals shaping their own paths forward, at times with the individual creativity of wildebeest pushing across the savanna during migration season.

It was in 1976 that Tom Wolfe—chronicling the boomers from the vantage of the wiser preceding generation—described the group's behavior using an ungenerous term that stuck: the "Me" generation.

His story, the cover article for *New York* magazine that August, began with a scene at the Ambassador Hotel in Los Angeles, where some 250 young people were participating in an Erhard Seminars Training course, popularly known as "est." As a non-boomer reading this 45 years later, I was struck first by the incongruity of attending a self-improvement program held however many yards from where a Kennedy had been murdered eight years earlier. Then there's est itself, a cultish fad that was probably a fraught reference to the magazine's readers. For me, though, it is associated with a collection of *Doonesbury* strips I stumbled across in a closet as a kid. Certainly familiar with the newspaper-comic format, I diligently tried to parse out the jokes buried in things like Duke's reference to "dropping acid on the Great Wall," as cryptic a phrase as when my father once scrambled to chase away some kids who were "smoking pot" behind our garage. I was unsuccessful in those attempts to disentangle Garry Trudeau's wit, as I was when, in one of the cartoons, some character discussed how another character had become consumed by est. This, like 80 percent of the other jokes, lodged itself in my brain to be deciphered only accidentally decades later.

In Wolfe's telling, the particular seminar at the Ambassador was derailed by one woman's shouted excoriation of her hemorrhoids after having been prompted to let go of her repressed emotions. This exceptional event, part of an exceptional process, spans some 2,000 words as Wolfe makes his point: the generation was exceptionally focused on its tumbling evolution through this universe.

As did others with whom I spoke, Wolfe ascribes the generation's inward turn to the decades-long economic boom that "pumped money into every class level of the population on a scale without parallel in any country in history." Time is money, so[23] that money allowed some time for self-reflection and self-care, fertile territory for religious consideration.

What Wolfe then describes is a new kind of religiosity that emerged—or, if not new, then renewed, picking up on the spirit of nineteenth-century religious revivals. (It would be overly cute to draw a line to the reformist magazine *Millennial Harbinger*, which served as a written forum for one branch of that movement, so I won't.)

"Ever since the late 1950s both the Catholic Church and the leading Protestant denominations had been aware that young people, particularly in the cities, were drifting away from the faith," Wolfe wrote. "At every church conference and convocation and finance-committee meeting the cry went up: *We must reach the urban young people*." But the young people wanted *ecstasy*. They wanted new ways of living and being and expression that were not always disconnected from psychoactive drugs. They wanted to lie on the carpet near a murder scene and scream away their anal maladies. So, Wolfe argued, it was "the most rational, intellectual, secularized, modernized, updated, relevant religions . . . that are finished, gasping, breathing their last."

This was wrong. That there were no small number of boomers who were lured into groups like the Hare Krishna—enough to become a quickly stale staple of the era's comedy—was in part the boom again flexing its size. Brought to New York City in 1966, the movement ballooned to a self-reported 40,000 members in the United States by 1973,[24] a big group to suddenly be ubiquitously visible (more than three for every American airport in service at that point![25]) but still a number equivalent to only 5 out of every 10,000 boomers.

The boomers were less inclined to embrace religious identifiers than their elders, yes, but they still embraced them. And they did and do so to a more robust degree than their own kids, over whom religious institutions have been wringing hands and for whom those institutions have been crafting appeals.

There has been a deterioration in the extent to which people identify with organized religious traditions over the past 70 years. In 1954, about three-quarters of respondents identified themselves as Protestant in the quadrennial American National Election Studies (ANES) survey. But, as Wolfe pointed out, that figure soon began slipping downward. This was a potentially existential problem for religious institutions, certainly, but it was also a challenge to America's self-identification. It was only a decade earlier, after all, that then-president Franklin Roosevelt told a senior member of his administration—Leo Crowley, who held the title of alien property custodian—that Crowley

CHART 34
Religious Self-identification by Generation

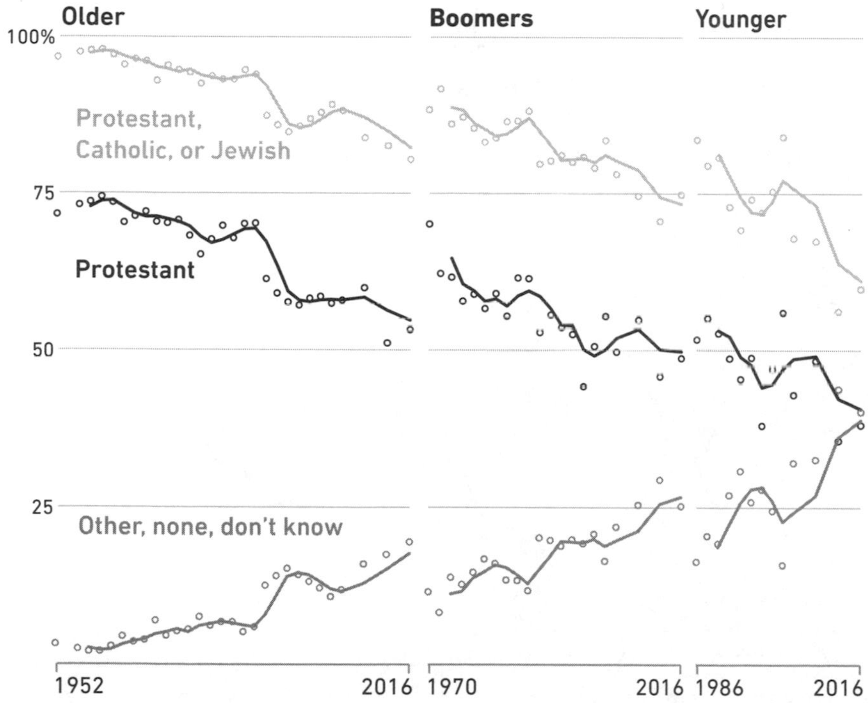

HOW TO READ THIS CHART Each dot indicates the percentage of respondents selecting a religious identifier in ANES polling. Since those values jump around a lot, the lines show the average of the three most recently assessed values. Those lines more clearly show the trends over time.

and Treasury Secretary Henry Morgenthau, Jr., would need to "go along with anything that I want at this time" because the United States "is a Protestant country, and the Catholics and Jews are here under sufferance."[26] Crowley fell into the former category; Morgenthau the latter.

What was replacing Protestants in the country wasn't Catholics or Jews, neither of which group has shifted much as a portion of the country according to the ANES surveys. Instead, the erosion of Protestantism has been matched with an increase in smaller religious identities and those who aren't religious at all.

That decline is not itself solely a function of younger Americans. Within generational groups, the density of Protestants has dropped over the decades. But the combination of younger people being more likely to identify as "other"

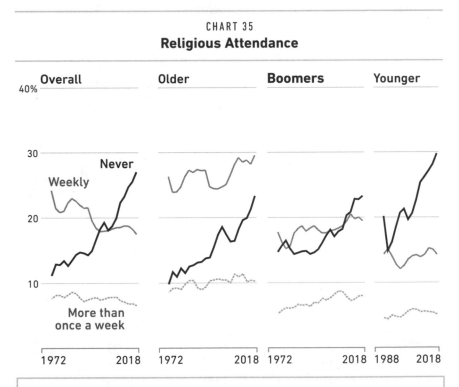

CHART 35
Religious Attendance

HOW TO READ THIS CHART The graph above simply shows the average, which, here, covers six years of surveys from the General Social Survey. Values for 1992 are averages of the surveys conducted in 1991 and 1993.

or "none" and the decreasing number of older, more religious Americans means a rapid overall drop in Protestantism.

Among respondents to the ANES survey in 2016 who are younger than the boomers, about as many said that they were Protestant as said they weren't a member of one of the three major religious groups included in the survey.

It's important to remember that there are a lot of things that can fall into the category of "other." The erosion in identification as Protestant was in part due to religious beliefs splintering into more exotic territories, albeit still religious ones. Not to belabor the point, but the Hare Krishnas mentioned above would fit into the "other" grouping.

Other national surveys, like the General Social Survey, measure religious belief in other ways. The GSS, which, like the ANES, is supported by the National Science Foundation, looks at social behaviors and attitudes. Things like how often Americans go to church.

Since 1972, when the GSS began, the number of people saying they never go to church has increased dramatically. In 1972, about a third of the country went to church one or more times a week. Only about 10 percent didn't go at all. Now, more than a quarter say that. And, again, that's powered heavily by Americans who were born after the boom.

More boomers go to church one or more times a week than never go. Among Americans born in 1965 or later, more say they never go to church. Meanwhile, the number of Americans who say they definitely believe in God has declined over the period in which the question has been asked in the biennial General Social Survey—with those younger than baby boomers being less likely to say they do.

This trend is projected to continue. In 2015, Pew Research Center released a report titled *The Future of World Religions*.[27] It estimated that between 2010 and 2050, the density of Christians in the United States would decline from 78 percent to 66 percent of the population. The density of religiously unaffiliated individuals in the population—which includes atheists and agnostics—is projected to rise from 16 percent of the population to 26 percent. Pew estimated that by 2070, the number of Christians globally will be passed by the world's Muslim population. By 2050, America is projected to have more Muslims than Jews.

Despite the evolution toward disaffiliation and the apparent erosion of belief in God, America is still a heavily religious country and will remain

CHART 36
Believe in Existence of God Without Doubts

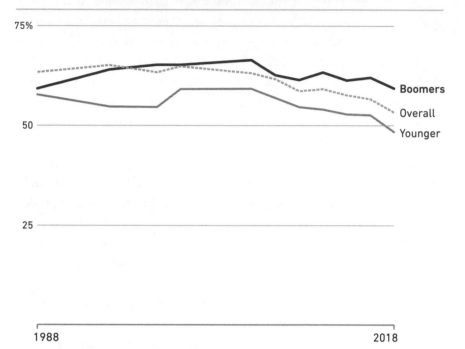

HOW TO READ THIS CHART Since the GSS didn't ask this in every survey, the graph above connects those years in which the question was asked. In other words, this is not an average but reflects actual responses.

so. But the shortness of breath experienced by religious denominations in Wolfe's telling is probably still afflicting those for whom some very particular religious tradition is seen as essential. Even in 1973, adherents to the diaspora of emerging religious cultures were often seen as aberrant. Wolfe was telling that story about the woman and her personal affliction not because it represented a norm but because it was an exception that bolstered his point about boomer solipsism. Members of his "Me" generation are now America's traditionalists—by definition, to a large extent, but also because many of those religious fads disappeared like so many boomer fads before them.

6. BOOMERS ARE MORE LIKELY TO BE MEMBERS OF TRADITIONAL INSTITUTIONS

It's useful here to step back and remember the point of this exercise. To wit: there are a number of ways in which the characteristics of the baby boom generation differ from younger Americans. Some of those characteristic differences are stark, like age and race. Some, like the difference in faith, are more subtle.

In his seminal book *Bowling Alone,* Robert Putnam differentiates between *life cycle* and *generational* effects. The former are things that distinguish between people of different age groups because one group is older or younger than the other, things like deteriorating eyesight, the example Putnam uses. Generational differences, by contrast, are things that happened to groups of a certain age, like serving in World War II. The density of veterans in the generation that preceded the boom remains unmatched; it sets that generation apart.

Putnam introduces this difference as he seeks to establish why boomers were particularly *dis*engaged from American civic culture. The boomers' parents engaged in a broad array of social and cultural activities that led Putnam to label them the "long civic generation" (though the moniker that stuck was, instead, the "silent generation," in part apparently due to their diminished voice as a relatively small group). The boomers themselves, though, were the leading edge of a "downward trend in joining, trusting, voting, newspaper reading, church attending, volunteering, and being interested in politics"—a decline that at the time of the book's release had been continuing "for nearly forty years," meaning since the 1960s.[28] When *Time* magazine marveled over the boomers in the middle of that decade, it noted the group's "disengagement": "Few organized movements of any description, from the John Birch Society to the A.F.L.-C.I.O. to the Christian church, have the power to turn them on."[29] When even the John Birch Society isn't compelling!

The shifts that occurred with the boomers appeared to be more generational than life-cycle in Putnam's analysis, though the two can overlap. On a number of metrics, including those he delineated, young boomers were less engaged than their parents' generations had been at the same age. As was the case with religion: boomers were less engaged with organized religion at a young age and that gap remained even as they reached ages when life-cycle habits would suggest more engagement.

Now, two decades after *Bowling Alone*, most boomers have reached an age when religion has historically been common (thanks to the grim realities explored in the preceding chapter) and that correlates with recent measured increases in church attendance. Younger Americans, meanwhile, trail even where the church-averse boomers were at the same age. So while Putnam is correct that the boomers began or accelerated an unusual shift away from membership in organizations and cultural activities, the continuation of that shift means that they're still disproportionately engaged with a number of key institutions relative to their own kids.

For all of the implied authority of data, such questions can be murky. When we talk about church attendance, for example, it obviously implies a level of religiosity—but what does it tell us about institutional loyalty? Are church attendees necessarily committed to one religious institution? Putnam takes a Wolfe-ish view of the generation's religious commitments, albeit with significantly fewer verbal flourishes. He describes the effort to find a bespoke religious identity that seems to have emerged with young-adult boomers, writing that the habit of "surfing" between congregations means that "while they may still be 'religious,' they are less committed to a particular community of believers."[30]

We can suss out from the General Social Survey the places where church attendance and religious identity overlap. About 8 in 10 of those who in 1978 said they attend church at least once a week also identified particular religious institutions with which they associated. By 2018, that number had dropped to 7 in 10. In 2018, 56 percent of boomers said they both identified with a religious group and attended church weekly, down from three-quarters in 1972. Among those younger than the boomers, less than half met both those criteria.[31]

There are other ways in which boomers are almost accidentally more likely to be overrepresented in institutions. Membership in labor unions has declined fairly steadily since the 1980s, for example, but boomers have consistently been among the age groups with the heaviest union representation, meaning both direct membership and coverage under a union contract. Representation has consistently been higher among those aged 45 to 64 since the government began breaking out age data in 2000.[32] During that same period, boomers' ages ranged from the midthirties to the midseventies.

CHART 37
Membership in Labor Unions by Age

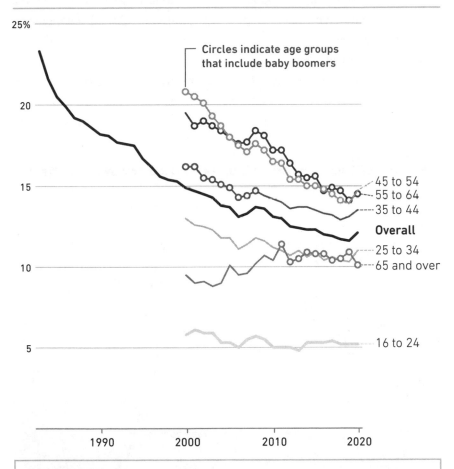

HOW TO READ THIS CHART A relatively simple line graph with three noteworthy details. First, that age-group data are only available since 2000. Second, that the uptick in membership in 2020 is in part a function of the coronavirus pandemic, since union members were better protected when millions of Americans lost their jobs. Third, the circles indicate an intersection of age group and the boomers' age range.

It is not the case that boomers are more likely than not to be members of unions, mind you. Only about 3.2 million people aged 55 to 64 were represented by unions in 2020, compared to more than 10 times as many boomers who overlapped with that age range. It is, instead, the case that boomers are more likely to be union members than, say, millennials. That same year, there were about 13 times as many millennials aged 25 to 34 as there were workers with union representation.

The increased density of boomers in this group is again something of a fluke. A lot of union members in those age groups have likely been members a long time and remain represented by a union contract. As union density has waned, those left skew older.

Boomer institutional affiliation manifests in other ways, too. While not to the same extent as their parents, members of the baby boom generation

CHART 38
Percent of Each Generation That Is Married or Never Has Been

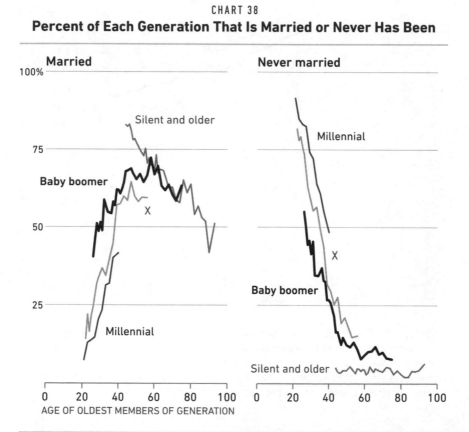

HOW TO READ THIS CHART Using data from the General Social Survey, the percentage of each generation that reports being currently married (at left) or never having been married (right). Instead of tracking this by year, the values for each year of GSS data are pegged to the age of the oldest members of the generation in that year. So, baby boomer data for 1976 are shown at the 30-year-old mark.

are more likely to be veterans than are younger Americans, for example—mostly because members of the generation were both subject to the draft and actually drafted during the Vietnam War.[33] That carries with it other institutional connections, like participation in veterans' groups such as the Veterans of Foreign Wars organization. This pattern also holds for familial institutions: older Americans, including boomers, are more likely to be married or to have been married than younger generations—as was the case when boomers were the same age that younger generations are now.

CHART 39
Partisan Identification

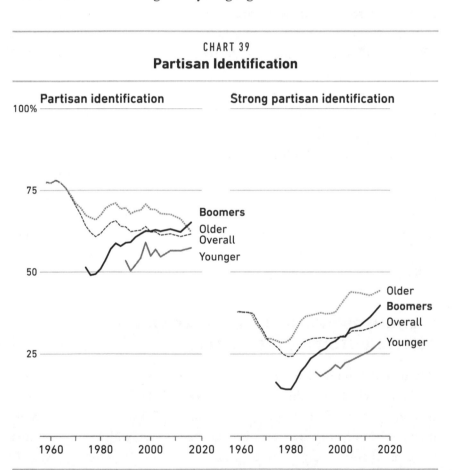

HOW TO READ THIS CHART Two simple line graphs showing the running average of the three most recent values for each age group. At left, a combination of strong and weak partisan alignment from both sides of the spectrum; at right, only the strong identifications.

Then there's partisan identification. In 2020, Pew Research Center reported that 62 percent of registered voters were members of one of the two major political parties. But, again, this varied by age group. Boomers were more likely to be members of one of the parties, with 67 percent identifying as Democrats or Republicans. Among millennials, only 54 percent did so.[34]

We can approximate how this evolved over time by looking at ANES data. In 2016, about 69 percent of boomers identified as Democrats or Republicans, higher than the overall figure and both older and younger Americans. Interestingly, this is in part a function of a steady increase in the identification of boomers as strong Democrats or strong Republicans. In 1980, only 17 percent of boomers identified themselves that way. By 2016, nearly 46 percent did.

While party membership has waned, partisanship—the manifestation of partisan sentiment—is very strong. This distinction between the institutions and the sentiment will come up in chapter 9.

What we see repeatedly in these numbers is a country that's slipping out of its institutional bindings, as Robert Putnam articulated. But within that pattern, there's still a generational gap: younger Americans are further along the path toward rejecting institutions than are older ones. Down in Florida, in fact, there's an entire community for those at the upper end of the boomer age group. No one is bowling alone at the Villages, not when there are so many available leagues to join.

7. BOOMERS ARE SLIGHTLY MORE LIKELY TO LIVE OUTSIDE LARGE CITIES

Reaching the thinner part of the tail of our generational differences, we get to one I touched on in the last chapter. With all due sheepishness, I noted that boomers would be less likely to encounter full cemeteries in their communities because they are more likely to live in places with less competition (in terms of both supply and demand) for that particular resource. Expanding on that, we see here the tilt of boomers toward less densely populated counties.

Buried in that graph—even obfuscated by it—is the way in which America has redistributed itself over the past several decades. The "big sort," as it was dubbed by Bill Bishop in his 2008 book of that name, has

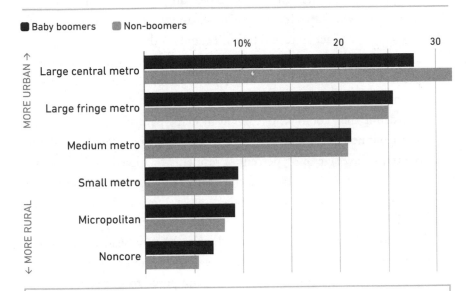

CHART 40
Where Generations Live

■ Baby boomers   ■ Non-boomers

MORE URBAN →

Large central metro

Large fringe metro

Medium metro

Small metro

← MORE RURAL

Micropolitan

Noncore

10%   20   30

> **HOW TO READ THIS CHART** Here we use bar graphs to compare the distribution of the boomer and non-boomer populations. A longer bar indicates that more of the population group lives in that type of county, using descriptors and designations from the Centers for Disease Control and Prevention, which for perhaps unexpected but understandable reasons categorizes counties.[35]

seen Americans increasingly move to areas in which they see their own values and experiences reflected.

Here the interplay of environment and institutions gets a bit more nuanced. There are a lot of practical motivations for the sorting Bishop and his colleague Robert Cushing documented, centered on job opportunities or proximity to family and cultural interests. But Bishop sees something deeper in this distribution, a rootlessness stemming from the erosion of social bonds and definitions documented in part by Putnam.

That erosion of institutional and social associations is to some extent an erosion of a sense of identity. The Villages is the exception that proves the rule; its surfeit of available recreational clubs allows its residents to define themselves through their associations, down to a club dedicated solely to women named Elaine. But what about the rest of us?

Bishop sees the erosion of social bonds and boundaries leaving people looking for communities that reflect their own identities. "That to me is the big shift," he told me. "That is part of—along with the economics and the education—what's driving people increasingly into these communities where people sort of act alike and talk alike and do the same thing."

Often, that means moving to a neighborhood where you're comfortable in expressing yourself or, at least, not uncomfortable in how others might express themselves. But part of the sort is also the people who don't move, who help define their communities simply by being part of the collective that *doesn't* seek out new surroundings. In the most densely populated counties in the country, an average of 55 percent of residents had lived in their homes for less than a decade in 2019. In the least densely populated counties, the ones that are home to a quarter of boomers, an average of 57 percent of residents had lived in the same place for *more* than a decade.[36]

Here, too, there's a lot of overlap: these sedentary residents are often older, more rural, more White. (Those least-dense counties were an average of 78 percent non-Hispanic White in 2019, compared to 48 percent White in the most dense counties.)[37] While the baby boom generation is by no means heterogeneous, it does keep a consistent beat. And that can help those curious to figure out if they themselves are part of this maligned generation.

MILLENNIALS ARE NOT JUST YOUNG BOOMERS

The distinctions between older and younger Americans are often relatively subtle. Of the White Americans in the 2016 and 2018 General Social Surveys with college degrees who identify as members of a political party, attend church at least once a week, and are native-born Americans with native-born parents, about 56 percent were boomers or older. But 15 percent were millennials. In other words, picking such a complex individual out of a hat means a 1-in-7 chance you're getting someone born in the 1980s or 1990s.

With that in mind, we distill the differences between the generations into a handy chart.

Boomers are 1.3 times as likely to be White; millennials are 1.9 times as likely to be immigrants or have an immigrant parent and 1.3 times as likely to have a bachelor's degree or higher. Boomers are twice as likely to attend

CHART 41
Comparing Characteristics of Two Generational Groups

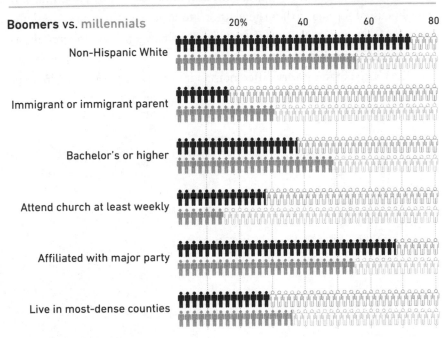

Boomers vs. millennials

| | 20% | 40 | 60 | 80 |

Non-Hispanic White

Immigrant or immigrant parent

Bachelor's or higher

Attend church at least weekly

Affiliated with major party

Live in most-dense counties

HOW TO READ THIS CHART Each silhouetted person represents 2 percent of the entire population of the generation.

church at least weekly and 1.2 times as likely to identify as members of a political party. Millennials are 1.3 times as likely to live in the most densely populated counties in the country.[38]

It's important to note, by the way, that these percentages are not moderated by the fact that there are so many more boomers than millennials. In fact, Pew Research Center reported in 2020 that, using its definition of "millennial"—an important caveat—millennials were more numerous than boomers in 2019.[39] Boomers are not only less likely to have a college degree; there are also fewer boomers with college degrees than there are millennials with one.

That those two groups are so similarly sized and relatively disparate in composition is certainly part of the reason for the current sniping between them. Friction between young people and old people isn't new, but it is unusual to have nearly half the population fall into one of those two groups. It is also unusual for one of those generations to have seen the country reshape itself to accommodate them, only to have it reshape again, more broadly, as they enter their twilight years.

The United States is very different than it was in either 1946 or 1964. For many boomers, those changes seem to be very much not OK.

4

The Politics of the New Generation Gap

I f you ask Google how to get to the U.S. Capitol from anywhere to the south or west of D.C., it instructs you to drive along the southern edge of the complex and then turn onto First Street SE, between the Capitol grounds and the Library of Congress. Which may be why, on the morning of August 19, 2021, Floyd Ray Roseberry turned onto First Street, parked his pickup truck on the sidewalk outside the library, and declared that he had a bomb.

As it turned out, Roseberry didn't have a bomb. Broadcasting live on Facebook, he claimed that he had a device that would be triggered by a loud sound—like a bullet shattering his vehicle's window. This would prove to be as hollow as his insistence that there were four more potential bombers scattered across the city or that he was the leading edge of a revolution. By the time he surrendered to police five hours after arriving at the scene, it became clear that Roseberry was no more than one angry, frustrated man in a country riddled with them, whose actions were amplified both by social media and by his targeting the Capitol seven months after the violent riot in January of that year. Roseberry wasn't entirely clear on what building he was aiming for; at one point in his livestream he showed viewers "a capitol over there"—the actual Capitol—and then "another capitol over here," which was apparently a reference to the library. He assured viewers, though, that his alleged bomb would eradicate precisely two and a half city blocks, so identifying the specific building didn't really matter that much.

As soon as the news broke about Roseberry's threat, it was fairly easy to predict what his objections might be. That he was a White man driving a pickup truck offered a not-insignificant hint about his political leanings. There was, after all, a book published in 2018 called *Prius or Pickup?* that explored the simple indicators—in both personality and personal consumption—that aligned with partisan identification. "Pickup" means "Republican." The book cites a 2016 survey conducted by an online auto-repair site called YourMechanic that identified the most popular cars in Republican and Democratic congressional districts.[1] In both, Honda sedans were most popular. But pick out the makes and models most likely to appear in one district and not the other and you get the book's titular sorting. None of the 10 vehicles disproportionately found in Democratic districts were pickups; three of the top four vehicles found in Republican ones were. The fourth most common was the Chevy Silverado 1500, the specific truck driven by Roseberry.[2]

Such tea-leaf reading, however trivial, wasn't really necessary. Roseberry's Facebook videos were an extended articulation of his hodgepodge of rationalizations, most of which centered on various right-wing tropes and misinformation. His wife had gone in for a medical procedure, he said, but his insurer wouldn't cover it, even while they "keep on letting all these illegal Mexicans in here" who are given "free health care."[3] He insisted that the South was "fed up" with Joe Biden[4]—he lived in rural North Carolina, within walking distance of the South Carolina border—and that Biden and others in his party would be imprisoned after Donald Trump was returned to office following Labor Day weekend.[5] Trump, his wife told a reporter, was the first candidate for whom he'd ever voted.[6] In early August, the Department of Homeland Security had warned local law enforcement organizations that the rampant false claims about election fraud and a resumption of the Trump presidency might lead to acts of violence. Roseberry appeared to be an ultimately innocuous iteration of that pattern.

But there was something else Roseberry said in a Facebook video recorded from his truck prior to his arrival on Capitol Hill, while it was still dark out.

"It's time for us to take a stand, fellas," he said off camera, his phone slowly scanning the cab of his Silverado. "We're the last generation. We're the last fucking generation that's going to have the balls to stand up [to] what's fucking wrong with this government."[7]

Roseberry, born in 1972, is too young to have been a boomer. But this sense of generational aggrievement, that something had snapped to break the United States along some temporal line, is exactly the point. What the otherwise unremarkable events of August 19, 2021, make clear is the subtext to the divides between old and young that I have detailed previously: it overlaps robustly with partisanship, too.

The chapters you've read have articulated the scale of the baby boom and how it differs from the America that's emerging. What we haven't yet explored is the tangible effect of that difference, the manifestation of the country's current generation gap.

"Every generation has a little bit of rebel, pushback, 'I'm not my parents, I'm not going to do it the way they did,'" Miami University business professor Megan Gerhardt pointed out to me. "That's been true through all of time." Gerhardt's work focuses in part on how to bridge that current generational gap, one she acknowledges as significant. "The tension is very real," she explained. "And the differences in the way people see things generationally is very valid and real." Part of the current tension, she said, is the "perception of scarcity," a perception of imbalance that isn't always inaccurate. That is particularly clear now, as a generation defined by its scale finds itself less able to use its electoral and cultural strength to preserve that imbalance.

So before exploring what we might expect to see as the power of the baby boom fades—as that perceived scarcity shifts—we should look at the way in which partisan politics broadly serves as its Alamo. What happens in the United States in future decades depends heavily on the toxic politics of the present, politics that broadly pit an older, Whiter, more Republican group against a younger, less White, more Democratic one.

Before we focus on that divide, though, it's useful to focus more specifically on the ways in which the baby boom itself isn't monolithic, exploring the exception before the rule. And perhaps the best lens through which to do so is to consider a very small subset of the generation.

THE BOOMER PRESIDENTS

For nearly thirty years beginning in the early 1990s, the United States was led by members of the baby boom generation. Four have been elected president, as of this writing. Three of them were born within a span of about two months.

The oldest of those three was Donald Trump, born in Queens in June 1946. This was actually a bit before the demographic boom itself began; birth rates began to skyrocket in July. Trump was atypical as a boomer in another way, too. The baby boom was stuffed with firstborn children, and Trump became, in the words of family biographer Gwenda Blair, a "faux firstborn"— a child who stood apart from his three older siblings as particularly "assertive, ambitious, and, above all, successful" as he moved with a huge cohort that bore the same confidence.

Of course, Trump was also born into a family that for more than a century rumbled through American capitalism with an eye toward the next score. His grandfather, Friedrich Trump, immigrated from Germany before briefly settling down in the Seattle area, where he eventually ran a restaurant that, according to Blair, likely doubled as a brothel. (He became a citizen in October 1892, just in time to vote in the first presidential election for which Washington submitted electors.)[8] After attempting to return to Germany and finding himself unwelcome for having decamped for the United States at precisely the moment he would have faced conscription in the German military, Friedrich returned to New York City. Donald Trump's father, Fred, was born in an apartment in the Bronx.[9] Fred Trump became a real estate developer, focused mostly on New York's outer boroughs. By the late 1970s, Donald was in charge and turned his attention to Manhattan. Flush with a lot of fame and somewhat less money, Trump became a celebrity and then a politician.

In early July 1946, three weeks after Donald Trump was born, another boomer was born whose path to politics was far more direct. That was George W. Bush, son of a future president, grandson of a future senator, brother to a governor, and himself destined for the White House. When he was 10, his grandfather casually introduced him to Lyndon Johnson.[10] The Bush family business was politics, and they were good at it.

A month after Bush's birth, America's first baby boomer president was born to a father he'd never know. William Jefferson Blythe, Jr., was killed in a car crash while his wife was pregnant with their only child, William Jefferson Blythe III. When the child's mother remarried, he took his stepfather's last name: Clinton.

Bill Clinton's family didn't have a business. He lived with his grandparents in Hope, Arkansas, while his mother studied to be a nurse. When she remarried, the family moved to Hot Springs, into a neighborhood that Clinton in his memoir *My Life* described with bottomless intentionality as "a class-A advertisement for the post–World War II baby boom."[11] For no one on this planet is more aware that Bill Clinton was the first baby boomer president than William Jefferson Clinton.

After parlaying a successful academic and legal career into several terms as governor of his home state, Clinton ran for president in 1992. In his memoir, he suggests that his generation might actually have been somewhat skeptical of his candidacy.

"Our baby-boom ticket did best among voters over sixty-five and those under thirty," he wrote. "Our own generation apparently had more doubts about whether we were ready to lead the country."[12]

They may have had "more doubts," but they still voted for him over his opponents. The election that year was upended by the strong third-party candidacy of Texan Ross Perot, with Perot pulling 19 percent of the national popular vote. Even with that chunk sliced off, Clinton's Democratic ticket beat his Republican opponent—George W. Bush's father, George H. W. Bush—in every age group. It's just that he won those in the 28-to-46 range, which the boomers then were, a bit more narrowly.[13] By 1992 the baby boom generation had started to vote more heavily Republican than Americans overall, though, a pattern that expanded through the 2016 election.[14] Then, of course, the Democratic candidate for president was Bill Clinton's wife, Hillary, who lost to Donald Trump. Small world.

It's worth lingering for a moment on the cosmic strangeness of having 3 of the country's 46 presidents born within a period of 66 days of one another—though we might remember that they arrived during the summer of a year that bears the historical stamp of seeing an unusually large number of births.[15] More interesting are the distinct paths to power the three men took. Bush was born into it, seemingly arriving at the White House at the predetermined point on his career path (after a few detours). Trump dropped into politics after expanding on his father's economic success and converting it into the currency of attention. Clinton got there the way Americans were always promised: overlapping his natural skills with the theory that any child could someday be president. The differences in their trajectories were matched by the divergence in their politics. Clinton, a Democrat, moderate by today's standards. Bush, a Republican, with the same qualifier. And Trump, staking out a position much further to the right.

Where they weren't different was in nearly everything else. Each of the three was a well-educated White man who, like 2.2 million other U.S. residents, turned 75 in 2021.[16] Which brings us to the fourth boomer president.

That's not Joe Biden, as you might assume. Biden has the unusual distinction of being the country's only president who's a member of the generation Pew Research Center defines as the one prior to the boom, the silent generation. Writing about possible contenders for the 1988 presidential nomination, *The New York Times* included Biden in its assessment of how candidates were hoping to court baby boomers, a group it says that Biden referred to as "our generation."[17] He would eventually drop out of the race after having been found to have plagiarized from other politicians.[18]

The fourth boomer president is, instead, Barack Obama. Born in Hawaii in 1961, he arrived just before the boom began to fade. Obama's personal story is probably familiar: his midwestern mother and his father, a native of Kenya, met in college and married shortly before he was born. He was also raised with the assistance of his mother's parents and, like Clinton, seemed destined at birth neither to elite universities nor to the executive mansion.

Obama earned that latter accomplishment with a resounding victory in the 2008 presidential election. That contest overlapped with another demographic first: it was the first in which most millennials could vote—and they preferred Obama to his opponent, Republican senator John McCain of Arizona, by a lot. If Clinton could boast of doing best among those under 30, Obama could tout winning that age group by a better than 2-to-1 margin. In fact, it was the widest gap between the youngest and oldest voters seen in exit polling since the modern exit polling system was first put in place.

In the moment, Obama's election seemed largely to reflect then-president George W. Bush's deep unpopularity, an unpopularity centered on the war in Iraq and exacerbated by the crumbling economy. Obama's strength with young voters was understood and the role of younger voters was a feature of post-election analysis. But observers could easily wave the victory away as representing less a seismic shift than a one-off, given the political mood.

There were rumblings before the election itself of the political fault lines that would soon rupture. McCain's selection of Alaska governor Sarah Palin

CHART 42

Difference in Presidential Support Between Age Groups

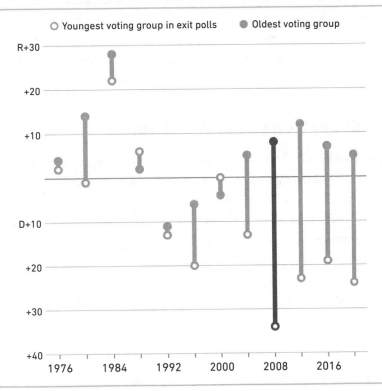

○ Youngest voting group in exit polls   ● Oldest voting group

This graph shows the margins of support recorded among the youngest and oldest voting groups in exit polling following each presidential election since 1976.[19] The distance between the dots—or, if you prefer, the height of the connecting line—indicates the gap in support between young and old.

as his running mate had been an explicit effort to energize the party's far-right base; by early October, it was obvious that the heat might have gotten a bit too high. At a town hall event in Lakeville, Minnesota, McCain was repeatedly forced to rebut conspiracy theories about Obama's background and intentions. One woman described Obama as an "Arab." A man told McCain that he believed Obama "cohorts with domestic terrorists." Another fretted that Obama would "lead this nation to socialism."[20]

McCain politely and gently rebutted each claim. His insistence to the woman's baseless assertions—that Obama was a "decent family man" and a "citizen that I just happen to have disagreements with on fundamental issues"—moved back into the spotlight when it became useful to contrast the senator with the 2016 Republican nominee for president, Donald Trump. McCain was hailed as a fundamentally different sort of politician than Trump, which is unquestionably the case. But like McCain himself, McCain's politics lost. The undercurrent at that event in Minnesota soon became the driving force of his party, eventually helping to bring Trump to power.

THE GENERATIONAL FAULT RUPTURES

It didn't take long for hostility to Obama and what he represented to become a central focus of the right. Less than a month after he took office, one strain of criticism that would soon threaten his presidency and consume the Republican Party crystallized within the unexpected confines of CNBC's financial coverage.

On the morning of February 19, 2009, the network's hosts and a guest were discussing Obama's plan, announced the prior day, to use funding from the Troubled Asset Relief Program to help Americans suddenly unable to afford their mortgages to stay in their homes. Reporter Rick Santelli, joining from the floor of the Chicago Mercantile Exchange, was indignant.

"The government is promoting bad behavior," he insisted before turning to the traders around him and asking how many wanted "to pay for your neighbor's mortgage that has an extra bathroom and can't pay their bills?" The traders booed.

Back in New York, the laughing hosts suggested that things were getting rebellious in Chicago's financial center. Santelli embraced the idea.

"You know, Cuba used to have mansions and a relatively decent economy," he said. "They moved from the individual to the collective. Now, they're driving '54 Chevys, maybe the last great car to come out of Detroit."

What Obama had proposed, it's worth noting, was a process in which the government would encourage lenders to reduce mortgage payments for struggling homeowners to no more than 31 percent of their monthly income.[21] Part of the difference resulting from that decrease would be covered by government funding. With 4.3 million private-sector jobs having been lost from January 2008 to January 2009[22] and unemployment at 7.8 percent and climbing,[23] the program was intended to offer a cushion to those suddenly struggling. Or, as Santelli framed it: socialism.

"We're thinking of having a Chicago Tea Party in July," Santelli added at another point, to more laughs. "All you capitalists that want to show up to Lake Michigan, I'm gonna start organizing."

"Rick, I congratulate you on your new incarnation as a revolutionary leader," CNBC's in-studio guest said, adding to the merriment. That was Wilbur Ross, who eight years later would be Trump's commerce secretary.

Santelli's speech was credited with being the trigger for what became the Tea Party movement. The idea was quickly picked up by conservative commentators on social media and local radio, who championed a series of protests like that proposed by Santelli. Conservative groups and activists recognized the potential for organizing. One round of protests followed in late February. By the time of the protests centered on Tax Day in mid-April, Fox News was explicitly promoting a number of them as "FNC TAX DAY TEA PARTIES"—where "FNC" stood for Fox News Channel.[24]

The movement was ostensibly a reaction to the idea that government was getting too big and government spending too generous. There was an obvious strain of anti-Obama sentiment, however, opposition that was often centered on the person and not the policies he promoted. Opposition that was driven by his being a Black man with a foreign-born father who'd captured the hearts of this young generation as he explicated and advocated for change.

Harvard University political scientist Theda Skocpol has written repeatedly about the movement, conducting hundreds of interviews with members of the Tea Party in an effort to gauge how the movement emerged and what motivated its participants. What she found, she explained to me, was a complicated interplay of concerns that had at its center the ways in which America was changing—as manifested in the man who had just been elected president on the strength of votes from a generation of which most of them weren't a part.

"If you go across the course of American history, all the way back, anytime you see a previously subordinated group of different ethnic and racial composition making political gains, you see a reaction to that," Skocpol said. "And anytime you see a period of rapid immigration into the country you see a period of nativist reaction."

Obama came into office as those factors overlapped with a collapsing economy and a sudden generational divergence, Skocpol said, layering multiple political stressors on top of one another. Santellian rhetoric about government spending was a catalyst for this tension, though given the role of existing groups like the libertarian Americans for Prosperity, it's not entirely bizarre that the ostensible focus for the Tea Party should be on taxes and outlays. Often, though, they weren't the emotional drivers of the movement.

"We found that Tea Partiers were most angry about immigration. And I still find that. When I go out and talk to Tea Party people now they will stress that," Skocpol said. "But the arrival of Blacks in political power is even more threatening, in some ways. And when you combine those two, and you combine it with young people who aren't doing what their elders expect them to do anymore, all three of those things were constantly present in the way Tea Party people talked about Barack Obama."

It's useful to quickly drill down a bit on that generational point and how it overlaps with concerns about race. Whites are generally older than the population overall because younger Americans are less likely to be White (as should have been firmly imprinted earlier). But this is a development that has occurred within the boomers' lifetimes. In 1920, there wasn't a significant gap in race between the oldest and youngest: the youngest tenth of the population was about 89 percent White while the oldest tenth was about 93 percent White. By 1970 that hadn't changed much. In 2020, though, the oldest tenth was only about 77 percent White—and the youngest tenth was more than half non-White.

This intertwines with the fact that the baby boom arrived during a period of restriction on migration to the United States. At the boom's outset, the relatively small foreign-born population in the United States was largely White and largely old. When the restrictions lifted, that changed. Immigrants from Latin America have consistently been younger than immigrants overall[25] and, relatedly, it is Hispanics who make up the largest portion of the younger non-White population.

Put another way, when Americans express concern about demographic change or immigration, intentionally or not they're often expressing generational concerns. This is what Skocpol saw in the Tea Party, and it is still detectable in the public debate.

CHART 43
The Growing Age Divide Between
White and Non-White U.S. Residents

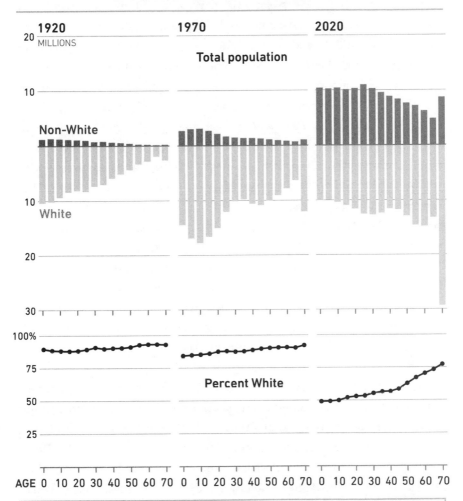

1920   1970   2020
20 MILLIONS

Total population

10

Non-White

10

White

20

30

100%

75

Percent White

50

25

AGE 0 10 20 30 40 50 60 70 0 10 20 30 40 50 60 70 0 10 20 30 40 50 60 70

HOW TO READ THIS CHART Here we show the same relationship in two different ways. The top graphs indicate actual population of the country by age, broken out into ten-year groupings. Because data from 1920 stop separating population by age at 75—itself an indicator of how the country has aged—the final indicated group is those aged 70 and over. (Notice how densely White the boom itself was as seen in the 1970 graph.) At bottom, the percentage of each age group in that year that is non-Hispanic White.

Demographer William Frey describes a "cultural generation gap" in his book *Diversity Explosion*—a gap that is dependent on the way in which age and race are braided. "The gap is not a result of racist attitudes per se. It reflects the social distance between minority youth and an older population that does not feel a personal connection with young adults and children who are not 'their' children and grandchildren . . . ," Frey writes. "It should not be that surprising, then, that baby boomers are resistant to the new demographic changes among the country's younger population, with whom, for the most part, they do not share close personal or family relationships."

In her book *The Tea Party and the Remaking of Republican Conservatism*, written with Vanessa Williamson, Skocpol summarizes Tea Party members as being mostly White, mostly male, mostly married, and the vast majority middle-aged or older. "Not surprisingly, given their age," they write, "Tea Party supporters and activists are better-off economically and better-educated than most Americans. Many are regular church-goers."

Perhaps this pattern sounds familiar.[26] In a phone conversation with me, University of Oklahoma assistant professor Rachel Blum described why the Tea Party engaged so many older Americans. "The boomers were particularly susceptible to any kind of claim that they weren't getting what they deserved or that their country was going to be taken away from them," Blum said, "because they were the rightful, dominant class"—at least in their minds.

The stressors that Skocpol identifies as driving engagement with the movement didn't decline over the course of Obama's presidency. Instead, they were amplified in ways that set the stage for a presidential candidate seeking to play specifically to the anxieties that Skocpol identified in the Tea Party. Most traditional politicians shied away from the sort of rhetoric and demagoguery required to directly elevate concerns about race and immigration. Donald Trump—who'd already loudly and dishonestly questioned Obama's nativity—was not a traditional politician.

AN AUTOPSY—AND THEN A RESURRECTION

A few days before the election that brought Trump to power, a new bookstore opened in Tallahassee, Florida. Called Midtown Reader, it got a generous write-up in the *Tallahassee Democrat*, with the newspaper praising its capacious shelves and a section dedicated to Florida authors and poets. The article's primary focus, though, was the store's owner, a woman named Sally Bradshaw.[27]

"Book retailer" is Bradshaw's second career in Tallahassee. The first was politics. She served as a senior adviser to former Florida governor Jeb Bush and worked in his father's White House. At other points, she advised Republican candidates for office, including Mitt Romney during his 2008 presidential run. Later she worked for the Florida Republican Party.

After Romney won the party's nomination in 2012 and then lost the general election by a wider-than-expected margin, the national GOP decided to regroup. Obama's election in 2008 could be explained as a response to his predecessor and the recession. But his victory in 2012, despite four years of the Republican Party throwing everything at him that they could and with the economy still only slowly recovering, suggested that there was something more fundamentally wrong with the party's national approach. It convened a group of experts, elected officials, and activists to develop a plan to revamp the party for the new political environment. It was formally called the "Growth and Opportunity Project" but was known colloquially as the "2012 autopsy report." Bradshaw was one of its co-chairs.

She went into the project understanding it to be an effort to stave off a dramatic evaporation of the party's relevance. "I think we really believed that not only would we not win the presidency—that was the number-one focus—but we wouldn't maintain or increase majorities in the Congress. We wouldn't be able to govern."

Bradshaw and the others leading the effort were given a broad mandate to assess how the party was approaching campaigns. Her background was in the mechanics of vote getting, like voter targeting and polling, so she took responsibility for the report's recommendations on that front. (At least one of those recommendations was adopted; the GOP quickly poured resources into improving its voter database.) Responding in part to the election of a Black president by an increasingly non-White electorate, the final report not only recommended that the party do a better job "promoting the inclusion in the Party of traditionally under-represented groups and affiliations"—which is to say non-Whites—but also explicitly called for the Republican Party to "embrace and champion comprehensive immigration reform."

This proposal was not particularly contentious in March 2013, when the final report was released. In the immediate aftermath of Romney's loss, many on the right saw the erosion of Hispanic support for the party as a clear signal that change was needed. (In 2008, exit polling showed Hispanics preferring Obama by 36 points.[28] In 2012, Hispanics made up slightly more of the total pool of voters and backed Obama by 44 points.[29]) The day after the election, Fox News host Sean Hannity told listeners of his radio show that he had "evolved" on immigration. "The majority of people here, if some people have criminal records you can send them home, but if people are here, law-abiding, participating for years, their kids are born here, you know, first secure the border, pathway to citizenship, done," he said. "You can't let the problem continue—it's got to stop."

By January, he was calling a bipartisan Senate proposal that would have instituted a pathway to citizenship or migrants in the country illegally "probably the most thoughtful bill that I have heard heretofore."[30] This likely wasn't entirely a view he'd come to on his own; a number of prominent Republicans involved in the legislative effort privately lobbied Fox News hosts to soften their response to the bill.[31] The bill passed the Senate by a 2-to-1 margin that June.

By which time Hannity had already begun to waver. He began to more frequently amplify concerns about border security, as he did when he described Republicans as "suckers" for being willing to make a deal on immigration during an interview with right-wing commentator Ann Coulter.[32] That he was hosting Coulter at all was a signifier: she'd declared during a speech that March that, if "amnesty" was enacted, "no Republican will ever win another election."[33] As another guest, anti-immigration filmmaker Dennis Michael Lynch, said of the party, "They see America falling off the cliff. And if this bill as it's written passes the House, forget it."[34]

Hannity may have flirted with the sophisticated discussion of immigration reform, but he was married to the rowdy passions of the party's base. And that base didn't like the Senate bill. A *Washington Post*–ABC News poll conducted soon after its passage found that only 29 percent of Republicans supported the legislation. Nearly half opposed it strongly.[35] This, of course, also overlapped with race. If Congress didn't create a path to citizenship, 61 percent of Hispanics said they would be disappointed. Fifty percent of Whites said they would be relieved.

By the beginning of 2014, hard-right members of the Republican House and Senate caucuses were organizing to block *any* reform bill, a cast of characters that included a number of names that would rise to prominence in the Trump era: Senator Jeff Sessions (R-Alabama), Representative Louie Gohmert (R-Texas), Senator Ted Cruz (R-Texas), Representative Paul Gosar (R-Arizona). That the country was seeing a surge in children arriving at the border fleeing violence in Central America only made passage less likely. Republican immigration reform discussion flicked into nonexistence.

All of this suggested that the Growth and Opportunity Project was not going to be the path forward for the Republican Party. "Maybe that should have been a clue," Bradshaw told me, "that there was an opportunity for a Donald Trump figure to emerge and run on those issues."

As he did. Within minutes of his descent down that escalator into the subterranean foyer of Trump Tower, he was railing against purported criminal immigrants. Likely assuming that Trump would remain in the business world after 2016, corporations that had partnered with the Trump Organization began severing ties, drawing national attention to Trump's positions and spurring his surge in the polls. Suddenly, the theory posited by RealClearPolitics's Sean Trende in the aftermath of the 2012 election[36]—that the GOP might be suffering more from lack of interest among Whites than surging interest among non-Whites—became the Republican Party's lodestar.

Bradshaw and her colleagues didn't foresee such a path, telling me that she thought "there was only one direction that the party could go after Romney lost." What's more, she said, those with whom she spoke for her research wore similar blinders. "I look back on that time, and I just never remember a conversation with anyone we spoke with—and our team spent countless hours for about six months, interviewing, conducting focus groups, conducting a survey, speaking with party leadership, speaking with elected leadership, speaking with people who dealt with demographics for a living in that party—I don't think anybody anticipated that there was a fork in the road of that nature," she continued. "It was more, stay the same or broaden our appeal, engage with the changing demographic, increase the representation of minorities in the party and focus on women, etc., etc. So it still is sort of a shock to me where the 2016 primary went."

A student of the party's history might have been less surprised by the collapse of the inclusivity approach. In 1989, the Republican Party elected a new chairman: Lee Atwater, who the year prior had cemented his notoriety in deploying thinly veiled racial appeals to aid George H. W. Bush's successful presidential bid. In his first remarks in his new role, Atwater's rhetoric on race showed where Bradshaw's report and Trump's success overlapped.

"We are now presented with a very unique chance. Those very sectors which have historically given their votes to the other party"—meaning Black voters—"are now beginning to realize that they have won very little in return for the allegiance," he said. "The other party has taken minority Americans for granted. Our party must take them for real."[37] This, of course, was Trump's pitch to Black voters in 2016: Democrats didn't deliver, so vote for me. What do you have to lose?

By the point when Trump won, Sally Bradshaw was no longer a Republican. She left the party after the 2016 convention because, she told an interviewer in 2020, "I was so disgusted with the messaging that was coming out of the Trump campaign and the RNC"—the Republican National Committee.[38] To me, she expressed amazement at the path that the party had taken when it came to that fork after 2012. It was a path that entrenched its appeal with older, Whiter voters, but, she felt, at an obvious cost.

"I have four children. Two have graduate degrees. One is in law school in Colorado. One is at Northwestern, amazingly in journalism school. Not a single one of those children will vote for a Republican," she told me. "And this is having—they've grown up in a Republican family. We've discussed politics at the dinner table every night. They will just never, ever vote for Republicans."

As we'll discuss in a few chapters, that impulse might itself warrant some new reflection from the GOP.

WHITE AMERICANS WORRYING ABOUT WHITE AMERICA

It's useful now to step back and recognize the point that Harvard's Theda Skocpol made about the emergence of the Tea Party: that it mirrored past moments of "nativist reaction." Like the one a century ago.

In August 1925, Washington, D.C., hosted what *The Washington Post* described on its front page as "one of the greatest demonstrations this city has ever known."[39] Tens of thousands of members of the Ku Klux Klan marched silently up Pennsylvania Avenue toward the White House under the gaze of thousands of local residents, many of the marchers having arrived in the city by way of special trains run for the occasion.[40] It was, the *Post* declared, "a great intermingling of what the klansmen call Americans."

That's an important phrasing. The focus of their show of force was not Black Americans, a group who speaker A. H. Gulledge dismissed as being left to their own devices: "As long as the black remain black and the white remain white, all is well."[41] Instead, the Klan was focused on a different threat. A handbill distributed around the city on the day of the parade detailed a bevy of concerns, warning what the Klansmen call "Americans" to "be on guard."[42]

"The Jews control the moving picture, jewelry and clothing industries and own us financially," it read. "The Greeks control the restaurant and confectionery business, the Italians the fruit and produce business. The Irish Catholics control us politically and are trying to control us religiously. The public press is controlled by Irish Catholics and Jews. . . .

"New York is now a foreign state and America is being overrun by the scum of Europe who owe allegiance politically and religiously to foreign potentates," the leaflet stated. "Americans! Awake! Patronize and vote for Protestant native-born Americans!"[43]

If the glory of the White man was his white skin, as Gulledge put it, the immediate challenge in 1925 was protecting that glory not from Black people but from groups considered something less purely White, the groups identified in the leaflet.

"Nobody really pays much attention to European origins anymore," Princeton's Douglas Massey told me in an interview, "but in the 1920s there were very salient lines between Italians, Poles, Russian Jews, and Anglo-Saxon Americans. Now, they're all pretty blurred." Italians and the Irish, he said, were considered to be akin to non-White for some time (as well as being ostracized for not being Protestant).

By the time the baby boom arrived, immigration had stalled—but the immigrant population that was already in the United States was primarily made up of the blurry-edged groups Massey describes. Over the course of the boomers' lives, though, the density of foreign-born residents increased quickly and those immigrants were mostly not White Europeans.

For those who associate "America" with "native-born Whites," this

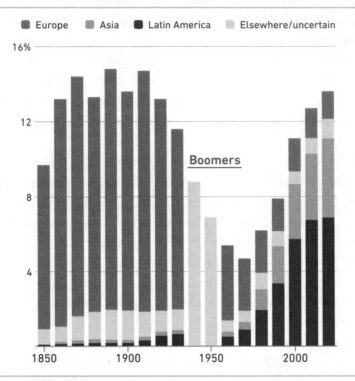

CHART 44
Composition of the Foreign-Born Population

Europe   Asia   Latin America   Elsewhere/uncertain

HOW TO READ THIS CHART This stacked column graph shows two pieces of information: the percentage of the population that was foreign born in each year and the regions of origin of those individuals. (As before, data for 1940 and 1950 aren't available because data on the foreign born in those years were "limited almost entirely to the White population," according to the Census Bureau.) The era in which the baby boomers were born is indicated.

evolution was not only jarring but a subversion of what America itself meant. And then the country elected that Black man with an immigrant father who, according to folks on Fox News, hoped to implement socialism.

People primed to look for signs of White America's collapse could see several accompanying Obama's ascendence. Shortly before he was elected, the Census Bureau announced its projection that the United States would be majority non-White by 2042, nearly a decade sooner than it had previously predicted. This, demographer Dowell Myers told *The New York Times* in 2018, "really lit the fuse" on concerns about changing demography.[44] Then came that surge of tens of thousands of migrant children from violence-wracked Central America in 2014, triggering a crisis for the administration as it tried to accommodate them and sparking the backlash on the right. The increase in migration that began that year introduced a pattern that has since continued.

There was a more subtle milestone passed during Obama's administration as well. The twin declines in the density of the non-Hispanic White population and the percent of Whites who were Christian meant that, at some hard to pinpoint moment after Obama's election, White Christians no longer constituted a majority of the U.S. population.

CHART 45
White Christians as a Percentage of the Population

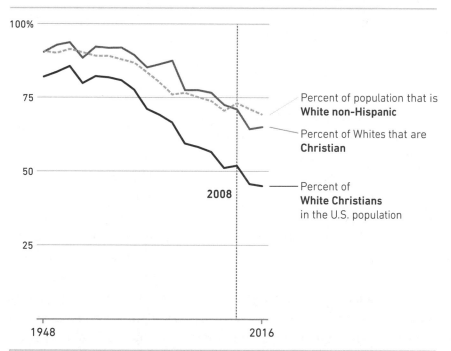

HOW TO READ THIS CHART This graph, using data from the American National Election Studies survey, shows how the percentage of Whites, Christians, and White Christians has declined consistently since the late 1960s. In essence, the top two lines combine to form the third line: fewer Whites in America and fewer Christians means a faster decline in the density of White Christians.

But these are second-order concerns. For many White Americans, the immediate challenge posed by Obama was Obama himself.

Soon after Obama took office, radio host Rush Limbaugh riffed on the meaning of his ascent. "The days of them not having any power are over," Limbaugh said of minorities, "and they are angry, and they want to use their power as a means of retribution. That's what Obama's about, gang. He's angry. He's gonna cut this country down to size. He's gonna make it pay for all the multicultural mistakes that it has made, its mistreatment of minorities."[45] When Obama was reelected in 2012, then–Fox News personality Bill O'Reilly made a similar comment, declaring that "the White establishment is now the minority."[46]

Notice that Limbaugh extrapolates outward from a Black president to the empowerment of non-White people generally. For a significant part of American history, that was the fundamental divide: non-White Americans were generally Black Americans. That's how the Census Bureau broke out its measurement of race until 1860. In 1960, before immigration laws were loosened, more than 94 percent of non-White U.S. residents were Black[47]— though this was also before Hispanic ethnicity was separated from the overall White category. In 1970, about 2 in 3 non-Whites (a group now including Hispanics) were Black (including Black Hispanics). By 2010, though, when Obama was president, only about a third of non-White residents were Black. By 2020, that density had fallen under 3 in 10.[48]

It's also true that the most significant political battles over race in U.S. history centered on the rights of Black Americans. The civil rights movement spawned a number of systems and structures aimed at protecting Hispanics, Asians, members of the LGBTQ community, and others, but its genesis was the restoration (or, at times, introduction) of fundamental rights for Black Americans. It was a push to give equal power to Black Americans that was viewed by some White Americans—usually but not always incorrectly—as a diminishment of their own power. After all, if Black voters are disenfranchised in a town, its decisions will be made by votes from its White residents. I stumbled across an old political ad that ran in the *Montgomery Advertiser* in 1967 that showed how this translated into direct political appeals. Promoting a candidate named Walter Bamberg, it proclaimed that Bamberg "believes in equal treatment for all citizens." The candidate would not "promise special privileges" for Black voters, the ad insisted—with the obvious implication that the special privileges tacitly enjoyed by Whites would be maintained.[49] (Bamberg was later appointed to serve with the U.S. Marshals Service by George H. W. Bush.[50])

As with the shift that occurred in immigration, the baby boom emerged into a nation where race was also being reconsidered. You'll recall from chapter 1 that the arrival of millions of kids demanded a spike in new school construction. That increase overlapped with another significant change in American education: the mandated end of segregation following the Supreme Court's 1954 ruling in *Brown v. Board of Education of Topeka, Kansas*. The court's decision spurred a backlash that included efforts to memorialize Confederate leaders as a sign of defiance. So, of the 146 schools identified by *EdWeek* in a 2021 analysis for which the year a school was named for a Confederate general or politician could be determined, more than a third were slapped onto schools during the years of the baby boom.[51]

Despite that history and associations like the one drawn by Limbaugh, America's non-White population is now mostly *not* Black. This makes it facially odd to assume that a theoretical erosion of White power will benefit

CHART 46
Schools Named for a Confederate Leader in Each Year

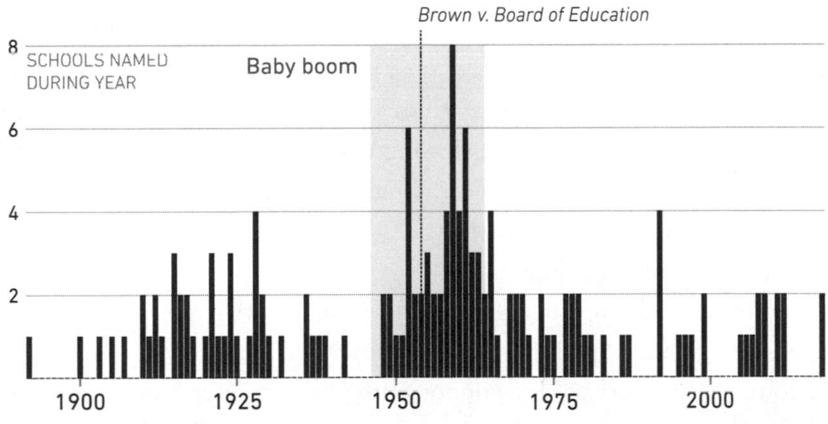

HOW TO READ THIS CHART On this graph, the vertical columns indicate the number of schools named for a Confederate leader in a year according to *EdWeek*'s analysis. The *Brown* decision is indicated with a vertical line.

the conglomeration of non-Whites, as though the zero-sum calculus of politics will reward "non-Whites" as a group. Finding this idea puzzling, a group
of researchers including New York University's Eric Knowles examined precisely that assumption—and found clear evidence that it was one being made,
particularly by White Republicans.

"When you think about it, what does it mean for Whites, White Americans to become a minority? Well, it doesn't mean that they're going to not
be the largest single group anymore—unless you sort of lump everybody else
together," he said when we spoke by phone. (Indeed, even in the Census
Bureau's projection for the population in 2060, Whites still outnumber Black
and Hispanic U.S. residents combined.) "So there's 'us,' and then there's
'everyone else,' and that 'everyone else' forms some sort of coherent whole.
That would be, it seems to us, kind of a prerequisite to feeling that sense of
threat. If you think that you're still the largest player in the game, and it's
just that there are a lot of other, smaller players, it's not logical to feel all that
threatened by it."

Knowles and his colleagues conceived of a way to measure what they
dubbed the sense of "minority collusion," the idea that non-White Americans
have a shared dislike and jealousy of Whites and that they work together to
peel away power and resources to which Whites are entitled. They surveyed
a nationally representative pool of White people multiple times from 2015
to 2018, asking them to respond to statements like "Minorities may disagree
about some things, but one thing they agree on is that they don't like White
people" or "Different minority groups are willing to cooperate with each
other in order to take power away from White people." The research team
also offered statements explicitly endorsing White identity politics like "Blacks,
Latinos, and Asians often vote for politicians from their same racial group
because that's who has their best interests in mind; Whites should not be
criticized for doing the same thing."

"What we ended up finding," Knowles said, "was that there was a marked
increase in agreement with the idea that minority collusion is happening over
the course of the survey." But, importantly, that increase "was driven *only*
by an increase in this minority collusion belief among White Republicans."
The measurement of acceptance of White identity politics showed a similar pattern. Republicans viewed those sentiments more favorably than did
Democrats—and that favorable sentiment increased over the course of the

study. The respondents' overall views of the racial groups, meanwhile, "stayed pretty flat," according to Knowles, suggesting that the shift wasn't a function of increased prejudice against specific racial groups.

Looking for evidence that White Americans might interpret changes in demography as posing a concrete threat to their own power, rather than a theoretical one, Knowles and his team found fingerprints. Conducting their research during the period when Donald Trump was ascending to lead the Republican Party—and using the emergent Black Lives Matter movement as

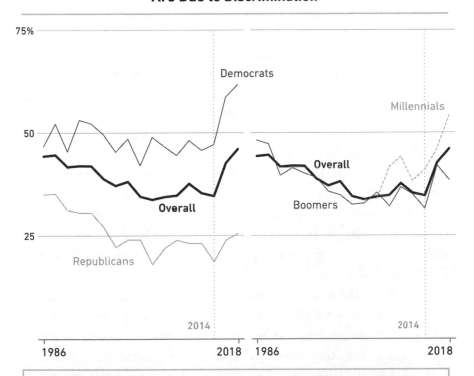

CHART 47

Belief That Racial Economic Differences Are Due to Discrimination

HOW TO READ THIS CHART Two simple line graphs showing the percentage of each group that thinks differences in income, housing, and employment between Blacks and Whites are mainly due to discrimination. Values are shown every two years; the values for 1992 are an average of 1991 and 1993. Note the uptick in this response after 2014, the year in which Black Lives Matter became a national force.

a foil—increased its salience. We know, for example, that there was a measurable shift after 2014 in how Americans viewed the economic disadvantages faced by Blacks. In the biennial General Social Survey conducted that
year, about a third of Americans said that they viewed those disadvantages
as mostly being a function of discrimination. By 2018, that had surged to
46 percent, largely thanks to a jump among Democrats from 47 to 62 percent. The percentage of Republicans holding that view had been slipping since
the mid-1980s, rebounding to only 25 percent by 2018.[52]

There are parallels elsewhere, too. Research from a team at the University
of North Carolina Greensboro published in 2021 found that White Republicans had less knowledge of historical racism than did White Democrats.
Republicans also "identified more strongly with their racial group."[53]

During the period that Knowles's research was in the field, the idea that
White Americans were embattled became more pronounced in the public
conversation. Polling repeatedly showed that supporters of Donald Trump
in particular were concerned about "reverse racism," racism targeting Whites.
A Quinnipiac University poll released in September 2016 found that nearly
two-thirds of those who planned to vote for Trump that November were at
least somewhat concerned about reverse racism.[54] Polling conducted for *The
Economist* by YouGov in 2019 found that Republicans were more likely to say
that Whites faced a great deal or fair amount of discrimination than they
were to say the same of Black Americans, Mexican Americans, women,
members of the LGBT community, or immigrants.[55] The only group that
Republicans identified that year as facing more discrimination than White
people was Christians. (A poll that June, though, had Christians about tied
with Jewish and Muslim people as perceived targets of discrimination among
Republicans.)

The Public Religion Research Institute has asked a similar question in
polling conducted since 2010. The pollsters offer a statement—"Today discrimination against whites has become as big a problem as discrimination
against blacks and other minorities"—and ask respondents if they agree. In
November 2010, 56 percent of Republicans did, compared to 28 percent of
Democrats, a 28-point gap. By September 2020, after a summer of protests
centered on race and with the presidential election looming, the percentage
of Democrats agreeing with the statement had fallen to 22 percent. The

CHART 48
How Much Discrimination Demographic Groups Face

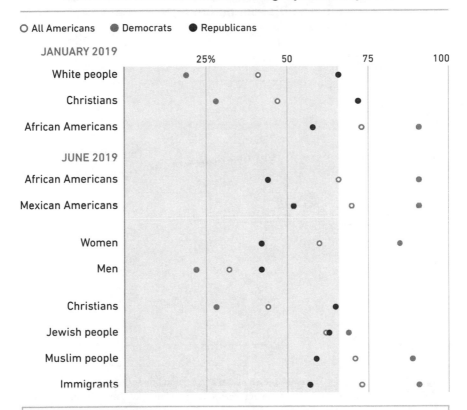

○ All Americans   ● Democrats   ● Republicans

JANUARY 2019

| | 25% | 50 | 75 | 100 |

White people
Christians
African Americans

JUNE 2019

African Americans
Mexican Americans

Women
Men

Christians
Jewish people
Muslim people
Immigrants

> **HOW TO READ THIS CHART** Two polls are shown above in which respondents were asked to evaluate the level of discrimination faced by various demographic groups. A dot farther to the right indicates that more of that partisan group—e.g., Democrats or Republicans—saw the identified demographic group as facing a fair amount or great deal of discrimination. Any dot in the shaded gray area indicates a level of perceived discrimination lower than the number of Republicans who viewed Whites as targets of discrimination. Notice that nearly every other Republican dot is in that shaded section.

number of Republicans agreeing, though, had climbed to 73 percent, a 51-point gap between the two parties.[56]

Shortly before Trump secured the Republican nomination in 2016, *The Washington Post* and ABC News asked Americans if they were struggling

CHART 49

Belief That Discrimination Against Whites Is as Big a Problem as Discrimination Against Blacks

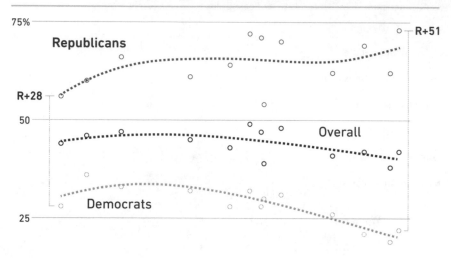

HOW TO READ THIS CHART The lines shown above are a trend line fitting the points of PRRI's regular polling on the question of discrimination against Whites. The difference between the Democratic and Republican views in 2010 and 2020 are highlighted.

economically and/or if they felt that White Americans were "losing." The latter sentiment was a much better predictor of support for Trump, with those indicating that they thought Whites were "losing out because of preferences for blacks and Hispanics" being three times as likely to support Trump as those facing economic challenges.[57] This overlaps with Knowles's research: White Republicans see themselves as embattled and perceive minorities— collectively—usurping their power.

The history of Whites fearing precisely that is long and violent. Writing for *The Washington Post* in 2019, Michael Miller traced the pattern just within the United States from prior to the formation of the nation itself through to the modern day.[58] From colonists using fears about Native Americans as a spur for violence to slavery-era concerns about uprisings to the emergence of the original Klan in the post–Civil War era, the history of settlement in the United States is interwoven with Whites seeing non-Whites as a threat. The modern manifestation is at its most toxic in White nationalist or neo-fascist ideologies, but it also appears in less overtly dangerous forms, like discussions of "great replacement theory," the idea that immigrants are being intentionally brought to the United States to reshape our politics and culture. An Associated Press–NORC poll conducted in December 2021 found that nearly half of Republicans agree to at least some extent that an intentional "replacement" is underway.[59]

Marquette University professor Julia Azari points out that Barack Obama's election triggered something that his candidacy didn't. "Having actual power was a whole other matter," she told me. "And there's always this sort of deep suspicion whenever a president tries to act on civil rights or whatever, that this president has been captured and is acting primarily on the interests of people of color, and specifically Black people, and that engenders backlash."

This is measurable. By 2016, immigration and race relations were viewed by Americans as bigger issues than unemployment—both because the economy was doing better and because the public conversation had shifted to focus on the non-White population. Donald Trump, recognizing the political value of stoking concern about how America was changing, elevated both immigration and race as subjects during his campaigns and presidency. His focus on building a wall on the border with Mexico in response to an increase in migration, for example, prompted more than 1 in 5 Americans to describe immigration as the most important problem America faced by early 2019.[60]

To Theda Skocpol's point, the recent pattern echoes how White Americans approached immigration 100 years ago, though with the unpalatable edges smoothed down. No longer is anti-immigrant or racist sentiment necessarily manifested as a group of Klansmen participating in a Memorial Day march through Jamaica, Queens, as they did in 1927. Instead, it is often more subtle, in the way that Lee Atwater put it in an interview in 1981—less than a decade before he pledged to lead the GOP to a new era of racial outreach.

"You start out in 1954 by saying, 'N——, n——, n——,'" Atwater explained. (He, obviously, used the actual word.) "By 1968 you can't say 'n——'—that hurts you, backfires. So you say stuff like forced busing, states' rights, and all that stuff." By the point at which he was speaking, he continued,

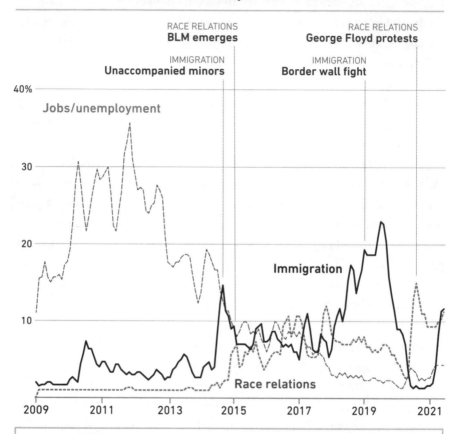

CHART 50
America's Most Important Problem

RACE RELATIONS
BLM emerges

RACE RELATIONS
George Floyd protests

IMMIGRATION
Unaccompanied minors

IMMIGRATION
Border wall fight

40%

Jobs/unemployment

30

20

Immigration

10

Race relations

2009   2011   2013   2015   2017   2019   2021

HOW TO READ THIS CHART   Every month, Gallup asks Americans to identify the country's most important problem.[61] Often, economic issues spur the greatest concern. From late 2014 to early 2021, though, both race and immigration were frequently mentioned by respondents, as indicated by the lines on the graphs above. Key political moments are indicated.

it was all abstract, with Republican rhetoric centered on tax cuts, for example—things where "a by-product of them is, blacks get hurt worse than whites."[62]

The above quote wasn't simply an observation Atwater was offering. It was the game plan he was executing, the Republican Party's decade-plus-old "southern strategy"—appealing tacitly to racial anger in campaigns. He's the guy who made the Willie Horton campaign ad, centered on the specter of dangerous Black criminals, which staggered Michael Dukakis in the 1988 presidential race. "Atwater's tactics were a bridge between the old Republican Party of the Nixon era, when dirty tricks were considered a scandal," *The New Yorker*'s Jane Mayer summarized, "and the new Republican Party of Donald Trump, in which lies, racial fearmongering, and winning at any cost have become normalized."[63] After helping Ronald Reagan win reelection, Atwater joined a prominent Washington consulting firm, the partners of which included Paul Manafort and Roger Stone.

Overt racism and racial slurs became far more socially unacceptable as baby boomers grew older. Racism manifests systemically today in part because it was hidden in systems, shielded from the opprobrium of an enlightened America even though many Americans still supported its outcomes. Late in the Trump era, though, that sense of White Americans being under attack by non-Whites led to a reversal of the sort of subtlety Atwater described. Prominent figures on the right like Fox News host Tucker Carlson increasingly argued explicitly that Whites were being disadvantaged by a focus on addressing inequities.[64] Trump claimed that he was the target of anti-White racism from Black prosecutors investigating his business and his reaction to his 2020 loss.[65] This sentiment pervaded. A few months after the 2020 election, the nonprofit public opinion firm Democracy Corps asked supporters of Donald Trump how they felt about politics in the moment. One participant, a man from Wisconsin, was blunt. "I have six grandkids; they don't have a future," he said. "With the race riots and Antifa, California passed a tax law and Californians are now getting taxed to give straight to the African American community."[66] This was broadly untrue, though rooted in specific concerns being amplified in conservative media. It nonetheless captured the way in which near-formulaic fretting about the future of younger generations overlaps with rhetoric about race.

In a 1981 essay, Robert W. Terry described an informal experiment in which he would ask White people about their Whiteness. Often, they would be flummoxed by the question. "To be white in America is not to have to think about it," Terry determined. "Except for hard-core racial supremacists, the meaning of being white is having the choice of attending to or ignoring one's own whiteness."[67] In 2022, White Republicans in particular were thinking about race a lot. That, in turn, contributed to a renewal of an old idea: that America—or, at least, a particular vision of America—requires an immediate defense.

The march of 1,000 Klansmen in Queens nearly a century earlier didn't end as peacefully as the one in D.C. It led to a brawl in which seven of the "berobed marchers" were arrested, as the *Long Island Daily Press* reported.[68] In response, someone distributed handbills throughout the community that "[gave] the Klan's side of the matter," according to *The New York Times*.[69] The flyers excoriated the "Roman Catholic police of New York City" for the heavy hand deployed against the marchers, including their having clubbed and beaten "[n]ative-born Protestant Americans."

"Liberty and Democracy have been trampled upon," it continued, "when native-born Protestant Americans dare to organize to protect one flag, the American flag; one school, the public school; and one language, the English language." Save the word "Protestant," that could have been a campaign slogan from Donald Trump's 2020 reelection bid.

America was changing. The flyer ended with a stark question for readers—"What will you do?"—and a post-office-box address. Asked who owned the box, the postmaster would only tell the *Times* that the application for it was signed by "two of Jamaica's most prominent men."

The identities of those arrested at the parade, though, are known. One was local resident Fred Trump, the future president's father. He was released without facing criminal charges.

THE PREDICTABLE REASON FOR REPUBLICAN DEFENSIVENESS ON RACE

It's useful here to point out the extent to which "White Republican" is broadly redundant—an overlap that necessarily has generational implications as well.

Pew Research Center has a variety of polling and analysis that speaks to this correlation. Its 2020 assessment of the electorate in 2018 and 2019 found that 81 percent of Republicans were White, a significantly higher percentage than there are Whites in the population overall. The Republican Party, in fact, was more densely White in 2019 than the Democratic Party was in 2012 . . . or 2004, or 1996. In 1996, Pew's data indicate, about 24 percent of the Democratic Party was non-White. A quarter of a century later, only 19 percent of the Republican Party fell into the same category. Most of those

White Republicans were also Christian; two-thirds of the party were both White and Christian in 2019. Only a quarter of Democrats were.[70]

In large part because of that overlap, most of Donald Trump's votes in both 2016 and 2020 came from White voters. About 7 in 10 voters in the 2020 election were White; they preferred Trump by a 12-point margin. Pew's analysis estimates that 85 percent of the votes cast for Trump in 2020 came from White voters, down slightly from 88 percent in 2016.[71] This was in part because Trump performed slightly better with non-White voters, losing Hispanic voters by 21 points in 2020 after losing them by 38 points four years earlier. But it's also because he did slightly worse with White voters, a group that made up far more of those who came out to vote.

Most Republicans are White—and most Whites in 2019 were Republican or Republican-leaning independents.[72] This latter category of voters has taken on increased importance in recent years as the number of self-identified independent voters has increased. Most independent voters still consistently vote with one party or the other, usually more for the opportunity to vote against the party they dislike.[73] This tendency creates a blurry, semipartisan category of voter often called a "leaner." White leaners tend to lean Republican. And in part because older Americans are more likely to be White than non-White, and are more likely to be White than younger Americans, older Americans also tend to be more Republican or lean more to that party.

This touches on another issue that will be more important in a bit: How much of the overlap between older voters and the GOP is a function of the racial demography of that older group and how much a function of the fact that they're older? The former presumes that the group votes Republican because of characteristics and beliefs it represents or embraces; that presumption undergirds much of this chapter. The latter, though, presumes that politics shift to the right as people age, a presumption that would have significant long-term implications given what we know about younger voters at the moment. For now, let's just assume the former and worry about the latter in a few chapters.

Whichever direction the arrow points, it is generally the case that boomers are White and Whites are Republican and Republicans are often boomers. None of these statements is uniformly true, certainly, but the Venn diagram of the three has a lot of overlap. Seven in 10 boomers are White.[74] Fifty-three percent of Whites in 2019 were Republican or Republican leaning.[75] Fifty-six

CHART 51
Where Party, Generation, and Race Overlap

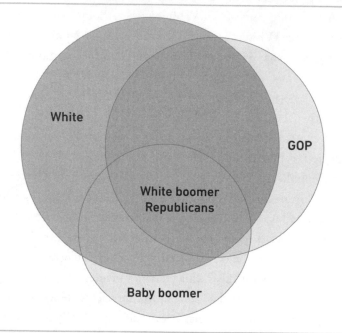

> **HOW TO READ THIS CHART** Using data from the 2020 American National Election Study, the Census Bureau and Gallup (from which we get partisanship data), the diagram above provides an estimate of how these three groups overlap. Just under a fifth of White American adults are also baby boomer Republicans. About a quarter of Republicans are White baby boomers. And about 4 in 10 baby boomers are White Republicans. About 1 in 9 Americans overall were White baby boomer Republicans in 2020.

percent of Republicans in 2019 were aged 50 or over.[76] Working the other direction, a quarter of Whites are boomers,[77] 8 in 10 Republicans are White,[78] and a plurality of those aged 55 and over were Republican or Republican leaning in 2019.[79] That year, Pew estimates that White boomers specifically were about 9 points more likely to identify as Republican than Democrat and about 16 points more likely to identify as Republican or Republican leaning than Democrat or Democrat leaning. By 2021, Republicans had gained a 13-point advantage with the group.

In 2020, Donald Trump won boomers by 3 points, about the same as his margin of victory in 2016.[80] Boomers were 36 percent of the electorate that year, also equivalent to 2016. The difference came among those older than boomers, who backed Trump by 17 points in 2016 and about the same margin in 2020. But in the latter election, they made up only 8 percent of the electorate, half of what they had in 2016. The passage of time had thinned their ranks, replacing them with millions of young liberals. Trump lost.

HOW WE EXACERBATE THE FOCUS ON RACE

In August 2021, the Census Bureau released detailed demographic data from the prior year's census. It is always an important political moment, since those data are used at the state level to redraw the boundaries of political districts, potentially reshaping the balance of power in state legislatures and the House of Representatives. This particular year was an important cultural moment, too, because, for the first time in the history of the United States, the population of Whites declined between decennial censuses.

That became a common focus of news reports about the bureau's announcement. The front page of *The Washington Post*, my employer, blared "First Drop in U.S. White Population" above the fold. *The New York Times* sent a push alert to phones: See where the racial composition of the United States changed the most over the last decade! The decline in the White population was the lead-in to jokes on the late-night shows, with one mock lamenting that this "has got to be a scary time for racists—and Applebee's."[81]

Not that it was really a surprise, except perhaps in scale; the bureau estimated that the non-Hispanic White population dropped by 2.6 percent— or 6 percentage points when considered relative to the national population. The growth of the White population had been slowing essentially since the end of the baby boom, so this reversal was a matter of when, not if. (Whites still outnumber non-Whites substantially.)

The data released in 2021 carried an important caveat, however, that shades those percentages a bit. "Data users should use caution when comparing 2010 Census and 2020 Census race data," it read, "because of improvements to the question design, data processing, and coding procedures for the 2020 Census." You will recall that,[82] between 2010 and 2020, the bureau researched how it might better capture the range of ways in which people describe their racial identity. That effort led to a recommendation that the 2020 census

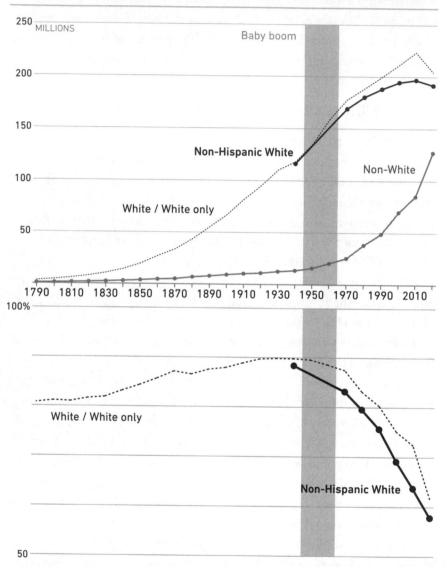

CHART 52
The Actual and Relative Sizes of America's White Population

HOW TO READ THIS CHART The top graph shows the raw count of each group of U.S. residents: those identifying themselves as White, those who are White but not Hispanic (a category that's been consistently isolated only since 1970), and those who are not White (regardless of whether they are Hispanic). The bottom graph shows the percentage of the total population that is White or non-Hispanic White.

include a unified question that included "Hispanic" as a race—a recommendation that was tabled by the Trump administration. In the bureau's presentation announcing the new race data, Nicholas Jones, the bureau's director of race and ethnic research and outreach, conveyed some subtle frustration with the failure to adopt the single-question format.

"While the Census Bureau tested an alternative question design in 2015," Jones said, "we must ultimately follow the 1997 [Office of Management and Budget] standards and use two separate questions to collect data on race and on ethnicity."[83]

So instead the bureau tweaked how it asked those two questions. For example, it added fields for those identifying as White and Black to identify their origins, allowing the bureau to, among other things, make clear that those of Middle Eastern heritage would generally be considered White. It also changed the literal number of characters it would accept from a submitted origin. In 2010, the bureau explained in a news release, someone submitting their origin as "MEXICAN AMERICAN INDIAN AND PORTUGUESE AND AFRICAN AMERICAN" would have only the first 30 characters recorded, meaning that the person would be considered "MEXICAN AMERICAN INDIAN AND PO" and only be categorized as Mexican American Indian.[84] In 2020, the entire response would be included and logged, including multiple racial identities. The percentage of Americans who were identified as "two or more races" by the bureau's analysis soared from 9 million in 2010 to nearly 34 million 10 years later—an increase of 275 percent.

When announcing the new data, Jones attributed that shift to "some demographic changes over the past 10 years." However, he wrote, the differences were "largely due to improvements in the design of the two separate questions for race data collection and processing"—that the change in how the question was asked and handled yielded a more accurate picture. (He was also confident, he explained a bit later, that using a single question for race "would ultimately yield an even more accurate portrait of how the U.S. population self-identifies.") It's a bit like the difference between asking, "Which king was more effective: William IV or George V?" and asking, "Which king was more effective: William IV, George V, or do you not care?" That additional option will change how your results are distributed. The question of self-identification is an important one, to which we'll return. But consider what the methodological shift alone means: a great deal of emotional energy centered on changes in the population of the United States is dependent to a large extent on how the bureau asked the question.

This is a vitally important consideration. Sociologist Richard Alba, who's been focused on the nuances of demographic change for years, argues in his book *The Great Demographic Illusion* that the "growing diversity of the United States is certainly making whites more conscious of their membership in an ethno-racial group that is just one part of the American population."[85] Undercutting R. W. Terry, Whites are thinking about Whiteness more.

In 2018, the demographer Dowell Myers published research with Morris Levy, his colleague at the University of Southern California, that looked at how the presentation of America's growing diversity affected the response that evolution evoked.[86] That work noted that news updates on the diversification of the country in the mid-2010s was also in part due to a function of shifts in methodology, though the top-line reporting centered on the declining heft of the White population. So Myers and Levy decided to see if there was a difference in how people responded to the change in demography depending on what they learned about it. They presented survey subjects with news reports about the shift using one of three frames.

"One story presented a bare discussion of continued rises in racial diversity, without any references to majority status"—the *diversity* frame, as their published research explains. "A second foretold a persistent or continuing white majority under an inclusive definition of whiteness that counts people from mixed backgrounds as white if they so identify themselves"—*inclusive.* "A third resembled the dominant media treatment that emphasized the exclusive white definition and forecast a white minority by 2044"—*exclusive.*

After being presented with the diversity or inclusive frames, more than 6 in 10 White respondents indicated hope or enthusiasm about the demographic changes. When presented with the exclusive frame—the one undergirding many news reports about the shift—6 in 10 Whites expressed anger or anxiety.

The researchers also drilled down one level deeper. About half of White Democrats said they felt angry or anxious when presented with the prospect of a declining White majority. About three-quarters of Republicans said the same.

Why were so many Democrats fairly sanguine about Whites losing power? Myers explained one reason in a 2018 interview with *The New York*

CHART 53

Emotional Response to News Stories
with Different Framing Applied

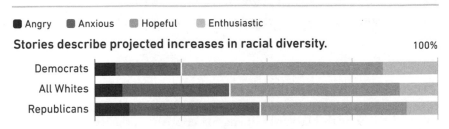

■ Angry   ■ Anxious   ▨ Hopeful   ▨ Enthusiastic

Stories describe projected increases in racial diversity.   100%

Democrats

All Whites

Republicans

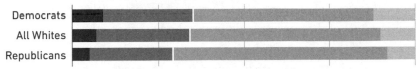

Stories describe persistent White majority using a definition that counts mixed-race people as White.

Democrats

All Whites

Republicans

Stories emphasize that Whites will become a minority.

Democrats

All Whites

Republicans

> **HOW TO READ THIS CHART** Each of the three sections describes a different manner in which the country's evolving demography was presented to White respondents. The third focused on the decline of the White majority and it was viewed the most negatively overall, but particularly by White Republicans.

Times. Progressive Democrats, he said, saw the change as "conquest, our day has come"—that, as theorized with the election of Barack Obama, demographic changes were permanently disadvantaging Republicans. The left "wanted to overpower them with numbers," Myers said. "It was demographic destiny."[87] More on this later, but notice the calculus: more Whites mean more Republicans.

Myers and Levy's research ends with an important point: the "exclusive" presentation of the shift in demography is probably *less accurate* than the alternatives, given that it treats non-Hispanic Whites as a rigidly identified group that ignores the sort of blurriness that the Census Bureau has actively tried to evince. It distills that Mexican American Indian Portuguese individual to one or the other. That this oversimplification is so common suggests that an enormous part of the tension and frustration that exists among White Republicans about changing demography might be a function of having the salience of race elevated and then misunderstood.

THE GENERATIONAL SPLIT ISN'T ONLY ABOUT RACE

When I spoke with Harvard's Theda Skocpol about the Tea Party movement and the energy that powered it, she was clear that her research indicated that it wasn't just demography or Obama.

"There's a religious side to it. Varieties of Protestantism even. And that was the start of the move to Trumpism." And another, related factor: "Right now, one of the biggest divides is between metropolitan America and—rural is not the right word—exurban and small-town America. And that interacts with age and generation and race."

Concerns about the future, about where things are headed, are wispy and vague until they come into contact with some reagent: a young person expressing support for Obama, a segment about immigration on Tucker Carlson's show, a new rumor about crime in New York. It's in part the eternal frustration of those who are aging, that just when they'd gotten things mostly the way they wanted them here come younger people interested in upending it all. At any moment it might be that those people look different, have different values, have a different culture. Republican politics are often built on those divides, on those seven traits separating the boomers from those who are younger.

Let's take education as an example, the fourth of those seven traits. That's one that former Barack Obama data guru David Shor highlighted as particularly significant when we spoke in 2021. The rapid increase in education levels in the United States "has created this really big cultural divide between people who have degrees and people who don't," Shor told me. He now runs data analysis for a nonprofit research organization, offering him access to reams of polling data each year. "It's not that having a degree is causal, but there are really big differences in terms of values, in terms of how they see society, things like racial resentment, social trust, culture, a bunch of other things. There are a bunch of different divides." Often, those sentiments over-lap with liberal politics.

Pew Research Center found that Americans who have college degrees were increasingly likely to describe themselves as liberal over the last several decades. In 1994, 7 percent of those who had undertaken some postgraduate work (seeking a master's or doctorate, for example) identified as "consistently liberal." By 2015, 31 percent did. Among those who stopped at an under-graduate degree, the increase was from 5 percent to 24 percent.[88]

While Donald Trump is often credited with a Reaganesque luring of non-college-educated Whites to the Republican Party, that's not actually what happened. For the first 10 years of this century—until about the time that the Tea Party emerged—the partisan identities of Whites with and without college degrees moved in tandem. From that point forward, though, data from Gallup show an increasing partisan divide between those two groups. As recently as 2006, both Whites with and without degrees were equivalently split in their party identifications. By 2019, there was a 38-point gulf, with college-educated Whites identifying as Democrats by a 13-point margin and Whites without degrees leaning Republican by 25.[89]

It's probably futile to try to disentangle this shift from the Trump-era rejection of college education by Republicans. In 2015, with the most-educated Americans having already moved so much to the left, about 56 percent of Republicans said that college had a positive effect on how the country was progressing. By 2017, views had inverted: 58 percent now said that colleges had a *negative* effect. That held through 2019, when the most common reason that Republicans expressed opposition to colleges was that "professors are bringing their political and social views into the classroom." (The most common negative factor expressed by Democrats? That tuition was so high.)[90]

Then there's religion, the fifth trait. When Donald Trump first ran for office in 2015, his candidacy was a nonstarter among many religious leaders. A guy who never went to church and who called the Bible his favorite book (just ahead of *The Art of the Deal*)[91] but couldn't name a Bible verse?[92] Who'd been pro-choice? Who'd been married three times? *That* Donald Trump?

But religious *voters*—specifically White evangelical Protestants—didn't seem to care. His polling with evangelical voters tracked with support from Republican primary voters overall once he became the front-runner.[93] He

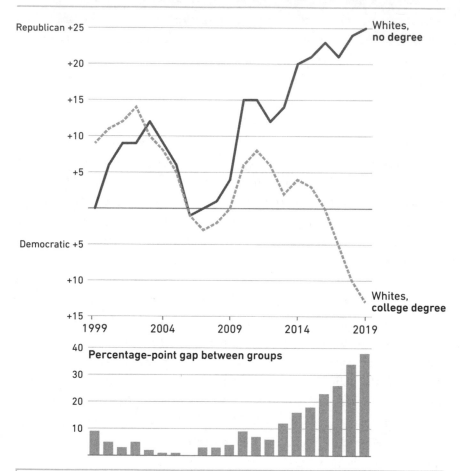

HOW TO READ THIS CHART These two graphs show the same data in two ways. At top, a line graph showing the margin between Republican and Democratic partisan identification among Whites, as measured by Gallup. At bottom, the actual gap in identification—essentially a measure of how far apart the two lines are in any given year.

won evangelicals by 61 points in 2016 and 69 points in 2020.[94] One reason was obvious: Trump pledged an unabashedly transactional relationship. Vote for him and get an unwavering champion for their interests, however divergent from moral perfection he happened to be.

On January 23, 2016, Trump gave a speech at Dordt University in Sioux Center, Iowa, shortly before that state's presidential caucuses. He was introduced by Robert Jeffress, an evangelical minister from Texas and Fox News contributor. Jeffress insisted he wasn't endorsing but summarized Trump's appeal to evangelical Christians: "Evangelicals, like most Americans, are sick and tired of the status quo."

When it came time for him to speak, Trump described having seen one of Jeffress's interviews the prior year. The candidate walked through a litany of rationales that he said Jeffress had offered, before getting to the crux of the issue. "'He may not be as pure as we think, but he's really good. And he is a great Christian,'" Trump described Jeffress as saying. "And that's what I wanted to hear."

This comports with polling. In 2011, 44 percent of Americans told Public Religion Research Institute (PRRI) that they believed an elected official who behaved immorally in private could nonetheless behave ethically in their public roles. Among White evangelical Protestants, only 30 percent did. By late October 2016, as Trump was on the brink of election, acceptance of such foibles had risen. Now, 61 percent of Americans overall thought such an official might still behave ethically in office—as did more than 7 in 10 evangelicals.[95]

Speaking in Iowa, Trump transitioned to his central point. "I will tell you: Christianity is under siege, whether we want to talk about it or we don't," Trump said. He later claimed that, had he proposed barring the entry of Christians to the country instead of Muslims (as he had the previous December), no one would have objected. This is of course not true, but it reinforced that sense of embattlement that his audience at the religious university likely felt.

He went on to bemoan that Christians—a group larger than the pool of American men or American women—didn't use their collective power, that there wasn't a "Christian lobby." But, then, they soon wouldn't need one. "If I'm there, you're gonna have plenty of power," he told the audience. "You don't need anybody else. You're gonna have somebody representing you very, very well, remember that."

In 2014, Pew found that more than a third of evangelicals were members of the baby boom generation, more than any other generational group. Three-quarters were White.[96]

Elizabeth Dias of *The New York Times* interviewed Iowans prior to the

2020 election, exploring Trump's relationship with the evangelical community and the rural communities around Sioux Center.[97] Reading the story, interspersed with professionally shot photographs of small towns, small-town farms, and families in small-town farmhouses, one of my first thoughts was of children's books. Even if you don't happen to have young children at the moment—which I did at the time the story was published, no doubt contributing to the connection—you're familiar with the books written for them. It's all Peter Rabbit and tales of Old MacDonald and here are the noises made by cows, chickens, and horses. Kids' puzzles and toys are often in the same vein, as are children's songs; one farmer, you may have been informed, has a dog named Bingo. The introduction of *Sesame Street*—a function of the emergence of television and the creation of a public broadcasting system in 1967[98]—elevated an unconstrained urban sensibility within children's entertainment. Otherwise, much of what kids are exposed to is a deluge of traditional educational material familiarizing children with what is for most of them today an otherwise unfamiliar culture. A lot more people now live in *Sesame Street*'s New York City than on Old MacDonald's farm.[99]

The life depicted in the photos in Dias's article, in other words, was the norm but no longer is. This is very much to the point, that even within the lifetimes of the people with whom she spoke that universe was growing smaller and more isolated.

"I feel like on the coasts, in some of the cities and stuff, they look down on us in rural America," a man named Jason Mulder told her. "You know, we are a bunch of hicks, and don't know anything. They don't understand us the same way we don't understand them. So we don't want them telling us how to live our lives."

Metropolitan versus small town, with religion overlaid. It also veers into the educational divide. "Cities are much more educated than rural areas," David Shor said, "and our electoral system heavily advantages, overweights the views of rural voters in a lot of different ways." Overweights the views of Republicans, in other words—and underweights the actual choices of voters.

THE TOXIC EFFECTS OF POLITICAL ISOLATION

The month of the 1964 election, pitting incumbent Democratic president Lyndon B. Johnson against Arizona senator Barry Goldwater, *Harper's Magazine* ran an essay from historian Richard Hofstadter. It was called "The Paranoid Style in American Politics" and it explored the way in which the extremism Goldwater and his supporters both reflected and embraced —"extremism in defense of liberty is no vice," the candidate said at the Republican convention that year—was a recurring theme in American history. What Hofstadter didn't know at the time, of course, was that his insights into the moment that brought Goldwater to power would resonate again 50 years later.

There was one difference between the previous derangements that had rippled through politics and the one represented by Goldwater, Hofstadter wrote. "The modern right wing . . . feels dispossessed: America has been largely taken away from them and their kind, though they are determined to try to repossess it and to prevent the final destructive act of subversion. The old American virtues have already been eaten away by cosmopolitans and intellectuals; the old competitive capitalism has been gradually undermined by socialist and communist schemers; the old national security and independence have been destroyed by treasonous plots, having as their most powerful agents not merely outsiders and foreigners as of old but major statesmen who are at the very centers of American power.

"Their predecessors had discovered conspiracies," he added: "the modern radical right finds conspiracy to be betrayal from on high."[100] A powerful Deep State fighting alongside socialists against Real America? It's essentially a Donald Trump tweet.

Hofstadter was insistent that he wasn't equating the term "paranoid" with genuine mental instability, though he did mean it pejoratively. But he was also clearly describing some delusional beliefs and activities, ones that might become acutely dangerous. "The situation becomes worse when the representatives of a particular social interest—perhaps because of the very unrealistic and unrealizable nature of its demands—are shut out of the political process," he wrote. "Having no access to political bargaining or the making of decisions, they find their original conception that the world of power is sinister and malicious fully confirmed."

He was referring to situations in which the derangements of advocates were understandably not treated seriously, prompting them to become more convinced than ever that power was arrayed against them. But what if the delusion is less exotic? What if, for example, a huge swath of the population becomes falsely convinced that free and fair elections have evaporated in the face of rampant fraud? One thing that happens is that hundreds of people push past or beat police in order to swarm into the U.S. Capitol and block the finalization of the results of a presidential race. Another thing that happens is there is a sharp diminishment in the idea that elections are the proper conduit for allocating power.

There are a lot of reasons that one might believe that the results of an election were tainted or upended by fraud. One is that someone you trust—say, the president of the United States—is telling you that they were. This becomes easier when he himself is building on decades of allegations about fraud. It's long been the case that fraud allegations were used as a rationale for disenfranchising undesirable voters; for years prior to 2020, Republicans hyped overblown or unfounded claims of fraud while pushing legislation that would make voting more restrictive (and, generally, disproportionately disenfranchise Democratic voters). Trump's claims were less strategic, centered in 2016 on the fact that he lost the popular vote (he repeatedly claimed that millions of illegal votes had been cast in California that year, for example[101]) and in 2020 on his loss overall. But they had fertile soil in which to take root, tilled by Republicans for decades prior.

Another reason that a Trump voter might be skeptical that Biden had won is that she knew relatively few Biden voters. This is what might be called Pauline Kael syndrome, after the movie critic who apocryphally expressed amazement at Richard Nixon's 1972 reelection by declaring that she didn't know anyone who'd voted for him.[102] In 2020, Pew Research Center found that 6 in 10 Trump voters said they had a lot of friends who similarly supported the incumbent president, while 4 in 10 had no friends who were supporting Biden. (The numbers for Biden voters were similar: about half said they had a lot of friends who supported Biden; 4 in 10 had no friends backing Trump.)[103]

You're telling me that Biden got 81 million votes despite literally everyone I know voting for Trump? I'm supposed to trust the mainstream media telling me that?[104] Ridiculous.

We've discussed partisan clustering, of which this is clearly a by-product. Part of the reason that 40 percent of Trump supporters said they didn't know anyone who supported Biden (and vice versa) is that Americans are heavily clustered geographically: Democrats into cities, Republicans into rural areas.

"Something happened in the mid-1970s that began to segregate everything except race," Bill Bishop, coauthor of *The Big Sort,* explained when we spoke by phone—"everything" meaning politics and cultural values and even prominent retail chains. He and his coauthor, Robert Cushing, found that the number of counties in the United States that were competitive in presidential races—having a margin between the Democratic and Republican nominees that was 20 points or smaller—decreased since the mid-1970s. In 1976, for example, about 27 percent of the country lived in counties where the margin was more than 20 points. By 2004, nearly half did. In other words, Americans have been increasingly likely to live in places that vote overwhelmingly for one party or the other and, therefore, presumably increasingly unlikely to know anyone who didn't vote the way they did.

We can see Bishop's sorting in the 2020 results. Precinct-level data compiled by researcher Ryne Rohla show that about 27 percent of votes cast in 2020 were from precincts—neighborhoods, in essence—where the margin between Biden and Trump was at least 50 points. More Democratic than Republican voters lived in those lopsided places, with about 27 percent of the

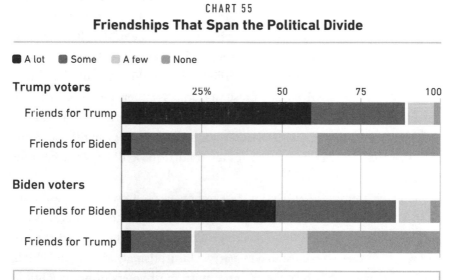

CHART 55
Friendships That Span the Political Divide

■ A lot ■ Some ▨ A few ▨ None

Trump voters

| | 25% | 50 | 75 | 100 |

Friends for Trump

Friends for Biden

Biden voters

Friends for Biden

Friends for Trump

HOW TO READ THIS CHART Each row represents the distribution for one group, from Trump voters identifying how many of their friends supported Trump to Biden voters doing the same. The lighter colored bars indicate fewer friends who support the candidate; in each case three-quarters of each candidate's supporters say that they have few to no friends who supported the other candidate.

votes cast for Biden coming in places he won by at least 50 points and 18 percent of the votes cast for Trump coming in places he won by the same margin.[105] The numeric difference, of course, is in part because so many of the places that voted overwhelmingly for Trump are much less densely populated and much more rural. Winning 10 percent of the vote in a crowded, pro-Biden New York City neighborhood could nonetheless yield more Trump votes than sweeping part of a county in Wyoming.

At the state level, places that voted for Trump—again, often more rural states—tended to see a higher percentage of cast votes coming from those lopsided precincts. About 39 percent of all votes cast in states Trump won came from lopsided precincts, including 31 percent of the votes cast for Trump himself. In states Biden won, 26 percent of all votes came from lopsided precincts, including 21 percent of the votes cast for Biden.

It's important to recognize the extent to which Trump laid the groundwork for the assumption that fraud was rampant. The weekend before the election in 2020, I was in Scranton, Pennsylvania, speaking with voters and tracking what the campaigns were doing to ensure victory. Biden's team was running a traditional operation to ensure that their voters actually cast votes. Trump's supporters were instead picking up signs or, at one point, participating in a raucous parade of vehicles down one of the city's (largely empty) main streets. In interviews, those who planned to vote for Trump told me that they were generally confident he would win—unless widescale fraud occurred. Given that presumption, a focus on a loud parade and putting out lots of Trump signs made some perverse sense. While Biden's team was trying to win more votes, Trump's team was creating the appearance that the president had so much support that those Biden votes became suspicious.

Shortly after the 2020 election, researchers Jacob Brown and Ryan Enos published a study that took Bishop's "big sort" analysis to its microcosmic endpoint. They looked at individual registered voters and measured the extent to which they were clustered by party. Unsurprisingly, they found "high partisan segregation across the country, with most voters of both political parties living in partisan bubbles with little exposure to the other party." In an interview, Enos explained that this can happen from both directions, with people moving to places where most share their politics or as the politics of a neighborhood's residents shift over time. Places with high densities of

CHART 56
State Results in 2020 vs. Partisan Insulation

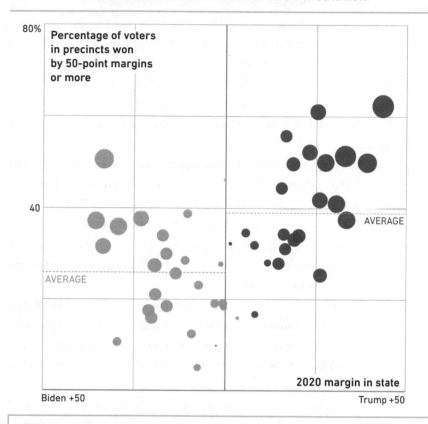

80%

Percentage of voters
in precincts won
by 50-point margins
or more

40

AVERAGE

AVERAGE

2020 margin in state

Biden +50

Trump +50

HOW TO READ THIS CHART There are a lot of data conveyed in this graph, probably the most complicated we've seen so far. Each dot represents a state, arrayed from biggest margin for Biden (left) to biggest margin for Trump (right). States at the bottom had fewer voters in precincts one candidate won by at least 50 points; those toward the top had more. The size of each circle represents how many more voters lived in precincts lopsided toward one candidate, indicated by color: darker-colored states had a higher percentage of voters in lopsided precincts that preferred Trump, lighter-colored ones in precincts lopsided toward Biden. A smaller circle, then, had a smaller percentage of voters in lopsided counties.

White college graduates, for example, would have become more Democratic as that group's voting patterns changed.

As an example of the former phenomenon, he pointed to the increase of explicit and implicit political signaling in neighborhoods, from political lawn signs to signs advocating the Black Lives Matter movement or even, during the pandemic, expressing confidence in science—signifiers that might encourage or dissuade people from moving in. "I would have people tell me, 'Well, I was thinking about moving somewhere, but then I saw that there were too many Trump signs, so I moved somewhere else,'" Enos told me. Neighborhood choices were an example of how partisanship can be epiphenomenal, he said, manifesting in ostensibly apolitical things like jobs and lifestyle choices. Like another example he offered of the sort of visual flag that might inform someone about a neighborhood's politics: the presence of pickup trucks.

Loosely speaking, the effect is that America becomes not a collection of united states but of aggregated and at times discordant political clusters—clusters that themselves overlap with demography. Speaking to *The New Yorker* after the 2020 election, a senior AFL-CIO official named Michael Podhorzer homed in on the way in which acceptance of the idea that rampant fraud had occurred overlapped with a galaxy of institutions and groups that aren't definitionally downstream from politics.

"What animates it is the belief that Biden won because votes were cast by some people in this country who others think are not 'real' Americans," he suggested, an assumption bolstered by a wide range of ostensibly apolitical institutions including "white evangelical churches, legislators, media companies, nonprofits," and others.

"Trump won white America by eight points. He won non-urban areas by over twenty points," Podhorzer argued. "He *is* the democratically elected President of white America. It's almost like he represents a nation within a nation."[106]

A GENERATION DIVIDED AGAINST ITSELF

We should end where we began, with recognition that the baby boom generation is not monolithic. A generation that gave us Bill Clinton, Donald Trump, and Barack Obama hardly could be. And we can appreciate the particular political divide in the generation's power by considering the political movement that emerged in opposition to the Tea-Party-to-Trump stream: the group that often called itself "the resistance."

"Those are people who feel just as intensely that the country is being betrayed and sold down the river," Theda Skocpol said of that collective, one disproportionately made up of boomer-aged women. Nor did those sentiments fade with Biden's election, she believes: "I think both sides feel profoundly threatened by the other."

Her research, conducted with her Harvard colleagues Caroline Tervo and Kirsten Walters, found that, largely given its politics, the resistance was relatively effective at crossing generational lines. "Most national resistance organizations are headquartered in big cities and liberal states, and function through paid professional employees who tend to be racially and ethnically diverse college graduates in their late twenties to early forties," they wrote in a paper published in January 2021. "Grassroots groups are spread across communities of all sizes and partisan compositions, and their leaders and most devoted participants are mostly older white women who might be (and sometimes actually are) the mothers or grandmothers of the youthful metropolitan advocates."[107] The latter are broadly self-identified progressives; the former more moderate traditional Democrats driven to activism by the concern Skocpol articulates.

Another paper Skocpol authored with Harvard's Leah Gose looked more closely at the demographic composition of participants in the resistance movement that kicked into high gear in 2017. The median age of participants was 61 years—meaning a birth year of 1956, in the heart of the baby boom. A large majority held college degrees. Many were retired. Nearly all were women.[108]

That this group would be a center of anti-Trump sentiment is not surprising, given what polling tells us about their politics and their views of the former president. For example, the American National Election Study survey conducted before and after each presidential election included a question in 2020 asking respondents to measure their views of Trump on a Celsius-like scale ranging from 0—very cold—to 100. On average, baby boomer women with college degrees rated Trump a 32. Boomer men without degrees rated him a 54.

It has consistently been the case that baby boomer women lean more Democratic than baby boomer men. Pew's analysis of the partisan lean of generational groups—meaning the extent to which members identify as members of a party or as independents who lean toward one party or the other—shows a consistent gap in the party identification of baby boomer men

CHART 57
Views of Trump, Measured as Temperatures

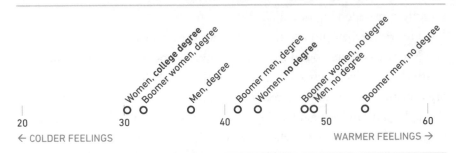

← COLDER FEELINGS   WARMER FEELINGS →

HOW TO READ THIS CHART   Each circle marks the average measurement of feelings about Trump for the indicated group in the 2020 ANES.[109] Circles farther to the left indicate colder feelings for him. Notice that, for the displayed groups, those with college degrees uniformly held more negative views.

and women. At no point has it been smaller than 15 points, with boomer women more likely to identify as Democrats or Democrat-leaning independents. One of the two points it was at its widest was in 2016, the year Trump was elected.[110]

While the resistance effort can be seen as something of a mirror image of the Tea Party movement, Skocpol notes that the effect on politics was different.

"The impact on the two parties is opposite, because the Tea Party tended to push ethnocentrist extremism in the Republican side, made the Republicans more extreme," she told me. "The opposite effect existed if you take the resistance as a whole. If you get beyond the people who appear on MSNBC and you look at the actual older women who organized all over the country, in blue and red areas as well as purple areas—in all the areas—they created a surge but a *moderating* surge on the Democratic side."

This is also measurable. Women, particularly college-educated women, are far less conservative than men, according to the 2020 ANES. Boomer women were more conservative than women overall—but far less than boomer men.

For all of the focus on the tension between baby boomers and other generational groups, one of the most potent tensions in recent politics was

CHART 58
Partisan Gap Within the Baby Boom by Gender

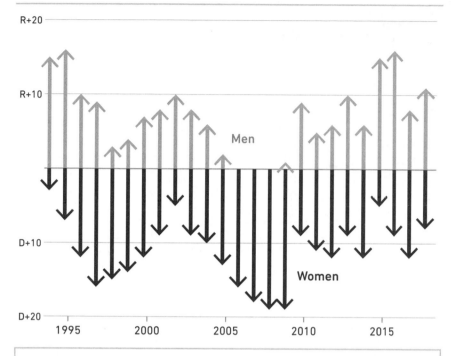

The arrows indicate the net partisan lean of baby boomer men and women by year—in other words, the extent to which the group is more likely to lean to the Democrats or to the Republicans. So in 1994, for example, baby boomer men were 15 points more likely to identify as Republicans or Republican-leaning independents than as Democrats or Democrat leaners (as the vernacular has it). The last displayed values are for both 2018 and 2019.

between the baby boom and itself. Trump's election had something of a catalyzing effect within the generation; boomers were often at the center of the impulses and activism that brought him to power—and then were at the center of the organized pushback against him.

That tension has since evolved, occasionally manifesting early in Joe Biden's presidency at the extreme, as threats of political violence like the one presented by pseudo-bomber Floyd Ray Roseberry in Washington. The question that follows is whether that's sustained or if Roseberry is right, if his generation of (in particular) older White men is the "the last generation" that

CHART 59

Baby Boomer Ideology by Education and Gender

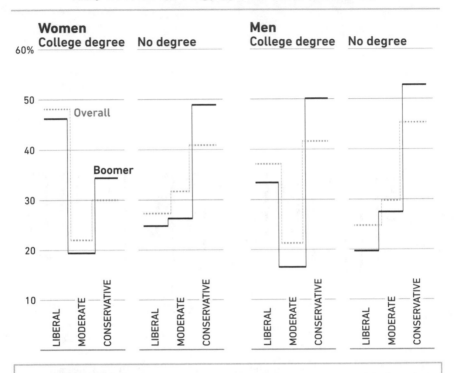

HOW TO READ THIS CHART The lines shown measure the percentage of each indicated group that identifies as liberal, moderate, or conservative. You can see that, among baby boomer women with a college degree, the level of identification as liberal is higher than the level identifying as conservative. For baby boomer men without degrees, the opposite is true—by a wide margin.

will defend the country in the way that might prompt someone to threaten to blow up the Library of Congress. The question further is whether the generation that follows will maintain its unusual political uniformity or be similarly split by the influences of demography and fear and power. That's one facet of the question that drives the rest of this book: What happens next?

II

THE AFTERMATH

5

The Post-Boomer
Cultural Era Has Arrived

Kathleen Casey Kirschling, canonically America's first baby boomer, was born in Philadelphia just after midnight on January 1, 1946. Her family lived south of the city, across the Delaware River in Pennsauken, New Jersey. Her father was in the navy, stationed at the nearby training center at Bainbridge, Maryland. Either due to some sort of perfect cosmic alignment or to the universality of the experience, Kirschling describes a thoroughly stereotypical boomer childhood: doors left unlocked, roller-skating and biking with friends. Her family was Irish Catholic, devoutly so, and she attended Catholic schools from childhood until she earned her master's degree. When she was a teenager, that meant Camden Catholic High School, a short walk away in Cherry Hill with its front entrance positioned beneath three large crosses as though the hill were Calvary. The faculty at the school were members of the faith, like Sister Mary Gregory, the school's "dean of discipline." Students took confession during the school day. In her 1964 senior-class yearbook there was a memorial to John Kennedy, America's first Catholic president, assassinated the prior November.

Despite the obviously strict environment, the teenaged Kirschling was (and remains) a fan of pop music. (Her senior yearbook entry wisely pronounces that "jazz and hamburgers make a winning combination."[1]) Happily for her, there was no better place to be a teenaged fan of music than in that town, at that moment, because one short bus ride over the river was the place

where those two interests most forcefully collided: WFIL, the local Philadelphia television station where a young Dick Clark was hosting *American
Bandstand*.

"We would go over there, a group of us," she told me, obviously still
thrilling from the memory. She and her friends would leave from school,
covering their uniforms with sweaters. "We'd take the bus and go over and,
no matter how cold it was, stand in line. You had to wait for them to let you
in. Not every teenager in America could do that."

Nor could she, for long. Early in 1963, when Kirschling was a junior,
Clark switched from taping after school to putting a week of episodes in the
can each Saturday.[2] Later that year, he'd decamp for California, where he
remained. Her days of dancing on camera were over.

As someone who grew up listening to music from that era via my parents,
I was curious whom she'd seen live. This was in the 1962 season, she said,
when the featured performers ranged from the fleeting (Timi Yuro) to the
eternal (Dionne Warwick). But she didn't remember. The experience, that
was what stuck, and the general sense that it didn't get much better.

"The music of the boomers is awesome music," she told me. This observation wasn't offered wistfully, as you might expect. It was direct, with the
honed assertiveness of someone who's spent a lot of time describing her life
to curious writers. "I mean, we're still playing it."

Well, yes, but that does depend on what "we" you're referring to. The
footprints of the baby boom are obviously still visible all around us, but
they're fading to different degrees in different places. The boom's cultural
dominance is eroding in the face of the natural shifts of age and dramatic,
rapid changes in how the world communicates.

BOOMER MUSIC FADES TO THE BACKGROUND

Bandstand had been on the air for a decade by the time Kirschling was waiting to get in. It operated in tandem with another still-young institution, the
popular music charts in *Billboard* magazine. Artists would appear on *Bandstand* and then on the charts shortly afterward, a smooth runway to success
that ensnared Clark in the late-1950s payola scandal.

Billboard's weekly rankings are convenient for our purposes because they allow us to see how musical acts rise and fall with generations. Or they could if we had access to that information, something that, as of this writing, *Billboard* doesn't make easy. Institutions that predate the internet sit in a sort of limbo between the Dark and Information Ages, possessors of enormous amounts of useful information that can't be used until it's transcribed or scanned or interpreted. *Billboard*'s efforts to present its own history in an accessible way has progressed slowly.

Where there exists an obstruction in the flow of information, though, the information finds a way around it, to paraphrase a truism about the internet. And in the case of *Billboard*'s old data, the way around the blockade was a crowd-sourced effort to hand catalog all of the magazine's past entries. The Whitburn Project began in 1998, as writer and technologist Andy Baio explained when he elevated it to the world's attention a decade later.[3] Its name comes from a series of books documenting popular music and the fluctuations of music charts started by researcher Joel Whitburn. The Whitburn Project was oriented around collecting audio files of the songs that landed in those books, but it also involved compiling an extensive spreadsheet of popular songs. The result was a garishly colored Excel document that, by the end of 2015, included nearly 40,000 songs from about 9,000 unique artists, beginning in the late 1800s—in other words, to a period well before *Billboard*.

These data allow us to do something interesting. We can measure the longevity of artists in popular awareness over time by tracking how often they charted as the years passed. Instead of looking at the artists who appeared on *Billboard*'s lists during the years of the boom, though, it makes more sense to look at the artists popular when the boomers were teens—and, later, when members of Generation X or the millennial generation were aged 13 to 19. There's some overlap: a boomer born in 1964 would be a teenager at the same time as a Gen X-er born in 1965. But with that in mind, we can track how long the artists who were popular when the boomers were teens stayed popular.

Appropriately enough, the last four years of the twentieth century saw a brief resurgence of boomer-era stars. In 1997, Elton John (who first charted in 1970) hit number one by reworking his tribute to Marilyn Monroe, "Candle in the Wind," into a memorial for Princess Diana. The next year, Aerosmith had a chart-topping song, 25 years after its first *Billboard* single. In

CHART 60
When the Most Popular Bands in a Year First Appeared

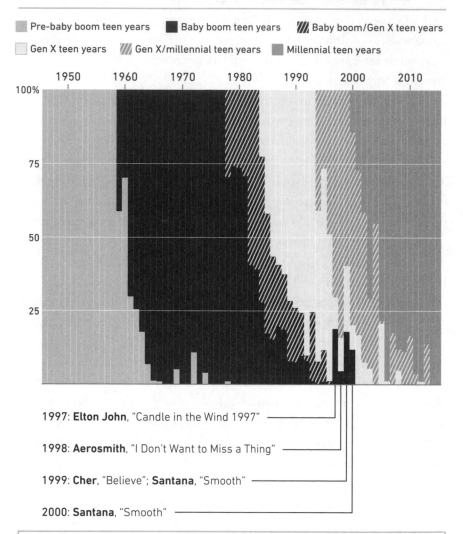

Pre-baby boom teen years   Baby boom teen years   Baby boom/Gen X teen years

Gen X teen years   Gen X/millennial teen years   Millennial teen years

1997: **Elton John**, "Candle in the Wind 1997"

1998: **Aerosmith**, "I Don't Want to Miss a Thing"

1999: **Cher**, "Believe"; **Santana**, "Smooth"

2000: **Santana**, "Smooth"

HOW TO READ THIS CHART Each vertical column represents a year of top-three charting *Billboard* artists, colored by the era in which they first appeared on *Billboard*'s charts at all.[4] You can see the darker-colored section emerge in the late 1950s as artists who first reached the charts in 1959 or later hit the top three. By the mid-1970s, the charts are almost entirely made up of artists who first charted between 1959 (when the oldest boomers were 13) and 1983 (when the youngest boomers were 19). By 2015, the millennials had taken over.

1999, both Cher (first on the charts in 1965) and Santana (1969) had number one songs. Santana's—"Smooth," with the singer Rob Thomas—stretched into 2000.

After that? A desert. For the next 15 years, no artist who first emerged when the boomers were teenagers was back on top of the charts. There was an artist from that era who reached the top 10 a few years later, though it's not someone whom you'd either associate with the baby boom or expect to be releasing music in 2014. That was Michael Jackson, who first charted in 1971 when he himself was a young boomer teenager. His song "Love Never Felt So Good" reached number 9 in May 2014 on the strength of a posthumous duet with Justin Timberlake. But now the era of boomer music dominance on the charts is over.

For another generation, the shift in popularity would merit a shrug. Yeah, teenagers aren't listening to music written by people now in their seventies? Shocking. But that underplays the extent to which music was a central unifier in the baby boom generation. In his aptly named book *No Peace, No Place: Excavations Along the Generational Fault*, journalist Jeff Greenfield summarized its importance succinctly. "Nothing we see in the Counterculture, not the clothes, the hair, the sexuality, the drugs, the rejection of reason, the resort to symbols and magic," he wrote—"none of it is separable from the coming to power in the 1950s of rock and roll music."[5]

It traveled with the generation as surely as the Beatles shifted from "Love Me Do" to "I'm So Tired." If you were 23 at Woodstock (or when Woodstock occurred, regardless of whether you were actually there or not), you were likely listening to the Coasters sing "Charlie Brown" when you were newly a teenager. Landon Jones probably wasn't the first person to declare that "rock was the sound track in the movie version of their lives," but he'll do to make the point.[6] I've never seen the 1973 movie *American Graffiti*, a film that "milks the boom generation's nostalgia almost rapaciously," in Jones's phrasing, but I've certainly heard the soundtrack.

There's an element of this, though, that's self-fulfilling, like the record viewership television shows enjoyed in the pre-internet era. The limitations of identification, production, and promotion that existed in the scout-to-vinyl era no longer apply, just as few families sit around on a weekday evening to choose between ABC, NBC, and CBS. Millennials aren't slavishly centered on rock music in part because they have a lot of other available options,

options that appear not only on well-established labels in record stores but are uploaded to SoundCloud. The emergence of these varying streams (pun intended) of production meant that *Billboard* had to change its methodology a few years ago. Instead of simply counting sales, its rankings now also tally the number of times songs are played online. And, of course, the fractalization of the media landscape also provides new opportunities for old things to find new audiences. When the streaming service Disney+ aired hours of footage from a Beatles recording session, the new interest pushed the band's songs back onto the *Billboard* charts, if only briefly.[7] Part of this, of course, is that same baby boomer nostalgia. The nostalgia that let bands like the Rolling Stones continue to sell out concert venues even with Mick Jagger pushing 80.

In 2009, Pew Research Center surveyed Americans about various musical acts, finding that even among those aged 16 to 29—Gen X and millennials, under its own definition—three of the five most popular acts emerged during the 1960s: the Beatles, the Stones, and Jimi Hendrix.[8] The sheer weight of the boomers' influence still has gravity. "Try imagining young adults back in the 1960s putting the big jazz bands of the Roaring '20s at the top of their list of favorites," Pew's Paul Taylor and Rich Morin wrote. "Not very likely"—true for numerous reasons centered on technology, on generation size, and on culture.

The most popular performer among that 16 to 30 age group in Pew's poll, incidentally, was Michael Jackson.

STANDING ON THE SHOULDERS
OF A GIANT GENERATION

That Pew poll was tied to the fortieth anniversary of Woodstock but focused more broadly on the way in which generational interactions had evolved during those four decades. One question asked in the survey presented respondents with various ways in which younger and older Americans might be different, like on politics or moral values. At that point—in August 2009, before the backlash against Barack Obama's presidency had reached high gear—only a third of those polled said that younger and older Americans were very different in their attitudes toward different races and groups. Instead, the widest divergence was seen on what might loosely be described as cultural issues: the music they like (69 percent said old and young were "very different" in this regard) and on the way in which they use technology and computers (73 percent said the generations were "very different"). To the point of the boomers' diminished cultural dominance: when asked if they knew what Woodstock was, only about half of those under the age of 25 said they did. Woodstock! And that was more than a decade ago.

It is harder to measure cultural influence than things like economic and political power. Earlier, we evaluated the amount of wealth held by generation and the density of each generation in Congress. How do we measure cultural power beyond things like tracking top-40 music? What's the specific index we can apply? Or is it necessarily ineffable?

Ann Larabee, the editor of *The Journal of Popular Culture*, is uniquely well positioned to consider such a question. So I asked her: Have the boomers lost their cultural dominance? And her answer, fittingly, was an intricate one.

She offered that mass production offers an immediately useful index. "In that regards, you can see who has the most consuming power," Larabee said. "Who are the marketers gearing their pitches towards? And then you could also look at who appears the most. Certainly, that's young people—but I would say that the boomers kind of pioneered that idea that popular culture is about youth. I'm not sure that holds before the postwar period."

In other words, evaluating the decline of boomer influence by pointing out that popular music is now dominated by younger, newer artists is itself a reflection of the cultural influence of boomers, who helped cement the idea that new pop music was a measure of culture in the first place. The boomers were "the first, true youth consumer group," she explained, something we considered in the first chapter. That was compounded by the boom's intersection with the growth in television; when Mr. Potato Head appeared in a 1952 ad targeted directly at children, it for the first time created a blend of medium, message, and market that continues today.[9]

Again we can quote Landon Jones: "Fads used to be started by young adults and then spread up and down to younger and older people. But the fads of the fifties, almost without exception, were creations of the children. They flowed *up*."[10]

They often still do. The river, reversed, continues to flow in its new direction. And the boomers, Larabee argues, deserve some credit for the reversal. Granted. So today what group is most visible—or, perhaps more intriguingly, who is most coveted by advertisers?

Barbara Kahn teaches marketing at Wharton. She agreed that the emergence of the baby boom had reshaped how capitalism approached its most basic function of selling things to people. Instead of simply thinking about young adults or the elderly, it now applied the idea of cohort analysis, "the idea," she explained, "that people who are born at a certain time and face certain milestones, think more similarly than people who are the same age but face different life events." In other words, a 30-year-old in 1945 who'd grown up during the Depression and global conflict was dissimilar from a 30-year-old in 1985. "What was different about them at the time," she summarized, "was that they were a big generation and they did seem to be markedly different from their parents."

The question about influence, then, is whether boomers are still a disproportionate target of marketing efforts. To a large extent, that's a function of how much money boomers spend.

There are two trends working against each other here. On the one hand, older people tend to spend less money than younger ones. On the other hand, there are a lot more old people, as may have become apparent elsewhere in this book. The federal government collects data on consumer spending through the Bureau of Labor Statistics. The Consumer Expenditure Survey (CES), as that measure is known, allows us to evaluate how the size of age groups compares to their spending over time.

In recent years, the data have been broken down by generation. In 2020, boomers made up about a third of consumer units (to use that accurate but robotic appellation), the most of any generation. But they made up slightly less of spending, at 32 percent, while members of Generation X, who were 28 percent of consumer units, were more than a third of consumer spending.

The CES data are also broken out by spending category, allowing us to see how boomers compare on spending in particular categories. They made up a disproportionately small percentage of transportation spending in 2020 and a disproportionately large portion of spending on health care—unsurprisingly, given their age. But they also made up a disproportionately large percentage of spending on entertainment. Digging a level deeper, we see where that disproportionate spending occurs: often on expensive things, like audio and visual equipment or the broadly drawn category of sporting goods and photographic equipment. And, for good measure, on pets.

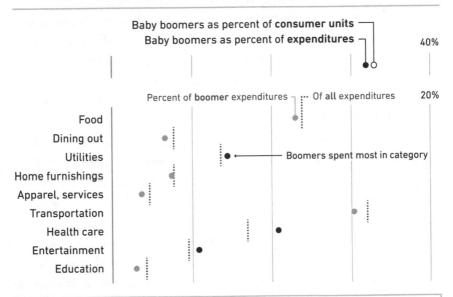

CHART 61
What Boomers Are Spending Money On

Baby boomers as percent of **consumer units**
Baby boomers as percent of **expenditures**   40%

Percent of **boomer** expenditures   Of all expenditures   20%

Food
Dining out
Utilities ← Boomers spent most in category
Home furnishings
Apparel, services
Transportation
Health care
Entertainment
Education

HOW TO READ THIS CHART   This shows 2020 data from the Consumer Expenditure Survey. At the top (on a scale from 0 to 40 percent), the fraction of consumer units who are boomers, followed by the (lower) fraction of spending made by boomers. At the bottom (on a scale from 0 to 20 percent), the fractions of all baby boomer spending going to select categories compared to the fractions for all Americans in those same categories.

Clearly there still exists a lucrative baby boomer market. What's more, it exists at a moment, as Kahn pointed out, in which technology has reshaped ad targeting to the extent that a company looking to sell to customers over 65 can simply check a box on Facebook's or Apple's or Google's automated marketplaces and reach that audience. That can happen, in fact, without having to consider how the ad might land with younger audiences, who would likely never see it.

That advertisers can target older Americans (and that they often should) doesn't mean that they do so effectively. Alison Bryant, senior vice president of AARP Research, advocates for businesses to focus more on older Americans. When we spoke by phone, there was an almost frustrated urgency to her voice. "This is not a core demographic that's hot, typically," Bryant said of the 50-plus consumers who are a target of the organization's outreach. AARP no longer stands for "American Association of Retired Persons," in case you hadn't heard; its constituency is about a third of the country.

Bryant thinks too many businesses have written them off. "Imagine that no one ever talks to you," she said. "That there's all these products and services and no one just tells you about them. And that's really where we still are with older adults." On those occasions when older Americans *are* targeted, it's often ham-handed, the equivalent of starting an ad with a large, flashing "HEY OLD PEOPLE!"

One way in which her team measures marketing outreach is by tracking the images used in ads. When we spoke, their figures had older adults as 40 percent of the market (in 2020, 42 percent of consumer units were aged 65 and over) but only constituted 15 percent of images used in advertising. She thinks the problem lies largely with the demographics of the people making decisions about whom to target and how. "Advertising, marketing, media, tech, gaming— all those are sectors where the age of the person who is doing that work is very young," Bryant explained. "In fact, there are a lot of age diversity issues in media and advertising. And so that's not their lived experience."

In 2020, the median age of working Americans was 42.5. In advertising and public relations, it was 40. In internet publishing and broadcasting, it was 34.3, a bit younger than the median age of employment at bars.[11]

AND THEN, ONCE AGAIN, THERE'S THE INTERNET

There is one industry that was particularly unlikely to include images of older Americans in its advertising, according to Bryant: technology. Only about 5 percent of images selling tech products did so. Worse, she said, "most of those images are either younger adults helping them or them being guided or taught."

The irony of being relegated to doddering status is that boomers were once at the forefront of the overlap of technology and culture. This was another point of Larabee's, that the boomers "lived through these amazing technological changes, including media entertainment." Radio had become near universal in homes, but the invention of the consumer transistor radio in 1954[12] and its introduction to cars in 1963[13]—when the oldest boomers were just turning 17—integrated music into their lives. Teens engaged both passively as an audience and actively as amateur (and, less often, professional) performers. Television brought the Beatles in 1964 to amplify that effect. Oh, and then five years later, TV brought the moon.

The baby boom would not have been the baby boom without television; the generation and the technology boomed together. There were more than 6,000 times as many households with televisions at the end of the boom as at the start. By the time the boomers were out of their teens, not only did nearly every household in America have a television, most were in color.

It turns out that there is a pattern to the adoption of new technologies, one that industry analyst Horace Dediu stumbled onto when he was working for Nokia in the early 2000s. "I had been observing the iPhone and video smartphones," he told me when we spoke in 2015, "and I'm looking at smartphones and I'm noticing that the way they're growing is according to this curve called an S curve."

Interrupting Dediu (in a manner of speaking), it's worth explaining this. It's not the case that a technology adoption generally expands arithmetically: 1 percent in 2010 and then 2 percent in 2011 and 3 percent in 2012. Instead, adoption starts slowly, then reaches a tipping point where it grows much more quickly. As deployment of the technology nears universality, a version of the last-mile problem kicks in—those who won't or can't adopt produce obstructions that slows the curve back down. What Dediu was curious about was whether the adoption curve for smartphones was particularly fast or particularly slow.

"So in order to answer that question, I started to collect other curves and try to calibrate whether the smartphone is extraordinary or not," he explained. "And when I started collecting, I got to twenty, and I was like, wow, there's also a pattern over time here: things are seemingly getting faster."

As an investor, that speeding up is a problem. You want to get in on the ground floor, not try to catch the express elevator halfway up the building. But those curves and the speed at which they rise also helps us understand the baby boom a little better.

Dediu provided me with a number of the curves he'd collected. They come from a variety of different sources, sometimes from federal agencies, sometimes from marketing organizations. For some technologies, the adoption curves are measurable on very specific metrics. Dediu used the example of international shipping containers. If a port upgrades to handle moving shipping containers on and off boats, the adoption of that technology ticks upward an increment. The results are charts that show how quickly different technologies were adopted and what else gained ground at the same time.

CHART 62
Technology Adoption as the Boomers Grew Up

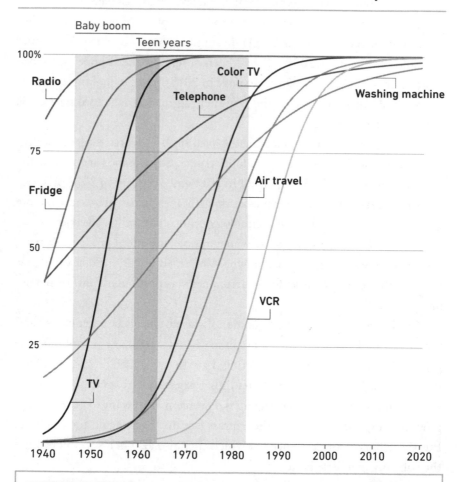

HOW TO READ THIS CHART Each line shows the saturation of a technology in the United States (from none, 0 percent, to complete) during the year indicated along the bottom axis. The years of the baby boom and the years during which boomers were teenagers are indicated by shaded areas.

When the boom began, most households had radios, and about two-thirds had refrigerators. Only about a quarter had washing machines. Air travel was very uncommon. By the early 1980s, when the youngest boomers moved out of their teen years, all of that had changed. Sometimes that change came slowly, as with washing machines. Sometimes it was fast, as with color television.

In the abstract, this is a fascinating evolution. But remember what we're talking about here. When 1 out of every 14 Americans alive in 2020 was born, they not only had no iPhones, it was a coin toss whether they had any phone at all. Using Dediu's curves, we can visualize the digital revolution. The boomers hit adulthood and then, suddenly, the entire world changed. In 1990, about 4 percent of households had cell phones. By 2015, adoption of cell phones matched traditional phones.

Anyone born in the twentieth century will recognize how things have shifted as the world transitioned from the shadowy analog age into the digital one. When I was in college in the early 1990s, for example, I had a job working overnight in a computer lab, helping students navigate word processors, save files to disks, or print out papers. When I returned to the school a few years ago, I figured I'd stop by the lab—failing to realize that of course it no longer existed. Everyone has her own computer now and probably only rarely needs to even print out her work. That personal computer curve spiked along with the internet one and, had Dediu somehow assembled a "large rooms filled with IBM desktop computers" curve, it would by now have withered into dust.

It took 22 years for color television to go from 10 percent adoption to 90 percent adoption. It took smartphones 10 years. Justin Timberlake's song "SexyBack" is older than the iPhone.

We can analyze adoption not only by rate but also demographically. Pew regularly measures technology use among Americans, breaking down their findings by age group. So we know, for example, that in 2021 nearly everyone under the age of 65 said they used the internet. Among those aged 65 and over, only 75 percent said they did.[14] That year, boomers were aged 57 to 75; it's fair to assume that it was the oldest segment of the 65-and-up group that was least likely to be online. But that trickles down into internet usage, too. The oldest Americans are the least likely to say that they go online "almost constantly," God bless them.[15] They're also less likely to use social media tools—often significantly—and YouTube.[16]

You'll remember that the divide in usage of TikTok is what powered the

CHART 63
Technology Adoption After the Boomers Grew Up

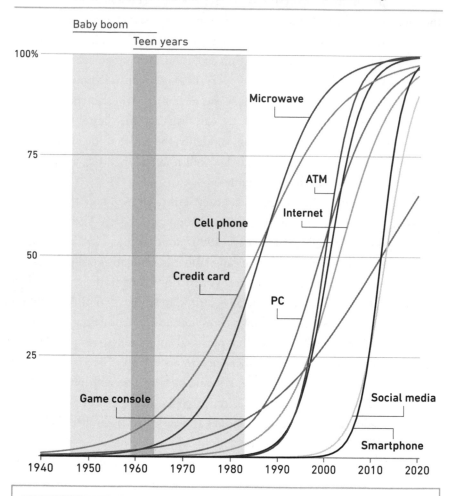

Baby boom

Teen years

Microwave

ATM

Internet

Cell phone

Credit card

PC

Game console

Social media

Smartphone

HOW TO READ THIS CHART The graph above is read the same as the preceding one, but it reflects innovations that mostly grew in use after the boom ended. To Dediu's point, notice how quickly many reached saturation.

"OK boomer" dismissal in the first place.[17] Young people saw middle-aged people show up and start doing middle-aged things, and they rolled their eyes. Miami University professor Megan Gerhardt, who studies the way in which the generation gap can affect organizations, framed the use of technology in this way as part of a power struggle.

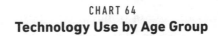

CHART 64
Technology Use by Age Group

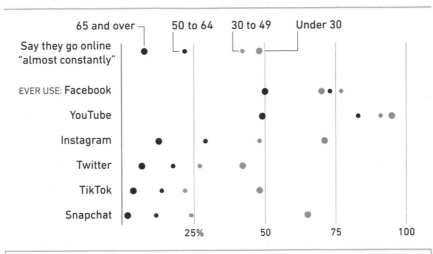

HOW TO READ THIS CHART Usage of the internet and platforms in 2021 by age group. One interesting detail: notice that the youngest group is actually slightly less likely to report using Facebook than those aged 30 to 64.

"They said, Well, we know how to use social media, we know how to use digital marketing," Gerhardt said of younger Americans, "and we're going to put you back in your place."

In these spaces, boomers can very tangibly feel that they are not the driving force, not the majority—something that, at least implicitly, must be an unusual sensation. For decades, the baby boomers were the center of the American universe. The arrival of the internet was a bit like learning about heliocentrism.

A NEW WORLD WITH NEW RULERS AND NEW RULES

The thing about the emergence of rock and roll is that it was infectious. Teenagers were listening to the music on the radio, "picking up these sounds and this musical energy," Larabee said of that moment, "and they're making their own thing out of it." By 1956, there were hundreds of teenaged bands according to a report in *Ebony* magazine, inspired to pick up instruments and join the movement.[18] Over the following years, that figure unquestionably grew. That meant a new source of competition for established artists, competition that natively understood the genre and the mediums—radio and television—that created stars. And there were plenty of older people in the industry eager to take advantage.

"Rock 'n' roll gave unprecedented power to teenage performers," Glenn Altschuler wrote in his book *All Shook Up*. "'Rejuvenating juveniles,' *Ebony* crowed, were 'dethroning and retiring veteran artists faster than you can say "oou oou I love you."'"

Unprecedented to that point, anyway. There were still gatekeepers, people who had to sign you to a label and take a cut. People who had to agree to give you airplay or to allow you to lip-sync in front of a crowd of Philadelphia-area teenagers. There were a lot of young people and they were leveraging new technology to create new cultural touchpoints (like 45s, which allowed individual songs to go viral) but they still couldn't become phenomena without a boost.

Now? "You can be in Cleveland, Ohio, alone in your bedroom, and you can get a million followers overnight. That's fucking crazy. That's never been possible."

That offering comes from an unnamed public relations person quoted in *Harper's* by Barrett Swanson. Swanson went to Los Angeles to live with a house of "influencers," young people who are given that title because they have a large number of followers on social media. The influence to which the term refers, of course, is marketing influence, the most important influence known to capitalism. But the PR guy wasn't wrong. It is the case that a random person can post a video and 12 hours later be a worldwide phenomenon. It is the case that a guy from a small village in Kazakhstan can remix a years-old hip-hop track from an artist born in Guyana, post it on Russian social media,[19] and see that remix earn a spot on the *Billboard* charts.[20]

There are still gatekeepers, of course. Tech companies are gatekeepers. The public relations guy worked for a company that put together a house full of influencers and invited Swanson to come write about it, a form of gatekeeping, certainly. But it's also often the case that established entities find themselves coming along for the ride. This is why *Billboard* began including YouTube streams in its charts. News outlets write stories based on firsthand social media posts. Late-night hosts invite teenagers famous for doing dances to popular songs to teach them the dances. All of the awkwardness of Ed Sullivan flexing his arm toward John, Paul, George, and Ringo, none of the learning instruments or writing songs.

And, often, none of the inventing of the dances. In another mirror of teen culture in the 1950s and 1960s, Black dancers who were often the creators of dance trends that became popular on platforms like TikTok became frustrated when others, often White girls, became famous from them. (Talk about repeating historic patterns.) So a number of dance creators went on strike in 2021, refusing to create new dances.[21] This wasn't simply an idle threat meant to punish White influencers. It also posed at least some economic threat, the traditional target of strikes.

"The dances on TikTok—without a doubt, without a question—is what is selling records," choreographer JaQuel Knight told *The Hollywood Reporter*. "In return, the records are making money. In return, *only* the records are making money, and not the choreography."[22] In this ecosystem, cutting the catchy choreography means fewer streams of the songs and less free advertising for the artists and their labels. When the singer Dua Lipa performed during the Grammys in March 2021, writer Grace Spelman speculated that the simple, vertically oriented dance moves Lipa deployed were intended[23] to prompt imitators to use the song with their TikTok or Instagram videos, each a little ad for the track. The next month, Lipa's song "Levitating" was the seventh-most popular track[24] on TikTok. By September, it had been played over 880 million times. That's probably more because of the lyrics than the dancing; a snippet in which Lipa sings, "You want me; I want you, baby" became a jumping-off point for both earnest and joking tributes to beloved people and objects. But the point about the power of the platform stands. "Levitating" ended 2021 as the top song on *Billboard*'s annual charts[25] in a year where Dua Lipa made a reported $30 million in sales and endorsements.[26] "I really believe TikTok gave it a humongous jolt back into the pop-culture forefront," one radio station music director told the magazine. "There was a period as it was re-emerging at radio when you couldn't open TikTok without seeing it all over your feed."

"The loss of gatekeeping has been profound across all of the media industries," Larabee said of the shift in power to those who create content. "I teach the generation that now grew up with video games, which most of us—I'm sure that boomers play video games, but to have been conversant with those modes of entertainment from the time that you're, like, five, is a stunning change. I don't know if anybody can really get their minds around that because we're right in the middle of it. We don't have any kind of distance for understanding these enormous technological changes"—changes she compared to the advent of the printing press.

These are also changes centered in a realm where boomers are for once underrepresented, a realm that also overlaps with nearly everything else. Ubiquitous technology affects what we learn and how we learn it in a way that requires those born before it to adapt as surely as they might have to figure out the controller for a PlayStation.

That includes the galaxy of options for information about the world itself.

THE DISINFORMATION AGE

"When I grew up, there was *the* news, right?" Megan Gerhardt said when we spoke. "Pick a channel, like ABC, NBC—it was basically the same news. I'm sure it wasn't objective necessarily, but it wasn't like you just chose your news channel and then that dictated the way that your news was shared with you. This is a whole generation who has grown up understanding that there's a lot of different versions of the truth or of news or of information and you can't just sort of blindly believe whatever you read."

Pew has Generation Z starting in 1997, meaning that by the time they were teenagers the social-media S curve was already at 28 percent.[27] By the time the oldest members of the generation became adults, it was at two-thirds saturation. It's a generation that literally grew up with social media. (The millennials have at times been referred to as the "digital natives" generation.) Not surprising, then, that Pew should also find that 40 percent of those under the age of 30 said they had at least some trust in information from social media, compared to only 15 percent of those aged 65 and over.[28] (There was not a significant difference in trust of national news organizations, though other research has found that younger people now are less trusting of mainstream news than young people were two decades ago.[29]) About 1 in 6 of those under 30 said that their social media platforms were their primary method of following the 2020 election. Only 2 percent of those 65 or over said the same; instead, 45 percent identified cable news.[30]

In part, younger people may have more trust in social media because they are better able to filter false information out of the medium, in the way that native English speakers might better appreciate the nuances of a joke. A 2019 study from researchers at Princeton and New York Universities found that sharing of articles from purveyors of false information on Facebook was relatively uncommon during the 2016 presidential election. When it occurred, though, it was more likely to come from older Facebook users. About 3 percent of those under the age of 30 shared an article from a fake-news website, compared to 11 percent of those over the age of 65.[31]

"[B]eing in the oldest age group was associated with sharing nearly seven times as many articles from fake news domains on Facebook as those in the youngest age group," the researchers found, a discovery that held even when controlling for education, ideology—and partisanship.

Here politics seeps back in. When we talk about the effects of internet culture on older Americans we are again also talking disproportionately about the effects on Republicans. And, sure enough, the researchers found that Republicans were far more likely to share stories from the identified domains than Democrats, something that was correlated to "the pro-Trump slant of most fake news articles produced during the 2016 campaign." This came up a lot in reporting about the prevalence of misinformation that year. *BuzzFeed News* looked at a group of teenagers in Macedonia who'd built a lucrative ecosystem of misinformation sites centered on the year's election, using the money to buy sneakers or music equipment. Most of the sites hyped false stories celebrating the Republican presidential nominee, though only after some trial and error.

The teenagers had "experimented with left-leaning or pro–Bernie Sanders content, but nothing performed as well on Facebook as Trump content," Craig Silverman and Lawrence Alexander reported. A 16-year-old summarized it neatly: "People in America prefer to read news about Trump"—though it's probably also in part because Facebook's audience skews relatively older.

It's useful to consider the other generational angle here. We have internet-savvy teenagers in Europe hustling (disproportionately) older Americans for page views and, by extension, advertising revenue. The gap on internet awareness helped create an opportunity for the unscrupulous.

Of course, the effort to grift older, often more conservative Americans isn't entirely centered on the internet. There are plenty of dubious nutritional supplements and non-FDA-approved medications pitched on right-wing television, lots of investment opportunities and recommendations to buy gold.[32] The Tea Party movement itself was notorious as a sinkhole of political contributions that went to line the pockets of consultants.[33] But nothing has proven as internationally lucrative in this regard as the internet, given the size of the head start it allows disinformation as the truth is still poking around for its boots.

And who better to embody the tendency of older Republicans to share fake news articles than Trump? At times it could be hard to tell if his false tweets were an effort to mislead or simply a function of his being misled. When a man at a rally in Ohio rushed the dais where Trump was speaking in March 2016, Trump quickly picked up a bogus claim from social media and alleged that the man had ties to a terrorist group.[34] Pressed on it by NBC's Chuck Todd during an appearance on *Meet the Press*, Trump shrugged. "What do I know about it?" he said. "All I know is what's on the internet."[35]

Trump was able to navigate the unfamiliar world of political communication thanks to the assistance of aides like Kellyanne Conway. Conway joined his campaign shortly before the 2016 election and left the White House shortly before the 2020 one. Her departure is salient to this discussion: Conway announced her intention to focus more on her family after her teenaged daughter, in addition to criticizing Trump, had made embarrassing allegations about her mother.[36]

The daughter had made them on TikTok, where they rapidly went viral.

AN ASIDE ABOUT JAMES BOND

The baby boom may have helped create the modern film economy, but that economy has shifted its attention to younger viewers. It's akin to Pepsi's targeting of boomers in the early 1960s as the "Pepsi Generation"—which, in the mid-1980s as Generation X emerged, became "The Choice of a New Generation." In 1997, a year into the millennials, Pepsi announced a new slogan: "Generation Next."[37] It wasn't the boomers; it was whoever was now young.

There's an interesting lens through which to consider the generational evolution of Hollywood. In 1962, audiences met James Bond, the dashing British spy who came to embody a very particular form of masculinity. During the years that boomers were in their teens, 13 Bond films were released, selling an inflation-adjusted $3.3 billion in tickets in the United

States.[38] The franchise is still pushing forward, Hollywood trying to figure out what that masculinity should look like now.

One aspect hasn't changed. Over the course of the movies released between the first film, *Dr. No*, and 2021's *No Time to Die* there were about 50 women who played love interests of Bond's (admitting how loosely that descriptor might at times fit).[39] On average, the women who played those roles were about 15 years younger than Bond. On only three occasions, including in 2015's *Spectre*, were the love interests older than Bond, never more than four years. In two cases, the spread between Bond and his love interest was at least 30 years, a period that is often used to demarcate an actual generation.[40] If we use modern definitions of generations, we can track the gap. The first Bond, Sean Connery, was a member of the silent generation, as were most of his love interests. Connery was also Bond when the first boomer women appeared opposite his character, in 1971's *Diamonds Are Forever*. The first boomer Bond appeared in 1995.

That pattern repeated frequently. The first member of Generation X to play a love interest in a Bond movie was in 1989's *Licence to Kill*; the first X Bond didn't show up until 2006. Two years later, the first millennial love interest made her appearance. It's not clear when or if a millennial will play the title character.

It does seem clear, though, that we've seen the last boomer love interest: Monica Bellucci in *Spectre*. Given that Roger Moore played Bond until he was nearly 60, we certainly can't rule out the possibility that we might see another boomer Bond.

ALL CULTURE IS POLITICAL CULTURE

Not to sound too much like a T-shirt that's advertised at the bottom of a tabloid website, but there are a few stages of growing older. There's the stage when you're young and you venerate those who are deeply familiar with popular culture. There's the stage when you join that group and can converse on any new movie or musical act or book or article with the best of them. There's the stage when you discover that you've missed a step and you're suddenly hearing about directors or musicians—and later musical styles— that you aren't familiar with. You scramble to keep up. Then there's the stage when the scrambling is replaced with shrugging. The things you like aren't

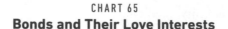

CHART 65
Bonds and Their Love Interests

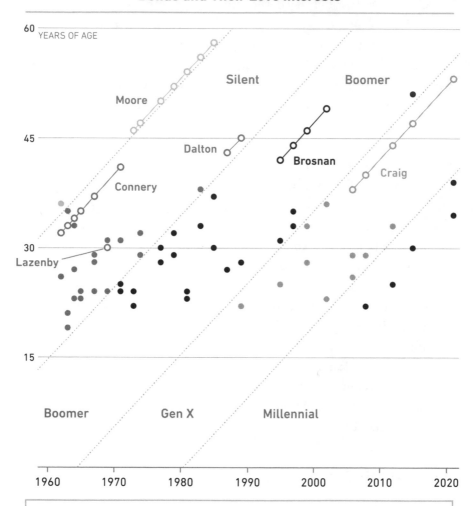

HOW TO READ THIS CHART Each solid dot represents one of the women costarring in a James Bond movie; each outlined dot is a Bond. The circles are positioned relative to the age that person would be at the end of the year in which a Bond movie was released. You can see generations indicated as diagonal slices, showing young boomers in the 1970s, for example, aging as the years pass.

what people younger than you like, and that's fine. Now you stumble across favorite songs not at clubs but when they come up in ads targeting your age demographic.

Culture changes and people often don't. Bond's sexism ages and those new to it view it quite differently than earlier audiences. Jokes and beats and fashion flicker through the years like waves, sometimes leaving us stranded. In the case of the baby boomers, plenty of other people were stranded on the same islands, so it was probably both less jarring and less immediately obvious that culture had moved on without them.

But some of those changes have unavoidable repercussions. Homophobic slurs are no longer something that casually populate conversations, any more than we still make quips about the intelligence of people from Poland. There was a joke about casting couches in the closing credits of a *Toy Story* movie that, only a few years later, was so obviously off tone that Disney quietly excised it from streaming versions.[41] It's clearly the case that some element of the "cancel culture" consternation, like the furor over "political correctness" that predated it by two decades, is a function of people who used to say and do things being frustrated at society suggesting they no longer do so. Extrapolate being told that your sense of style or music or your beliefs are archaic or grating to a population that still numbers in the millions and has been used to deference for 60 years. Imagine that group being told that its conception of American culture itself is out of date.

Even the technological changes that we've seen over the past two decades reinforce that same insecurity and that same political backlash. Young people can and do organize national protests. The universality of internet-connected cameras (more concisely referred to as cell phones) has meant that systemic affronts that were once hidden in the dark—like the killing of Black men by law enforcement officials—are brought into the public glare. Moments of interpersonal tension, including those with political or racial overtones, are captured and shared instantly and universally.

The phrase "culture wars," the succinct description of the increasingly expansive zone where culture and politics overlap, began gaining traction in the 1990s, as Generation X was assuming control of popular culture.[42] The first instance of its use in *The New York Times* came in a review of the 1991 book of the same name by James Davison Hunter. Andrew Greeley, a sociologist and Catholic priest, considered the book insightful, but was skeptical of the book's premise that progressive and orthodox religious traditions would align on either side of a political divide. His broadest rationale for that skepticism has aged poorly.

"The American people's reaction to cultural conflicts is much more complex, nuanced, ambiguous and ambivalent than any two-category typology might suggest," Greeley wrote. "The pro-con format so loved by television programs like 'Nightline' and the morning news shows does great violence to the 'blooming, buzzing' pluralism of American culture. Thus, it seems to me, Mr. Hunter's engaging and challenging book falls substantially short of making a convincing case for the realignment he thinks he sees."

As it turned out, the pluralism of American culture eagerly enlisted in a much broader culture war than even the one centered on religion that Hunter predicted.

BACKING INTO NEW RELEVANCY

From the outset, the baby boomers were darlings of advertisers. But it was only when they reached adulthood—and after Tom Wolfe's nudge toward calling them the "Me" generation—that boomers were targeted as "the baby boom." Christopher Andersen updated his best-selling book *The Name Game* to create a version "completely revised and updated for parents of the 80s": *The Baby Boomer's Name Game*.[43] This was neither the first nor the last book centered on the generation. Baby Boom clothing, trademarked to a company in Passaic. James Taylor released a syrupy, saxophone-heavy track called "Baby Boom Baby." A musical based on the comic strip *Doonesbury* that was released in 1983 included a song called "Baby Boom Boogie Boy." United Artists released a Nancy Meyers movie in 1987 titled *Baby Boom*, starring Diane Keaton and Harold Ramis. The show *Muppet Babies* had a 1988 episode called "Muppet Baby Boom." Endless.

Few products better capture the generation's solipsism than the release in 1983 of the Baby Boomer Edition of the board game Trivial Pursuit. The game itself was near the peak of its popularity; offering an expansion set of two boxes of questions specific to the boom must have earned someone at the game's parent company a bonus. I was raised on Trivial Pursuit, though growing up in western New York, we'd somehow obtained a Canadian edition that led to a house rule allowing players to pass on a turn by declaring it to be a "Canadian question." But even applying that generous flexibility, those in the baby boomer edition are near impossible for a non-boomer to answer 40 years later. It's like trying to parse inside jokes with no context.

One question, for example, asks, "Who played Mr. Novak?" while another asks his first name. It would be useful if one knew who Mr. Novak was in the first place. (If you do, I suspect I can guess your generation.) In 1987, the new owners of the brand shredded unsold sets of questions, with a spokeswoman dubbing them "just too trivial."[44] Other questions reveal the sort of painfully anachronistic worldview described above, as when players are at one point asked, "Whose house did Roman Polanski get into trouble with that jailbait at?"—an obviously grotesque way to refer to the movie director's rape of a 13-year-old.[45]

It's tricky to measure the extent to which baby boomers were explicitly targeted by marketers (outside of the context of age) in each of the past 70-plus years, but it seems safe to assume that the wave crested at some point in the 1990s. (Most of the copyrights recorded by the federal government that include the phrase "baby boom" are from that period.)[46] Suddenly, though, discussion of the boom is seemingly everywhere once again, a function both of the generation reaching retirement age and, more important, the emergence of a younger, larger generation, the millennials, that offers a point of contrast and tension. So now we have products in which boomers are pitted against millennials, leveraging the same energy seen in the "OK Boomer" phenomenon. The baby boom is back as a force—but this time as a foil.

The millennial generation is large enough that it's getting some of the same treatment as the boomers did. In 2018, Hasbro announced a new millennial-centric version of its board game Monopoly. On the cover of the box, Rich Uncle Pennybags—the mustachioed, top-hatted mascot of the game—is updated with sunglasses, white headphones, and a "participation" ribbon. Instead of real estate, which the box joshes that millennials "can't afford anyway," players collect "experience points" by visiting destinations like "Parents' Basement" or "Vegan Bistro."[47] It's all a joke, Hasbro insisted to CNN.[48]

In response, the British satire site *Daily Mash* proposed a version of the game centered on boomers. In this game, players receive "a free house on every square and £3,000 in pension cash whenever they pass Go."[49] A sharp joke that gets to a significant part of the generational tension, but one that misses an important cultural point: no one's making board games about boomers anymore.

6

Who Will Inherit the Economic Boom?

The morning was bright and the sky blue, as mornings in the Villages are supposed to be: nice to the point of surreal. The streets were empty, a repeating pattern of lawn, driveway, lawn, driveway in front of a repeating pattern of ranch houses and attached garages with their white doors closed.

Except for one house. At one house, the garage door was open, quietly exposing a small bit of personality to anyone who for some reason happened to come by, which I did. On a narrow walkway next to the garage, Dolores Buguliskis was bent over some sort of plant, holding herself up with a cane. I remember her wearing a housecoat, but that may be incorrect. My notebook confirms one detail of her house, though: a large Philadelphia Eagles flag on the wall of the garage.

That's where she was from, Philadelphia. She and her husband slowly moved down the eastern seaboard until they retired to the Villages in Florida a few years earlier. As was the case with the others with whom I spoke in the complex, she embraced the community aspect of living in the area, speaking fondly of nights playing dominoes with the unseen other women on the street, of meals made by her neighbor, a "very excellent cook."

That said, she couldn't vouch for everyone. "We've had a lot of new neighbors on the block, though, so I couldn't honestly tell you who they are or anything. There's like four or five new people within the last two or three years," she said, an unusual level of turnover. "In the second house, the husband passed on," she explained, "so she gave up the house. Over here"—pointing—"was an elderly couple, they passed on. They had to give up the house, of course. Over there, the man had also cancer so they stayed with the family. They gave up their home." A few more stories about a few other houses, all on the same theme.

"It's quite a turnover just from deaths alone, you know what I mean?" the 76-year-old explained. "But we're all up in age, you know, so it's expected."

Not to be macabre, but: sure, makes sense. The question that follows is, what happens next? For all of the traditional values on display in central Florida, the Mayan tradition of leaving homes abandoned for fear of the spirits of the deceased is probably taking things a bit far.[1] There were about 47,000 houses in the Villages in 2019[2] and, while they may eventually suffer the fate of Tikal, it's more likely that most of those thousands of homes will simply churn through various owners. Those plants being tended by Dolores Buguliskis will eventually be watered by someone else; some other team's flag might hang in that garage.

What was particularly interesting about the conversation, though, was where it went next. I was there in the spring of 2021 because I was curious how the people who lived in the self-described bubble of the Villages understood the world to be changing around them and how they foresaw the future. So, once she mentioned them, I asked Dolores about the concerns she felt for her grandchildren. Her answer was simple: financial stability.

"Are they actually going to have all the Social Security? Are they going to take away the IRAs and stuff?" she said. "It's really, just—the way things are going, to send my grandson to Drexel is over seventy thousand dollars a year. I said thank God for my daughter, but, I mean, we've helped out a lot."

This brief conversation, a few isolated minutes in the shade of Dolores Buguliskis's garage, drew in a number of threads relevant to the question of how the economy might evolve once the python has finally finished digesting that pig. What happens to their houses and to the housing market? Would younger generations be able to climb out from under student debt? Will there still be a social safety net? Any effort to distill the effects of the baby boom on the economy into a book, much less a chapter, is necessarily leaving things out. But these questions are central not just to that generation's impact but to the question of where it and other generations are in tension, so they seem like good ones to try to answer.

Before we do, though, we should answer another question. The baby boom has accumulated an enormous amount of wealth during its three-quarters of a century of existence. What happens to that wealth once the boom is gone?

THE OPPOSITE OF BABY BOOM

By the middle of 2021, baby boomers held just shy of $74 trillion in assets, according to analysis from the Federal Reserve, slightly under half of all assets held by Americans in total.[3] If you imagine that this was all in one-

CHART 66
The Distribution of Assets in the United States

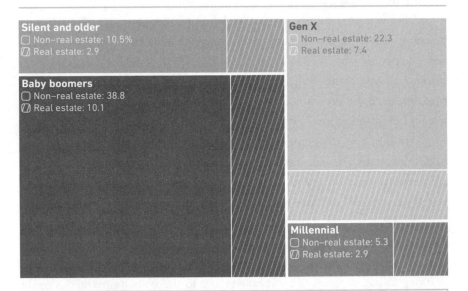

HOW TO READ THIS CHART The total area of this graph represents the $150 trillion in assets held in the United States in the second quarter of 2021. The four colored sections represent the proportion of those assets held by each generational group; the striped subsections the portion of assets made up of real estate.

dollar bills, it would be *just* shy of 5 million miles high. But it's not all cash, of course. About a fifth of it—10 percent of all assets in the United States—was real estate owned by members of the generation. Boomers held more in real estate assets than millennials held in assets overall.

A staggering total in the abstract, but also only an estimate. Microeconomist Gray Kimbrough of American University has spent a lot of time evaluating the Federal Reserve's generational data and, when I spoke with him about it, offered an immediate and useful qualifier. When the bank generates its analyses of wealth, he said, those assets are assigned to the head of the individual household. And while "households" are not exclusively living arrangements in which one member is the homeowner (about a third of housing units in the United States are rented[4]) that can mean that baby boomers get more credit for wealth than they're due.

"One thing that we've seen with millennials and younger people is they're much more likely to live with their parents," Kimbrough explained. "So if you are living in the same household, then you end up not having any wealth attached to you—which kind of is your situation at that point."

Pew Research Center has analyzed Census Bureau data going back to 1900. Its estimate is that, prior to the pandemic in 2020, 47 percent of 18- to 29-year-olds lived with their parents. That jumped to over 50 percent once pandemic restrictions were introduced. By comparison, when the oldest boomers were in that age range (from 1964 to 1975) only about 30 percent of young adults lived with their parents.[5]

Given that, the wealth of the boomers might be somewhat overstated by including the wealth of their offspring. If you own a million dollars of stock while you're living with your boomer parents, that's counted as boomer wealth. (I will admit that this particular scenario is probably unlikely.) This was not so significant an effect that the pandemic retrenchment shown on the above graph had a noticeable effect on asset distribution, however; from the third quarter of 2019 to the third quarter of 2020, millennials and members of Generation X saw more relative growth in their assets than did boomers.

Probably more important is Kimbrough's addendum: "The delays in household formation that we've seen"—the increase in the percentage of adults living with parents—"have made it much harder for people to build wealth." If you're 29 and living at home, you're unlikely to be married and

CHART 67
Percent of Adults Under 30 Living at Home

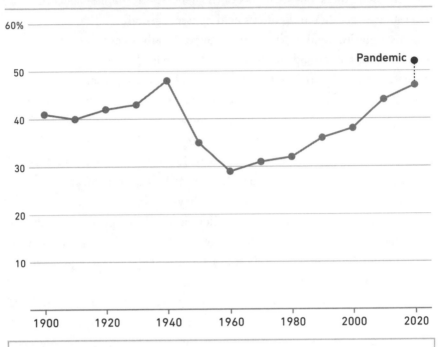

HOW TO READ THIS CHART This is perhaps the most straightforward graph in the book. The points reflect the estimated percentage of young adults living with parents at each census. That jump in 2020 reflects the aforementioned increase due to the pandemic.

probably even less likely to have a mortgage of your own. But more on this in a bit.

Assuming that the Federal Reserve data broadly capture the assets held by boomers, we should remember that even those non–real estate assets don't amount to trillions sitting in bank accounts. The balance sheet also included liabilities, nearly $5 trillion in total, most of which is home mortgages. Subtracting those from the $74 trillion in assets yields an estimate of $69 trillion that will eventually be redistributed out of the baby boom generation.

That figure aligns with a 2022 estimate from Cerulli Associates, a research and consulting firm that specializes in wealth and asset management.

Cerulli's analysis posited that there would be a transfer between households of $72.6 trillion in the quarter century ending in 2045, mostly through post-humous bequeathments—the six-syllable version of "inheritance." That includes wealth transfers originating with the generations prior to the boom, of course, a group that in mid-2021 was estimated by the Federal Reserve to have an accumulated wealth of $19 trillion. But most of it was from boomers: Cerulli's almost $73 trillion in transfers included $53 trillion that would be transferred solely from that generation.

If I can impose on you to do a bit of math twice within three paragraphs, you'll notice that the transfer of $73 trillion over 25 years comes out to about $2.9 trillion a year. That's not what's being moved at the moment, according to Cerulli's analysis, again in part because boomers are still relatively young. When I spoke with their analysts in 2021, the annual figure was closer to $1 trillion, including gifts to charity. By early 2022 it had jumped to $2 trillion.

"Since baby boomers are the wealthiest generation in the United States and they still have some life to live here, we find that a majority of that transfer is going to come in the back half of the 25 years," Cerulli's Chayce Horton explained. By the early 2040s, the pace is projected to be nearly $5 trillion annually.

Of that figure of $1 trillion in 2021—a bit under $32,000 a second, just to add some context—Cerulli's estimate was that about $100 billion (10 percent) was being transferred by members of the baby boom generation. But that's not solely from those unlucky baby boomers who are dying. Cerulli segments out these transfers of wealth into four categories, forming a sort of grid: bequeathments to younger members of family, bequeathments to charity, and inter vivos transfers to family and charity—that is, transfers made before death (inter vivos meaning "while alive").

Those inter vivos transfers are an enormous part of the calculus, and not just for the implications about the size of eventual estates. It's a reminder that what the boomers have now is not what they will have when they die in nearly every case. Before they go they will be spending money both on themselves and on others (even as they often also see real estate and security asset values increase). Cerulli figured that about 90 percent of the annual $1 trillion being passed along at that point was transferred after death—but that means $100 billion wasn't. (This likely overlaps heavily with the $100 billion being transferred by boomers.) That number, too, will fluctuate, often in ways the boomers can't always predict or control—but focusing on the figure understates how such shifts unfold.

Stephen Morgan, now a professor at Johns Hopkins University, coauthored a paper that looked at intergenerational transfers of wealth in 2006. When we spoke by phone in 2021, he was picking up his 15-year-old son, Vincent, from work. Vincent was patient as his father and I discussed the research with which he shared a birth year, but the situation was also symbolic: here was a father spending his time and energy on his son, itself a form of investment.

"In many ways, to me, the baby boomers don't look that unusual relative to what our sort of baseline expectations were for the way in which they transfer wealth to their offspring," Morgan explained. As expected, there is a near-constant transfer at varying scales and of varying directness. Yes, it took the form of checks cut when needed. A 2018 report from Country Financial revealed that more than half of Americans between the ages of 21 and 37 had received some financial assistance since turning 21, with a third of that group receiving money every month.[6] But it was also paying for a better college education, helping pay for cars, even moving to areas with better schools in order to give their children whatever advantages they could. Those inter vivos transfers were at times simply investments in improving their children's lives, early bequeathments (if you will) that often just seemed like living.

A critical point that now arises is that Americans live longer today than they did a century ago. They live a lot longer than they did even when the baby boomers were born. A child born in 1950 would have been expected to live about 68 years. By the time they hit 65 in 2015, however, they would have been expected to live not another three years but another 19[7]—five more years than a 65-year-old in 1950 would have been expected to live.

Those extra five years for a 65-year-old now versus in 1950 are more years the boomers can or will have to spend down their assets. It's also five more years in which their families might get bigger, bringing us back to Vincent Morgan.

"Vinny's fifteen, as you just heard, so he'll have kids one of these days! That'll be a scary moment," Stephen Morgan said. (This being a phone call, I was unable to record Vinny's reaction.) "And as I think about inter vivos

CHART 68
How Life Expectancies Change over Time

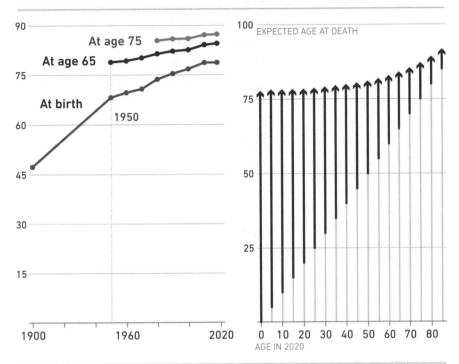

At left, the upward trend in estimated ages at death from birth, at 65, and at 75 over the past several decades, using data from the National Institutes of Health.[8] Each line increases over time, if occasionally only subtly. The year 1950 is indicated as the first census year that included boomers.

At right, life expectancies by age in 2020. As the age of the individual increases (left to right), so does the expected age at death. The dark arrow is the additional expected life for people at each age (lighter-colored line).

transfers, I'll be thinking about helping him buy a house and putting money in his kids' college fund."

As a sociologist, if not immediately as a father, Morgan was excited about the prospect of grandchildren. "I think the most interesting stuff—and where we're now getting data and research that allow us to really start to look at these things—are really how the baby boomers are going to participate in their grandchildren's education and early livelihood," he said.

There are three overlapping patterns that come into play with implications for transferring wealth. Living longer means potentially being introduced to—and investing in—more grandchildren. That's offset by the fact that Americans are having fewer children than they used to. Over the past 50 years, it has become less common for Americans to have three or more children and more common for them to have only one or two—or none. That means fewer outlets for inter vivos transfers for direct progeny than in years past; you're only sending two kids to college instead of four. Perhaps, though, you'll get to see their kids graduate, too.

You'll remember Kimbrough's warning: young people are starting their households later than they used to. This is the third overlapping trend. Baby

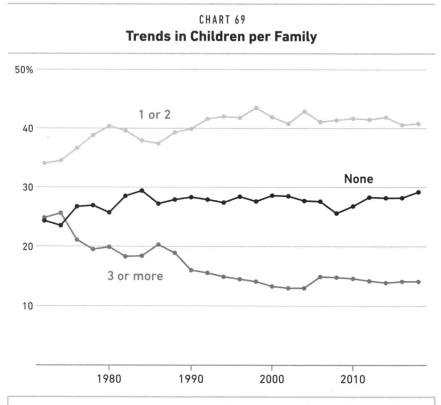

CHART 69
Trends in Children per Family

HOW TO READ THIS CHART The number of children reported by respondents to the General Social Survey over time.[9] In 1972, about as many people reported having three or more children as reported having none. Now, respondents are more than twice as likely to report having no children.

boomer grandparents are living longer, but their kids are waiting longer to have kids of their own. Between 1970 and 2000, the average age of an American woman at the time of her first child increased by 3.5 years, from 21.4 to 24.9.[10] During the same period, the life expectancy of a 65-year-old increased by 2.4 years, from 15.2 to 17.6 additional years of life.[11] It's also likely the case that some younger Americans are not forming families as early in part *because* their parents are living longer. Inheritances offer lump-sum benefits that inter vivos wealth transfers don't (as the Internal Revenue Service would be happy to remind you).

As I was exploring the financial fallout of the end of the baby boom, there was a complicating factor that was mentioned repeatedly and that has been an undercurrent to the analysis above. College funds and car buying, transfers of assets and wealth—these imply that there is existing wealth to be transferred, a financial situation that isn't the case for many Americans and many baby boomers. In 1990, the Federal Reserve estimated that the top 1 percent of American households in terms of wealth collectively had about seven times the net worth of the least-wealthy half of American households. Seven times as much wealth; one-fiftieth as many households. But by 2021, the advantage of the wealthiest 1 percent had doubled: at that point, their collective wealth was 14 times the poorest half of households. As we explored in chapter 1, boomers hold a lot of wealth collectively, but not necessarily individually.

The enormous gap in wealth between the richest and the poorest Americans is neither closing nor likely to erode significantly as the boom ends. Fabian Pfeffer of the University of Michigan studies how inequality evolves across generations, and he's confident that the inequality currently seen in wealth in the United States will not weaken solely because the baby boom is gone. This is in part because of how bequeathments work: the beneficiaries tend to be family, not random strangers, and the wealth of children often mirrors that of their parents. The average age at which people receive inheritances these days is 50, he said, by which point they've already accrued much of their own wealth—boosted, among the more wealthy, by their parents. Bequeathments are simply "the cherry on top."

"Kids tend to be similarly wealthy as their parents," Pfeffer said of this research. "But a lot of that correlation arises from processes earlier in life and more indirectly." These are your inter vivos transfers, paying for better schools

and helping with down payments on houses, which itself aids wealth accu-
mulation in other ways. "A lot of the intergenerational transmission of wealth
has already happened," he said. "It's happening today."

That "cherry on top" descriptor was the one he used when contextualizing
the process above with one of the country's most obvious examples: Ivanka
Trump. Ivanka, he pointed out, "will be fine anyway, whether she inherits
something or not." She's already reaped the benefits of privilege that come
with wealth.

Ivanka Trump is a useful example for two other reasons: she's American
and she's White. To the first factor, Pfeffer's research shows that the United
States is unequaled in its inequality. No other country has as large a gap in
household wealth between young and old, for example. Children often *erode*
wealth in the United States, due to the costs of early childhood care and, eventually, college. To the second factor illustrated by Ms. Trump, the racial wealth
gap is even starker. The median net worth of a Black American child is about
1 percent of a White child's median net worth. What's more, even for Black
children in the middle segment of wealth in the United States, "there's pronounced downward mobility in terms of their own wealth attainment as
adults"—in other words, even outside of the poorest Black Americans, the trend
over time is down, not up. In the second quarter of 2021, the Federal Reserve
estimates that White Americans held nearly 18 times as much of the country's
assets,[12] despite only representing about 5 times as much of the population.[13]

Wealthier people will transfer not only more wealth, as you'd expect, but
also a larger *percentage* of their wealth, mainly to their families. That there will
soon be a large transfer of wealth that mirrors existing lines of inequality has
not been lost on younger generations. Writing for *New York* magazine, Eric
Levitz, himself a millennial, mused that inequality exacerbated by the transfer of assets between generations might trigger an intragenerational "civil
war."[14] The tension between boomer and millennial was always interlaced with
tensions about wealth and power. When the boom is gone, those tensions will
simply shift downward to be between members of the same generation.

BOOMERS AND AN UNCERTAIN FUTURE

Unsurprisingly, economic inequality is also reflected in Americans' expressed
confidence in their future retirements. Gallup polling found that only a third

of those who earned under $40,000 a year in 2021 thought they would have enough money to live comfortably. Among those earning $100,000 a year and more, three-quarters were confident they'd be OK.[15]

To be fair, it's been a rocky few decades. In chapter 2, I briefly mentioned the increase in pessimism about retirement that Gallup recorded in polling since the beginning of the century—years that followed a broad economic expansion.[16]

(It's worth noting that identifying 65 as the expected age for retirement is largely an artifact of the passage of the Social Security Act of 1935, in

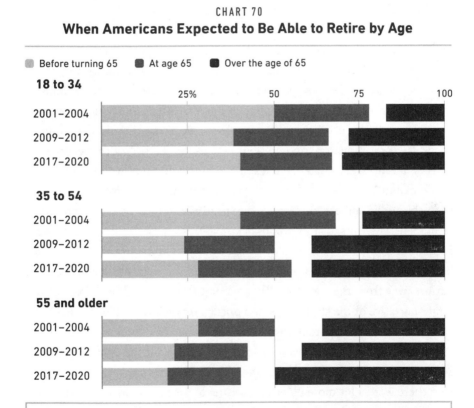

CHART 70

When Americans Expected to Be Able to Retire by Age

HOW TO READ THIS CHART Gallup has polled regularly over the past several decades to measure how optimistic people were about their ability to retire. Three polling periods are shown for each of three age groups. Lighter-colored bars indicate the belief of that age group in that polling period that they would retire before age 65. Gaps indicate respondents who had no opinion.

which that age was set. After a tweak in the early 1980s, the Social Security Administration doesn't pay out full retirement to baby boomers until they reach 66 or 67.[17])

The obvious reason for the shift in expectations measured by Gallup was the deep recession that began in 2007. That shock had "a two-pronged impact" on older workers, in the words of researchers Alicia Munnell and Matthew Rutledge.[18] Workers saw retirement savings and home values erode, prompting the need to work later in life—but the weak labor market made that difficult to do.

To the first point, we can wring still one more pertinent detail out of Stephen Morgan's expectations for his teenage son's future family. Morgan would be able to transfer his own wealth to Vincent's kids, he explained, because his own income was relatively liquid. As a university professor, he at one time would likely have depended on a pension during his retirement; his income would have been fixed. But the era of 401(k) accounts and other securities-based retirement options allows him and boomer retirees to transfer more of their wealth earlier. "Liquid retirement wealth is much more common now," he said. "It's not 1962 when people are thinking that they're going to spend their retirement period on their pension savings. Not that everyone's pension has been eliminated, but it's really quite a different world now."

Flexibility means risk. To some extent, this was the point: employers in both the public and private sectors were finding themselves having promised retirement payments to large groups of employees approaching retirement age. Moving to plans that gave employees the ability to invest in the stock market both increased the workers' potential upside and shifted the risk and the obligation away from the company. This, Fabian Pfeffer noted, was "part of the larger narrative of the shift of risk and uncertainty to American families."

This has been a potent element of how the country responded to the aging of the baby boom. A system largely built during the post–Depression New Deal and centered on protecting older Americans suddenly discovered that there were a lot more older Americans to protect. Institutions that had prioritized paying short-term bills over preparing for long-term pension obligations began to see the inevitable result of such policies looming. Part of the shift was ideological: particularly in times when markets were growing, transitions to defined contribution plans were pitched as rewarding individual initiative over less-lucrative stability.

When markets collapse, as during the 2008 recession, the downside risks become obvious. Equities held in 401(k) plans and individual retirement accounts dropped by $2.8 trillion, according to Munnell and Rutledge,[19] though the market later recouped those losses. Pension plans were also hit hard by the recession, of course. About half of the assets held in public pension funds are stocks, according to Greg Mennis of Pew Charitable Trusts. After decades of state and local governments shorting pension funds, the imminent retirements of boomers spurred them to try to make up the shortfall. State and local government funds are still short by about $1 trillion, Mennis said; they will face "much less significant" pressure moving forward than they did over the last decade.

The darker cloud lingers over the Social Security system. Gallup also found that nearly half of Americans aged 55 and over expected Social Security to be a major source of income in retirement,[20] more than the 4 in 10 who said the same of 401(k) accounts, to which boomers have had less time to contribute, as Catherine Collinson, president of the Transamerica Center for Retirement Studies, told me. Her organization's polling found that about a third of employed boomers expected Social Security to be their primary source of income in retirement.

If you look at the amount of money held in Social Security trust funds over time—and particularly if you look at how much money is projected to be in those accounts over the next decade—you might justifiably be concerned about the extent to which Social Security will be able to provide the safety net it promised. In August 2021, the Social Security Administration announced that the combined Old-Age and Survivors Insurance and Disability Insurance Trust Funds would be depleted by 2034.

As Monique Morrissey of the Economic Policy Institute told me, though, running out of money is largely the point. Workers pay into the system when they're working and draw from it when they retire. It's a "pay-as-you-go" system, she explained, and the swollen trust fund by 2020 was "only built up because the baby boomers were a big generation." In other words, the increase was to be expected as boomers entered the job market—and the decrease is to be expected as they leave it.

That this is the system working as intended and not representing some sudden collapse is important. Depletion itself isn't really the problem.

"There's often this idea that millennials or Gen Z are going to be left

CHART 71
Social Security Assets and Recipients

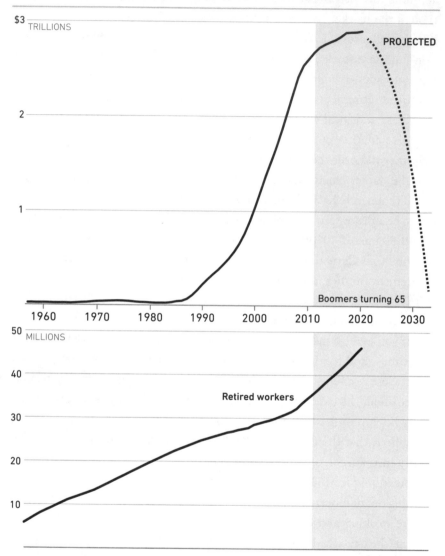

The top graph shows the measured and projected (the dashed line that quickly drops off) holdings of the Social Security trust funds at the end of each year, according to the Social Security Administration.[21] At bottom, the number of retired workers drawing benefits in December of each year. Notice that the surge in retirees predates the point at which the boomers began turning 65; it instead lines up with the 2007–2008 recession.

holding the bag with Social Security," she said. "I don't believe that. I think that's a lot of scaremongering." Particularly since political scrutiny of Social Security's solvency has waned with the Republican Party finding itself representing a lot more retiring Americans than it used to. We'll come back to this in chapter 9.

If the fund does run out in 2034, it will nonetheless still be taking in revenue from existing workers, those millennials and members of Generation Z to whom Morrissey referred—but only enough to cover about 80 percent of payments. For the Transamerica Center's Collinson, *that* sort of adjustment is a problem. "If you're an individual who's expecting—let's hypothetically say a twenty-five percent reduction in benefits—and if you're expecting twenty thousand dollars a year and only getting fifteen," she said, "that's a huge hit."

Again, these are less-risky forms of retirement planning. Morrissey explained a rule of thumb used in estimating retirement needs that accounts for risk: you'd need twice as much in an individual account like a 401(k) as in a pension to have the same level of security. There are a number of reasons for that: it's one pool of money and not fixed income, the market might be down when you retire, you might live longer than you expect. (To measure this sort of preparedness, Collinson's group asks survey respondents what age they plan to live to, which she says often evokes some quizzical responses.)

"The boomers are drawing down more of their savings than previous generations," Morrissey explained, "partly because they're living longer, partly because they thought they had more before 2008 hit"—that is, before the recession.

Retirement has long had an element of spending baked into it. Morgan, for example, wondered whether, post-pandemic, boomers were "going to be able to find consumption opportunities, more cruises, more enjoyable leisure activities, buy that RV and drive to the West Coast"—stereotypical retirement activity. But living longer and (often relatedly) unexpected medical costs can upend spending plans, consuming accumulated wealth faster than expected. A tragic example can be found in the story of Nobel laureate Leon Lederman. In 2011, he moved with his wife to Idaho, to a cabin they'd purchased with the money that accompanied his prize. The move was one of necessity: Lederman was suffering from dementia and his doctor recommended calmer environs. By 2015, though, his finances were strained to the point that his Nobel Prize medal was sold for more than $765,000 at auction, the proceeds earmarked for future medical costs. He died three years later at the age of 96.[22]

In one bleak sense Lederman was lucky: he had something valuable to sell. In 2002, Health Services Research published a study looking ahead at the way the retirement of the baby boom generation would reshape the economy. Called "The 2030 Problem," it anticipated that older Americans would need to expect four "aging shocks" centered on health care: out-of-pocket costs for prescription drugs, uncovered medical expenses, the cost of insurance itself, and uncovered costs for long-term care.[23] If we consider just the

CHART 72
The Increased Cost of Getting Sick

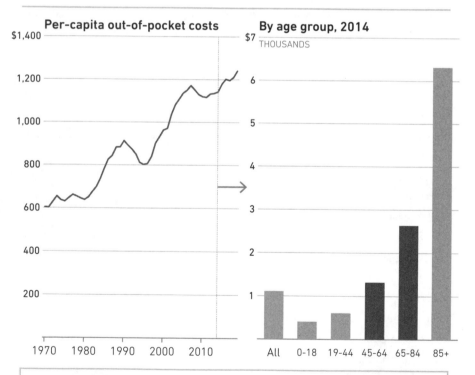

Per-capita out-of-pocket costs   **By age group, 2014**

HOW TO READ THIS CHART The chart at left shows inflation-adjusted out-of-pocket health care costs in each year, as calculated by the Kaiser Family Foundation from National Health Expenditure data.[24] The year 2014 is isolated because the data at right, showing per-capita out-of-pocket costs by age group, are from that year.[25] In 2014, baby boomers fell into the 45-to-84 age range.

question of out-of-pocket medical costs, federal data show two trends that certainly seem to suggest a significant risk of economic shock. Over time, inflation-adjusted out-of-pocket costs for American health care have steadily increased despite the introduction of the Affordable Care Act—and those costs are significantly higher for older Americans.

Having accumulated wealth "wiped out by medical care and end-of-life care," Kimbrough said, has "become a bigger problem for society—at least below the top few percentages of households that will have plenty of wealth to pass on." In other words, these, too, are the plights of non-rich boomers. For the least-wealthy half of the country, a group that held only about $8 trillion of the $151 trillion in assets in 2021,[26] retirement can be a patchwork of Social Security and savings and eyeballing costs and worrying about a medical crisis. For most people, in other words, the worry is less about what they leave behind than about paying their bills now.

Collinson's concern is that those extended lifespans and spiking medical costs will mean a legacy not of wealth but of debt and indirect financial hardships to children and their families. "What we see is an aging boomer population, many of whom are financially vulnerable and would lack the financial resources to cover long-term care," she said. "At the same time, their adult children are likely at their peak earning years, juggling family, juggling their work." But some of those children may need to become caregivers, disrupting their own lives and employment. (According to AARP research, a quarter of caregivers for older adults are millennials.)[27] It also disrupts "their own financial situation at a time where they need to be really focused on saving for their own retirement," she said, "so there's a risk of creating a cycle that's difficult to break out of."

This balance between those needing and those offering care is a much broader problem than simply within families. In fact, it's a central question for American society and the U.S. economy moving forward. So let's consider it.

WILL THERE BE ENOUGH YOUNG AMERICANS?

By 2018, most retired Americans were members of the baby boom generation as the number of boomers who were retired more than quadrupled over the preceding decade. By 2021, about 1 out of every 11 Americans was a retired baby boomer.

This is what will spur that depletion of Social Security benefits. But it also risks depleting other resources, like the size of the labor force. Retirees, by agreed-upon definition, are not working. As the number of older Americans who will need services grows, there will be proportionally fewer younger people to provide or pay for them.

For decades, the number of older Americans and the number of younger Americans was in a sort of stasis. Demographer Dowell Myers uses a ratio that compares the number of people aged 25 to 64—prime working age—with those 65 and over. From 1970 to 2010, that figure, generally referred to as the "dependency ratio," was about 24 seniors to 100 working-age people.

CHART 73
Who America's Retirees Are

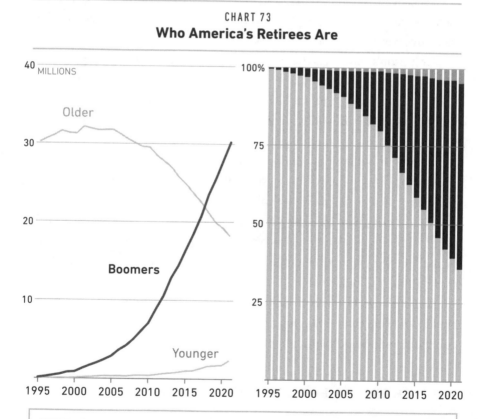

HOW TO READ THIS CHART   The graph at left shows the number of retirees from each of three age groups over time: boomers and those both older and younger.[28] At right, the density of each group in the total pool of retirees.

In 2011, when the first boomers hit 65, "that ratio started to skyrocket," he said—the boomers once again breaking the system.

The ratio is projected to rocket higher still, nearing one senior for every two workers, particularly if immigration to the United States slows.

The implication as Myers sees it? Those workers now have to "carry twice the load." The amount of tax revenue one younger person had to generate in 2010 in order to support those over the age of 65 (largely through Medicare, Social Security, and other programs) will by 2060 have nearly doubled.

In his book *Diversity Explosion*, demographer William Frey points to a compounding problem. While the ratio of workers to retirees is important

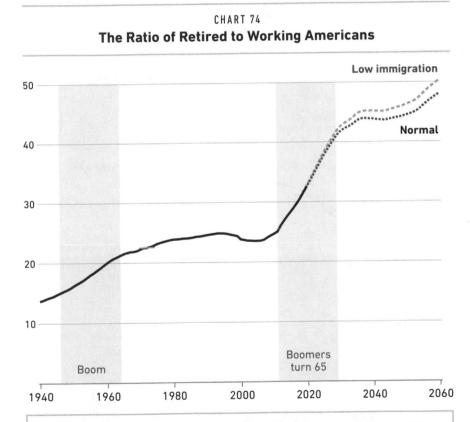

CHART 74
The Ratio of Retired to Working Americans

HOW TO READ THIS CHART The past and future ratio of seniors to 100 adults of working age. The upward spike in the ratio occurs right at the point that the baby boom starts joining the 65-plus ranks. The projected values are from the Census Bureau's 2017 estimates.

in general, it's also important (as per Collinson's concerns) to consider how those ratios evolve within families. Since older Americans are more likely to be White, the ratio of retired to working-age populations among Whites is projected to be far narrower than among non-White Americans and, particularly, Hispanics. The ratio of older to working-age non-Whites is projected to be lower in 2060 than it is among Whites now.

Collinson's concern that older people will burden younger family members assumes that there are younger family members to burden. Those without family might be expected to draw more on social resources.

James Knickman, lead author of "The 2030 Problem," uses a less expansive group of retirees in calculating the same ratio, including only those 75 and older in the pool of seniors—both because the younger subset of the

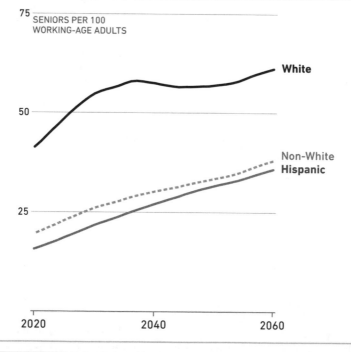

CHART 75
The Ratio of Working to Retired Americans by Race

75 —
SENIORS PER 100
WORKING-AGE ADULTS

White

50

Non-White
Hispanic

25

2020   2040   2060

HOW TO READ THIS CHART Using Census Bureau projections, this graph shows the ratio of working-age (using Myers's 25-to-64 range) to retired people.

over-65 population has lower long-term-care costs and because boomers would likely continue to work past the age of 65. (That is a trend reflected in Gallup's polling, but also anecdotally from the Transamerica Center's Catherine Collinson.) This metric makes another important change: it also includes those under the age of 20 in the pool for whom working-age people would need to provide. Comparing those aged 20 to 74 with everyone else, the ratio stays fairly flat from 1990 on because of how America is aging, both getting older and seeing fewer young people.

In other words, Myers's concern about workers soon bearing twice the

CHART 76
Another Way of Considering Working-Age Ratios

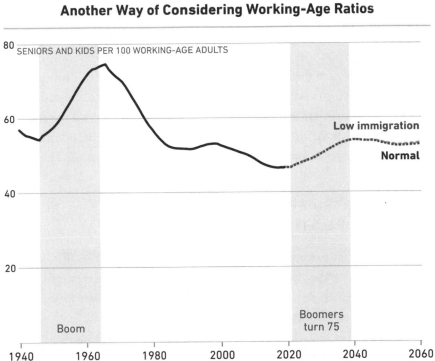

HOW TO READ THIS CHART The past and future ratio of seniors and those under 20 (whom I will condescendingly call "kids") to adults of extended working age. The ratio surges with the boom as huge numbers of Americans under the age of 20 are added to the population. As the boomers age, though, this ratio stays fairly flat, regardless of population projection. The projected values are again from the Census Bureau's 2017 estimates.

economic load is ameliorated when expanding our understanding of what that load looks like. "The point of that, in some ways, is to say this is not a macroeconomic problem," Knickman said of his modified ratio when we spoke by phone. "We can afford this." That depends to some extent on young and old Americans incurring the same costs, which isn't the case. And *can* afford doesn't mean *will*, given the isolated funding streams for children and seniors and long-standing debates over how resources are allocated. More on this in a bit.

Knickman and I spoke at a point closer to the 2030 cutoff point than when he wrote the report in 2002. He marveled that little had changed in what he foresaw, including that seniors weren't retiring with more money. "If anything," he said, "there's probably more people who have very little financial safety net in terms of expenses."

With all of this, we get a different picture of what awaits many non-rich members of generations after the boomers. Uncertain inheritances coming later in life. Wealth depleted by longer life spans and health care costs. In some cases, having to help family members with their medical needs directly. A greater societal burden as the number of elderly Americans swells. All layered on top of their own existing financial struggles: debt, housing constraints, and lower incomes.

THEY STARTED FROM THE BOTTOM
AND THEY'RE STILL THERE

As we transition to considering younger workers, let us rise first to their defense. One popular theory holds that it is their own fault that millennials and younger Americans are less wealthy, that they make poor financial decisions or are less likely to stay at jobs over the long term.

While the internet has upended any number of norms about working, it has not been the case that younger people are more likely than prior generations to job hop at this point, even with the emergence of an economy that allows people to piece together their own income streams. "Young people always switch jobs more than older people at the same time," Gray Kimbrough told me, pointing to data that he'd pulled from the Census Bureau's Current Population Survey. "If we compare twenty-five-year-olds now to twenty-five-year-olds thirty years ago, they are not switching jobs more." Uber, long the quintessential side-hustle occupation, wasn't founded until 2009. By that time the drop in the number of young people who were holding multiple jobs per year was already near its recent minimum.

This is a useful place to start because it's a reminder, once again, that cross-generational perceptions are not necessarily accurate. It's also useful because it's one reminder among many that younger Americans hold less wealth for reasons that are not primarily downstream from their personal choices.

In 2017, a group of researchers from Stanford University, Harvard University, and the University of California, Berkeley, published research indicating that a central component of the American dream was often out of reach.

CHART 77
Percent of Age Group Holding Multiple Jobs in a Year

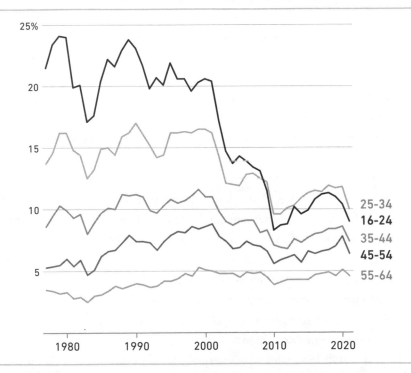

HOW TO READ THIS CHART Each line indicates the number of people in each age group who held at least two jobs during the given year.[29] As Kimbrough points out, the decline among young people began at the turn of the century.

"[C]hildren's prospects of earning more than their parents have faded over the past half-century in the United States," the researchers found. "The fraction of children earning more than their parents fell from approximately 90% for children born in 1940 to around 50% for children entering the labor market today." That decline was seen across income ranges but largest in the middle class. Again, a familiar problem appeared: "[T]he rise in inequality and the decline in absolute mobility are closely linked."[30]

Robert Manduca, one of the authors of the paper, explained the underlying problems in a phone call. The decline in upward mobility, he said, "is driven to some extent by overall economic growth. Is [gross domestic product] growing as quickly as it did back in the fifties and sixties? The answer is no. But it's also the case that economic growth is being really concentrated at the very top of the distribution." Other countries didn't see a similar contraction of incomes in younger generations; in several Scandinavian countries, for example, the percentage of children outearning their parents had been near 75 percent for decades, even though economic growth in those countries had been slower than in the United States.

For baby boomers, the situation was different. The economy expanded quickly after World War II, and by the time boomers reached age 30, which is when the research team measured their incomes, they'd benefited. By contrast, millennials began reaching age 30 in 2011, after the great recession. They were often earning less than their parents—not the steady generational improvement that had so often been promised.

Baby boomers had other advantages, too, like growing up in an era of much higher interest rates. The money they saved could itself generate more money. Catherine Collinson, for example, described working summers at the Ohio State University faculty club in college, income she would deposit in a certificate of deposit that earned double-digit interest. This also meant that boomers needed to set less money aside earlier in their lives in order to meet their needs for retirement; their money compounded more over the long term than the savings of younger people are likely to. A 2021 paper assessing the effects of interest rates explained the decreased benefit for retirees succinctly: "A 50-year-old in 1982 who wants to spend $10,000 per year for the next 30 years had to set aside $125,000. In 2012, a 50-year-old with the same desire needs $291,000, or 2.5 times as much financial wealth."[31]

CHART 78
Comparing Median Incomes Between Parents and Children

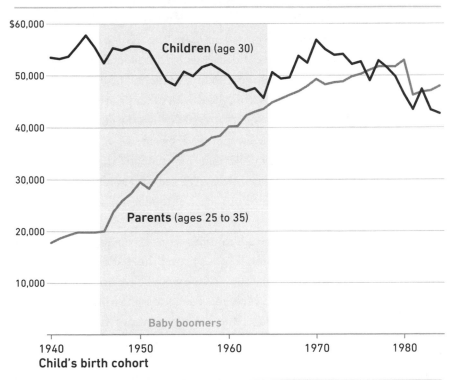

HOW TO READ THIS CHART The paper on which Manduca worked includes estimated
median incomes for parents and children based on the child's birth year. The median
income for children born at the start of the baby boom, where the darker line crosses
into the gray box, was more than twice that of their parents when their parents were
aged 25 to 35. For children born in the 1970s and 1980s, those median incomes were
equivalent or lower than their parents'.

As Monique Morrissey put it, "Millennials should have more savings
because their expected returns are lower. Millennials should have more
savings because they have less secure future income streams as a share of
everything"—meaning more reliance on things like 401(k)s.

Accruing hefty savings for retirement is easier said than done, particularly for a generation often grappling with large outstanding college debts.
This story has been told often before, but it bears repeating. In the second

quarter of 2021, Americans under the age of 50 held about $1.2 trillion in student-loan debt—about $33,000 for each of 36.7 million borrowers.[32] That's about a quarter of Americans aged 16 to 49.

The reasons for the increase in debt are myriad. In his book *The Debt Trap*, which looks at the growth of student-loan debt, *The Wall Street Journal*'s Josh Mitchell considers a series of decisions by the federal government in which the effort to encourage college enrollment (and, as the baby boom aged, bolster universities' bottom lines) conflicted with other priorities, like reducing federal spending. The result was a system in which the government made it easier to obtain financing for education and, by extension, to accrue debt. For schools, there was less downside than for students: the availability of loans allowed them to expand their offerings, increasing adult and advanced-degree enrollment among other things. Risk shifted, once again, to the individual.

At the same time, college was becoming more expensive. Stories about people in the 1960s working summer jobs to cover the cost of tuition are not entirely apocryphal. In 1969, for example, one would have had to work about 200 hours at minimum wage to cover the average cost of tuition, room, and board at a public four-year college. The cost of a private school was higher, requiring nearly 900 hours. But 50 years later, thanks both to stagnant minimum wages and rising college costs, one would have to work nearly 1,300 hours to afford tuition, room, and board at a public school and nearly 4,400 for a private one.[33] That's more than two years of 40-hour workweeks.

That ratio rose more quickly as baby boomers moved out of the typical age of college attendance, which is not a coincidence.

The inclusion of room and board in that metric is intentional. Adam Looney of the Brookings Institution, a former official with the Treasury Department, studies student loan debt in the United States. He pointed out that, for many borrowers, college loans are more akin to salaries than to something like car payments. The loans often cover rent and daily needs, meaning both that the amount of loans (and therefore the accrued debt) is larger than just the amount needed to cover tuition but also that it builds something of a dependency on college attendance—leaving school means giving up support for other basic needs. When the for-profit Argosy University collapsed in 2019, Looney said, a common complaint among its former students was that they lost the ability to pay their rent.

CHART 79
Costs of College Compared to Minimum Wage

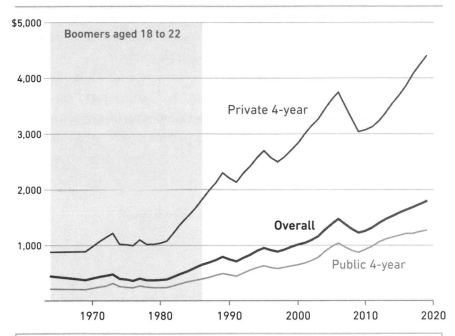

HOW TO READ THIS CHART Each line shows the number of hours of minimum wage employment needed to afford the average tuition, room, and board at an undergraduate institution.[34]

Loan debt has become particularly problematic in recent years because of the expansion of nontraditional institutions and programs. When enrollment increased a decade ago, partly in response to the recession, many of those new students were accommodated at for-profit schools and places that allowed for more flexible attendance, including online.

"They didn't add seats at Harvard. And they didn't add seats at the University of Michigan," Looney said. Nor were there seats added at community colleges, given budget constraints. The increase in debt, then, was because "there were a lot more students at nonselective four-year institutions, at for-profit schools, at two-year schools like community colleges. On average, those students who are lower income and older are more likely to have previously been unemployed or to be first-generation students or kind of in any index of disadvantage." And, therefore, in greater need of financial assistance and loans.

While we tend to think about student debt as a problem centered on young people—which, of course, it often is—that actually tends to understate the amount of debt held by older Americans. In 2021, nearly a quarter of student loan debt was held by Americans aged 50 and over.

This debt takes three forms. The first is loan debt for adult borrowers seeking degrees, something that Looney says has become prevalent. Much of it, too, he suspects, is debt from when older Americans first went to college but that went unpaid, debt for which the "department has ceased collections

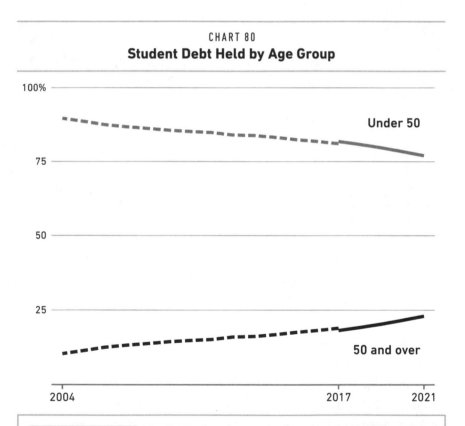

CHART 80
Student Debt Held by Age Group

HOW TO READ THIS CHART   The distribution of accrued college-loan debt by age group. Prior to 2017 (the dashed lines), the data are from the Center for Microeconomic Data at the Federal Reserve Bank of New York, using data from Equifax. Data from 2017 forward are from the Department of Education (and include only those aged 24 and older).

and people ceased paying," Looney said. The third segment of debt is from loans parents have taken out for their kids—more inter vivos transfers of wealth—using the federal PLUS loan program.

Reporting on those loans in 2021, *The Wall Street Journal* noted that parent recipients owed more than $100 billion,[35] money given mostly to schools that will either be repaid by borrowers or, in the case of default, taxpayers. Once again: the shift of risk from institutions to individuals.

"Unlike undergraduate loans that have limits, there is no cap on what parents can borrow through the fast-growing Parent Plus program, no matter their income," the *Journal* reported. "Some parents wanting the best schools available for their children sign on the dotted line unaware how the debt can burden them into retirement." A 2019 report from the Congressional Research Service put that burden in a context that came up earlier in this chapter. "Student loan debt can be especially problematic for older Americans," it read, "because, in the event of default on federal student loans, a portion of the borrower's Social Security benefits can be claimed to pay off the loans."[36] It overlaps.

THE HOUSING QUESTION

Standing in the shade of Dolores Buguliskis's garage down in Florida, I was struck by the way in which she summarized the central economic questions at issue. What retirement income will look like. The cost of her grandkid's college. And, of course, what happens to all of the surrounding houses and their occupants.

It would be fair to assume at the outset that the passing of the baby boom would lead to an enormous glut in the housing market. Millions of people from the largest generation in American history moving to long-term-care facilities or dying, finally freeing up inventory. Instead of a scramble for housing, there would suddenly be a scramble for buyers. But as with everything else about the baby boom generation, this simple calculus is likely not what will unfold.

I will note at the outset that predicting the future of the housing market is not just fraught, it is legendarily fraught. In 1989, N. Gregory Mankiw and David N. Weil predicted that, with the baby boomers beginning to shift to middle age, there would be a collapse in demand in housing. After all, their research indicated that demand peaked when people were in their late thirties. From then on, they found a slow and then rapid collapse in desire for housing, suggesting that the 1990s and 2000s promised to be periods in which prices dropped.

This was quite incorrect. In January 1989, when the paper was published, the Case-Shiller U.S. National Home Price Index was at 73.9. By January 1999, the index was at 93.2, an increase of 26 percent. Ten years after that, even as the recession was clobbering home sales, the index was over 151. In January 2021, it was at 236.4,[37] following the surge in home sales driven by the coronavirus pandemic—a surge that continued through the autumn of that year.

Benjamin Keys, an economist in the Real Estate Department at Wharton, was one of multiple people to offer the Mankiw and Weil paper as a point of caution. In our first conversation, he rattled off a number of factors that the paper understated or missed: supply-side constraints, geographic differences, the effects of demand for second homes or retirement residences. "Making projections based on demographics is really fraught," Keys said, with admirable succinctness.

So let us begin cautiously looking at the state of the market in 2019, a subject we touched on in the first chapter. At that point, before the pandemic, baby boomers made up about twice the number of homeowners as did millennials, a much larger gap between old and young than existed when boomers were millennials' age.[38] But this, yet again, is in part a function of the scale of the baby boom. About 78 percent of boomers were homeowners in 2019, compared to about 44 percent of millennials. Three decades earlier, in 1986, about 48 percent of baby boomers owned homes, while 79 percent of the preceding silent generation did—about the same proportion. This is not much consolation to those looking to purchase homes, of course, particularly given the real and obvious challenges that younger Americans have faced in doing so.

For example: that student debt. The Federal Reserve published research in 2019 suggesting that the increase in student loan debt from 2005 to 2014 led to a 2-percentage-point drop in the homeownership rate among those aged 24 to 32. Had the increase in student debt not occurred, the researchers estimate that some 400,000 more people in that age range would have purchased homes by 2014.[39]

For example: efforts to curtail new home construction, particularly in places with high demand for housing. Keys pointed me to analysis from the Building Industry Association of the San Francisco Bay Area—a group with an obvious stake in home construction, certainly—that found that the region had added more than half a million new jobs from 2011 to 2017 but only about 124,000 new housing units.

Other research has demonstrated that restrictions in home construction have effects on the economy more broadly—even just from limits in certain geographic areas.

A 2019 paper from Chang-Tai Hsieh and Enrico Moretti found a significant effect from limited access to housing in places with high productivity like New York or San Jose, California. A model of 220 metropolitan areas determined that growth in the *national* economy from 1964 to 2009 was 36 percent lower than it would have been had those housing constraints not been in place. A third of potential national growth, sliced away.

"It really comes back to this disconnect between where opportunity is for young workers and where houses are," Keys explained. "In the past, prior to the 1970s, when you have a big influx of job creators, you build houses to help creators. That's just not happening in the same way that it used to in the past."

Katherine Levine Einstein wanted to figure out where politics was obstructing the expansion of new housing. The Boston University political scientist worked with colleagues Maxwell Palmer and David Glick to develop a novel mechanism for measuring input on housing policy decisions at the local level: comparing identified speakers from public meeting minutes to voter files to determine residency and demographic information. These meetings have become a critical point of influence for developers, as municipalities and local governments have sought to build community consensus by mandating public input on projects. Often, that's not what they get.

"To build more than one unit of housing almost anywhere in the country you as a developer end up having to present your plans in front of one of these public forums in order to get a special permit or variance from existing zoning," Einstein explained in a phone call. "So because of the way that we set up land use in this country, these public meetings in practice service as a really important veto point that decides what gets built and where it gets built."

The problem, though, is that those who actually participated tend not to look much like the broader community. "There were two important ways that the folks who showed up to public hearings about housing are really unrepresentative," Einstein explained. "The first is that they tend to be disproportionately older, Whiter, and homeowners. The second piece is that they're overwhelmingly opposed to the construction of new housing. So rather than serving as forums that maybe empower underrepresented interests and serve the broader community, instead public meetings in practice serve as a way for privileged White homeowners to protect their investments and control who lives in their communities."

This tension between a group of older and Whiter residents with the population overall is, of course, a tension that should by now be familiar, as should the fact that they are consistently overrepresented in the electorate.[40] In a 2020 paper, Stanford University's Andrew Hall and Jesse Yoder found that homeowners were significantly more likely to participate in local elections.[41] This isn't simply a function of having more stable voter registrations and voting locations. It is also a function of focus. When zoning issues were on the ballot, the boost in turnout doubled. "[H]omeowners have special influence in American politics in part because their ownership motivates them to pay attention and to participate," Hall and Yoder wrote.

The pandemic provided an interesting opportunity for Einstein and her colleagues to extend their research on public-meeting participation. After all, one could see how older homeowners might be more likely to have the time to attend hours-long meetings on a weekday evening. The transition to virtual meetings conducted on platforms like Zoom that followed the emergence of the coronavirus, then, seemed as though it might be an opportunity for other groups to weigh in.

But they didn't. "What our Zoom results suggest is that the problem with these hearings isn't just barriers to participation," Einstein said. "We could make it as easy as you want and it doesn't fix the interest and sense of advocacy problem." In other words, the reason that older homeowners were more likely to participate wasn't simply that they were older and had the time to do so. It was because they were homeowners. Their contributions, Einstein said, regularly amounted to efforts to try to "control their neighborhoods," constantly invoking the neighborhood's character in defense of rejecting any changes to it.

"I could get, maybe at some level, why, if someone was proposing a hundred-unit apartment building, you think that that's going to be a huge change to your neighborhood," she said. "But people use that same kind of language for a three-unit building. Sometimes people even talk about the *traffic* from a six-unit building." An effort to build more housing necessarily means introducing some change to a community and it is much easier, if not more natural, to assume that a change to a community will have a negative effect rather than a positive one.

Part of the concern, certainly, is the keen understanding of homes as investments. About a quarter of respondents to Gallup polling from 2017 to 2020 said that they expected home equity to be a major source of their income in retirement. The National Retirement Risk Index, an assessment of how ready Americans are for retirement, determined in early 2021 that about half of households would not have enough income to maintain their current standards of living, "even if they work to age 65 and annuitize all their financial assets, including the receipts from a reverse mortgage on their homes."[42] Even with the option of converting the value of their homes to usable income, in other words, many people will see their economic positions degrade. In light of that, it's easy to understand the drive to protect house prices. But blocking new development is protectionist in two ways: first by avoiding perceived degradation of communities and second by limiting supply.

Protecting real estate investments is not only a function of individual objections. You'll remember Alex Lee, the California state assembly member who still lived in his mother's Silicon Valley home when he was elected. Among the factors he's focused on as exacerbating the problem is real estate speculation that leverages the constraints on availability and the surge in homes prices—the conversion of houses into "an investment commodity rather than homes for people," as he put it. In early 2021, a *Wall Street Journal* report isolated an example of that phenomenon. The market for single-family homes was so robust that investors were scooping up blocks of new construction, expecting to turn a nice profit. One investor told the newspaper that "you now have permanent capital competing with a young couple trying to buy a house," a dynamic that he expected would "make U.S. housing permanently more expensive."[43] In other words, this was not simply a pandemic-related surge, in his estimation.

Among the institutional investors making this play? Large pension funds, ensuring they had enough money to fund their former employees' retirements.

ANSWERING THE HOUSING QUESTION

None of this answers the question of what happens when boomers start to give up their homes at a faster clip. Would the effect be an oversupply, pushing prices lower? Or would all of the constraints above—investors, pent-up demand, etc.—stabilize prices?

Wharton's Keys suspects the latter.

"I think it's a little bit overblown that there's going to be a big disruption to the housing market on an aggregate level," Keys said. For one thing, there may not be a big glut of homes that follows the aging of the baby boom, in part because boomers are living longer. In addition to slowing the erosion of the generation, it also gives boomers more of a chance to time their home sales strategically, if they wish to do so. The dam won't collapse; water will be shunted out through spillways.

But Keys made another important point: there are also a lot of millennials. "In terms of the need for single-family homes in the United States, the millennial generation—just in terms of the size of the generation—it doesn't seem unreasonable to me that you'd have close to one for one: for every boomer house that's vacated there's a millennial, or the generation behind millennials, Gen Z, around the corner who would scoop that up," he said. And that's largely true. The baby boom constituted a huge increase in the population of the United States, but the country's population has continued to expand. So while the millennial mini-boom made up a smaller percentage of the country's population, for every 100 boomers alive when the middle of that generation turned 40, there are expected to be 96 millennials alive when the middle of *that* generation reaches the same age.[44] Nearly 1 to 1—but a smaller percentage of a larger total population.

In his book *Immigrants and Boomers*, Dowell Myers frames what's next as something of a symbiosis: "This great transfer of real estate assets will join the two generations in mutual dependency," he wrote, "matching older sellers with younger buyers." The transfer of homes from older to younger Americans is indeed already underway—or, really, is continuing as it generally has.

The question that remains unanswered, in Keys's mind, is whether those younger buyers will continue to want the same sorts of houses in the same places—what he called "less of a cohort size story and more about a changing

CHART 81
Who's Selling and Who's Buying Houses

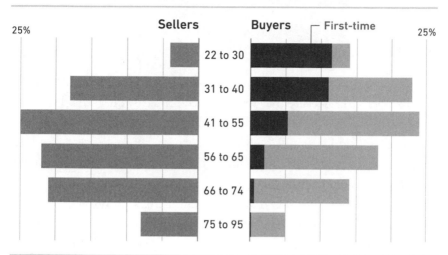

HOW TO READ THIS CHART To the left, the percentage of home sellers in each age group. To the right, the percentage of home buyers. The darker sections of the buyer bars indicate those who were making their first purchase of a home, according to the National Association of Realtors data.

tastes story." If they don't, the demand for houses generally might not align with the demand for the houses that are available. If younger people arc inclined to stay in cities rather than seek out more space in the suburbs, or if they'd prefer new construction to midcentury modern, we might still see dips in the housing market.

Desirability was an undercurrent to the objections of those public-meeting attendees that Einstein's research examined. "That's for sure a part of people's concerns, that you put your life savings and your net worth into these homes," she said, "and then are totally dependent on other people wanting to buy into that neighborhood and that community for your investment to essentially be worth it."

The good news for Dolores Buguliskis is that she lives in a community, the Villages, where, all else aside, sales of homes are limited to those aged 55 and over. Over the next few decades, there will be more people in that age group than at any previous point in American history. By 2060, there are projected to be more people aged 55 and over in the United States than there were people in total at the start of the baby boom.[45] The market will be there.

IT'S THE POLITICS, STUPID

It's safe to assume that voters in Miami-Dade County did not go to the polls in November 2012 because they were focused primarily on a school funding question. Barack Obama was up for reelection and the result of the presidential contest in Florida would likely be decisive in what was expected to be a close contest. Obama ended up winning the state by only 74,000 votes, far fewer than his winning margin in Miami-Dade.[46]

Lower on the ballot was that schools measure, a proposal that would issue a $1.2 billion bond paid for by extending an existing property tax. About 140,000 people who voted in the presidential race didn't bother voting on the bond but it passed anyway—easily, earning more than two-thirds of the vote.[47] But there was an interesting aspect to how that vote broke down: the larger the density of older voters in a precinct in the county, the less support the measure earned.

In the 163 precincts that had the lowest density of older voters, three-quarters of voters supported the bond. In the 159 precincts that had the highest density of older voters, only 6 in 10 did.

It shouldn't come as a surprise that older voters are less supportive of educational spending. In 1989, James Button and Walter Rosenbaum of the University of Florida looked at every school bond vote in the state over the preceding 20 years, finding that the density of voters over the age of 65 was a strong predictor of opposition.[48] This makes logical sense: older voters are less likely to have children in school and, therefore, may be less likely to want to fund education.

Those I spoke to about how shifting demographics would change the economy repeated this point. Take Monique Morrissey, for example, whose husband worked for years for the labor movement in Florida, including representing employees at Disney. "He would go to places like the Villages," Morrissey told me, "and they were like, we paid our taxes up north, we don't want to pay taxes for schools and the schools in Florida suck. And there's a reason for it: snowbirds come down, they don't want to pay taxes."

CHART 82
Votes for the Miami-Dade School Bond by Age

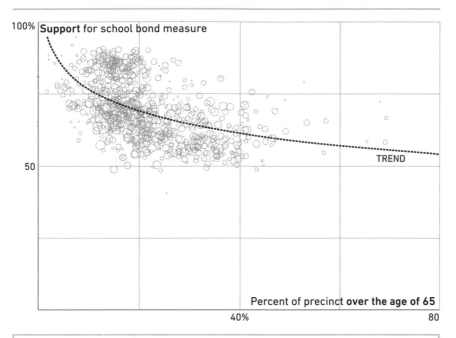

HOW TO READ THIS CHART This is a scatter plot, positioning the results from each precinct in Miami-Dade County during the 2012 general election on two axes. The vertical axis shows the percentage of votes cast that were in support of the bond measure. The horizontal axis shows the density of the population that was over the age of 65. The size of the circles is scaled to the number of voters in the precinct. Overlaid on top of the circles is the trend line, a rough delineation of the pattern that the circles form. That it drops down from the upper left as it moves to the right is the key point; as the density of older voters in precincts increased, support for the bond measure fell.

Beth Mace, who works on senior housing for the National Investment Center, noted that the tension works in both directions. Mace pointed out that parents of young children might wonder, "With the limited dollars that are available, who gets that money? Does it go to the retirees? Does it go to get schoolbooks for the kids? Why should I be paying taxes for, you know, Mrs. Smith down the street who is 90 years old when I can't get books for my kids?"

Such tensions increase when resources grow thin—a strain to be expected if there are fewer people paying taxes and more people needing support in retirement. A 2020 report from researchers at Deutsche Bank described the problem succinctly: "an ageing population means that the working-age population will face an increasing burden to pay for age-related spending, ranging from state pensions to public health costs."[49] When we fret over those changing ratios of old to young Americans calculated by Dowell Myers and James Knickman, in other words, this is what we're fretting about.

In Myers's assessment, there's at least one straightforward solution to this problem: increase the number of young people in the United States, shifting the ratio back downward. If birth rates remain flat, the easiest way to do that is to move America back onto a track of welcoming more immigrants. In fact, as mostly White boomers increasingly retire, immigrants are already filling the gap, making up a growing share of the country's workforce. In 2007, data from the Bureau of Labor Statistics indicated that about 82 percent of workers were White (including Hispanics) and 15 percent foreign born. By 2021, a bit under 78 percent of workers were White while more than 17 percent (mostly non-White) were born outside of the United States.

Myers contributed to a 2017 report, *The Economic and Fiscal Consequences of Immigration*, produced by the National Academies of Sciences, Engineering, and Medicine.[50] Among other things, it evaluated the role of immigrants in bolstering the workforce by decade, using data from Pew Research Center. During the 1960s, the number of immigrants leaving the workforce outnumbered those joining. This was during the period in which immigration was tightly controlled and immigrants mostly older, so that finding makes sense. By the 2000s, though, about 10 million more immigrants joined the workforce than left. It was also during that later decade that second-generation Americans began adding to the workforce more than they were leaving, as the children of those who arrived after immigration laws were loosened in the 1960s reached working age.

The biggest shifts came among third-generation Americans and higher, those whose immigrant relatives were no closer than grandparents. This included much of the baby boom. As the boomers aged into adulthood, net additions to the workforce surged—before soon beginning to drop off. In this decade, more third-generation-plus Americans will leave the workforce than join, and the net overall increase in workers will be entirely due to immigrants and their children.

As demographer William Frey put it when we spoke, immigration is already backstopping the economy. "The White population, especially the native-born White population, is aging much more rapidly than all the rest

CHART 83
Net Change in the Workforce by Immigration Status

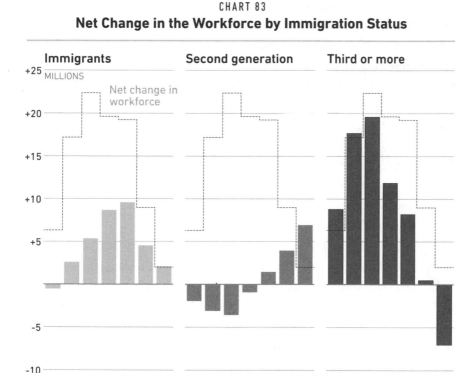

The 2016 report *The Economic and Fiscal Consequences of Immigration* used data from Pew Research Center to estimate the change in the workforce by decade from the 1960s to the 2020s. Those numbers were broken out into three groups: new immigrants, native-born children of immigrants, and Americans who were three or more generations removed from immigration. Those groups are broken out above, showing the net number of members of each group who would join (bar points up) or leave (points down) the workforce in the indicated decade. The dotted line that appears on all three graphs shows the overall net change in the United States, so that outline remains the same for each group.

of the population," he said. "That's why it's so important that we had all this immigration over the last several decades, because we would be a much older, even more age-dependent population today, were it not for all of those immigration waves, irrespective of what happens from now on."

Often, increases in immigration are viewed as threatening specifically because new arrivals are seen as competition for employment. The National Academies of Sciences, Engineering, and Medicine report on which Myers worked, though, indicates that this concern is generally not warranted. As one researcher involved in creating the report explained to *The New York Times*, their analysis found that immigrants had "little to no negative effects" on the number of native-born people working or how much they made.[51] But even beside that analysis, the sheer number of retiring boomers "nullifies the threat of competition," in Myers's estimation. If you're worried there aren't enough jobs to accommodate new arrivals, simply consider that, as illustrated above, native-born Americans skew older and are therefore leaving the workforce. Instead of the question being about scarcity of jobs, it will likely be about scarcity of job *fillers*, particularly given that a decline in births in the United States that began in 2008[52] will begin to show in the workforce in the mid-2020s. And, lo: the need for more immigrants.

"Within two years, we're going to be gasping for workers again," Myers said when we spoke in early 2021. "So that's a great environment in which to have racial harmony." Indeed, the number of job openings by the end of 2021 was more than 50 percent higher than it had been the year before.[53] Myers's optimistic assessment was that we might see a sort of generational détente as older and younger Americans begin to recognize their codependence. Myers did write a book titled *Immigrants and Boomers*, after all, the cover of which (at least in the edition sitting on my desk) shows a white hand shaking a brown one.

The good people in Deutsche Bank's research department, however, are less sanguine. "The widening generational divide should be a key source of alarm for investors, financial markets and society as a whole," that 2020 report from the bank's analysts began. Its title is somewhat grimmer than Myers's—"Intergenerational Conflict: The Next Dividing Line"—as is the content. "The widening gap between the generations is simply unsustainable," it reads at one point. "In the absence of something to redress the balance, the building resentment of younger citizens towards their elder counterparts will lead to a backlash. Already, we see this beginning to happen as political parties with heavy redistributionist policies gain support." One root cause identified by the analysts? Housing prices.

Notice that point about the "redistributionist" policies gaining traction. Deutsche Bank has a particular audience, for whom increased taxation is anathema (you may have noticed the hierarchy with which its warning began: looming alarm for investors, markets . . . oh, and everyone else), but it is nonetheless the case that the higher costs of an increasingly elderly population could be attenuated with an increase in taxes. Some increase in tax revenue is baked into the aging process itself, with 401(k) withdrawals and (a small percentage of) estate transfers generating money for the government. The increase in income inequality offers a tempting target, too. From 1992 to 2016, the number of people reporting at least $10 million in assets to the IRS jumped from 36,300 to more than 209,000.[54] Part of this is inflation. Part of it isn't.

The report's inescapable point is that those in power can either make changes now or potentially have changes forced upon them. Our current politics, often hostile to spending, are malleable. That they haven't been re-shaped is, in part, because of inertia from those dominant boomer voters.

"The boomers have had more and more lasting influence because they're a larger generation," as Robert Manduca put it. "And so in a democracy, they have more voting power and more cultural weight or economic weight. So you can imagine that the beliefs and the ideas about how to run the economy that they grew up with or came to in the seventies or eighties, when they were starting to gain some influence, those are perhaps stickier or have lasted longer." Even if those beliefs or ideas are outdated or fail to address the needs of younger Americans. Even if we've since experienced the detriments of policies that reinforced income inequality or which limited new home construction. Doing something is always politically harder than doing nothing.

"There are a lot of issues that our current ways of thinking about the economy we've had for the past four decades are unable to solve," Manduca argued. "So we're sort of starting to look around for alternatives. It does seem to be caught up in part with generations of policymakers."

It is not only younger legislators who are focused on addressing some of these issues. During his first 18 months in office, President Biden expressed openness to forgiving some student loan debt, a campaign promise advocated by many of his allies as the 2022 midterms approached. The broader political focus on redistributionist policies in recent years stemmed from Senator Bernie Sanders of Vermont, like Biden a member of the pre-boom silent generation. But those policies have been advanced in part due to the advocacy of a number of younger members of Congress, like Representative Alexandria Ocasio-Cortez, the millennial from New York.

Or like Alex Lee, who sees the political tension of housing costs in his California State Assembly district. There, home buyers experience a very specific, localized version of the sort of protectionism—pulling up of the ladder, as various people phrased it to me—that has since become something of a hallmark of boomer-generation policy making.

In 1978, just as the oldest boomers were reaching their peak home-buying years, California passed a constitutional amendment radically reducing property taxes. Those things are not disconnected; the baby boom pushed the population higher, as well as demand for housing and government services. Largely to protect existing homeowners—and to the detriment of things like public schools—Proposition 13 set the tax rate at 1 percent of a house's sale price and limited annual increases in property taxes until the home was sold. That's created disparity in the current market. Surging home prices mean that two adjoining and otherwise equivalent homes today might see wildly different tax assessments: the one last sold in 1975 for $100,000 pays no more than $2,500 a year in property taxes, while the one that sold in 2021 for $750,000 pays three times as much.

"When people finally become first homeowners in the Bay Area, they also realize that their tax bill is perhaps several hundred percent higher than their own neighbors," Lee told me. "That inequality rubs people so badly. Obviously everyone would love to have lower taxes, but they're like, this is not fair. I worked really hard, I bought my own house, and now because of something they passed in the seventies, my tax rate is like twenty times my neighbor's. And that's completely unfair. It's not based on anything except for when you bought the house."

Lee was confident that a backlash against the policy was brewing. A 2018 poll from the Public Policy Institute of California, however, found that most adult Californians still supported the policy. Of course, there were some sharp divides in opinion: homeowners liked it far more than renters, and older Californians liked it more than younger ones.[55]

It's also true that economic frustrations are often limited in scope. Anger among young home buyers in California is still anger among home buyers. In our conversation, Morrissey pointed out the significance of housing availability affecting "knowledge-economy places in blue states" like Silicon Valley and New York, where young people want to live. "The resentment of millennials to boomers," she said, "is largely a resentment that reflects how millennials from relatively privileged backgrounds are struggling much more than boomers from relatively privileged backgrounds."

The group that holds the most college debt? The wealthiest quintile of Americans.[56]

WHAT THE COMING DECADES WILL BRING

As the baby boom ages, we can expect to see a few patterns emerge. An increase in wealth transfers downward that primarily benefit the already wealthy. More older Americans struggling with debt, particularly if the stock markets that hold so much retirement wealth change direction. We'll see funds being drawn out of Social Security at a rapid—though not necessarily dire—clip. A bumpy housing market as seniors give up homes that don't always match with younger Americans' demand. An increase in the ratio of elderly to working-age Americans that both strains employers looking to fill positions (as was already evident by the end of 2021[57]) and, later, strains government budgets as the number of elderly people seeking care increases. That assumes that the economics of government services aren't overhauled, which may not be a fair assumption.

The American economy after the baby boom, after all, will be heavily shaped by the choices the boomers make until then. It will be affected in part by the choices boomers make about how they spend their retirements and how and when they pass their wealth on to younger Americans. But it will also be a function of political decisions being made, decisions that will still bear the boomers' fingerprints. For the next 10 years, boomers will be at least a fifth of the adult population and a higher percentage of the electorate.

With his own son waiting for his interview with me to wrap up, Johns Hopkins's Stephen Morgan mused about how those decisions would be made. Would immigration be increased, for example, bolstering the tax base and, by extension, Social Security, keeping less-wealthy Americans from having to decide between spending on their immediate families or caring for their elders?

"That kind of stuff to me feels much more important than just 'are these boomers going to think differently than we expect on how they save or consume,'" Morgan said. "It may be that the political choices that boomer voters make will be more consequential than their own financial investment and consumption behavior."

How American politics evolves as the baby boom fades, of course, is a complicated question of its own.

7

The Importance of What We Don't Know

A t some point in 1871 or thereabouts, a series of fusion reactions occurred in one of the four stars of the Regulus star system, emitting photons of light that, unbeknownst to anyone, would travel 464.4 trillion unimpeded miles through empty space until their path intersected precisely with the lens of a telescope at the University of Alabama on June 16, 1950, at eight p.m.[1]

The university existed when that light left Regulus, but the telescope didn't. It had been installed only shortly before the light arrived,[2] an overdue upgrade to the school's observatory after the old one was damaged in the final days of the Civil War.[3] What *might* have existed when the light left Regulus in 1871 was the Alabama city of Birmingham, founded on June 1 of that year. For the sake of poetry, let's imagine that the photons were created on that actual date, making the light from Regulus *precisely* as old as Birmingham itself when it arrived on Earth in 1950. The chance of such serendipity is why scientists at the university gathered light from the star that evening. They used it to spark a flame that lit a lamp eventually carried by Hill Ferguson, president of the Birmingham Historical Society, from Tuscaloosa to his home city.[4] Ferguson was tasked with keeping the flame lit for a month and a half so that it could be used in what was at that point likely the largest civic celebration in Birmingham's history: the dedication of a massive new city hall. Just to the left of the main entrance of the building is its cornerstone, bearing a plaque that recognizes the city's 1950 mayor and commissioners and marks the date of its erection. And within that cornerstone is a large iron box, filled with letters and memorabilia from the period and fused shut at the dedication ceremony that summer with a welding torch lit with the fire ignited by those photons from Regulus. The cornerstone plaque includes instructions for what to do with the box: "To be opened August, 2050 A.D."[5]

Ferguson and other officials cast a wide net in soliciting letters for inclusion in the time capsule. Frederick Othman, Washington columnist for United Feature Syndicate, described his pride in being asked to participate until he learned how many other people had been similarly honored.[6] Heads of civic organizations, elected leaders, even schoolchildren, all tasked with offering Birminghamites a century hence a sense of their own lives and expectations. The Kiwanis Club earned national press by including a $1,000 endowment to Birmingham-Southern College, a sum to be held in trust until 2050, at which point they expected it to be worth more than $300,000.

What's fascinating about the letters is how specific they were to the moment in which they were written. Othman's letter (or, at least, his column about the letter) centers on how there likely won't be newspaper columnists in 2050, not because newspapers will have evaporated but because his job would have been taken by a robot. "When readers phone to complain about the pieces he's written about 'em," he joked, "he'll buzz insultingly." But this led to some hopefulness. "The trouble with people is they're always getting into arguments, putting on uniforms, and shooting each other," he wrote. "This is wasteful practice which a modern electric brain would not tolerate."

Othman's optimistic words about the futility of violence is sitting in that box in that cornerstone in that building next to a letter written by one of the names that also appears on the cornerstone plaque. "From the police and fire departments of the city of Birmingham of 1950, I send greetings across the span of a century," it begins. The letter details the "motorized equipment" the departments had at their disposal, including the "shiny, new, red riot car" that earned its own article in *The Birmingham News*'s special section about the dedication ceremony.[7] The author mulls what likely changes would be expected in 2050, like the emergence of an international police force that could operate across borders. After all, he speculated, future criminals "will probably be able to steal a jet plane in Birmingham and in a short time conceal it in a hideaway in Rome."[8] (Interpol was founded in 1923, if you were curious.[9])

"May those values that have made Birmingham a great city in my generation and in yours," the letter concludes, "be cherished and guarded to the end that another hundred years will find Birmingham an even better place in which to live."

Then it is signed: Eugene "Bull" Connor, commissioner of public safety.

Suddenly, the entire exercise snaps into a different focus. Connor was the official who, 13 years after the dewy-eyed dedication of city hall, deployed his officers from that building to a nearby park to drive away Black civil rights protesters with dogs and who sent out crews to disperse Black residents with fire hoses. That riot car drove out of the city hall basement as part of the effort to contain the protests that followed.[10] *The Birmingham News*'s matter-of-fact description of the accessibility of the room where the tear-gas guns were kept in the new city hall lands differently in that context, as does the little blurb boasting that the mayor of Jackson, Mississippi, visiting for the dedication ceremony, praised the city's jail, "Bull Connor's bastille."[11] This was the jail from which Martin Luther King, Jr., wrote his famous letter.

There were hints about what was to come even amid the hoopla over the dedication. A column from April 1950 that describes the iron box that will be used for the time capsule follows a more somber discussion about an incident in which a member of the state legislature was threatened by armed Klansmen for supporting a law targeting the racist group by barring the wearing of face coverings in public. (During the pandemic, Alabama's attorney general had to formally establish that medical masks were exempted from that law.)[12] One of the time-capsule letter writers, Birmingham Bar Association head Harvey Deramus, informed his successor in 2050 that one of the "vexing problems at this time is the zoning between the white and the colored population. Presumably you will have solved this problem by 2050."

What the letter writers foresaw for the city that would come to be called "Bombingham," due to frequent acts of racial violence, was continued upward movement within the unmentioned context of the city's deep segregation and the narrow understanding of how modernity would unfold. A century hence would be a wondrous age of robots running on atomic power but, as far as might be gleaned from many of the more prominent letters, one in

which White and Black Alabamans were content to still use separate drink-
ing fountains. Granted, the group's collective vision of the future was informal and amateurish, often centered on sci-fi optimism. It's still notable that
even relatively thoughtful participants seem to have failed to consider not just
what Birmingham would be like in the twenty-first century, but failed to
understand what lay only about a decade ahead. Deramus just figured it
would be resolved, the deus somehow arriving ex machina.

The lesson is straightforward. Evaluating how the United States will
experience the post–baby boom era necessitates recognizing that we (admittedly primarily meaning me) are necessarily limited in what we can anticipate. These are the Rumsfeldian unknown unknowns, the things we can't
anticipate—Othman's expectation that his 2050 journalism robots would
obviously still be engaged in producing newspapers. He didn't see internet
publishing coming.

But we must also consider our *known* unknowns, the things that we
already understand to be tensions and evolutions that will redirect our path
forward. For many reasons, we would be wise not to emulate Bull Connor,
including by not ignoring the looming crisis in favor of comforting forecasting. So even if we can't answer the questions we know the country will face,
we must at least acknowledge them: questions about lifespans, about the
effects of climate change, and about American democracy itself. The country's future depends heavily on how those known uncertainties are eventually
resolved.

HOW LONG WILL THE BABY BOOM LAST?

Let's begin with an unknown introduced earlier. We have established that
the question of how long baby boomers will live is of importance to the
boomers themselves, both for the extremely obvious reason of self-interest
but also because of how longevity intertwines with resource allocation. Stay-
ing alive, it turns out, costs money—ours and other people's.

It is also hard to predict. I'd mentioned[13] that Catherine Collinson, president of the Transamerica Center for Retirement Studies, conducts surveys
in which her organization asks respondents what age they plan to live to, but
I didn't include what they answer. So here it is: "not sure." That's the majority response, very fairly, but it's one that was offered by only 53 percent of

respondents (all retirees aged 50 or older) in the group's 2020 poll. The median among all other respondents is that they expect to live to the age of 90; 14 percent expected to hit triple digits.

This is, unfortunately, probably optimistic. A 1996 Census Bureau report determined that about a quarter of 65-year-olds at that point were likely to live to 90; by 2040, the percentage was expected to be just over 40 percent.[14] Most of those retirees surveyed by Collinson, then, likely *won't* reach age 90. But how many will? And if they do, what does that suggest about how long the effects of the boom might last?

Shripad Tuljapurkar has some thoughts on this matter. He's the dean and Virginia Morrison Professor of Population Studies at Stanford University, and, in a phone call, he explained that the upper bound of human lifespans is uncertain, if it exists. His suspicion was that "110, 120 would easily be achievable if we continue at this rate. I see no sign that we're going to slow down significantly." When he says "this rate," he means the pace at which life expectancy in the United States has increased since 1950 or so: "about two-tenths of a year of added life per calendar year." In other words, every five years, life expectancies have historically increased by a year. Getting to 120 puts us somewhere past the year 2220.

Those improvements have largely been a function of our better understanding of heart disease and more effectively spotting cancer, changes that allow us to at least delay death, if not prevent it. "We're just getting better at keeping people alive longer and keeping them healthier," Tuljapurkar said. "And they"—the boomers—"are getting the fruits of it."

Except for those members of the baby boom generation who aren't. Except for the more than 300,000 baby boomers who died of Covid-19 by the beginning of 2022,[15] a large chunk of the 1 out of every 100 elderly Americans killed by the disease by that point.[16]

Except, too, for those who died younger than they might otherwise have, including during the pandemic, because of drug overdoses, substance abuse, and suicides—deaths that researchers Anne Case and Angus Deaton describe as "deaths of despair." In their 2020 book on the subject, Case and Deaton describe those affected by the pattern in a familiar way. "Our story of deaths of despair; of pain; of addiction, alcoholism, and suicide; of worse jobs with lower wages; of declining marriage; and of declining religion is mostly a story of non-Hispanic white Americans without a four-year degree," they write.[17] Like Tuljapurkar, they note the cultural achievement of a decades-long increase in life expectancies—an achievement that makes the exception to that pattern that they unearthed all that much more remarkable. It's not just that suicides increased. It's that all deaths among middle-aged White Americans were increasing—the group that's the focus of much of this book.

A central point of Case and Deaton's research is that the causation of those deaths overlaps. Suicides and accidental drug overdoses alike "show great unhappiness with life, either momentary or prolonged," they write.[18] While Case and Deaton link the trend to the state of capitalism in the United States—explicitly, even on their book's cover—they emphasize that the pattern is not entirely dependent on the recession that began in 2007.

Katherine Hempstead, a senior policy adviser at the Robert Wood Johnson Foundation, has looked specifically at the issue of suicide. With baby boomers, she said, "we saw an increase in the proportion of completed cases—that is, deaths—where people were citing or there were circumstances about economic dislocation, legal problems, job problems, financial problems." But "the big, long secular trend that we see in the U.S. in the recent past," she said, suggested a pattern that's less tangible.

When we spoke, Tuljapurkar emphasized the importance of the disparity in death rates by education and income—that the disparities that affect us in life are echoed in how our lives end. That's starkly demonstrated in Case and Deaton's data. Mortality rates are already higher for those without a college degree than for those with one. Considering only deaths of despair, the difference widens. In 2019, the death-of-despair mortality rate for those without a degree was more than 3.5 times that of those with a degree.

As we consider a generation that's relatively less educated, the importance of this gap becomes clear. Alison Bryant of AARP put it succinctly: "The whole idea of longevity only works right now in certain sectors of the population."

Case and Deaton's book was published in mid-March 2020, just as the coronavirus was starting to appear across the United States. Eventually, the CDC announced that life expectancies had dropped by 1.8 years in 2020,[19] mostly due to the coronavirus pandemic but also because 100,000 Americans died of drug overdoses in the pandemic's first year.[20] More deaths

CHART 84
Mortality Rates Relative to Education

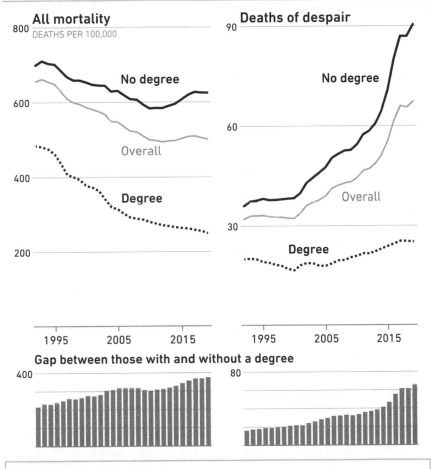

All mortality
800 DEATHS PER 100,000

No degree

600

Overall

400

Degree

200

Deaths of despair
90

No degree

60

Overall

30 Degree

1995   2005   2015   1995   2005   2015

Gap between those with and without a degree
400   80

> HOW TO READ THIS CHART At left, the overall age-adjusted mortality rate for the 25-to-74 population as calculated by Case and Deaton, both overall and by educational status.[21] Below that, the difference between those with and without a college degree by year. At right, the same charts, but showing only deaths from suicide, drugs, or alcohol.

among the non-elderly, Tuljapurkar pointed out, has a disproportionate effect on life expectancies: someone who dies at age 80 is not driving down the average in the way that someone who dies at 40 does.

The life expectancy of those aged 65 in 2020 fell to 18.5 years, down from 19.6 years in 2019. As of this writing, data for 2021 have not yet been released, but the trend is not encouraging: more people died of Covid-19 that year than in 2020. In other words, the baby boom will almost certainly wither more rapidly than we would have expected.

HOW WILL CLIMATE CHANGE UPEND THE COUNTRY?

While we're considering grim themes, there is another slow-moving catastrophe that will reshape the geography, politics, and economics of the post–baby boom world, quite literally: climate change.

As advocates for controlling the greenhouse-gas emissions that are accelerating warming will be quick to tell you, it's tricky to attribute any particular negative event specifically to increased atmospheric heat, much less a specific event in a particular place. We do not know that our continued dumping of carbon dioxide and methane into the air will lead to 80 percent more hurricanes in New Orleans, or anything like that. We might someday be able to; a group of researchers has been lobbying for a massive investment in computing power that would improve the international scientific community's ability to forecast the effects of warming.[22] Until then, we're left with a relatively broad understanding of what we might expect.

Broad, but detailed. Temperatures will increase, obviously, but that is simply the top level of the flowchart. That warms air, which then holds more moisture, which then means more precipitation from storms—though when and where rain might fall and trigger flooding is hard to predict. It warms the ocean, which expands the water in the ocean and contributes to sea-level rise even as melting ice on land adds additional water volume. It dries out the Earth's surface, affecting crops and increasing drought. Increased drought means drier vegetation and more fires. The effects trickle out from there: warmer temperature means disease-carrying insects survive more winters. It means that permanently frozen ground in the Arctic thaws, destabilizing the built environment and, more problematic, allowing vegetation to decompose and release methane back into the air.

For our purposes, the questions are more specific than the available answers. Where might habitability decrease? How might that affect migration, both into and within the United States? How will that migration affect politics? What effects might there be on longevity, to our point above? How do our actions now potentially compound or ameliorate the negative effects of the future?

We can make some assumptions. Sea level rise, for example, will be more of a problem near the ocean, for obvious reasons. Data from the research organization Rhodium Group analyzed by ProPublica and *The New York Times* evaluated the risks from various likely climate effects by county across the United States. Heat, fires, sea levels—each county was assigned a value from 1 to 10, with 10 indicating that under certain predictive climate models,

CHART 85

Where Climate Effects Are Likely to Hit Hardest

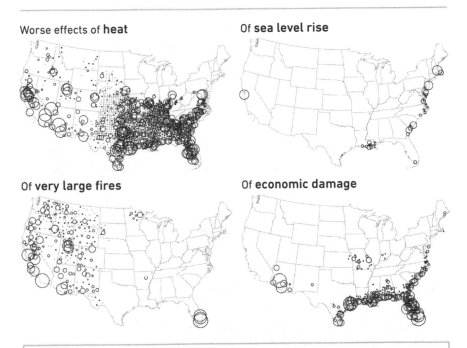

Worse effects of **heat**

Of **sea level rise**

Of **very large fires**

Of **economic damage**

HOW TO READ THIS CHART Using the county-level data from the ProPublica–Rhodium Group's indices,[23] the maps above show counties rated between 6 and 10—higher levels of risk. The population of each county is shown as a circle, with larger circles representing more populous counties. The climate risks have varying effects: about 38 percent of Americans live in counties where heat is likely to have worse effects, while only about 2 percent live in counties where sea level rise will.

that county would see the worst negative effects within the 2040 to 2060 time frame. That allows us to approximate how Americans will be affected by these anticipated shifts.

When we spoke in 2018, Alexander Halliday, director of Columbia University's Earth Institute, offered an important bit of caution. "As we discover more, we are discovering how much more complicated it is and how much more we've got to think about," he said. "But also the potential that actually it could be far worse than we've considered before." When scientists revise prior estimates of the effects of the warming climate, they are generally revised to be more dire, not less.

Some of the effects above will affect baby boomers disproportionately. In 2019, 12 percent of baby boomers lived in counties that are expected to experience the largest negative effects of heat. Extreme heat is more dangerous for older people.[24] But some effects simply raise more pointed questions about the future. What happens if large cities along the Gulf Coast become significantly less habitable? What happens if it becomes infeasible to live in huge portions of the West, where fires and drought are endemic? If tens of thousands of Americans—hundreds of thousands—are forced to move, where do they go? How does it reshape their destinations? Where they came from? How does it affect the economy?

We have recent examples of how weather-related disruptions reshape communities and politics. After Hurricane Maria hit Puerto Rico in 2017, the Census Bureau estimates that more than 123,000 more people moved from the island to the mainland than vice versa, twice what the figure had been over the prior several years.[25] Many moved to Florida,[26] where there were large existing Puerto Rican communities. New Puerto Rican arrivals were credited with helping to elect the first Hispanic mayor of the city of Kissimmee[27]—though one Democratic consultant with whom I spoke found that the government's much-criticized hurricane response wasn't a potent political consideration for Puerto Ricans even in the 2018 midterms. Many Puerto Ricans displaced by the storm eventually moved back, of course. But this is also the point: the upheaval destabilizes both the point of origin and the point of destination. Research conducted several years after Hurricane Katrina hit New Orleans showed that those who returned were more likely to be older, wealthier, and better educated.[28] The city changed, however subtly, as did those cities to which refugees fled.

Munich Re, a firm that insures insurers, began warning its customers about the increased costs of climate change–related disasters nearly a decade ago.[29] Since then, the problem has only been exacerbated. Again, despite typically being manifested as weather events, climate change is not something that emerges from natural forces. These exceptional events are a function of our spending decades burning fossil fuels and emitting heat-absorbing gases into the air. More specifically, it is a function of our having done this fairly recently.

The Global Carbon Project is an international effort to index and estimate the release of greenhouse gases by country and year. By the end of 2020,

---

CHART 86
Who Produced Greenhouse Gases—and When

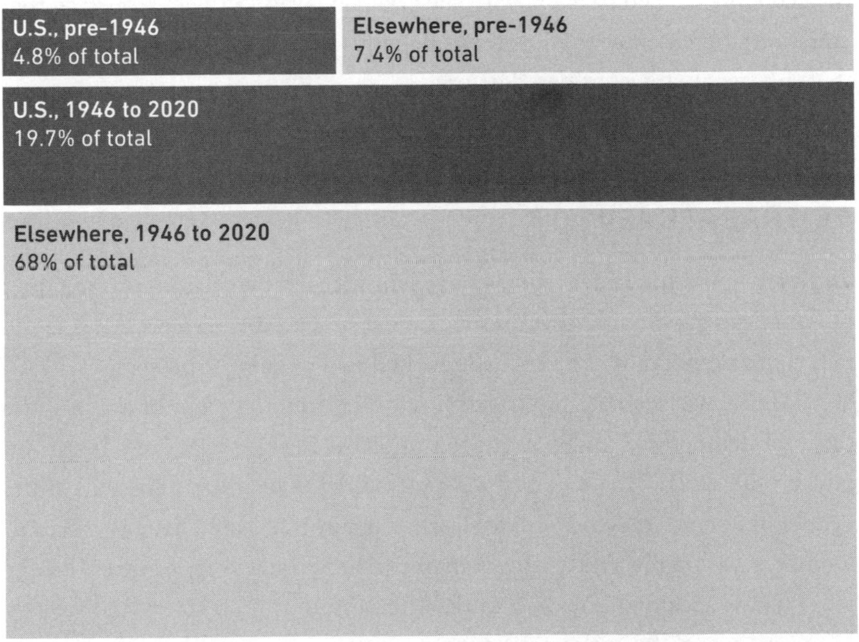

U.S., pre-1946
4.8% of total

Elsewhere, pre-1946
7.4% of total

U.S., 1946 to 2020
19.7% of total

Elsewhere, 1946 to 2020
68% of total

HOW TO READ THIS CHART The entirety of the shaded areas represents the nearly 1.7 trillion tons of carbon dioxide emissions since the beginning of the Global Carbon Project's analysis period.[30] The darker-colored segments are emissions just from the United States.

it estimated that about 1.7 trillion tons of carbon dioxide had been released since the eighteenth century. About a quarter of that total had been emitted just since 2008. And no country has contributed more to the total than the United States. Nearly a quarter of all emissions originated here, including just under a fifth of the global total that was emitted by the United States just within the lifetimes of the oldest baby boomers.[31]

For decades, Americans have migrated away from the Northeast, toward warmer states like Arizona and Texas. If the negative effects of climate change unfold as indicated in the Rhodium Group's analysis, that trend could shift or reverse, once again reshaping politics and the economy. It depends largely on where the dice land.

And on how big that graph above gets. The economic slowdown that accompanied the arrival of the coronavirus in the United States in 2020 helped push carbon dioxide emissions lower, closer to the trajectory scientists suggest is necessary to reduce the likelihood of the worst effects. And then the economy opened back up, with the Global Carbon Project reporting that emissions increased nearly 5 percent globally in 2021.[32] It could be far worse than we've actually considered before.

HOW MIGHT AMERICAN DEMOCRACY ITSELF BE THREATENED?

The first words Joe Biden said as president focused overtly on a component of American governance that's normally just subtext to a new presidency: the fact that a democratic election had resulted in a change of power.

"Today, we celebrate the triumph not of a candidate, but of a cause, the cause of democracy," Biden said soon after his inaugural address began on January 20, 2021. "The will of the people has been heard and the will of the people has been heeded. We have learned again that democracy is precious. Democracy is fragile. And at this hour, my friends, democracy has prevailed."[33]

He was speaking only two weeks after a riotous mob spurred to fury by Donald Trump's false claims about the election, and called to Washington by the president himself, had stormed into the U.S. Capitol in a failed-if-not-doomed effort to prevent Biden's victory from being cemented. He was speaking only feet from where the mob two Wednesdays before had attacked police officers and dragged one, Michael Fanone, into its midst to be beaten and tased. So Biden's "at this hour" was meant to be triumphant, an our-flag-was-still-there declaration that the American system had won. It also reads as a warning: at this hour, democracy prevailed—but the hour may be changing.

In researching this book, I spoke with a broad range of political scientists and observers of the complexities of American culture and systems. And one caveat arose repeatedly: here's what we might expect in the future . . . if American democracy remains intact.

You'll remember New York University's Eric Knowles, who conducted that research discussed in chapter 4 showing how White Americans, particularly on the political right, often view non-Whites as a threatening aggregate. That chapter looked at the ways in which the particular characteristics of the baby boom often overlap with the demographics of America's political right. In our conversation, Knowles drew the connection between his work and the perils of the moment explicitly.

"The postwar generation was highly committed, at least in the abstract, to democratic institutions. What we're seeing is a softening of those commitments," he told me. "I don't know whether the kinds of changes in racial attitudes that I'm seeing in my research are a product of that or one of the things that is driving it. But it seems to me to at least be a symptom of a really, really frightening trend, and that's the idea that it's okay to sort of deprive other people of rights, if that's what's necessary to protect the group."

Vanderbilt University's Larry Bartels looked at YouGov polling shortly before the 2020 election and found that a subset of Republicans embraced anti-democratic responses to the loss of power and voice they perceived. Republicans who exhibited the most "ethnic antagonism"—defined by Bartels as "concerns about the political power and claims on government resources of immigrants, African-Americans, and Latinos"—exhibited the highest levels of support for illiberal measures to protect power. The more "ethnic antagonism" expressed by a survey respondent, the more likely they were to say, "The traditional American way of life is disappearing so fast that we may have to use force to save it" or "A time will come when patriotic Americans have to take the law into their own hands."

"One of the most politically salient features of the contemporary United States is the looming demographic transition from a majority-White to a 'majority-minority' country," Bartels wrote. "Several years ago, reminding

White Americans of that prospect significantly altered their political attitudes. Now, President Trump and Fox News remind them, implicitly or explicitly, on an almost-daily basis."[34]

Over the past 20 years, the Republican Party has joined the parties of
Hungarian prime minister Viktor Orbán and Turkey's Recep Tayyip Er-
doğan in shifting away from an embrace of liberal democratic traditions,
as measured by the Varieties of Democracy Institute at the University of
Gothenburg.[35]

The practical effect of this shift is to deprioritize the connection between
political power and free and open elections. This manifests in a number of
ways. In the wake of the 2020 election, for example, hundreds of laws aimed
at curtailing voting access to some extent were introduced almost exclusively
by Republican legislators. By June 2022, more than 50 laws had been enacted
in 24 states.[36] Over and over, the rationale used to justify those changes was
the purported fraud alleged by Trump and his allies, something that, by that
same point in time, had been demonstrated to have occurred the prior year
on only a smattering of occasions.[37]

Whether by design or remarkable coincidence, the new laws made or
proposed changes that would disenfranchise and encumber low-income and
other more heavily Democratic voting constituencies. To some extent, *any*
constriction of voting access has such an effect, because those most likely to vote
tend to be older (meaning more time to get to the polls), wealthier (meaning,
among other things, that they work more predictable hours and have fewer
transportation issues), and homeowners (meaning less subject to changes
in registration status or change in polling place). In unguarded moments,[38]
though, Republican legislators have directly described past proposals to restrict voting as specifically unhelpful to their opponents or embraced new
restrictions as necessary for holding power.[39] If your base is primed to think
that fraud is substantial to the point of affecting results—3 in 5 Republicans
held that view of the 2020 election by the following June[40]—there's not going
to be a substantial outcry over changes that kneecap opposition voting.

Overhauling voting procedures became easier in some states because of
the Supreme Court's 2013 decision in *Shelby County v. Holder*. That decision
removed the Voting Rights Act's requirement that changes to election law in
a number of mostly southern states be reviewed by the Justice Department
before implementation. Even as he credited the act for being "immensely

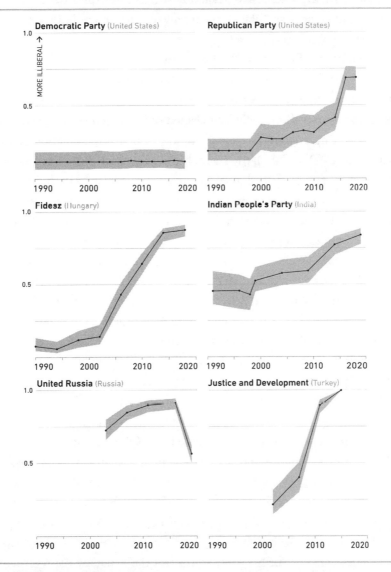

CHART 87
Illiberal Tendencies in Global Political Parties

Democratic Party (United States)

Republican Party (United States)

Fidesz (Hungary)

Indian People's Party (India)

United Russia (Russia)

Justice and Development (Turkey)

MORE ILLIBERAL →

HOW TO READ THIS CHART Each graph above shows the evolution over 30 years of a political party's embrace of illiberal tendencies, like a tendency to demonize opponents or to refrain from discouraging the use of political violence. The higher the line rises, the more illiberal the party is determined to be. The shaded areas indicate the boundaries of estimates. Note the rise in the GOP in 2016, the second-to-last marked data point.

successful at redressing racial discrimination and integrating the voting process," Chief Justice John Roberts advocated stripping out a component of it that had been used to achieve that success. This, Justice Ruth Bader Ginsburg wrote in a dissent, was "like throwing away your umbrella in a rainstorm because you are not getting wet."

Republican efforts after 2020 went further than new restrictions. The focus of Trump's efforts on January 6 was not simply leveraging his lies about voter fraud in order to affect future elections but to unwind the preceding one. Some Trump allies, including elected officials, subsequently advocated for empowering state legislators to undo or undermine election results.[41] Writing for CNN in 2022, the staunchly conservative former federal judge J. Michael Luttig described a deliberate effort to create a path for the Supreme Court to affirm the ability of state legislatures to determine election processes and results unilaterally. He was not reserved in how he framed this push: Republicans aimed at "stealing the 2024 election."[42]

"What you're seeing right now inside the Republican Party elected elite," Harvard's Theda Skocpol told me, "is an argument about whether they should go back to simply manipulating the Electoral College and the state-level ability to shape voting rules to make it hard for Democratic constituencies that are demographically on the rise to vote."

In part because Republican political strength is heavily weighted to rural areas, the party enjoys disproportionate power in the Senate and the Electoral College, which allows them to hold majorities or the White House despite winning fewer votes. Such imbalances can and have shifted over time, but the system currently works heavily to the GOP's advantage. Democratic data expert David Shor found that the advantage Republicans enjoyed from the Electoral College grew from 2016 to 2020.[43] These imbalances are a function of the system and have been since the founding of the country. It's disadvantageous, though, that they would be stacked in favor of one party, allowing, for example, for Donald Trump to be president in 2017 after losing the popular vote and for his party to control the Senate while representing less than half of the country's population and receiving less than half of the votes cast for Senate seats.[44] In essence, the country was being run by the political minority, something that Democrats were quick to point out. Often, the response that followed was along the lines of, yeah, well, tough luck. Sometimes, though, it was different.

"We're not a democracy," Senator Mike Lee (R-Utah) wrote on Twitter on the evening of October 7, 2020, less than a month before the presidential election.[45] He continued his thought a few hours later, writing that "[d]emocracy isn't the objective; liberty, peace, and prospefity [*sic*] are. We want the human condition to flourish. Rank democracy can thwart that."[46]

Lee (who would later quietly work to bolster Trump's efforts to hold power after the 2020 election) was drawing the familiar, facile distinction between a democracy and a republic that's common in such debates.[47] The latter is differentiated as a government run by elected leaders—leaders elected through a democratic process, which obviously blurs the line Lee's trying to draw. But his semantic differentiation was not aimed at spurring debate in an introductory political science class. It was instead meant to suggest that the idea that power should be allotted through the measured will of the people was not the desired outcome of American government. With the re-election of a president who took office despite losing the popular vote looming, it was a way to wave away concerns about a minority (specifically the minority of which he is a member) holding a majority of political power by arguing that this was an intended outcome of how America was constructed.

Writing for *The Atlantic* in response to Lee, Claremont McKenna College professor George Thomas saw through Lee's effort to justify the power imbalance his party enjoyed. He presented examples of the Founding Fathers explicitly rejecting the distinction Lee tried to draw, then dicing up the senator's subtext.

"High-minded claims that we are not a democracy surreptitiously fuse *republic* with *minority rule* rather than *popular government*," he wrote. "Enabling sustained minority rule at the national level is not a feature of our constitutional design, but a perversion of it."[48] Particularly given the history of centering power in an American minority: of White, male landowners at first and, later, of Whites generally. In 1910, both Mississippi and South Carolina were majority Black;[49] in neither state did Black residents hold significant political power. "Minority rule" is often euphemistic for preserving rule by the subgroup of Americans who've always ruled.

In their book *How Democracies Die*, Steven Levitsky and Daniel Ziblatt posit a future that looks much as Skocpol articulated. "Under this scenario, a pro-Trump GOP would retain the presidency, both houses of Congress, and the vast majority of statehouses, and it would eventually gain a solid majority in the Supreme Court," something made real in 2020. "It would then use the techniques of constitutional hardball to manufacture durable white electoral majorities," they write. "[. . .] Measures to reengineer the electorate would likely be accompanied by elimination of the filibuster and other rules that protect Senate minorities, so that Republicans could impose their agenda even with narrow majorities."[50]

For a largely White and heavily jingoistic Republican Party that's in part reacting to the perceived threat of a changing America, assurances like Lee's that This Is What the Founders Wanted are part soothing balm and part rationalization. The baby boomer–powered movement that cohered into the Tea Party and expanded into MAGA has metastasized.

There are also a number of more dire warning signs for our democracy. Polling from July 2021 showing that a quarter of Republicans approve of the actions at the Capitol six months before, if only somewhat.[51] Polling from February of that year showing that most Republicans see Democrats not as political opponents but as enemies.[52] (For most Democrats, the opposite was true.) Polling from PRRI released in October 2021 that found 3 in 10 Republicans agreeing with the statement that "because things have gotten so far off track, true American patriots may have to resort to violence in order to save our country." Among those who believed Trump's lies about election fraud, the figure was nearly 4 in 10.[53] This is not a feature of a stable democracy.

The most acute demonstration of that willingness manifested on January 6, 2021. Most of those who were eventually arrested for criminal activity that day were younger than baby boomers. But as Robert Pape, director of the Chicago Project on Security and Threats, told *The Atlantic*'s Barton Gellman later that year, the participants skewed far older than other insurgent groups he'd studied.[54] Normally, political extremists were in their twenties and early thirties.[55] Pape measured the median age of January 6 rioters at 41.8.

Kelly O'Brien, a 49-year-old woman from Pennsylvania, posted a call to arms on Facebook in December 2020, according to federal prosecutors. "Elders are cheering us on and believe that WE ARE GOING TO BE THE GREATEST GENERATION in their lifetime," the message read. "And they lived through WWII."[56]

Pape's analysis included other useful observations, as Gellman reported. "Other things being equal, insurgents were much more likely to come from a county where the white share of the population was in decline," he wrote.

CHART 88

Age, Gender, and Race Distribution of Those Arrested for January 6

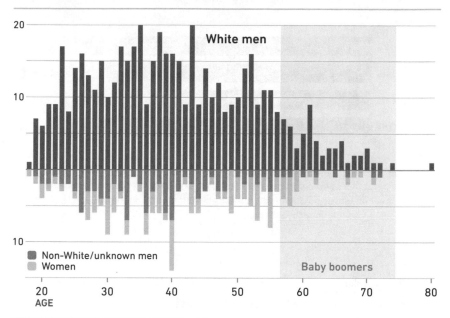

HOW TO READ THIS CHART Using data from the open-source group the Prosecution Project, arrests related to the Capitol riots (as of late January 2022) are shown as a stacked column graph. Above the horizontal line are White men, from youngest (18) to oldest (80). Below are women and non-White men. (Sixty-nine arrestees without known ages are excluded.) White men made up 81 percent of those for whom race or ethnicity had been identified; baby boomers were 1 in 9 of those for whom age data were available.

"For every one-point drop in a county's percentage of non-Hispanic whites from 2015 to 2019, the likelihood of an insurgent hailing from that county increased by 25 percent. This was a strong link, and it held up in every state." Polling conducted by Pape's group determined that supporters of the "great replacement theory," a racist assertion that the White population was being intentionally undermined by non-White immigrants, were four times more likely to say that violence was justified to reestablish Trump's presidency than those who didn't adhere to that theory.

In this context, concerns about the distribution of power within the democracy are the near end of the spectrum of how things might grow more

CHART 89
Perception of Democracy Under Threat

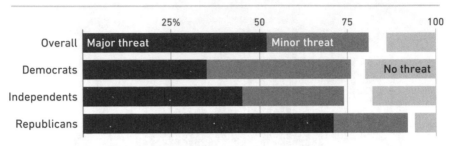

	25%	50	75	100

Overall — Major threat / Minor threat

Democrats

Independents

Republicans — No threat

HOW TO READ THIS CHART This stacked bar graph contrasts those who told pollsters from Selzer & Company in October 2021 that they saw American democracy being under threat (at left) or not (light-colored bar at right). Nearly all Republican respondents said that they thought it was.

dire. The broader concern is that underlying sentiment of embattlement. In October 2021, Iowa's Grinnell College commissioned a poll that evaluated confidence in American democracy. Republicans, not Democrats, were more likely to see the system as facing a threat.[57]

"The sense that democracy is under threat is characterized by deep, partisan polarization, with Republicans rather than Democrats describing our democracy as facing a 'major' threat," Grinnell political science associate professor Danielle Lussier said in a press release. "It appears as though baseless accounts of fraud and a stolen 2020 election have sharply eroded confidence in our system among Republicans and created a sense that democracy is facing a crisis."

Historian Thomas Zimmer studies political polarization and contextualized the moment with more breadth. The country is being tested to determine if it can simultaneously be a liberal democracy and pluralistic, a struggle that echoes elsewhere around the world.

"We're experiencing this very, very serious, very dangerous, authoritarian, anti-democratic onslaught on American democracy," Zimmer said. "But I don't think that's a result of liberal democracy being weak. I think it's actually a result of liberal democracy being stronger than it's ever been." Americans who are not White Christians have an increased presence in our population, creating more points of contrast to be evaluated through democratic processes—and creating more strain on the entrenched power of those White Christians.

"If you have a democracy and, just because of demographic and cultural developments, the electorate becomes less White and less Christian, that will probably result in diminishment of power for White Christians," he said. In other words, there may be a real threat to that established power. So many— and not just cynics, grifters, and those seeking trickle-down power from Trump, he said—"are reacting to that by ditching democracy. If democracy doesn't work for us anymore, then democracy has to go." If democracy goes (or even recedes significantly), then our forthcoming analysis of how political power is reshaped after the baby boom becomes rather moot.

"Post January sixth, the supposed moment of reckoning for the Republican Party?" Michael Steele, once the chairman of the party, said to me a few months after the riot. "There's been a reckoning all right. And those people who support democracy have left the party."

One of the architects of Trump's strategy to undercut Joe Biden's victory was a law professor named John Eastman. Eastman wrote memos articulating a process through which Vice President Pence could arrive at the Capitol on January 6 and simply reject the electoral votes cast by several states that had selected Biden over Trump.[58] He encouraged state legislators to demand that their submitted electors be rescinded.[59] Under scrutiny, Eastman at times tried to moderate this position, but the president of the far-right Claremont Institute with which Eastman was affiliated was adamant that they were collectively engaged in a just fight.

"The Founders were pretty unanimous, with Washington leading the way, that the Constitution is really only fit for a Christian people," Claremont's Ryan Williams told *The Atlantic*'s Emma Green in 2021. The authors of that document, he assured her, "set up a republic, not a democracy. The rule of pure numbers was never the touchstone of justice for the Founders." Asked if he worried that the country was heading toward a "generationally defining conflict that could potentially be violent," Williams suggested that it was possible. "I worry about such a conflict," he said. "The Civil War was terrible. It should be the thing we try to avoid almost at all costs."[60] Almost.

"There's a reason why when Trump got elected in 2016, every far-right movement all over the Western world rejoiced," Zimmer told me. "They, I

think quite rightly, looked at America as sort of an advanced test case for
whether or not it would be possible to erect a stable, functioning multiracial
democracy. If the answer is yes, then that's bad news for far-right movements
everywhere."

What if the answer is no? This is also uncertain: What does an America
that backslides from liberal democracy look like? In an *Atlantic* essay published a few months before the 2020 election, former Obama administration
official Ben Rhodes articulated the ways in which Trump's administration
had already taken many of the steps deployed by authoritarians like Viktor
Orbán in Hungary,[61] someone who Trump ally and adviser Stephen K.
Bannon—whose post–White House career has been centered on further elevating far-right politics and politicians—called "Trump before Trump."[62]
Leveraging governmental power for his own benefit and as a personal reward-
punishment mechanism (an effort that expanded as the election neared).
Undercutting or polarizing the nonpartisan functions of government. Bolstering the judiciary with those who share your ideology. Lying repeatedly
and unashamedly, relying on allies in the media to amplify, defend, and trans-
mit your message.

In the wake of his 2020 loss, Trump consistently hinted that he might
seek a second term in the 2024 presidential contest. That prospect dramatically raises the acuteness of the question. His 2016 and 2020 campaigns were
centered on the unease and fear associated with America's cultural and demographic shifts; making America great again implies making it more like
what it used to be. Seventy-four million Americans voted for his proto-
authoritarianism in 2020, even after the actions delineated by Rhodes and
others. What happens if enough Americans support a 2024 campaign to
bring him back to power? Or what happens if the robust effort to make it
easier for him or another candidate to become president despite losing the
election—an effort that continued even after Trump left office—achieves its
desired outcome?

In 2017, the first year of Trump's presidency, the World Values Survey
Association asked Americans how they viewed a form of government in
which a strong leader could act without regard to a legislature or elections.
Most Americans rejected this idea, describing it as bad or very bad. Among
those who said they preferred voting for Republicans over Democrats, though,

44 percent said such a form of government was "very good" or "fairly good." Among Republican voters under fifty, a majority viewed the framework as good.[63]

"Americans are not conditioned to think that our political system might be transformed, and Trump's own incompetence offers false reassurance that there are limits to what he can do," Rhodes wrote. "But Trump's authoritarian impulses have fit into the Republican Party's illiberal tendencies like a plug into a socket, powering an authoritarian movement."

Zimmer has a similar view.

"I still see too much American exceptionalism in this discourse over what's going to happen to American democracy," he told me. "This idea that it's basically inconceivable that American democracy might end, might turn into something that is more adequately described as a sort of authoritarian system or a minority-rule type of system." It wasn't that there wouldn't be elections or a political left. It's that it wouldn't matter that there were.

It's important to acknowledge that this significant erosion of political comity and the decline of boomer political heft overlapped with a moment of remarkable social instability. American institutions and Americans' personal relationships were rattled by the coronavirus pandemic and a contentious election. Crime surged. It's fair to wonder if the warning lights that are flashing might be a function less of a trend than of a moment. A less reassuring alternative: the moment simply accelerated the trend.

THE PAST MAY BE PROLOGUE

At the same time that Ben Rhodes was writing for *The Atlantic*, University of London professor Sarah Churchwell wrote an essay for *The New York Review of Books* that offered an important reminder for those who might dismiss his concerns: America has already experienced fascism.[64]

Churchwell begins by quoting James Waterman Wise, who in 1936 argued that fascism would arrive in the United States "wrapped up in the American flag and heralded as a plea for liberty and preservation of the constitution"—a very Claremontesque articulation. (In a speech that year, Wise was reported to have also said that "any faction which works against the freedom of a minority is working against the very principles upon which our Constitution was founded.")[65] Her point, though, was that fascism is specific to the place in which it emerges. In the United States, that looked like the alternate power structure that emerged in the South.

She quotes Robert O. Paxton, who describes the Ku Klux Klan's rebirth a century ago as being "a remarkable preview of the way fascist movements were to function in interwar Europe," arising in purported defense of real American values and unafraid to use political violence to that end. The Klan's focus at that point was broader than skin color, including targeting immigrants and Catholicism. (The Klan rally at which Donald Trump's father was arrested, you'll recall, was predicated on a defense of Protestantism against Irish and Italian Catholics.) Nazis often pointed to racist rhetoric (like Lothrop Stoddard's *The Rising Tide of Color Against White World-Supremacy*) and southern segregation as a validation or defense of their system, Churchwell explains. During a debate in Florida's gubernatorial race in 2018, Democrat Andrew Gillum declined to say that his opponent, Republican Ron DeSantis, was racist. Instead, he said, "the racists believe he's a racist."[66] The parallel: a system viewed with approval by fascists is probably not a system too distant from fascism.

Churchwell's history is a reminder that a collapse of democracy even in parts of the country would not really be novel. Instead, it would be what Zimmer described as "a return to historical norm." Before the civil rights movement, "if you happened to be White and if you happened to be a White man in particular, then it was a fairly well functioning democracy," he said. "But if you happened to not be a White Christian male in America, pre-1965, then this country was certainly not a functioning democracy for you."

University of North Carolina political scientist Michael Greenberger was able to draw a direct line from White perceptions of racial threat to near-autocratic governance in the post–Civil War South. His 2022 research found that "[r]ace unquestionably played a key role in shaping the collapse of democratic elections in the South," with more-Black counties having "reported decreasing turnout at higher rates than other locales but also reported higher rates of voting for Democrats—the political vehicle of disenfranchisement." The region "never became a completely closed autocratic system for all its inhabitants, but it very nearly did for African Americans."[67] That it didn't he ascribed to concern over federal intervention. It was just autocratic enough to survive.

Well into the twentieth century, Blacks faced enormous roadblocks to voting in the South, including literacy tests, legal carve-outs, and, at times, the deployment of threats and violence. Expanding the franchise to broaden democracy was a centerpiece of the civil rights movement, one that led to the 1965 Voting Rights Act. That the legislation was eviscerated in 2013 shortly after White Christians moved from majority to plurality seems symbolic, if nothing else.[68]

Among the states freed by the 2013 decision to allow changes to voting laws without federal review was Alabama.[69] In 1960, before the act was in place, there had been a strong inverse correlation between the density of the

CHART 90
Voter Turnout vs. Race in 1960 Alabama

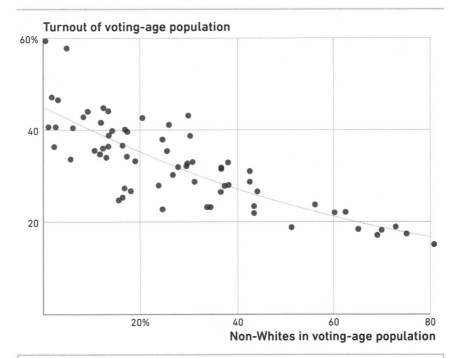

Turnout of voting-age population

Non-Whites in voting-age population

HOW TO READ THIS CHART Each dot represents one county in Alabama in 1960. The farther to the right the dot is located, the larger the percentage of non-Whites among those old enough to vote. The higher the dot, the more of that population that actually cast a ballot. The dotted trend line that moves from upper left to lower right shows the correlation: counties with more non-White adults voted less heavily.

non-White population in a county and turnout in the year's presidential contest.[70] In the quarter of counties in which non-Whites made up the smallest percentage of the voting-age population, an average of 42 percent turned out to vote. In the quarter of counties with the largest percentages of non-Whites old enough to vote, only 23 percent did.

This was 10 years in the future when Birmingham dedicated its new city hall in that optimistic, forward-looking 1950 ceremony. The city's first Black mayor lay another 19 years beyond that.[71] In between, it would be wracked by racial conflict as an explicitly subjugated population pushed for equality. Alabama would become the epicenter of the push to extend the unfettered right to vote to all American adults. It may also offer a preview of the future: by 2050, on the day that the time capsule is extracted from Birmingham city hall and opened, American democracy might in some places look less like it does now than it did in Alabama a century ago.

As Representative Adam Schiff (D-California) put it during one of the congressional hearings aimed at dissecting Trump's effort to retain power: "That we have lived in a democracy for more than 200 years does not mean we shall do so tomorrow."[72] In America's history, fair elections open to all men and women are the exception, not the norm. Restricted democracy is largely history, but it is not ancient history. If I walk outside tonight and find Regulus, the light I see will have left that star system before the civil rights movement and before Birmingham's new city hall was built. It will have left, in fact, before the baby boom even began. It is emitting light as I write. Who knows what America it will land on, if any?

The Importance of What We
Don't Know About Ourselves

Had Takao Ozawa been living in San Francisco in 1880, his family would have been faced with an odd situation. Ozawa was born in Japan five years earlier, but if a census taker that year had asked them to identify their race—or, as the census form put it, their "color"—they'd have been categorized as "Chinese." Twenty years before that, even "Chinese" wasn't an option; they'd have had to fit into one of the three available categories: White, Black, or mulatto. Of course, immigration from Asia to the United States had only just begun to pick up by 1860. The census that year found that about 1 in 1,000 U.S. residents had come from China.[1] By 1870, the number of Chinese immigrants had nearly doubled, and "Chinese" joined "Indian" (as in Native American) as a separate census category.[2] But Japan? Thanks in part to the nation's robust isolationism, the Census Bureau paid it no heed. And if the Census Bureau didn't count it, for governmental purposes there were no distinctly Japanese people in the United States.

From the beginning, the U.S. government's interest in cataloging race has been largely reactionary—but it was also foundational. "[R]ace was introduced with the first census," the Census Bureau's Karen Humes and Howard Hogan wrote in 2009, noting that the Constitution did not specifically demand it.[3] But politics did. If enslaved people were to count as three-fifths of a state resident in order to bolster the representative power of slave states—an accommodation that *is* specifically stipulated in the Constitution—then you need to know how many non-free people live in each state. And if you're counting enslaved people in 1790, you're counting people brought to the country from Africa. So, in that first census, enumerators were asked to tally the number of free Whites as well as the numbers of "other free persons" and enslaved people—Black people, though that wasn't explicit.

As the decades passed, other groups were added in some form or another: various Asian origins, Hispanic, Hawaiian and Pacific Islander categories (after Hawaii became a state), and, for a period, mulatto and other mixed-race categories like "quadroon," a person with one Black grandparent. This, Humes and Hogan write, was a function of a racist push for "more meticulous sta-

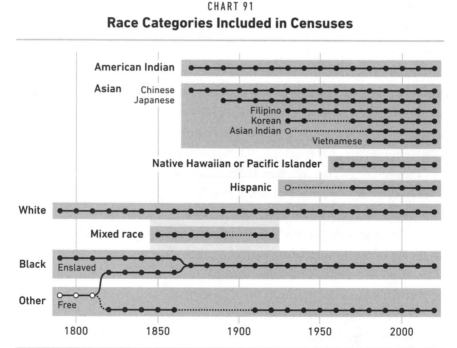

CHART 91
Race Categories Included in Censuses

HOW TO READ THIS CHART Each dot above indicates a racial or ethnic identity that was included in the indicated year's decennial census. Dotted lines indicate periods when the question wasn't asked. Outlined circles indicate that a question was asked in an exceptional way. In 1930, respondents were identified as being "Hindu," not Indian and as "Mexican," not Hispanic.

tistics on the black population, which could provide statistical evidence that blacks were inferior and unfit for freedom."

How America categorizes race is not fixed, but, instead, is buffeted by evolving politics, situations, and motivations. As we explored in chapter 4, that means that residents of the United States have often had to figure out which of the racial definitions provided is the one that best describes themselves. And this gap between how people see themselves and how the government categorizes them yields one of the more important uncertainties about America's projected future.

HOW TO BE LEGALLY WHITE

The question of self-identification is not simply academic. Takao Ozawa was tallied by the 1920 census at an address in Honolulu, Hawaii, his "color or race" listed as "Jap."[4] Two years later, Ozawa made a different assertion before the Supreme Court: he was White—White enough, at least, to be granted U.S. citizenship. At the time, the only people allowed to apply for naturalization were "free white persons" and "aliens of African nativity and . . . persons of African descent." Ozawa was not of African nativity or descent, but he was, he argued, both assimilated with (White) American culture and White in appearance, tracing those of Japanese descent back to White forefathers.[5]

The court rejected this argument. Associate Justice George Sutherland, writing for the unanimous majority, explained that simple skin color was insufficient evidence of Whiteness. "[T]he test afforded by the mere color of the skin of each individual is impracticable," he wrote, "as that differs greatly among persons of the same race, even among Anglo-Saxons, ranging by imperceptible gradations from the fair blond to the swarthy brunette." Instead, "the federal and state courts, in an almost unbroken line, have held that the words 'white person' were meant to indicate only a person of what is popularly known as the Caucasian race."[6] To that point, a circuit court in Massachusetts had in 1909 allowed four Armenian men to become naturalized[7] after accepting their argument that they were Caucasian and therefore not subject to the exclusions that "applied usually to the yellow race."[8]

Sutherland admitted that "Caucasian" was not as clear a delineator as one might hope—"[c]ontroversies have arisen and will no doubt arise again in respect of the proper classification of individuals in border line cases"—but also argued that Ozawa clearly fell outside of the category. Ozawa's application for naturalization was rejected.

A few months later, Sutherland again had the opportunity to clarify what counted as "White" in the eyes of the federal government. Bhagat Singh Thind, born in India, applied for and was briefly granted citizenship. When his case made its way to the Supreme Court, though, it was again unanimously rejected, despite Thind arguing effectively that he was, as a matter of geographic fact, Caucasian.

Suddenly, that wasn't good enough. "The word 'Caucasian' not only was not employed in the law, but was probably wholly unfamiliar to the original framers of the statute in 1790," Sutherland wrote this time. ". . . [A]s used in the science of ethnology, the connotation of the word is by no means clear, and the use of it in its scientific sense as an equivalent for the words of the statute, other considerations aside, would simply mean the substitution of one perplexity for another."[9]

So, instead, Thind was measured against the nebulous perception of what constituted "White."

"[T]he term 'race' is one which, for the practical purposes of the statute, must be applied to a group of living persons now possessing in common the requisite characteristics, not to groups of persons who are supposed to be or really are descended from some remote common ancestor," Sutherland argued. ". . . It may be true that the blond Scandinavian and the brown Hindu have a common ancestor in the dim reaches of antiquity, but the average man knows perfectly well that there are unmistakable and profound differences between them today." In other words, he was White by the Ozawa standard but not by the seems-White standard.

The 1930 census records a Bhagat Singh Thind of the same age as the protagonist of the Supreme Court case living in San Francisco. His race is marked as "Hindu."

A PROJECTION ONLY AS STURDY AS ITS FOUNDATION

The idea that White Americans will soon constitute a minority of U.S. residents is entirely dependent on how you define "White." In 2060, the Census Bureau projects that about 179 million of the country's 404 million residents

CHART 92
The Increase in Hispanic Population Density

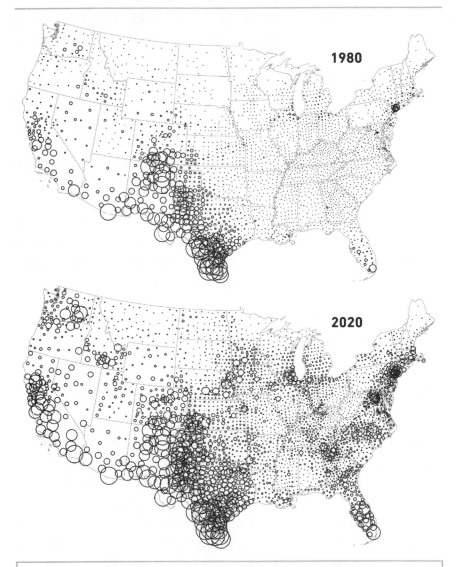

HOW TO READ THIS CHART The circles above correspond to the density of the Hispanic population per county, using data for 1980 from Pew Research Center's analysis of Census Bureau data and for 2020 from the bureau directly. The scale is the same on both maps, so a circle represents the same density on both versions. Notice the growth of the Hispanic population everywhere by 2020—but particularly in the Midwest, in the Pacific Northwest, and along the East Coast.

will be non-Hispanic Whites—about 44 percent. But, again, the bureau looks at race (e.g., White) and ethnicity (Hispanic) as separate measures. If you include Hispanic Whites, then 275 million residents will be White, two-thirds of the total. This distinction is not simply bookkeeping. It is, instead, one of the essential considerations for any discussion of how America's demography will change.

The country's Hispanic population in particular is at the center of the question of America's future diversity. From 2020 to 2060, the density of Hispanics in the population is expected to climb from 19 to 28 percent, the largest jump for any group. That would be a continuation of a trend. From 1980 to 2020, the number of counties in which the population was at least 10 percent Hispanic tripled; the number that were at least half Hispanic more than doubled.[10]

But, again, the census—then, now, in the future—records self-reported identity. A projection that Hispanics will make up an increasing percentage of the population depends on expectations about how those individuals identify themselves that might not hold up. What's more, the projection about when America will become majority minority depends on the at-times-iffy assumptions the government makes about the continuity of race between *familial* generations.

Pew Research Center has data that speak to that point. In 2017, it found that nearly all foreign-born Hispanic residents of the United States identified as Hispanic. But by the fourth generation—that is, the great-grandchildren of immigrants—only half did.[11] The identity was less common, perhaps because of intermarriage, perhaps because of assimilation. By the third generation, Pew reported at another point, grandchildren of immigrants were as likely to call themselves "Hispanic" as they were simply "American."[12]

The decline in the percentage of later-generation Hispanics who identify themselves as Hispanic or by their family's country of origin is roughly mirrored in research Heather Silber Mohamed conducted for her book *The New Americans?* She described the finding as being "consistent with existing scholarship that finds that given the stigma surrounding new arrivals, many established Latinos opt to distance themselves from their coethnics."[13] In other words, Silber Mohamed understood some of the shift to be driven by public perceptions of new Hispanic immigrants.

Americans who are not Hispanic or otherwise not obviously multiracial

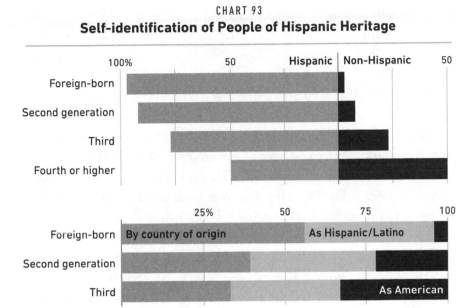

CHART 93
Self-identification of People of Hispanic Heritage

HOW TO READ THIS CHART The two sets of research by Pew (from 2017 and 2020) are shown as bar graphs. At top, lighter-color bars that extend to the left show the percentage of each generational group with some Hispanic ancestry that identifies as Hispanic. The darker-color bars that extend to the right show the percentage that doesn't identify that way. At bottom, a stacked bar graph displaying how self-identified Hispanics identify themselves most often.

might wonder how it is that someone could simply shift his racial identity. I can offer a personal example that illustrates the complexity. My wife's father is White and her mother Mexican and Native American. There's no inherent tension for her in this. It's just who she is. But when asked to identify her race, she is forced to pick; Erwin Schrödinger's cat can no longer exist in a state of uncertainty. Sometimes she identifies herself as Hispanic or White Hispanic. Sometimes she identifies herself as Native American. There's no real system to it, but, then, in those circumstances it's someone else who's making her decide.

The Census Bureau does tend to insist on such things, in its own way—but as is true with any survey, small changes in how it asks influence the results.[14] You'll remember that the bureau's 2020 questionnaire allowed respondents to provide much more detail on their racial backgrounds. In 2010, there were about 25 million more Hispanics who identified themselves as White alone than there were who identified themselves as White and some other race.[15] By 2020, after that change, 4 million more Hispanics identified as White and some other race than as White alone.[16]

This wasn't all a function of the change in the bureau's process, but it's a reminder of how categorization itself can influence our understanding of diversity—and how our understanding of diversity can influence categorization. How the results are presented also matters, of course. In this book, I've generally used "White" to refer to non-Hispanic Whites, then used "non-White" to refer to literally every other racial and ethnic combination. The bureau tends to do the same, meaning its discussion of the future of the country therefore often collapses into that same binary.

Sociologist Richard Alba has for years been considering how the country's demographic future will unfold and is someone who criticizes the bureau's approach to presenting its assessments of what it learns. While careful to note that the Census Bureau does a complicated task well, which is certainly true, Alba does take issue with its frequent majority-versus-minority framing. When the bureau announced in 2019 that most babies born in the United States were members of minority groups, for example, it depended on "a classification in which most mixed babies with a white parent are categorized as minority—not white, in other words," as Alba wrote in his book *The*

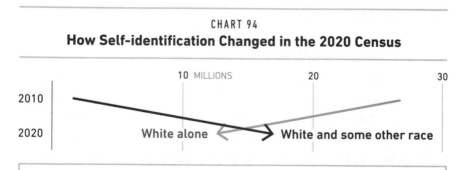

CHART 94
How Self-identification Changed in the 2020 Census

HOW TO READ THIS CHART The lines indicate the shift in the count of Hispanics who identify as White between the 2010 and 2020 censuses. The totals differ only slightly; there were about a million more Hispanic Whites in 2020 than in 2010. But there's a wide change in how they identify—or, at least, how they were recorded as identifying.

Great Demographic Illusion.[17] Again, maybe this seems right to you. But we've seen from Dowell Myers's research that this binary tends to exacerbate stress and frustration about immigration and the country's future.[18]

It's also necessarily simplistic. To demonstrate how this binary blurs a complex reality, Alba went through the more than 3 million birth certificates recorded in 2017, indexing the racial and ethnic identities of the child's parents. Most of those births involved parents of the same racial and ethnic group, including members of minority groups. About 15 percent, though, were births in which the parents didn't share the same background. The majority of those involved one White parent and one parent from a minority group.

Next, Alba looked at how 2017 parents actually reported their children's race or ethnicity when asked by the Census Bureau.[19] Most of the time, children of mixed-race couples were identified as mixed race or White instead of as members of minority groups. (This was particularly true for couples in which neither parent was Hispanic, since the Census Bureau asks about Hispanic ethnicity separately.[20] Children identified as mixed race and Hispanic would therefore be part of a minority group: Hispanic.) From this analysis, Alba estimates that 9 percent of children born in 2017 were born to one White parent and one parent who's a member of a minority group—and will be categorized by the Census Bureau as minorities.

"These babies are in between: they are both white and minority, with family roots on both sides of a still salient societal divide," Alba wrote. "In this respect, the idea that US babies are now mostly minority is an illusion fostered by arbitrary classification decisions." What's more, he added, "[b]ecause most of these prospective parents are already classified on the not-white side of a binary division, their children are likely to be classified this way as well."

Here, again, I can offer a specific example. My elder son was born in 2017 to a White father and a White Hispanic mother, a parental pairing that made up about 5 percent of births that year. He is fair complected and blond, with a truncated Anglo-Saxon last name.[21] But if he identifies as Hispanic or if we do on his behalf, presto. He's a minority.

"Anyone who's taken a college sociology course probably learned in the first week of Sociology 101 the distinction between ascriptive and achieved statuses," Alba said during a 2021 event on demography hosted by the American Enterprise Institute. "And that race was an ascriptive status, one that was a trait fixed over the life course and assigned at birth. Through much of our history that characterization of race has worked fairly well."[22] In an era with a far more diverse population, though, that distinction erodes.

WHO'S ALLOWED TO BE WHITE

Now we get into the more immediate question about the future of non-Whites in the United States. It's not just that self-identification shifts as time passes and families expand. There's also the question of when, if ever, particular groups are simply considered White. After all, we understand how people of eastern and southern European ancestry—like those Armenians in 1909—were incorporated into the country's sense of Whiteness. Can we expect that other currently understood boundaries will similarly break down?

"Hispanic" is already an "ambiguous category," Princeton University's Douglas Massey explained to me. Someone from Mexico is Hispanic. Is a Portuguese speaker from Brazil? A Spanish speaker from Spain? Massey points out that the group identity only emerged in the Census Bureau's assessments in 1970, in part after seeing how the civil rights movement established race-based protections for Black Americans.

Nonetheless, Massey's expectation is that it's "highly likely" that most Hispanics will assimilate into broader White America. Massey pointed to those rates of intermarriage between Whites and Hispanics, something that he identified as having been integral to the assimilation of eastern European groups. What's more, the country has seen a similar process centered on Hispanic immigrants in the past. There was a surge of migration from Mexico a century ago, the genesis of families that are no longer identifiably Hispanic. Mexican women married White men and took their husbands' names, for example, and Mexican families folded into White ones.

The most obvious remaining boundary is the one that's often most closely associated with race: skin color. In that first 1790 census, the government tallied the number of free White people, "other free persons," and the enslaved population. The boundary was drawn, with the juxtaposition to "White" being a largely homogeneous population of Black people. That boundary has through custom and care been maintained.

CHART 95
Frequency of Words in Published Books

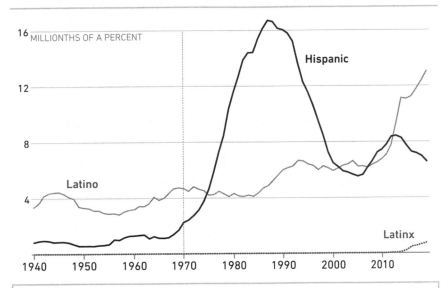

16 MILLIONTHS OF A PERCENT

Hispanic

12

8

Latino

4

Latinx

1940   1950   1960   1970   1980   1990   2000   2010

HOW TO READ THIS CHART An index of the frequency of various descriptors found in Google's scans of published books.[23] Use of "Hispanic" increased sharply after the term was added to the census in 1970. In recent years, "Latino" has become much more common.

Self-identification is the root of how government statisticians see you. The root of how everyone else sees you, however, is physical appearance. A key question in Massey's mind, therefore, is how variations in skin color might spur varying treatment for people from Latin America and Asia, populations we tend to categorize collectively. Phenotypically Black (that is, dark-skinned) Hispanics from Caribbean regions, for example, might see a different response than a light-skinned person from Venezuela.

Tanya Golash-Boza, a sociology professor at the University of California, Merced, pointed at the same dividing line and, in a 2006 paper, she made much the same point about Hispanics. "Those Latinos/as who appear 'white' and do not face discrimination are more likely to assimilate into U.S. society and become unhyphenated Americans," she wrote—meaning "Americans" instead of "Hispanic-Americans." "They, like immigrants from Europe, can disappear unnoticed into the melting pot, if they so choose."[24]

The paper included an interesting and important additional observation: Latinos who aren't perceived as White by others are more likely to face
discrimination. And discrimination, the research suggests, decreases the
likelihood of people *self-identifying* as White.

In another paper from 2008, Golash-Boza and coauthor William Darity,
Jr., explored this idea further. One of the more interesting data points they
highlighted involved research conducted as part of the 1989 Latino National
Political Survey in which respondents (all Hispanic, including people of
Mexican, Cuban, and Puerto Rican heritage) were asked to describe their
own race: White, Black, or something else. About 62 percent self-identified
as White; only about 2 percent identified as Black. What made this research
unusual, though, was that it also included a measure of the respondent's
observed skin color; that is, how light or dark skinned the interviewer *perceived* them to be. Even among those with the darkest observed skin color,
there was an impulse to self-identify as White.[25]

"As skin shade lightens, more and more respondents chose white as their

CHART 96
How People Self-identify vs. How Others See Them

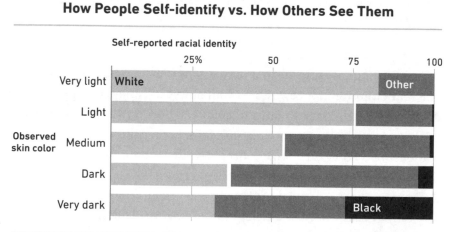

HOW TO READ THIS CHART These data from the 1989 Latino National Political Survey
compare how survey respondents viewed their own race (White, Black, or something
else in each set of bars) with how light or dark their skin was observed to be. So the
vast majority of respondents who were observed to have very light-colored skin
identified as White—but more respondents with very dark-colored skin identified as
White than as Black.

race," Golash-Boza and Darity wrote, "but significant proportions of darker-skinned respondents did so as well." Bear in mind that the "other" category in the research includes self-identification as "Hispanic" or "Latino," terms that were used more in subsequent years according to the researchers. But the findings, they write, indicate "a general . . . preference in 1989 to be identified as white." Among those who said they'd experienced discrimination, the prior research found, such a self-identification was less likely.

Speaking with me in 2021, Golash-Boza referred to the "capaciousness of Whiteness," an evocative way of describing the fluidity of the term as both a racial identity and a category with cultural and political significance. As Charles Mills put it in his book *The Racial Contract*, "Whiteness is not really a color at all, but a set of power relations."[26] Access to that space in the United States is often dependent on appearance, but appearance is not always the central consideration for how people identify any category to which they belong.

THE EYE OF THE BEHOLDER

For their book *The Diversity Paradox*, authors Jennifer Lee and Frank Bean conducted numerous interviews with parents of different racial backgrounds, exploring how they identified their children's race and what they expected over the long term.

"Many Asian-white and Latino-white couples who recognize and identify their children as multiracial or multi-ethnic feel nonetheless that the sheer force of incorporation into the non-Hispanic white culture is so powerful that their children will soon adopt a white or American identity," they write, "regardless of how hard they try to instill in them a multiracial or multi-ethnic culture and identity." But, they wrote, this was less true of Black parents. "Although they, too, recognize the multiracial backgrounds of their children, they are more likely to identify their children as black, in part because they claim that others identify them as such. Whereas the Asian-white, Latino-white, and Asian-Latino couples believe that their children will soon identify as white or American, none of the black intermarried couples identified their children as white, nonblack, or simply American, suggesting that the incorporative power of intermarriage operates differently for blacks than it does for Asians or Latinos."[27]

If we are to consider the political and cultural implications of a more diverse American population, we can't simply focus on the likelihood that the Census Bureau's projections will match future self-identities. We must also more immediately understand how other Americans are likely to identify them.

In our conversation, Golash-Boza used a specific example that illustrated the fungibility of "Hispanic" as a racial identity. "Here in Merced, it's certainly the case that darker-skinned Latinos do face more discrimination and people who work in lower-level jobs are more likely to be darker skinned," she said. "At the same time, though, there are people who live here, identify very strongly as Mexican American, are racialized as Mexican American in their everyday life"—meaning that they are treated like Mexican Americans—"but if they were in Washington, D.C., which is where I'm from, they would not be read as Hispanic and therefore they wouldn't face discrimination on the basis of their racial identity."

The Supreme Court's ruling in *United States v. Bhagat Singh Thind* notwithstanding, race is not like pornography; you don't necessarily know it when you see it.[28] Sociologist Wendy Roth, writing in 2016, uses the example of a New Yorker named Salvador, who is Puerto Rican. He's dark skinned, she writes, but classifies himself as White when prompted because of his complicated racial background and due to a lack of what he views as a more fitting option. Salvador assumes that people view him as Hispanic, given his name and accent, but as Roth points out, it will likely be a perception that he's Black that has the most direct effect on his life. His identity is a situational blend of how he sees himself, how others see him, how he assumes people see him, how he understands his heritage to determine his identity, and how he describes himself in official categorizations. Race, Roth writes, can "be thought of as something specific to each moment and each act of observing."[29]

There's a parallel here to generational identities that bears elevating. Most people have at least a broad sense of what generation they belong to, though some, born in marginal years, might be a bit flummoxed. Rarely if ever is that identity a central concern, anything that we think about or that is presented to us as an urgent question to answer. Sometimes, however, it can be a point of focus or negative attention: trying to avoid being labeled as a Gen X slacker or a flighty and avocado-toast-obsessed millennial. Sometimes, we can be labeled with a generation that we *know* is inaccurate but that an observer chooses to apply nonetheless. The "OK boomer" taunts didn't come from people who'd checked birth years on driver's licenses. They were reacting to demonstrated traits *attributed* to boomers. You see the parallels with race—down to the arbitrary delineations of the generations themselves.

The stakes for racial identity and perception, obviously, are far higher. A conclusion of Golash-Boza and Darity's research, remember, was the determination that discrimination against Hispanics decreases self-identification as White. Research from New York University sociologist Maria Abascal indicates that a corollary to that is also true:[30] outside observers primed to focus on America's increasing diversity (itself often a trigger for a negative reaction[31]) are less likely to categorize racially ambiguous people as White. Membership to that important political and cultural category is revoked when the perceived exclusivity of the group is threatened. The effect, Abascal found, "is actually much stronger among the kinds of people who we would suspect would be more threatened by this demographic information—that is, people who voted for Trump, people who identify as Republican."

Separate research published in 2015 by a team made up of Census Bureau staff and a sociology professor at the University of Minnesota offers a different lens for the question of third-party identification. In each census, some responses are provided by proxies for the residents at an address, people identified as being able to backfill information about residents if the bureau repeatedly finds that it can't reach anyone at the home. (Neighbors, for example.) The research team took proxy reports from 2000 and 2010 and compared them with the self-identification offered by the address's residents in the other census. In other words, if you weren't available in 2010 and your neighbor spoke to the bureau as your proxy, the researchers then compared the neighbor's description of your racial identity to the one you offered in 2000.

In 90 percent of cases, the categorizations matched. Those who identified as non-Hispanic White, Black, or Asian were generally identified in the same way by the proxies. Other identities led to different results.

"For black-white biracials, we found that proxy mismatches follow lines predicted by the one-drop-rule of hyperdescent; black-whites are often reported as black," the researchers reported. "Non-matched response for other single race groups (non-Hispanic American Indians, Asians, and Pacific

Islanders) were more often white than minority." The researchers ascribed this to a combination of factors, including that "centuries of interracial unions have created some people who may seem phenotypically white," though the people identify with other groups. They also note the possibility that the proxy and the resident hadn't discussed race, which "might lead them to assume the person is white."[32] (You'll recall Robert W. Terry's phrase: "To be white in America is not to have to think about it.")

One of the more interesting findings was that younger residents were more likely to be identified as multiracial than older residents, something that the researchers hypothesized was a function of observers being aware of the increasing occurrence of interracial marriages. A possible implication is that if too few older people are categorized in that way and too many younger people are, this might artificially lower the average age of the country's multiracial population. After all, if a 40-year-old father of mixed race is categorized by a proxy as White and his 14-year-old daughter, who shares his racial composition, is categorized as multiracial, the multiracial group gains one teenager and no adults for its total. Continue that pattern broadly? The average drops. Perceptions change.

THE PAST MAY NOT BE PROLOGUE

What's important as we consider the tensions and boundaries of the country moving forward is not how Roth's exemplar Salvador identifies his race but how everyone else does. It correlates to a line from Abascal's research: "Threats need not be objective—merely perceived—to be consequential." So what about the oft-mentioned historical analogy, those southern and eastern Europeans who successfully crossed the boundary from non-White to White a century ago? Might that not still be a possible trajectory for this evolution, one that blankets the benefits of Whiteness broadly?

In 2012, researchers Cybelle Fox and Thomas A. Guglielmo argued that it likely wasn't. The idea that immigrants from Italy or Greece were at some point considered non-White, they argue, is flawed. "[N]o boundary separated [southern and eastern Europeans, or SEEs] from whites; SEEs were not widely recognized as nonwhite, nor was such a boundary institutionalized," they write. "In fact, where white was a meaningful category, SEEs were virtually always included within it. . . . One could be considered both white (color) and racially inferior to other whites," they continue.[33] This is of course not to say that there were no negative effects from this distinction. Historian David Roediger wrote that "[w]hen Greeks suffered as victims of an Omaha 'race' riot in 1909, and when eleven Italians died at the hands of lynchers in Louisiana in 1891, their less-than-white racial status mattered alongside their nationalities."[34]

Put another way, there wasn't just one boundary between White and non-White, but many, enforced in different ways in different contexts. The treatment of these Europeans was also distinct from how immigrants from Mexico were treated at the time—a much blurrier situation that echoes Golash-Boza's depiction of Merced today.

"Mexicans might be considered white in one town and not in another," Fox and Guglielmo explain: "white in Santa Barbara in 1880 but not in the same city in 1920, white for the purposes of naturalization law but not for the school board, or white for the 1920 census but not for the 1930 one." As is probably obvious, these were often explicit connections between political capacity and racial categorization. The spectrum of "White" is, often, a spectrum of granted power. Toward one end, the Connecticut family tracing its roots through Plymouth Rock. Toward the other, a Black resident of Birmingham in 1950. Arrayed between, America, slotted into position based, among other things, on wealth and background and, of course, skin color.

When the 1930 census first included that category for "Mexican," the instructions to enumerators were explicit in recognizing the fluidity of the term: "Practically all Mexican laborers are of a racial mixture difficult to classify, though usually well recognized in the localities where they are found," census takers were told.[35] Even Massey's question of how intermarriage muted Mexican identity is subject to a chicken-egg problem: "Were these Mexicans categorized as White because they married Anglos? Or could they marry Anglos because they were racially categorized as White?"

Over the long term, the effect was the same. Roediger, who has written extensively on the process by which immigrants were assimilated into the White mainstream, summarized the effect concisely in a phone conversation. "Over time, as intermarriages proliferate," he said, "if you take the German Irish and then German Irish Italian and German Irish Italian Polish family, it really doesn't make as much sense for them to identify with a specific ethnicity as it does for them to identify as White in this situation."

That said, his expectations aren't exactly sanguine. "Taking history seriously . . . calls into question the proposition that demographic trends can easily be extrapolated into the future to predict racial change," he wrote in his book *Colored White: Transcending the Racial Past*. "Not only do trends shift, but the very categories that define race can also change dramatically. The idea that 'crossbreeding' will disarm racism is at least 140 years old."[36] Whiteness isn't that simple.

"We simply do not know what racial categories will be in 2060," Roediger later wrote, adding that "[t]he answer to whether there might be 77 million, or fewer, or three times that many, Latinos in 2100 will be decided historically and politically, not just demographically."

Duke University sociologist Eduardo Bonilla-Silva has speculated that the country might be expected to move from being stratified biracially— Black vs. White—to a triracial system "comprised of 'whites' at the top, an intermediary group of 'honorary whites' . . . and a nonwhite group or the 'collective black' at the bottom."[37] In our conversation, Roediger agreed that a restructuring of power would still likely leave Black Americans (and those perceived to be Black) out of the equation: "If we're going to look 40 years down the road, absent some kind of a social movement or social transformation, none of what we're talking about here really addresses the plight of the majority of Black Americans."

The poles of Whiteness are sturdy. Everything else is more fragile.

WHERE WE ARE HEADING AND WHO'S GOING

In future decades, we can anticipate an American population that in measure and manifestation is less centered on White people. What we can't foresee is how much of the political and cultural value of being White seeps into groups that now wouldn't generally be considered White or who now wouldn't consider themselves White. We can assume that the Census Bureau's projections of America's future demography are overly rigid, but we can't assume that we know how they should be loosened.

Again, and important for the discussion of politics that we're about to begin, a key part of the tension of the moment is the fact that the future remains uncertain. In our conversation, Massey centralized the perceived threat among members of his own generation.

"Most of the reaction against what people will talk about as the changing racial and ethnic composition in the United States, most of that's concentrated in the baby boomer generation," he said. "I'm a baby boomer. When I graduated from high school in 1970, entire sectors of the job market were reserved for White males like me. Women were out of the labor force and out of the professions. Blacks were about 10 or 11 percent of the population, segregated, out of sight. Latinos were only 4.7 percent of the population. Asians are less than 1 percent of the population. It was a really different world." The America into which the baby boom was born and in which it grew up has changed.[38] The generation's influence has waned as that change has occurred, and the two conflate. As Massey said of the demographic change, with some understatement, "I think that there's a lot of reaction against that."

For how long? To what scale? How might the political power centralized in being White—power that's not any more evenly distributed than the baby boomers' wealth—be doled out? Or will allies be recruited to rise to its defense?

Sociologist Richard Alba summarized the problem moving forward by neatly describing the present. "The enduring paradox of the U.S.," he said, "is the combination of racism for some and assimilation for others."[39]

The uncertainty lies in how those allocations are balanced.

9

A New American Politics

On paper, they seem quite similar. Both Alex Lee and Saurabh Sharma are children of immigrants from Asia. Lee's parents immigrated from Hong Kong before his birth; Sharma's from India shortly after. The fathers of both worked in technology. Both attended state universities—the University of California, Davis, and the University of Texas at Austin, respectively—and both then soon fell into the world of politics. At 25, Lee in 2021 became one of the youngest members of California's state assembly in nearly 80 years. At 23, Sharma founded an organization aimed at preparing young people for government service.

Both even identify similar problems that politics might address, including college debt and housing. But then, when considering responses, a seemingly uncrossable gulf emerges. Lee is a progressive who describes his political affiliation as Democratic Socialist. Sharma is a right-wing conservative—and a 2021 Publius Fellow at the Claremont Institute—for whom a traditional party label is similarly too moderate. Ask Lee how to reduce college debt and he advocates for reducing costs on the front end, including ancillary expenses like rent that can strain resources. Ask Sharma and he argues that fewer people should go to college, that it should once again be a "luxury commodity" that is not seen as a necessary benchmark for success. And, further, that it's not a great idea to "extend adolescence well into someone's twenties," given how that delays family formation and pushes women up against biological barriers to childbirth.

Lee and Sharma are extreme representatives of their generation, certainly. But how do we understand the gulf between them? What is it that made Lee Lee and Sharma Sharma? Is it the difference between growing up in California's Bay Area and suburban Dallas? Is it familial? Socioeconomic?

Sharma explains that his political emergence was intertwined with the 2016 presidential primary. He had just started college and, unlike most of his friends, stayed in Austin for the summer to add credits more quickly.

"I was watching a lot of YouTube videos," Sharma told me. "I watched a lot of Trump rallies. I watched a lot of Bernie Sanders's interviews." He said that he found a lot of what both candidates had to say compelling— both the leftist Vermont senator and the right-wing businessman who'd go on to win the presidency that year. "I sort of slipped into more kind of institutionalist or traditional right-wing institutions as part of my tangible political involvement as I got more involved," Sharma said, "but that was really my genesis, being very interested in the scene of both populist left and right."

Don't be misled by that reference to YouTube videos. Sharma is the sort of person who casually uses words like "salubrious" and "deracinated" in an impromptu conversation. In the case of his awakening, the medium is, largely, the message: Sharma was exploring politics through his own lens, at his own pace, again in keeping with others in his age cohort. The play button is their Walter Cronkite.

Where Sharma wound up, though, is far more unusual for someone his age. Most young Americans are much more liberal than Sharma if not necessarily as liberal as Lee, a fact that both readily admitted and that both see as a challenge to the political right as the years pass. But this belief, a common one, underappreciates how the electorate is changing and may change further as younger-than-boomer generations age into power.

THE END OF THE VOTER BOOM

The first president for whom baby boomers could vote was Richard Nixon. It's simple math: 1946 (the year the boom began) plus 21 is 1967. By the time Nixon was up for reelection, though, the electorate was joined not by four more years of baby boomers but by seven. The passage and ratification of the Twenty-Sixth Amendment in 1971 lowered the federal voting age to 18, increasing the number of Americans newly eligible to vote from a bit over 10 million in 1964 to more than 24 million eight years later.

Lowering the minimum voting age is often attributed to the Vietnam War, that young people were being plucked from their homes and dropped into Khe Sanh in defense of a democracy from which they themselves were excluded. But once again it's hard not to recognize the effect of the scale of the baby boom itself. In 1954, less than 6 percent of those over the age of 17 were aged 18 to 20. By 1971, more than 8 percent were. It was a group by then acclimated to unusual cultural power[1] and a group that by the late 1960s was regularly using its size to increase its volume on national political issues. By the time they got the franchise, young Americans had already presented a mature political voice at scale.

When the amendment was ratified, it wasn't clear what might result. Younger voters already didn't vote at the same rate as older ones and there was reason to think that these newly enfranchised voters—many of whom had developed a robust skepticism of government—might not turn out heavily. Sure enough, only about half of eligible 18- to 24-year-olds cast ballots in 1972. (By comparison, about 7 in 10 eligible 45- to 64-year-olds did.)[2] But that was more a function of age than generation. By 1984, baby boomers constituted a plurality of votes cast in federal elections, a position they have retained relative to other generations ever since.

We cannot say with certainty when that preeminence will collapse. Pew Research Center's analysis of the 2016 and 2020 elections found that the density of baby boomer voters held steady at 36 percent between those two years, with gains among younger voters (particularly Gen Z) being offset by the decline of members of the silent generation.[3] It seems likely, however, that there will be more voters in 2024 from the millennial generation and younger than there will be from the baby boom.

There are currently more adult millennials than there are baby boomers, at least using Pew's definitions. Add in the adult members of Generation Z and the gap grows. Yet in 2020, Pew's estimate is that 20 percent more boomers voted than members of the millennial or Z generations. Fewer people, but more votes.

"The Republican Party's competitiveness this century has really been propped up by differential turnout rates between younger and older voters," David Faris, author and Roosevelt University associate professor, told me.

CHART 97
The Boom as Percentage of the Electorate, Past and Present

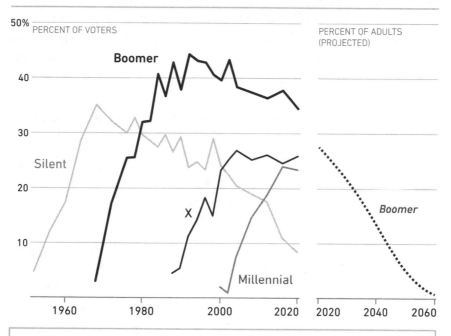

HOW TO READ THIS CHART   Consider the two graphs above to be something of a before and after for the 2020 election. At left, the composition of the electorate according to the American National Election Study for each available year from 1952 to 2020. (This includes some midterm elections, which explains the sawtooth effect on the baby boomer curve.) At right, the percentage of adults the baby boom is projected to include over the following 40 years. (From 2046 on, this percentage includes everyone over the age of 100 as a baby boomer, as the Census Bureau projections on which the data are based don't break down age by birth year for that age range.)

Notice the difference between the boomer percentage of the electorate in 2020 and its percentage of the population as shown in the right-hand graph: the former is much larger. Part of this is a function of comparing apples to oranges, since the ANES survey is measuring something different than the Census Bureau. Part of it, too, is that older voters vote more heavily and baby boomers are increasingly at the older end of the adult population, so they make up more of the voter pool than the public.

Shortly before the 2020 election, he'd written an essay for *The Washington Post* in which he argued that the Republican position with younger voters was worse than the party might acknowledge.[4] To his point about turnout, a rough estimate of the differential to which Faris referred suggests that the

Democratic presidential candidate would have netted about 3 million additional votes in 2016 and 2020 had voters under 30 turned out at the same rate as those aged 65 and up.[5]

This isn't some marker of apathy—at least, not an *unusual* one. It has consistently been the case that younger Americans are less likely to vote. ANES data show that millennial and Gen Z voters are registered to vote and actually vote at rates that are consistent with prior generations at the same age, if not slightly better.

Michael McDonald of the University of Florida publishes estimates of

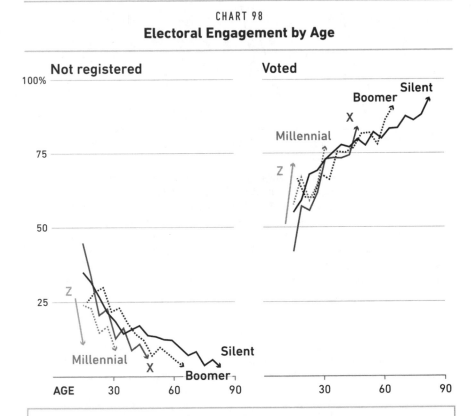

CHART 98
Electoral Engagement by Age

HOW TO READ THIS CHART The ANES asks respondents if they are registered to vote and, if so, whether they voted in the most recent election. Above, I've plotted those responses[6] for adults in the middle of each generational range over time (for example, for baby boomers born in 1955). As members of each generation age, the percentage who aren't registered to vote falls and the number who vote rises.

turnout based on Census Bureau data. In 2000, about 35 percent of voters under the age of 30 turned out to vote in the presidential election. In 2008, 48 percent did. By 2020, the figure was over 50 percent. Over that same period, though, older voters also increased their turnout rates, neutralizing some of the effect. On average, voters aged 60 and above have turned out about 28 percentage points more heavily in presidential election years and about 36 points more heavily during midterms since 1986. That's Faris's differential turnout.

CHART 99
The Difference Between Population and Voting-Eligible Population

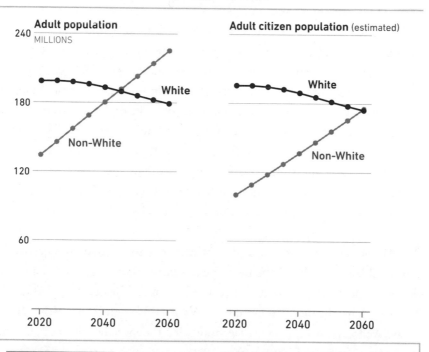

HOW TO READ THIS CHART The two graphs above compare the projected demography of the total adult population (according to Census Bureau estimates) with the population of adult citizens. In each case, we're working with future estimates that may not hold up, as explored in chapter 8. In the second graph, though, we're overlaying a separate assumption that naturalization rates will continue to be what they were in 2019, when nearly two-thirds of White immigrants were naturalized compared to just under half of non-Whites. In other words, consider these as the possible future scenarios that they're intended to represent.

As has hopefully been made clear by now, the transition to an electorate made up of a greater number of currently young Americans is a transition to an electorate that is less heavily White. But there's a hitch. According to the Census Bureau's projections, non-Whites (with all of the previously mentioned qualifiers that phrase demands) will be a majority of the country's adult population by 2045.[7] As sociologist Richard Alba pointed out to me, though, if the existing naturalization rates hold, they will not be a majority of the adult *citizen* population—and therefore its voting-eligible population— for more than a decade after that.

"What that implies is that Whites are going to be the effective political majority of the nation quite a bit longer than they are even if their numbers go exactly as the Census Bureau projects," Alba said. "They would still be the political majority past midcentury."

Shortly before the 2020 election, the left-leaning Center for American Progress published a lengthy examination of the future American electorate, exploring what demographic trends suggested about the country's political future. As part of that research, the authors (including demographer William Frey) estimated the percentage of eligible voters in each state in both that year's election and 2036 who would be non-White or members of one of the country's youngest generations. In each state, those percentages increased, with the percentage of millennial, Gen Z, and younger voters making up more than half of the electorate. In nine states, the number of non-White voters was projected to pass the 25 percent mark; in three it was projected to reach or pass 50 percent.[8]

Above, we have a discussion of whens, not ifs. When younger voters replace older ones. When the median American voter will be someone who doesn't identify exclusively as White non-Hispanic. The question that comes next is perhaps the more important one: When this likely future arrives, then what? We focus on who's in the electorate, but the more important indicator, of course, is how they actually vote.

ARE NOW-YOUNG VOTERS GOING TO VOTE DEMOCRATIC FOREVER?

David Faris's point about younger voters wasn't just that the imbalance in turnout between them and older voters defined electoral results. It was that

CHART 100
Change in State Electorates by 2036

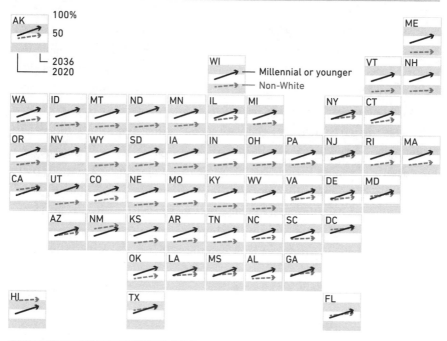

HOW TO READ THIS CHART A state-level look at how the density of non-White (dotted arrow) and currently young (solid arrow) populations are expected to increase between 2020 and 2036. States are roughly placed according to their actual locations, though the density of small states in the Northeast makes that tricky.

the imbalance *combined* with the sharply Democratic politics of the younger generation was skewing politics.

"If current trends continue, you've got the eighteen to twenty-nine demographic that voted for Biden by something like thirty points," Faris told me. "You can build in a little bit of erosion of that, but that's still a huge problem for Republicans because what's happening is you've got this natural demographic churn. The GOP has its greatest strength with voters over forty-five. The ones who are over sixty-five are going to pass away at some point and they will be replaced in the voting pool by much more liberal voters."

The Center for American Progress concurred. "By 2028," William Frey explained to me, "the Democrats are in hand, not just in the popular vote but the Electoral College vote because they take things like Georgia, Arizona, North Carolina, possibly Florida, and may slightly hang on to the purple states in the Midwest."

This is the path the electorate is on now—but the electorate does have a habit of taking unexpected detours. In this case, the momentum being described depends on those younger voters continuing to back Democrats like Joe Biden by wide margins.

What's happened in recent years with younger voters is exceptional. Pew calculates the partisanship of generations over time. For groups older than millennials, party identity has been fairly evenly split. For millennials, it's a Democratic blowout. The widest partisan gap seen among generations older than millennials since 1994 was the silent generation's 12 points in 2007. From 2006 to 2019, the gap for millennials was never narrower than 15.

What might also jump out at you in that data is the slow narrowing of the partisan identity gap among baby boomers. There's a popular assumption

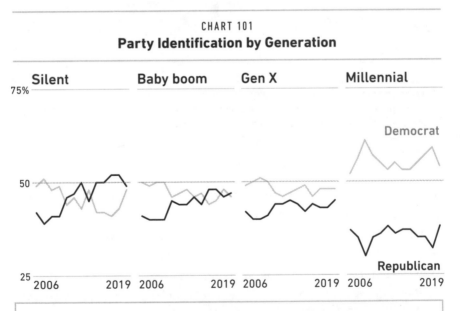

CHART 101
Party Identification by Generation

HOW TO READ THIS CHART Each line represents Pew Research Center's estimate for the percentage of each generation that identifies as Democrat, Republican, or an independent who leans toward one party or the other.[9] The figures for 2019 are a combination of both 2018 and 2019.

that people become more politically conservative as they age, which would obviously be significant to the future of millennial politics—but the chart doesn't actually demonstrate that. For one reason, starting at 2006 is misleading. It was a moment in which the backlash against the Iraq War and various scandals within the Republican Party powered an unusually strong Democratic performance that carried into 2008. But it's not just the chart. The idea that young left-leaning voters will eventually transform into old right-leaning ones isn't well rooted in evidence.

"We always had this vague idea of the young people being more liberal and older people being more conservative," Columbia University political scientist Andrew Gelman told me when we spoke by phone one evening in early 2021. "But at least when it comes to voting for Democrats and Republicans, it didn't used to be that way." The liberalism of the baby boom in the 1960s evolving into the more conservative electorate of the moment, he said, is "an interesting case of reality catching up to the stereotype."

I'd called Gelman because of research he'd done into the question of the stability of partisan identity. He and two colleagues, Yair Ghitza of the data firm Catalist and Jonathan Auerbach of George Mason University, looked at how political views have evolved relative to birth year since before the baby boom, comparing party preference to political experiences (as indicated by presidential approval ratings) over time. What they found was that the formation of presidential voting preferences was most heavily centered on the period from age 14 to 24. "At the height of their influence, around the age of 18," they write, political "events are nearly three times as meaningful [in forming voting preferences] as those later in life."[10]

Consider someone born in 1952, near the front half of the baby boom. Their most formative years were between 1966 and 1976, a Democrat-friendly period that began with Lyndon Johnson's relative popularity and ended with Richard Nixon's massive unpopularity. The Reagan administration then slowly pulled them back to the right, though by then they were out of the age range when events were most influential, and so the pull was relatively modest. Someone born in 1968, however, hit her formative years in 1982, carried through Ronald Reagan's second term and through George H. W. Bush's mostly well-received administration. She would be expected to have a more Republican-friendly view of politics.

Then consider millennials. Someone born in 1993 would have hit 14 right

CHART 102

Influence of Political Events on Voting Patterns by Age

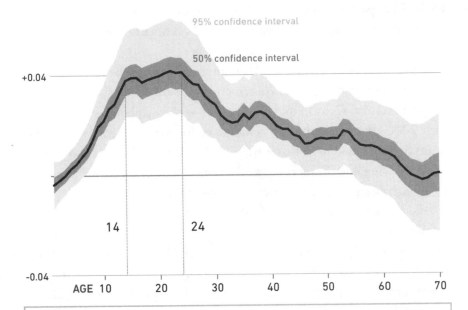

+0.08 AGE-SPECIFIC WEIGHTS

95% confidence interval

50% confidence interval

+0.04

14   24

-0.04

AGE 10   20   30   40   50   60   70

> **HOW TO READ THIS CHART** The curve above shows the varying importance of political events in forming long-term presidential voting preferences by year of age. A higher value for a year is one in which political events are more important in forming those views. Since this is a statistical model, confidence intervals are shown, ranges in which 50 or 95 percent of outcomes would be expected to fall.

as George W. Bush's approval ratings were collapsing and reached 24 just as Donald Trump's unpopular administration was beginning. "I don't know that I can think of the last time we've had that," Gelman told me when we spoke early in Biden's term, "two presidents of the same party being so unpopular for so long." In between was Barack Obama, whose approval ratings weren't exceptional but were far better than Bush's in 2007 or Trump's in 2017, particularly with younger Americans.

It didn't get much better after that, as David Faris pointed out in our conversation. "If a Republican president is in power and things are going well, presumably folks turning eighteen that year would have a more favorable view of the party, because that's just when they're starting to pay attention," he said. "What I think should really, really concern the Republican Party is that that did not happen in the first three years of the Trump administration—take Covid out of this. They never made inroads with these voters, even though the economy was booming and it was mostly a good time." Of course, it might similarly worry the left that younger voters were not particularly enamored of Joe Biden's first two years in office either.[11]

It's not as though there's *no* movement after age 24. The effects grow smaller, but they're still there. "[D]espite the decline—and the fact that a generation's preferred party is all but locked-in by 40—we find political events continue to influence voter preferences," Gelman and his colleagues write. "The age weights only return to zero around age 60." (So: baby boomers are probably not going to start switching parties.)

"The finding is fairly clear that by the time you're toward the end of your twenties, your partisanship moves very, very slowly over time," Columbia's Donald P. Green told me. Green has done extensive work both on political voting behavior and political campaigning. "It's not that it's immutable, or the unmoved mover or any of that kind of nonsense, but it moves so gradually that that kind of change we're talking about, appreciable change, where you switch parties or you move from a resolute partisan to an independent, is unlikely."

Singling out and measuring partisanship and presidential vote preference also misses nuance, as Green pointed out. "You might be surprised, if you looked at the public opinion profile of young people, how ideologically heterodox this otherwise largely liberal group is," he pointed out. "There are some specific issue positions in which young people are quite distinctive—for example, LGBT equality—but on other issues they're not."

In the future, then, it may be the case that younger voters hold fervent liberal views on a number of issues—but are more moderate on other questions. If it's the former issues and not the latter that serve as litmus tests for supporting a candidate, the road will be rockier for a politician hoping to focus on those more moderate views.

"That eighteen- to thirty-five-year-old crowd, we have no hold over. We have no sway with them." That was the assessment of Michael Steele, the former chairman of the Republican Party who'd worked to broaden the appeal of the party in the era prior to Donald Trump—unsuccessfully in the case of the demographic to which he was referring.

"These folks are a whole different breed. They don't look at politics the way my generation or your generation did. There's no way," Steele said. He pointed to the example of the activism that emerged in the wake of the mass shooting at a high school in Parkland, Florida, on Valentine's Day 2018. "They weren't defeated by the narrative. They leaned into it and pushed back against it and challenged the state legislature. You're looking at twentysome-things and early thirtysomethings beginning to run for elective office and heading up organizations, grassroots organizations—how do you think that materializes over the next few years? That's going to have a profound impact on public policy, it's going to have a profound impact on our economy. And they're going to be looking at the people who are weighing down their future and they won't want to be part of that."

Running for elective office? Yes. Amanda Litman cofounded the orga-nization Run for Something in 2017 with the aim of expanding the number of young people who were seeking elective office. (Which word of the orga-nization's name gets the emphasis highlights a different part of its mandate.) A key motivation for young people to do so, Litman told me, was a sense that "these are older leaders who do not understand the problems that me, my friends, my peers, my generation are facing." The drive wasn't just having younger leaders for the sake of generational diversity. Instead, she said, it was that "the lack of young people in the room is really affecting the policy out-comes in a way that's fucking over young people."

Heading up organizations? Yes. Melissa Deckman, a political science professor at Washington College, has done extensive research on activism among members of Generation Z in particular, finding not only a heightened level of activism but particularly among young women.

"Their formative socialization experiences are not just growing up in the Trump era," she told me, "but it's growing up as a lockdown generation.[12] They have lived these gun drills." Involvement in the response to Parkland "introduced them to what political organizing was. Many of them talk about climate change and the impact of Greta Thunberg and these climate strikes."

It's not only that the generation's formative years have overlapped with ones in which Republican leaders have been so unappealing to them (to Gelman's point). They have also overlapped with numerous large-scale leftist movements, including #MeToo and Black Lives Matter, which attracted and drew energy from younger Americans. The activism on the right, where it existed, was largely either reactionary or some flavor of Trumpism. "This is a key point," David Faris told me: "Every year that Republicans don't make inroads with eighteen-year-olds, then their overall position with the electorate gets worse."

There have been concerted—or at least well-resourced—efforts to entice young Americans to embrace the political right. There's an entire galaxy of groups focused on energizing young conservatives and building their ranks. The best known is likely Turning Point USA, which leveraged the high public profile of founder Charlie Kirk to vacuum up nearly $40 million in 2020.[13] Other groups include the Young America's Foundation, the Leadership Institute, and the now-defunct group Generation Opportunity, funded by the prominent conservative donors Charles and David Koch.[14] Those efforts, often tapping into demand from right-wing donors for some counterweight to the left's dominance with younger voters, don't seem to have made much of a dent. Representative Dan Crenshaw (R-Texas), elected to Congress in 2018 at the age of 34, has held summits aimed at encouraging young people to get engaged in conservative politics. Attendees at the 2021 iteration were encouraged to apply online, though only those in the on-the-nose 14-to-24 age group were welcomed.[15]

"What Dan is trying to do is incredibly admirable," Representative Peter Meijer (R-Michigan) told me when we spoke in 2021. "He's trying to communicate conservatism in a way that is—" He stopped himself. "He's actually trying to communicate it! There's an ideology there. Turning Point, I mean—it's a bit more reactionary. There's not actually anything underpinning it. It's filling a vacuum, but not really filling it."

Meijer—elected in 2020 at age 32—was pointing at the broader divide in his party between traditional political advocacy and the proto-authoritarian celebration of Trumpism that had defined the GOP since 2016. He was one of the few Republican legislators who voted to impeach Donald Trump after the violence at the Capitol, a decision that ultimately doomed his chances of being renominated by his party in 2022. He also criticized the party's establishment for its dearth of a platform, made obvious when, in 2020, it simply declined to outline any policy goals beyond support for Trump.

"There's no question that Democrats have better font choice or more stylized, Canva-centric graphic design, and better use of social media," Meijer said. (Canva is a user-friendly graphic-design program.) "I think the idea that the youth can't be persuaded is a false one. You need to have a compelling pitch, and I don't think that compelling pitch is being made."

Meanwhile, Run for Something's Amanda Litman and Melissa Deckman see an enormous amount of energy and organizing among young people on the left, particularly young women.

"For Gen Z women, this youngest cohort, they're far more confident about politics, they're far more interested," Deckman said. "If they continue to participate at higher levels than their male counterparts, we're going to see politics go definitely in a leftward direction." In Pew's assessments of the partisanship of the millennial generation, women are *far* more likely to identify as Democratic than are men.

Then there's that second shift in the population. *White* male millennials are actually more likely to be Republican than Democrat. It's perhaps the only bright spot for the right within that generation at the moment. But there are a lot fewer White males in the population of Americans who are millen-

CHART 103
Party Identification Among Millennial Demographic Groups

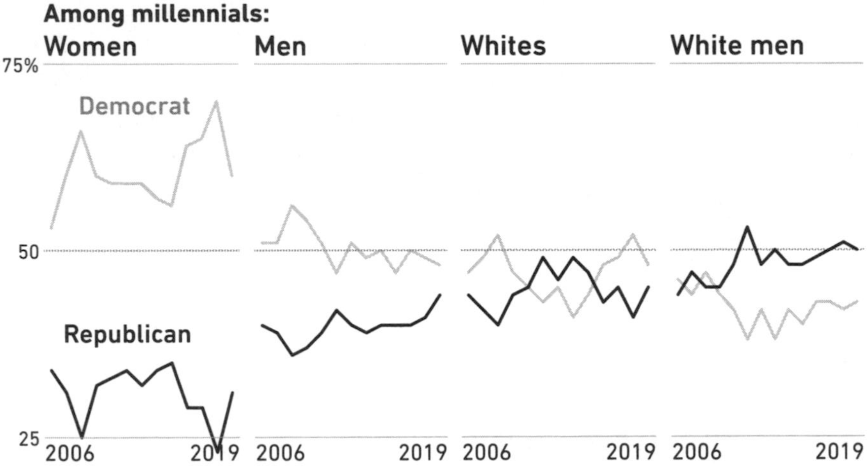

HOW TO READ THIS CHART Similar data as in the prior graph, but specific to members of the millennial generation. Again, the figures for 2019 are a combination of both 2018 and 2019.

nial age or younger (27 percent of the total, according to the Census Bureau) than in the group that is baby boomer aged or older (34 percent).[16]

This is where you slap your forehead and say, *Of course!* We can't talk about whether young people will remain consistent Democratic voters without talking about whether *non-Whites* will remain consistent Democratic voters.

Chris Warshaw is a political science professor at George Washington University. We spoke in 2021 about his observations about the consistency of ideology, thoughts that we'll get to in more depth a bit later in this chapter. But he highlighted the question of race in analysis of how young people vote in an appreciably succinct way.

"It is true that young people are disproportionately Democratic," Warshaw told me. "Often in the exit polls you see simple breakdowns like young people versus old people that are heavily confounded by race." If young people maintain consistent Democratic allegiances, it aids the party, he said, then adding a cautionary note: "It also isn't inevitable, given a lot of that actually is race, not age."

Which raises a much trickier question.

THE BIG-TENT PARTY SPRINGS SOME LEAKS

A crowd of several hundred people attending a rally in support of Donald Trump's 2020 reelection campaign were presented with what could fairly be described as an atypical speaker for a Republican campaign rally: a Latino UFC fighter sporting a mullet and a gold-and-black Adidas tracksuit. Not that the audience was surprised; the venue was Jorge Masvidal's gym.

Masvidal was there to introduce the president's son Donald Trump, Jr., but began by telling his own family's story. Casually slouched over the lectern, mouth close to the microphone, Masvidal described his father's six-day journey from Cuba to Florida in an inner tube at the age of 14.

"I'm going to let you in on something," Masvidal said near the end of his off-the-cuff comments. "The Democrats just think that they're entitled to the Latino vote. They think that we just have to hand it over to them. We sure as hell don't." Instead, he continued, "they got to show us what they can do for us, what they can do for our communities. We're not going to buy the same wolf tickets and false promises that destroyed great countries like Venezuela and Cuba. It's not going to happen."

If you live in Florida, you might have heard this riff before. Trump's team spent heavily to run it as an ad to YouTube users in the state prior to the election.[17] In the campaign's final days and on Election Day itself, the campaign featured Masvidal's comments as it bought out advertising on the YouTube homepage.[18] After all, the message squared perfectly with what Trump was saying elsewhere. He'd been using footage of violence and vandalism that occurred during his presidency and warning with great irony that it represented not the present but the future should Joe Biden win. He'd been insisting for years that Democrats were taking advantage of non-White voters. Here was a prominent Latino making a similar argument as he warned of social collapse.

There were signs well before that point that Trump was getting traction with Hispanic voters in Florida in particular. When his campaign tapped a Cuban American businessman to speak at the Republican convention about the "shadow" of socialism, it was piggybacking on polling that showed Trump outperforming expectations in the state.[19] By the time the election was over, Trump had seen marked improvement among Hispanic voters in 2020 relative to 2016 nationally, and not just where Trump invested in promoting Masvidal. Hispanic voters still preferred Biden by a 21-point margin,[20] but four years earlier they'd backed Hillary Clinton by nearly twice as much.

In the months that followed, Trump's success with Hispanics became a central point of debate on the left. What happened? Why? And, most important, was this a fluke—or, worse for Democrats, a permanent trend? If the latter, the results would be dire. As Democratic data guru David Shor told me, the GOP's gain in 2020 was "enough to wipe out a lot of these [Democratic] advantages to demographic growth." If the population grows to include more Hispanic voters but those voters vote less heavily Democratic, it's a wash for the party.

There's an inherent challenge to Democratic politics that Republicans don't face, a challenge spotlighted in 2020. As we explored in chapter 4, the GOP has remained a largely homogeneous composition of conservative White voters. The Democratic Party, by contrast, was already more racially diverse in 1996 than the Republican Party was in 2020.[21] It represents working-class White people in Wisconsin and college-educated

Hispanic people in New York. Republicans have been able to hold power largely on the strength of loyalty from rural White voters for whom one national message can be offered. Democrats must figure out how to get urban Black voters and rural Whites and suburban Hispanics to unite on a broad policy platform and, occasionally, on candidates—a prospect that's made trickier with the nationalization of elections, something to which we'll return. At the same time, the party also needs to balance its perceived focus among those constituencies. There is a well-established Black-Brown fault line in Democratic politics, one that was at times strained by the elevation of the Black Lives Matter movement. Not only is it not the case that minorities are colluding against Whites (as Eric Knowles's research examined), racial groups are and long have been jockeying against each other. But now there are far more Asian and Hispanic Americans than there were a few decades ago.[22]

For now, let's focus on the question undergirding the shift among Hispanics in 2020. If it was the start of a trend, particularly if it's one that applies to other non-White groups, it demands an overhaul of expectations for what American politics will look like in the aftermath of the baby boom—and in 2024.

A good place to begin is by thinking about how American politics has already changed as the electorate has gotten less densely White—or, more accurately, how it hasn't. Consider two of the more dramatic elections in recent years: Barack Obama's election in 2008 and the surprising success of Republicans in the 2014 midterms. That first election seemed to augur a new American electorate that was not only capable of propelling a Black man to the White House but one that would continue to reshape politics moving forward. That year, about 23.4 percent of voters were not White,[23] and not only did Obama win the White House but Democrats swept up 53 percent of the votes cast in House races compared to the GOP's 42 percent.[24] Six years later, though, Obama's party faced a midterm backlash, with Republicans picking up 51 percent of the votes cast in House races, about 6 points more than the Democrats. The Republican Party gained control of the Senate and expanded its margin in the House.

In 2014, about 23.1 percent of the electorate was non-White—0.3 percentage points lower than the density of non-White voters in 2008. In other words, the electorate that brought Obama to the presidency was almost exactly as diverse as the one that would punish Obama's party six years later.

CHART 104

House Results vs. the Diversity of the National Electorate

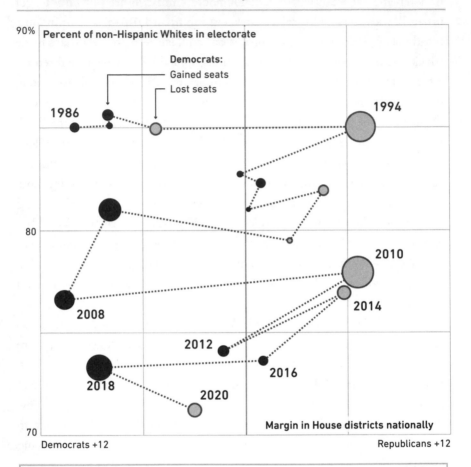

HOW TO READ THIS CHART This graph shows a path through history, if you will. We start at 1986, in the upper left corner. In that year, the density of Whites in the electorate (shown on the vertical axis) was 85 percent, and the Democrats won a much larger percentage of votes in House races (measured on the horizontal axis, with dots to the left of the center vertical line indicating that Democrats won more votes). They didn't pick up many seats, though; the circle for the year 1986 is small in order to denote that.

Then, over time, the dots start moving around—and, to the main point, drop lower. As the density of White voters falls, Democrats and Republicans are both gaining and losing seats and winning and losing the national House balloting. The composition of the electorate is from Michael McDonald's analyses of Census Bureau data and the House results from the Office of the Historian of the House of Representatives.

Since the density of White voters began to slip in national elections in 1996, there's been no consistent pattern in political outcomes. In some years, the electorate has gotten less densely White and Republicans have romped.

CHART 105

2020 Election Results vs. State Demography

Percent of population that's non-Hispanic White
Percent of adult citizen population that's non-Hispanic White

Margin in 2020 presidential vote — Biden +50 / Trump +50

HOW TO READ THIS CHART Each state is plotted according to the percentage of Whites in its population[25] on the vertical axis and its 2020 vote margin[26] on the horizontal. The chart also displays the percentage of Whites in the population eligible to actually vote in federal elections; that is, adult citizens. In some states, like Mississippi, those percentages are similar. In others, like Texas, there's a wide gap, a function of the state having a large population of younger residents and noncitizens. Remember this chart; it comes up again later in this chapter.

In others, the electorate has gotten more White and Democrats have seen big gains. It's literally all over the place.

Just to belabor the point, we can look at the results from one election: the aforementioned 2020 presidential race. States with lower densities of White residents voted more heavily for Joe Biden—but so did some states (like Vermont and Maine) that are heavily White. If race correlated neatly with Democratic politics, we'd expect to see Texas voting like California. It does not, even when taking into account the difference we noted above between a state's population and its adult citizen population.

Part of the muddle here derives from our grouping non-Whites as a unified electoral body, the purportedly colluding minority researched by Eric Knowles.[27] But that is the point: expecting declines in the percentage of Whites in the electorate to correlate neatly to Democratic gains is overly simple.

To gain one component of the appropriate nuance, we turn to Stephanie Valencia. A veteran of Barack Obama's administration, Valencia plays many roles in Democratic politics, including involvement with programs aimed at promoting Latino involvement in government[28]—sort of the inverse of Saurabh Sharma's work, in a variety of ways. Valencia is also a cofounder of EquisLabs, an organization aimed at understanding the Latino vote and sharing that understanding to improve Democratic campaign outreach.

"If you look at where Democrats are with Latino voters today, sixty-five percent—we always want to push, seventy, seventy-five percent but if it stays at sixty-five percent with the percentage of growth that's happening in population today? That is a deal that Democrats should take," Valencia told me shortly after EquisLabs had released a detailed analysis of the 2020 vote. The rationale is simple and aligns with David Shor's point about the gains that would be erased. "If there is this more fundamental kind of shift in baseline trend that is shifting in a different direction, toward Republicans," Valencia said, "then I think Democrats have bigger problems ahead of them."

Latino voters, she said, "may be one of the last true swing parts of the electorate," as evidenced at least to some degree by the shift from 2016 to 2020. One thing Valencia's research found was that many of those Hispanics who voted for Trump were "a more newly immigrated, less assimilated, potentially lower-information voter." Less partisan Latino voters, EquisLabs' final report argued, are "navigating their identities and values in ways that don't always map out neatly on the political spectrum and aren't always consistent."[29] Some Hispanic voters appalled by Trump's rhetoric on immigration in 2016, for instance, came into a 2020 election focused mostly on the pandemic and the economy. That made them willing to consider supporting the incumbent president when they wouldn't have four years earlier. After all, the economy was doing well before the pandemic emerged. In his endorsement of the incumbent president, Jorge Masvidal had argued that a team wouldn't change coaches when it had been "winning Super Bowls," a line quoted in EquisLabs' report.

It was Valencia who'd pointed out Trump's embrace of Masvidal to me. This overlapped with another important part of their report: that the Trump campaign made a concerted effort to communicate with Hispanic voters that was often unmatched.

"In a place like South Florida, where there was already a much more traditional media ecosystem in place, of radio and television that was more conservative leaning already—Radio Mambi, some of the local television stations," she explained, "and that on top of YouTube and aggressive digital recruitment, with disinformation or at least misleading information, helped to really accelerate in some ways what happened in South Florida."

The message about socialism was a particular focus of misleading information. Research conducted by the Cybersecurity for Democracy project at New York University identified Facebook ads targeting Spanish-speaking voters in Texas and Florida in which Biden was described as a "communist."[30] Research from the firm Avaaz found that Spanish-language misinformation was much more likely to go unchecked on the platform than was misinformation offered in English.[31] The team at WhatsApp, a chat application owned by Facebook's parent company, had pushed for a Spanish-language version of a voter misinformation hub, but Facebook CEO Mark Zuckerberg reportedly worried that such a tool wouldn't be "politically neutral" and could be seen as partisan.[32] EquisLabs' analysis later found that the best predictor that a Hispanic voter would think that socialism was a bigger threat than fascism was if they used WhatsApp for news—more than even those who got news from far-right cable networks.

Trump didn't win Florida or even improve his position solely because of misinformation. "This is a multiyear investment that the Trump campaign and the conservative media ecosystem made to communicate with Latino

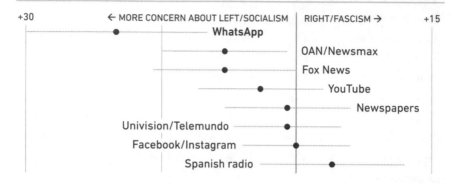

CHART 106
How Sources of Information Relate
to the Views of Hispanic Americans

+30   ← MORE CONCERN ABOUT LEFT/SOCIALISM │ RIGHT/FASCISM →   +15

WhatsApp

OAN/Newsmax

Fox News

YouTube

Newspapers

Univision/Telemundo

Facebook/Instagram

Spanish radio

> **HOW TO READ THIS CHART** The predicted extent to which a Hispanic adult would express more concern about socialism on the political left (dots to the left of the vertical center point) than fascism on the right.[33] The analysis is from EquisLabs' national survey of Hispanics, with statistical uncertainty indicated by the dashed lines.

voters," Valencia said. By contrast, "you had $14 million spent in the last two weeks from Democrats in South Florida. It was too much, too late. That's the kind of difference you see: you see an influx of cash in the last two weeks and you see a steady drip of Republican funding over a course of years, shifting and changing the way that people's views were developed."

Both parties recognize that long-term investments in Hispanic and other minority communities is a better strategy for success, and not, in the words of one Democratic Party official, "just waiting until a month before the election where we do bad copy-and-paste jobs and put 'AAPI for,' 'Black Americans for,' 'Latinx for' on signs, bumper stickers, and buttons."

In Florida in 2020, the Republicans did this better. EquisLabs identified the left's failure to counter the right's messaging in Texas and Florida as points of particular advantage for Trump's campaign and a contributor to his success in those states. If you give swing voters or a voter with limited political knowledge only one side of an argument, you shouldn't be surprised at the outcome.

The question for future projections is how much of this is *specific* to Trump. Some of it is, certainly. A number of people with whom I spoke pointed, for example, to Trump's brash appeal to a particular form of masculinity as a factor in his ability to peel non-White voters away from the Democratic Party. His biography was also helpful. Trump is often seen as an embodiment of the American dream, someone who became rich in business (though, of course, that's heavily a function of his father's carefully laid foundation).

"Many Latinos who are entrepreneurs and small business owners really aspire to be that and really want to aspire to build a business and build something for themselves and their families," Valencia said. "Many Latinos do that through entrepreneurship and small business and so they saw Trump as somebody to aspire to in that regard." Another predictor of increased concern about socialism on the left in EquisLabs' research was an embrace of the idea that hard work can lead to success for average people in the United States.

Over the long term, this particular rhetorical debate may be less important than the fact that there was terrain on which the debate could play out. *Texas Monthly*'s Jack Herrera wrote a perceptive analysis of the shifts seen in border counties in that state, pointing to an increased willingness to break with pro-Democrat tradition.

"[F]or decade after decade, part of being Hispanic in South Texas, just like wrapping tamales on Christmas Eve or listening to Selena at family reunions, meant voting Democratic, even as the party became less welcoming to those with conservative views," Herrera wrote. "What changed in 2020 is that conservative Hispanic South Texans voted like their non-Hispanic white neighbors. Ideology suddenly became polarizing for the group in a way it never had been before."[34]

Herrera's making a broader point here, but it's worth picking out that idea about the assimilating effects of community. When I was speaking to sociologist Richard Alba about how he expected racial identities to evolve over time, he highlighted an interesting bit of data.

"About forty percent of Hispanics live in census tracts where the Hispanic population is less than twenty-five percent of the residents," Alba said. "So there are a lot of people living in low-density Hispanic areas. They're much more assimilated."

With that idea in mind, I reached out to L2, a political data firm that compiles information about voters in the United States. In some states, voter registration data are offered by race—generally states that at one point were subject to the preclearance provisions of the Voting Rights Act that we discussed in chapter 7. In others, L2 uses statistical modeling to estimate a voter's racial or ethnic identity. The result is that we can compare Alba's observation about Hispanic density to actual or modeled registration data.

The result? Hispanics who live in less-heavily Hispanic counties are less likely to identify as Democrats. Hispanics who live in more-heavily Hispanic counties are more likely to identify as Democrats. That holds both for the

CHART 107
Party Identity Relative to the Density of Hispanics in a County

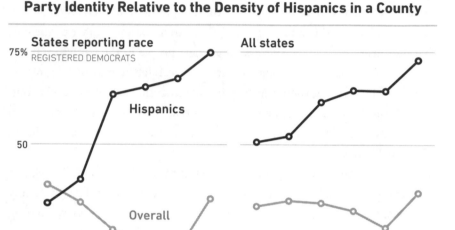

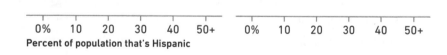

Percent of population that's Hispanic

HOW TO READ THIS CHART These simple graphs mask quite a bit of data analysis. They show the same thing, but with different universes. Using L2's data, I grouped each county into one of six buckets—those with a population that was 0 to 4.9 percent Hispanic, those with a 5 to 14.9 percent Hispanic population, etc.—and then averaged the percentage of Hispanics in each county that registered as Democrats. (The groupings were selected in order to have a significant number of counties in each group.) The graph at left shows the result for the states that report race data (Alabama, Florida, Georgia, Louisiana, North Carolina, South Carolina, Tennessee, and Texas) and the one at right for all states, using L2's imputed data. The registration data are from mid-2021.

states in which voter racial identities are reported and the ones in which they're imputed by L2.

We can't make assumptions about causality from this. Are Hispanics who are more likely to be Republican or independent also people who prefer to live in less-densely Hispanic places? Is this a reflection of the influence of community? Are there confounding factors that this doesn't capture? It's hard to pick out the direction of the arrow, but there is a clear correlation between Hispanic population density and politics.

Of course, all politics are local. Hispanic voters in South Texas and in Florida shifted heavily to Trump in 2020 and were targeted by the incumbent president's campaign with messages specific to the composition of the communities: border issues in Texas and socialism in Florida.

CHART 108

Shifts in Heavily Hispanic Counties from 2016 to 2020

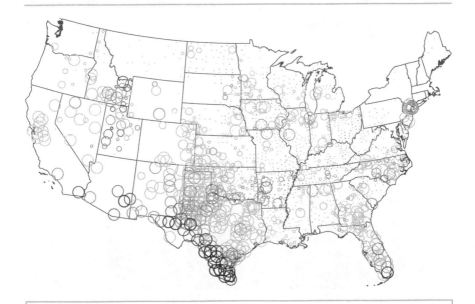

HOW TO READ THIS CHART Each circle represents a county where Trump's margin was wider in 2020 than in 2016. The size of the circle corresponds to the density of the Hispanic population in the county. The darker the circle, the bigger the shift to Trump. Some of the biggest shifts were in heavily Hispanic counties near the U.S.-Mexico border and in south Florida.

"Hispanic residents of our state are much more likely to identify as white than Hispanic residents of cities elsewhere in the country. With roots many generations deep in lands that were annexed from Mexican control to that of the U.S., many also actively reject being cast as immigrants," Herrera wrote for *Texas Monthly*.[35] A challenge for Democrats in 2020, he argued, was that it was *they* who treated non-White voters as a sort of unified entity centered largely in opposition to Trump.[36] "While Hispanic South Texans are proud of their Mexican heritage," he wrote, "many do not consider themselves to be 'people of color' at all."

CHART 109
Ideological Identification by Race and Party

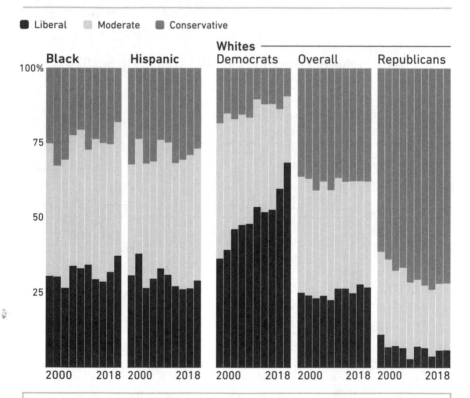

HOW TO READ THIS CHART The percentage of each racial (or racial and political) group that identifies as liberal, moderate, or conservative since 2000, using data from the General Social Survey. The obvious change over this period is the increase in liberal identity among White Democrats.

Beyond questions of identity and neighborhood, it's worth recognizing that both Black and Hispanic Americans are slightly more likely than Whites overall to identify themselves as liberal or moderate. White *Democrats*, though, are far more likely to identify themselves as liberal—an identification that has increased over time.

These sorts of self-identifications are fraught. A self-described moderate Democrat might support a strongly progressive House candidate; a liberal Democrat might be starkly conservative on the question of building afford- able housing. They are approximations of political worldviews that manifest differently in different contexts. They are also useful as a marker of receptiv- ity to an explicitly "liberal" agenda from the Democratic Party.

This difference in ideological identity may offer some insight into the shift seen between 2016 and 2020. Marquette University political scientist Julia Azari noted that there's long been tension between how Black and Hispanic Americans view political issues and their party loyalty.

"One of the things that's striking is that as Black Americans have become richer, they've stayed Democratic, which is not normally what happens," she said. "They also are quite varied in their ideology, their policy views—but not in their partisanship. One of the things I think we started to see in 2020 was Black and to some extent Latino voters just sorting a little bit more. So if they're conservative in their ideology then they're more likely to vote for Trump."

"Non-White voters have been trending against Democrats, and that de- crease, there's a lot of evidence, seems to be concentrated among younger voters," David Shor told me when we spoke, reflecting Chris Warshaw's cautionary point. The shift was likely in part because younger non-White Americans, who of course come from a more diverse generation, "are less susceptible to group appeals," Shor said. "Their race is less central to their identity than is the case for their parents or grandparents."

Shor also pointed to the erosion of participation in social organizations as having a potentially weakening effect on the loyalty of Black Americans to the Democratic Party. "A really underrated piece of this is that when you get ninety-five percent of any group, that is not due to people agreeing with you on issues. There is a peer pressure and social identity that plays a big role in actually getting you to ninety-five percent," Shor said. "That's true for African American voters in the same way that it's true for rural White voters in Mississippi. The mechanisms by which that kind of identity and social pressure manifests itself is having all of your friends be African American, going to a Black church. Something that I think is underrated is that young Black voters are much less likely to go to church than older voters."

Corrine McConnaughy is a political scientist at Princeton University whose work focuses on the role of institutions in protecting democracy—a subject we'll look at more closely in a bit. In our conversation, she also highlighted the importance of Black community and institutions in maintaining that shared political identity.

"Even as Black Americans became a more economically heterogeneous group, they managed to cling to cohesive behavior, political behavior. It's not because they all actually agree with each other. There's a social process of saying, We're interdependent. You're just as vulnerable to racism as I am," she said. "We have these institutions to basically keep us accountable to each other, to keep that as a coherent political priority. And without that social process, that's not what you get. You get an increasing heterogeneous behavior."

One of the people with whom I spoke who was most skeptical about the ability of the GOP to woo Black voters was Michael Steele, the Black former chairman of the Republican Party. He scoffed at Trump's lazy appeals to Black voters as president, including his reliance on Black stereotypes.

"If you can't put anything on the table, other than 'Black unemployment is the lowest it's ever been.' That's your go-to? All right. Okay, fine. That's your go-to," Steele said. "So tell me then, what do I say to my son when he comes back after his encounter with the police that didn't go so well? Do I just buck him up by saying, 'Hey, at least Black unemployment is the lowest it's ever been'?"

One of the appeals of Trump, he said, was playing to fears, like that "as a Black man you're losing your jobs to other people, to outside folks. The same is true for immigrants, playing the other end of that with immigrants who came through the process naturally, the right way. Legally," he said. "You saw it in the appeal to White women in the suburbs. Oh, they're coming for you. Well, who the hell are 'they'? I tell the White folks I live around, I'm already here, just so you know."

That mirrors the delineation offered by Ian Haney López, a prominent scholar in critical race theory, when we spoke. The heart of Trump's improved performance in 2020, he suggested, was "racial status anxiety, of a sort that is promoted by dog-whistle narratives about decent, hard-working, law-abiding people beset by undeserving violent, lazy people. We know that that language was crafted originally to appeal to racially anxious Whites." (You'll recall Lee Atwater's articulation of the transition in Republican rhetoric from chapter 4.) "But it's not racially explicit; it's coded. And it also draws support from a number of people in communities of color, who don't see it—and a majority of Americans don't see that language as racist. They see it as common sense."

He pointed to that *Texas Monthly* article as demonstrating his point. Those Hispanic Texans, he said, "are going to vote for somebody who's using anti-illegal language. Their own status depends on them saying, We belong. We did it the right way. We've been here for generations."

You can see how these things fold together, from Hispanics seeking to differentiate themselves from immigrant groups to Black Americans being encouraged to worry about their job security. That latter point was very much one that was amplified by the Trump administration. At one point in August 2017, Stephen Miller, perhaps Trump's foremost voice in opposition to increased immigration, was wheeled out to defend proposed legislation aimed at overhauling the immigration system. The current system, he claimed, had been "very unfair for American workers, but especially for immigrant workers, African American workers and Hispanic workers, and blue-collar workers in general across the country." Asked for evidence to defend his claim, he offered only one study that had already been challenged[37]—including in the research published by the National Academies of Sciences, Engineering, and Medicine[38] that found few long-term negative effects for American workers from immigration.[39] But the point was the argument, not the reality.

The salience of the discussion in chapter 8 to all of this should be clear. "The big question for me for the next decade is really how Latinos continue to relate to their own identity, and how that relates to their participation in politics," Stephanie Valencia of EquisLabs told me. If Hispanic Americans like those in South Texas increasingly don't consider themselves to be people of color, as Herrera wrote, that suggests both that appeals from Democrats centered on race will lose resonance and that those voters will vote more like Whites.

Shortly after the 2020 election, Ian Haney López wrote an essay for *The Washington Post* about research he and some colleagues conducted. Hispanic respondents were presented with three statements, including that Hispanic Americans were "more like African Americans who over generations remain a distinct group" or that they were "more like immigrant groups from Europe who over generations become part of the American mainstream." About a quarter of respondents agreed with the statement about African Americans and a third with the one about becoming part of the mainstream. Those who agreed with the statement equating Hispanics with Black Americans preferred Joe Biden by 61 percentage points. Those who disagreed with that statement preferred Biden by less than half as much. What's more, they found "resistance among Latinos to seeing themselves as primarily being allied with people of color"—particularly among those who saw Latinos as similar to European immigrants.[40]

"If I happen to have a set of political predispositions as a Latina, it's not because I'm a Latina." This observation came from Lisa García Bedolla, a political scientist and vice provost at the University of California, Berkeley, during a video call we had in early 2021. "It's because that social position in American society, rightly or wrongly, for historical and political reasons, makes me more likely to have had a certain set of experiences in my life." (All politics are local.) While García Bedolla saw a "tremendous opportunity" for the GOP to reorient their relationship with young Hispanics, she also thought that "what they're doing is just kind of digging in in a way that I think is going to alienate a whole generation of folks." That comports with EquisLabs' determination that the decreased importance of immigration during the 2020 election (providing space for Trump to run on the economy) didn't suggest that the issue was not important to Hispanic politics. "Signaling on immigration is really important for Latinos to understand whether a politician is for or against us," Valencia argued. "Do they see us as a threat to this country or do they see us as an asset to this country?"

Perceived threats often manifest politically. Not only in the sort of blunt-force rhetoric Trump often used about immigration and crime, but also in policy. William Frey of the Brookings Institution pointed to Arizona, where the Hispanic population grew by 177 percent from 1990 to 2015.

"Against that demographic backdrop, it is perhaps no coincidence that a great deal of animosity between whites and Hispanics erupted upon the 2010 signing of the Support Our Law Enforcement and Safe Neighborhoods Act, also known as Arizona State Bill 1070," he wrote in his book *Diversity Ex-*

plosion. "Although the law was later amended and the Supreme Court struck down key parts, it was one of the strictest anti-immigration laws ever enacted by a state. Provisions included requirements that residents carry papers verifying their citizenship; if they did not, they would be subject to arrest, detention, and potential deportation."[41]

Something similar happened in California. By 1996, the state was on the brink of being majority minority; Whites made up just over half of the population, according to the Census Bureau. Two years earlier, a ballot initiative, Proposition 187, passed by a wide margin, severely restricting access to state resources for undocumented immigrants. In 1996, voters narrowly passed Proposition 209, which eliminated affirmative action programs in California.

Exit polling released by the *Los Angeles Times* after the Proposition 209 vote revealed something interesting. The measure was broadly supported by White Californians and opposed by Black and Hispanic residents of the state. But since the electorate was overwhelmingly White—unlike the state's population—it passed by a 10-point margin. Had the electorate matched the composition of the state, it would have failed by a near-equivalent spread.

Remember that map of how the non-White population in states was expected to increase by 2036 from the research published by the Center for American Progress? It seems fair to assume, given recent history, that other states might propose similarly restrictive policies in response.

Released weeks before the 2020 election, the map was a product of contributions from Brookings's Frey, Rob Griffin of the Democracy Fund Voter Study Group, and CAP senior fellow Ruy Teixeira. Teixeira was the coauthor of an influential book called *The Emerging Democratic Majority*, which was published in 2002. Its thesis will be familiar: that the shifts in demography in the United States augured a potential new progressive dominance in the intermediate future. The CAP project echoed that idea, with state-level shifts suggesting that Democrats would build increasingly concrete majorities in the Electoral College. But even before the election and those shifts among Hispanic voters in particular, Teixeira's public rhetoric was less optimistic for the left.

The case made in his book, he wrote in July 2020, had been "bowdlerized." "Instead of focusing on the fact that this emerging majority only gave Democrats tremendous potential if they played their cards right, many

CHART 110
What Would Have Happened to Prop 209
if the Electorate Matched the Population

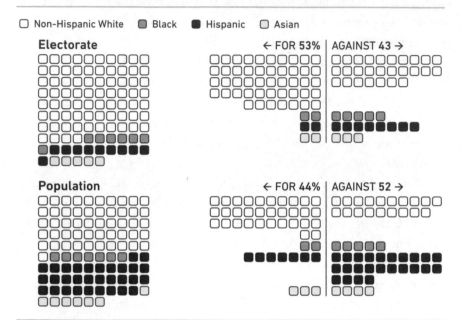

HOW TO READ THIS CHART   At top, the composition of the electorate in 1996 according to *Los Angeles Times* exit polling[42] is shown next to the approximate distribution of support for the ballot measure. (Each square represents one percentage point.) At bottom, the composition of the population of the state that year, with the adjusted distribution of support had the electorate been similarly distributed. In other words, if White, Black, and Hispanic Californians had voted as indicated by the exit poll but turned out proportionately to the population, the bottom right graph indicates the result.

progressives started to interpret it as a description of an inevitable future," he suggested. "The new Democratic majority, they believed, had already arrived. All they had to do to win election after election was to mobilize the growing segments of the electorate, and the demographic changes that favored them would take care of the rest." Biden's advantage, he suggested, was an ability to maintain the core Democratic base but bring back some of the White working class that Trump had seized.[43]

In the aftermath of the election, Teixeira wrote about shifts among working-class Black and Hispanic voters that he worried suggested a new set of potential problems for Democrats. "[T]he anchor of Republican strength among the working class is dominance among whites within that group, which only subsided slightly in 2020," he wrote in May 2021. "But it is startling to note that since 2012, running against Trump twice, Democrats have lost 18 points off of their margin among nonwhite working class voters."[44] There are other factors at play besides the passage of time, like the change in the candidate at the top of the Democratic ticket. But other polling, including Pew Research Center's validated post-election polling, shows shifts to the right among non-Whites without college degrees.

This divide on education is significant enough to break out on its own. But before we do, an anecdote to convey how the conventional wisdom on racial politics can shift.

You'll remember the GOP "autopsy report" that followed Mitt Romney's 2012 loss. It recommended the party invest more in outreach to the growing non-White voter pool. So ingrained was the idea at the time that a prominent Republican speaking to the right-wing media network Newsmax a few weeks after Romney's loss pointed directly to the party's failures with non-White voters as a flaw.

"Republicans didn't have anything going for them with respect to Latinos and with respect to Asians," he said. Democrats didn't have a proposal to address immigrants in the country illegally, he continued, "but what they were is they were kind." Romney's odd suggestion that those immigrants might be pressured to "self-deport" during a primary debate, this prominent Republican argued, meant that he "lost all of the Latino vote. He lost the Asian vote. He lost everybody who is inspired to come into this country."[45]

The speaker was Donald Trump. It was very much in keeping with his habit of repeating what was being said in conservative media; even Fox News's Sean Hannity had clambered onto the Republican bandwagon supporting the idea that immigrants in the country without documentation should be given a pathway to citizenship.[46] But then the tide turned, and Trump turned with it. Instead of moving to the left on immigration relative to Romney, there was enormous political value for a Republican presidential candidate in 2015 to move hard to the right. To be less "kind." Trump did.

THE COLLEGE GAP—AND THE GENDER ONE

If you are a woman who voted in the 2020 presidential election, the odds are that you voted for Joe Biden. If you're a *White* woman, though, the odds are that you *didn't* support Biden; exit polling found that White women preferred Trump by about 5 percentage points. If you're a White woman who has a college degree, however, you were probably a Biden voter, since 60 percent of that group supported the winning candidate.[47]

CHART 111
Presidential Support Relative to Gender, Race, and Education

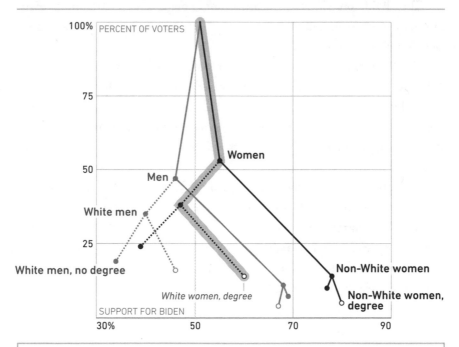

HOW TO READ THIS CHART Using Fox News Voter Analysis exit polling conducted in partnership with the Associated Press by the NORC, the chart shows how support for Biden varied as demographic characteristics are applied. At top, the total electorate is shown, giving Biden 51 percent of the vote. It's then split by gender, with women (who made up more than half the electorate, as shown on the vertical axis) supporting Biden with more than 50 percent of their votes. Then we overlay race (with White voters indicated using a dotted line) and, finally, education (with those with a degree indicated with an outlined circle). As the demographic groups are narrowed, the percentage of the electorate they constitute drops.

This demographic ping-ponging was unusually robust for White women, but not unique. Gender, race, and education were key determinants in how people voted in 2020, with a 46-point difference in support for Biden between White men without college degrees and non-White women with one. The election's result was in part a function of that gulf and in part of the gulf in the size of each voting bloc: there were about three times as many White men without degrees as non-White women who'd graduated from college.

We looked at the education gap in chapter 4, so this shouldn't be surprising. But it's important to recognize both that this divide in partisanship based on educational attainment is widening and that it overlaps with gender.

This isn't a U.S.-specific phenomenon. In late 2021, a group of researchers looked at how this split had grown in a number of Western countries. The 2010s had seen "a divergence between the influences of income (economic capital) and education (human capital): high-income voters continue to vote for the right, while high-education voters have shifted to supporting the left," Amory Gethin, Clara Martínez-Toledano, and Thomas Piketty

CHART 112
How Income and Education Overlapped with Vote Choice

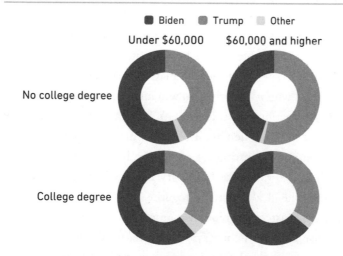

■ Biden   ■ Trump   □ Other

Under $60,000 $60,000 and higher

No college degree

College degree

HOW TO READ THIS CHART Vote distribution by income and education level, using data from the 2020 ANES. The only group that preferred Trump was that without degrees who had household incomes of $60,000 or more.

wrote.[48] The distinction here between income and education is important, because we often use education as a proxy for class in the United States. In the 2020 election, though, people without degrees from higher-income households preferred Trump to Biden.

"[P]arties promoting 'progressive' policies (green and traditional left-wing parties)," the paper reads, "have seen their electorate become increasingly restricted to higher-educated voters, while parties upholding more 'conservative' views on sociocultural issues (anti-immigration and traditional right-wing parties) have concentrated a growing share of the lower-educated electorate." The time frame here mirrors the one seen in Gallup polling: Whites with degrees began to diverge from Whites without degrees after the 2012 election[49]—as immigration and race gained new saliency in the national conversation, to Trump's eventual benefit.

For Democrats, the divergence is often disadvantageous, David Shor argues. "It's in the Democratic Party's interest to not have the national conversation be about those cultural divides and, instead, to try to make conversation be kind of a boring, technocratic question of, like, adopting commonsense policies that people care about," he told me. "It's in the Republican Party's interest to not do that." Democrats, he argued, should run on policy deliverables. Republicans should amplify culture-war fights.

The latter is often an easier political task, as Republican strategist Patrick Ruffini pointed out when we spoke. "It's very hard to get people to pay attention to a purely economic, bread-and-butter, kitchen-table issues message," he said. "There's a real temptation to play that culture war card" for Republicans, he added, "where, frankly, you win more often than you don't."

During the 2020 election and into Biden's first months in office, this was manifested in the national debate. The Republican Party had no specific platform as Trump was running for reelection beyond boosterism for their candidate; a year later, Senate Minority Leader Mitch McConnell (R-Kentucky) rejected the idea of putting together a policy platform for the 2022 midterms, relying instead on blocking proposals from the Democrats and receiving no pushback from conservative media for doing so.[50] As the party's former chairman Michael Steele said when we spoke, "We can tell you what we're against, and we've been very clear about that."

"The only reason any working-class people vote for Democrats is because

Democratic economic policies are more popular than Republican ones," Shor said. "To the extent to which [Republicans] shift their messaging to make it sound like they're looking out for working-class people standing up against these pointy-headed rich elites, they'll do better."

The GOP and other right-wing parties have been successful at precisely that. In their research, Gethin and his colleagues found that the left has "developed a more elitist approach to education policy" that spurs less-educated (and usually poorer) voters to see the left as worried primarily about defending those college-educated elites.[51]

Here the GOP may be aided by the fact that its base of support is aging and, therefore, less interested in the sorts of reforms to government spending programs that were once a focal point of the party. That aging base "has

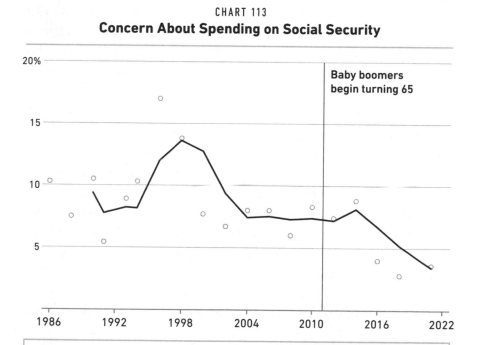

CHART 113
Concern About Spending on Social Security

HOW TO READ THIS CHART The percentage of baby boomer Republicans and Republican-leaning independents who said they believed the country was spending too much on Social Security on the General Social Survey. The line is the average of the prior three biannual values, indicated by the circles.

paradoxically made it easy for them to project an image that is more populist or more economically centrist—or even, dare I say, to the left," Ruffini said, "based on the fact that their constituency is moving so solidly in this direction, actually, depending on Social Security, Medicare." The shift in opinion among baby boomers is measurable.

Another important metric: Fox News mentioned Social Security in the context of cuts or reforms in more than 3,200 blocks of airtime from 2009 through 2013. From 2017 through 2021, it did so fewer than 400 times.[52] This change, Ruffini said, could "reshape the party if they are really seriously looking to double down on this 'party of the working class' and 'party of workers plus minorities' that are also heavily working class."

The inclusion of non-Whites in the latter formulation echoes one theory of how the GOP builds a new political coalition—one that depends on non-White Americans embracing the GOP more robustly. That Trump's numerous comments appealing to racial grievances or overtly expressing racist thoughts didn't dampen non-White support for him in 2020 suggested to Ruffini that perhaps there was "a certain conservatism that's animating this under the surface"—in keeping with the ideology-versus-party tension mentioned above.

There's an interesting exception to the voting patterns centered on college degrees, one pointed out by Ian Haney López when we spoke and that he framed as overlapping with race. "When you look at White evangelicals, which is the single most important voting bloc for the right, there is no difference between White evangelicals with and without a college degree," he said. That's true. In both 2016 and 2020, White evangelical Protestants made up one out of every three votes Donald Trump received.[53] Trump worked hard to secure that loyalty, you'll recall,[54] and it paid off. Trump received 77 percent of the evangelical vote in 2016 and a staggering 84 percent four years later—about the level of support Biden got from Black men. That's in part because there was no advantage to Democrats among college-educated evangelicals.

López's assessment is that, for Whites generally, having a degree is a proxy for a set of other correlated beliefs: "a greater familiarity with American history, a greater comfort with people of color, less of a sense of being locked into economic competition with non-White populations"—beliefs less resonant on the religious right.

CHART 114
Party Identification Among Evangelicals by Education

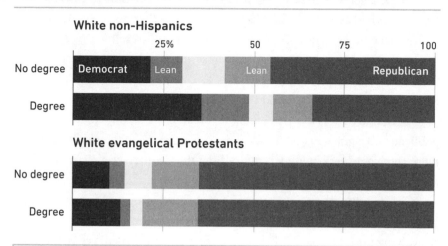

White non-Hispanics

| | 25% | 50 | 75 | 100 |

No degree — Democrat | Lean | Lean | Republican

Degree

White evangelical Protestants

No degree

Degree

HOW TO READ THIS CHART This one is straightforward. At top, the party identification of Whites with and without a college degree in 2020, according to the ANES. At bottom, the same divisions for White evangelical Protestants.

On this point, David Shor agrees. "It's not that having a degree is causal," he said, but for more liberal graduates "there are really big differences in terms of values, in terms of how they see society, things like racial resentment, social trust, culture, a bunch of other things." Recent research suggests that these days such distinctions may not be *derived* from college but *brought* to college,[55] which would help explain the evangelical data. As Shor later noted, for highly religious Americans, college "makes you more Republican/conservative because education helps you know what you 'should' believe."[56] The result is that conservative college-educated White evangelicals end up resembling conservative non-college-educated Whites.

The book *Jesus and John Wayne* by historian Kristin Kobes Du Mez opens with a moment from the 2016 campaign that we explored in chapter 4: Donald Trump's speech at a Christian college in Iowa. There, he pledged to defend the Christian right from the "siege" it was currently experiencing. The response Trump received in that election from conservative religious voters was "no aberration, nor was it merely a pragmatic choice," Du Mez writes. "It was, rather, the culmination of evangelicals' embrace of militant masculinity, an ideology that enshrines patriarchal authority and condones the callous display of power, at home and abroad."[57]

This is a central thesis of Du Mez's book, that many White evangelical Protestants had over the span of decades convinced themselves of the primacy of unchecked masculinity in leadership, that they "were looking for a protector, an aggressive, heroic, manly man, someone who wasn't restrained by political correctness or feminine virtues, someone who would break the rules for the right cause." They found that in Trump.

Of course he was mostly picking up on an existing undercurrent in Republican and right-wing politics, a sense among some men, including young men, that they were being left out of how the country was changing. This can manifest in varying degrees of toxicity, from acts of violence targeting women[58] to cultural cocooning in a shared sense of masculine importance. Writing for *Politico* in June 2021, Derek Robertson aptly described the GOP as evolving into the "Barstool" Party, a reference to the media company Barstool Sports.[59]

"[I]ts proudly Neanderthal, reactionary ethos aligns perfectly with the side of our political binary that Trump reconfigured: the one whose common denominator is a tooth-and-nail, middle-finger unwillingness to accept liberal social norms," Robertson wrote of Barstool. ". . . [T]he Barstool Republican now largely defines the Republican coalition because of his willingness to dispense with his party's conventional policy wisdom on anything—the social safety net, drug laws, abortion access—as long as it means one thing: he doesn't have to vote for some snooty Democrat, and, by proxy, the caste of lousy deans that props up the left's politically-correct cultural regime."

This meme-ish manifestation of masculinity has a superficial appeal that's rooted in a certain view of American culture. Football, cars, pretty women. Being right by virtue of being a man. Joe Rogan-ism. But it's inextricable from a desire to reclaim things that have been recast in less-flattering terms. Concussions, pollution, misogyny. It's another facet of the sprawling fight against the ways in which culture is sidelining traditional symbols of power, including male power.

"We absolutely know that for non-college-credentialed populations—and they're not all White men: some of them are Latino, some of them are African American—the changing gender dynamics, the fact that men cannot earn enough to support their families the way they used to be able to, and that women are out of place—and believe me, we are, we're all out of place—that is very disquieting," Harvard University's Theda Skocpol said when we spoke. "I think it's very disquieting to college-credentialed men, too, and to women, for that matter. This is not something that only affects one gender, but I do think it's been experienced as a source of anger and anxiety more by people whose economic prospects have not risen along with women in their minds. Who end up not even being in the same household with their children."

At the same time, women are increasingly found in the center stage of American politics. The resistance to Trump's presidency was rooted in the activism of middle-aged women. Melissa Deckman, who looks at politics among younger generations, pointed out that the gap in political participation between men and women had narrowed over the past decade. Young women in particular are politically engaged, in part due to seeing role models in politics who weren't older White men and in part because they're more motivated by salient issues like climate change and gun violence. Young women are also more likely to attend college.[60]

So we come back to where we started, with Biden's strongest support coming from college-educated women (among both Whites and non-Whites) and his weakest performance from men without degrees. Once again, though, this overlaps with other patterns that will likely affect politics over the short to intermediate term.

LOCATION, LOCATION, LOCATION

A quarter of Americans live in just 35 counties.[61] Those counties, collectively, voted for Joe Biden in 2020 by a 30-point margin. A quarter of White Americans, however, live in 62 counties, which preferred Biden by 27 points. A quarter of Black Americans live in 18 counties (Biden by 40 points) and a quarter of Hispanic Americans live in only 9 counties,[62] which Biden won by 26 points. A quarter of those with a college degree live in 28 counties, places that voted for Biden by a 32-point margin over Trump.

What the distribution of the college educated is most akin to, predictably, is the distribution of Democratic votes in 2020. A quarter of those votes came from 27 counties that also backed Biden by 32 points. The distribution of Republican votes looked like the distribution of the White population,

CHART 115
Education, Place, and the 2020 Results

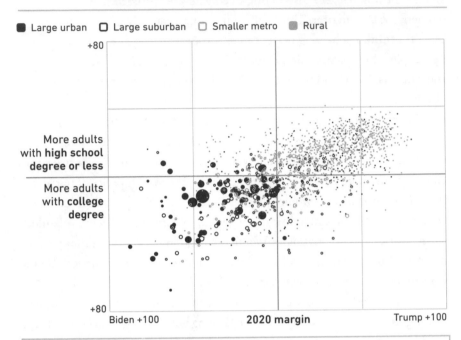

■ Large urban   ☐ Large suburban   ☐ Smaller metro   ■ Rural

More adults with **high school degree or less**

More adults with **college degree**

Biden +100   **2020 margin**   Trump +100

HOW TO READ THIS CHART   A scatter plot showing each county in the United States (except for those in Alaska) on two axes. The vertical axis shows the ratio of adults in the county with college degrees to those with high school degrees or less, with circles at the bottom having a much higher density of college-educated residents. The horizontal axis is the county's vote margin in the 2020 presidential race. Circles are scaled to the size of the total population and colored based on type, as categorized by the University of Wisconsin Population Health Institute. The dots are arrayed from lower left to upper right, showing the correlation between college degrees and Democratic vote choice in a county.

with a quarter of the total fitting into 62 counties that backed Biden by 21 points. (Most 2020 Trump voters live in Biden-voting states, after all.[63] The largest city to cast more votes for Trump than Biden that year was Oklahoma City.)

College-educated Americans converging in left-leaning states is not new. This is one of the elements of Bill Bishop's "big sort" theory, and it's one bolstered by data. A 2019 analysis of the migration of highly educated Americans showed that states that saw a net gain of more-educated residents were more likely to vote for Joe Biden in 2020 by a 15-point margin. States that saw a net loss with that group later voted for Trump by a 9-point margin.[64]

Just because it isn't new doesn't mean it isn't worrisome for the Democratic Party. Having strong constituencies heavily concentrated in relatively few areas dampens the party's political power. You're familiar with the way in which the Electoral College and the Senate disconnect political power from vote margins, of course. Biden won 7 million more votes than Trump nationally, but only won the Electoral College outright because of a 43,000-vote margin in three states.[65] Four years earlier, Hillary Clinton won by 2.9 million more votes nationally, but lost the presidency thanks to an 80,000-vote margin in states in the Upper Midwest. Widening the lens slightly, Democrats only held the Senate in 2021 thanks to a narrow margin of 55,000 votes in Georgia. That both institutions reroute power at the state level means that having a more broadly distributed base of support provides a political advantage—and that voters centered in cities in a few states presents a challenge.

So what happens moving forward? Does the erosion of the baby boom—whose members are less likely to live in big cities—mean a shift in this distribution? Are there other important patterns that might be less obvious?

There is an underappreciated element to how the United States sorts geographically that is relevant to the broader discussion of post-boomer America. Harvard University researchers Jacob Brown and Ryan Enos took national voter registration data and used them to evaluate how finely segmented Americans were by political party. That research included an interesting finding: White people tend to live near other White people, and that racial segregation ends up reducing *partisan* segregation.[66]

I asked Enos about that in a phone call. "White Democrats tend to live in more diverse neighborhoods than Republicans do, but not as much as probably a lot of White Democrats tell themselves," Enos said. "Your [typical] White Democrat lives in a place where most everybody else is White, just like White Republicans. We live in a very racially segregated country." White Democrats "are more willing to live around Republicans than they are around non-White people," he added. "They're trading off racial diversity and they're gaining some partisan diversity."

This isn't a function of necessarily explicitly choosing segregated communities; instead, it's often a function of factors that have themselves been downstream of race in the past, like school quality and access to resources.

Stanford University sociologist Sean Reardon noted that the increase in income inequality was mirrored in an increased polarization of communities. "There are fewer mixed-income neighborhoods than there used to be and more very affluent or very poor neighborhoods. So the rich are increasingly likely to live with the rich and the poor are increasingly likely to live with the poor," Reardon told me. "If you look at the intersection of racial and economic segregation, even if you take White and Black families with the same household income, do they live in similar kinds of neighborhoods? The answer is no. They live in very different types of neighborhoods. Black or Hispanic families live in neighborhoods that don't just have larger proportions of Blacks and Hispanics, but are also much poorer than an equal-income White family."

This fragmentation then influences politics. "One of the reasons we worry about segregation is because it means kids grow up in neighborhoods and people live in neighborhoods with people that are like them racially, economically, background or shared experiences or things like that," Reardon said. "The more you grew up with a bunch of like-minded people and live among them, the less likely you are to have neighbors who taught you to think about the world from a different perspective." It becomes easier, then, to exist within a limited, unchallenged bubble of information and familiarity. To assume that there's no way a presidential candidate received that many votes, given how few of his supporters you know.[67]

The flip side to White Democrats being more likely to live near White Republicans, then, is that they might be expected to build bridges across the parties. Except that Enos's research found that "even when Democrats and Republicans live in the same city—or even the same neighborhood—they are residentially sorted by political party."[68] Instead of bridges, we tend fences.

Asked if we might expect this sorting to accelerate, Enos noted two important considerations. The first was that most people don't actually care as much about politics as he or me or (probably) you. The second was that the existing partisan animosities are not as immediately obvious or potent as something like racism. "We know very clearly that White people in this country picked up and moved as soon as a Black person moved into their neighborhood," he said, referring to historic patterns from the mid-twentieth century. It seems less likely for a variety of reasons that someone encountering a member of the opposing political party would have that reaction. Americans are less likely to move these days in general,[69] for example, and racial cues often (though not always) present more immediately than partisan ones.

This comparison with racial sorting introduces an interesting though imperfect analogue. Chris Warshaw, the George Washington University political science professor with whom I spoke about the consistency of partisanship and ideology, pointed to the former Confederacy during our discussion. It was both very conservative and very Democratic until the civil rights era.[70] Then, thanks in large part to old conservative Democrats being replaced by young conservative Republicans, its partisanship came into alignment with its ideology. Democrats hope the same generational replacement moves the country to the left as the baby boom ages; they worry the same partisan realignment will happen among their less liberal members. When I asked Warshaw what areas might currently see an awkward fit of philosophy and party he pointed to the heavily Democratic, heavily rural, and heavily White Northeast, where the density of people without college degrees is relatively high.

Shortly before the Virginia gubernatorial election in 2021, researchers Zachary Hertz, Lucas Pyle, and Brian Schaffner wrote an essay for *The Washington Post* in which they tried to determine why there was such a wide and growing split between urban and rural vote preferences. They measured several possible factors: the increased likelihood that rural voters were White evangelical Protestants, the increased gun ownership in rural areas, and that urban voters were more likely to say that White Americans had certain advantages in society. The cultural divide that best explained vote choice, they found, was the one centered on race.

"[I]f voters in urban and rural areas acknowledged White privilege at the same rate, the urban-rural voting divide would be relatively small, just eight points," they wrote. "That the divide is actually 32 points speaks to the powerful role that racism plays in fueling this gap."[71]

Importantly, the urban-rural shifts in recent presidential elections have not been even, as David Hopkins, author of the book *Red Fighting Blue: How Geography and Electoral Rules Polarize American Politics*, pointed out when we spoke by phone.

Rural Whites, he said, "really have changed over a twenty-, twenty-five-year period, in a way that can't really be explained just by generational replacement or migration or anything like that." Instead, he said, "it seems clear

CHART 116
Change in Vote Margin by County Population Density

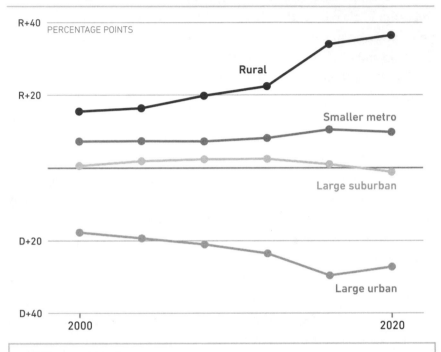

HOW TO READ THIS CHART How counties have voted in the past six presidential elections, according to urbanization definitions from the University of Wisconsin Population Health Institute. Each line represents the change in vote margin across counties of each type relative to the national vote margin, with rural areas seeing a larger shift.

to me that there are people who used to vote Democratic who are now voting Republican."

Hopkins wrote in August 2021: "Republicans' plight as the rural party of an increasingly non-rural nation has so far been balanced out by the fact that rural America has moved toward the GOP at a faster pace since the 1990s than urban America has shifted away. When combined with the structural biases of the electoral college and Senate in favor of rural voters, the current Republican popular coalition can easily remain fully competitive in national elections."[72]

It's likely that the increase in Democratic votes from urban areas over recent elections helped contribute to ongoing theorizing about rampant voter fraud occurring in cities. Rumors emerged about St. Louis in 2000.[73] About Philadelphia in 2012.[74] About Phoenix—and most other cities, it seems—in 2020.[75] Donald Trump, flustered by his election loss, hyped fraud repeatedly, often centering his claims on urban areas. His allies echoed his claims. In one highly scrutinized incident in Wayne County, Michigan, the top Republican on the county board of canvassers suggested that the vote results be certified for everywhere except Detroit.[76] This despite urban voters moving to the right in 2020.

About 41 percent of the 102 million people living in America's large urban counties are White. Of the 46 million in rural counties, 76 percent are.[77] "I think that we have to realize that this notion that rising Black voting power—and Brown voting power and youthful voting power, concentrated in cities—is illegitimate, is out there," Theda Skocpol told me shortly after the election. "It was out there for quite a while. It wasn't created by Trump; it was magnified by Trump."

This again is likely linked to the fact that so few Republicans live near non-White people, particularly in rural areas. Across the country, more than 3 in 10 Whites live in census tracts that are at least 85 percent White. In rural counties, 6 in 10 Whites do.

Some people in heavily White rural areas see heavily Black urban areas casting more than enough ballots to cancel out their margins and they get suspicious or feel wronged. In 2018, Republican Robin Vos, speaker of the Wisconsin State Assembly, was unusually blunt about this idea. "If you took Madison and Milwaukee out of the state election formula," he said, "we would have a clear majority."[78] Dropping Milwaukee and Dane Counties loses the state about a fifth of its White population—and about three-quarters of its Black population. The number of votes cast for Donald Trump in 2020 drops by 13 percent, but the number of votes cast for Biden declines by more than a third. Milwaukee, of course, became an epicenter of post-2020 conspiracy theorizing, none of it validated.[79]

Remember Ryan Enos's research showing that even neighborhoods demonstrate partisan divides. This segmenting sits alongside the erosion of social groups like Kiwanis or (in Robert Putnam's eponymous example) bowling leagues. But more general cultural activities also overlap with partisan categories: NASCAR, going to museums, hunting.[80] That you're reading this book makes it more likely that you're a liberal.

CHART 117

How Often Americans Live in Racially Heterogenous Neighborhoods

		Living in tracts that are at least 85%:				Living in tracts that are at least 85% White:	
		Asian	Black	Hispanic	White	Urban	Rural
Percent of the total population that is:	Asian	0.2%	0.1	0.4	3.5	0.9	28.1
	Black	0.0	10.4	0.3	2.1	0.5	6.1
	Hispanic	0.0	0.2	10.9	3.4	0.6	15.3
	White	0.0	0.1	0.2	31.5	9.8	60

HOW TO READ THIS CHART Census tracts are one of the smallest demographic units compiled by the Census Bureau, generally including no more than a few thousand people. Using the 2020 data, I looked at how much of the country's racial and ethnic populations lived in tracts that were dominated by other racial groups. Each row shows the percentage of a population (Asians, Whites, etc.) that lives in census tracts in which the population is at least 85 percent members of the group indicated at the top of the column. So 3.5 percent of Asians live in census tracts that are at least 85 percent White. The right two columns look only at tracts that are 85 percent White in either urban or rural counties. So 15.3 percent of Hispanic residents of rural counties live in census tracts that are at least 85 percent White.

In her book *Uncivil Agreement*, an exploration of how politics became so intertwined with identity, Lilliana Mason writes that in the middle of the twentieth century the blurring of partisan boundaries (as with those southern conservative Democrats) had an upside: "[S]ince voters did not receive clear cues about their partisan ingroups and outgroups, they did not treat their fellow citizens as enemies simply because of their party affiliation."[81] Now? That's not the case. "White, religious, and conservative people have little incentive to reach across to the nonwhite, secular, and liberal people in the other party," Mason writes. "What superordinate goals do they have? In which places do they mix with opposing partisans?"[82]

Put another way: In this era when America is so often being pulled apart, what's pulling us together?

AMERICA'S BRITTLE GLUE

We're far enough along by now that I think a little thought experiment is warranted. Say I gave you some demographic information about a voter: age, race, educational level, income, gender. Were I to describe 100 adults voting in elections since 1952 using those five characteristics, how often do you think you could correctly guess their presidential vote choice?

If you are as good at this as the computer model developed by researchers Seo-young Silvia Kim and Jan Zilinsky, then you would be right only about three out of every five times.

"The accuracy of this type of model is surprisingly low," Zilinsky told me when I called the pair to talk about their research. "With the five demographic attributes it's only 63.5 percent on average. As Silvia likes to say, if you just flip a coin, you wouldn't really do that much worse." What's more, this isn't simply a function of demographics having become more predictive over time, they found; demographics were about as useful a cue for guessing vote choice half a century ago as they are now.

But then you add in one more piece of information, and suddenly the model can guess right nearly every time. "We do show that, in our second model, where we include partisanship, it really rapidly predicts vote choice," Kim said. Specifically, combine demographics with party identification and you're suddenly able to predict vote choice 95 percent of the time. "Once you have partisanship," Kim added, "other variables tend to really pale in the further information they can give."

Well, sure, you think. *Tell me someone's a Democrat and I can guess that they voted for the Democratic presidential candidate.* But there are three pieces of context useful to remember here. The first is that this was not always as clear a connection as you might assume. In 1980, for example, exit polling suggests that only about two-thirds of Democrats voted for Jimmy Carter.[83] That was an exceptional election, yes, but it's also a reminder that the recent partisan loyalty in presidential voting is not the historical norm. (More on this in a moment.) The second thing to remember is that the point of the research was not to make a point about partisanship but, instead, one about demography.

The third is that the finding holds even despite the increase in nonpartisan and independent political identification in recent years.

Most independents tend to vote with one party or the other, but these are not simply indifferent allies. "The canonical finding in the literature is that so-called leaners actually behave in more extreme ways than, for example, weak partisans," Kim said, pointing to the 1992 book *The Myth of the Independent Voter*. Instead, those voters often form a sort of anti-party, focused more on opposition to one party than support for the other. In early 2022, Pew Research Center asked Democrat- and Republican-leaning independents whether they viewed each major party favorably or unfavorably. Independents who leaned toward a party were generally split on the party to which they leaned but disliked the other party nearly as vehemently as partisans themselves.[84]

Berkeley's Lisa García Bedolla pointed to this specific motivation as driving Hispanic support for Democrats. "There's growing independent identification in the United States, and especially among the immigrant-origin communities, so Asian Americans and Latinos are much more likely to be independent," García Bedolla told me. "In a weird way, you know, the support for the Democratic Party is more, well, *they* hate us. So I guess we have to go over here."

CHART 118
Percent of Each Group That Views Parties Unfavorably

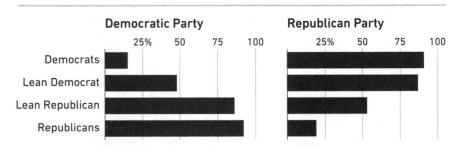

HOW TO READ THIS CHART From Pew Research Center's 2022 survey, the percentage of each group—Democrats, Democrat-leaning independents, Republican-leaning independents, and Republicans—who viewed each party unfavorably. Hostility to the opposing party among leaners was as strong as among members of the parties themselves.

CHART 119
How Hispanics View the Parties

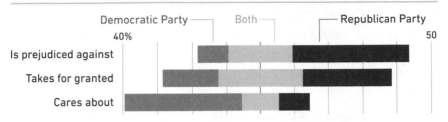

Democratic Party	Both	Republican Party
40%		50

Is prejudiced against

Takes for granted

Cares about

> **HOW TO READ THIS CHART** A December 2021 poll of Latino Americans evaluated their views of each party. Respondents to the poll, conducted by Ipsos for Axios and Telemundo, were asked which party, if either, was prejudiced against Latino and Hispanic Americans, took them for granted, or cared about them.[85] Because one of the accepted answers was "both parties," that response is shown straddling the midpoint between the parties evenly.

Not that weird, really, particularly given how Hispanic voters view each party. A poll released in December 2021 found that more than half of American Hispanics said either that the Republican Party alone was prejudiced against Hispanics or that both parties were.

And, again, not that weird given the negative partisanship displayed by leaning independents. This is a pattern that comports with a phenomenon that Marquette University political scientist Julia Azari succinctly describes as weak parties, strong partisanship.

"[W]hile parties as organizations are weak, parties as ideas—partisanship—is strong. This is what studies of Congress . . . are telling us. This is what obstructionist politics tells us," Azari wrote shortly before the 2016 election. "Polarized presidential approval, the Republicans lining up behind Trump—all of this is telling us that party identification matters to people. A lot. And much of these partisan feelings manifest in a negative way, with distrust and dislike for the other side."[86] This spills over into other institutions that begin to be perceived as similarly partisan. How did the average Trump supporter view the FBI by 2020, for example?

It does not seem likely that parties will strengthen over the intermediate term. You'll remember from chapter 3 that younger people are less likely to belong to political parties. They are also less likely to believe that even the party to which they belong (or lean) reflects the interests of people like them, according to 2021 polling from Pew Research Center. Overall, they are also about as likely as any other age group to believe that the Democratic Party represents their interests, but much less likely to say the same of the Republican Party—a relevant point to our earlier discussion about that party's need to woo members of this voting bloc.[87]

Speaking with me after the 2020 election, Azari suggested that the skepticism of younger voters had been made obvious with the party's schism four years earlier, when Senator Sanders lost the party's nomination for president.

"I don't know that [the Democrats] really have thought about how popular Sanders was, in particular with younger people," Azari said. "And it's because he, I think, was saying the system does not work for you. And younger people were saying, 'Yeah, that's right. It doesn't.'" This message appealed even to Saurabh Sharma, the young conservative I mentioned at the beginning of this chapter. Nor did the man who beat Sanders in the 2020 primary, Joe Biden, resolve the frustration. By the second year of his administration, some of Biden's most vocal critics were young people who felt that he had failed to make the systemic changes he'd promised or to defend basic rights like access to abortion—an indictment of both Biden and his party. If I might tailor Azari's point in service to my thesis: she is identifying a sense of disempowerment felt by an ascendant generation buried under and muffled by the scale of the baby boom.

Part of the strengthening of partisanship is rooted in the increase in what Lilliana Mason describes as "social polarization." "A single vote can now indicate a person's partisan preference as well as his or her religion, race, ethnicity, gender, neighborhood, and favorite grocery store," she wrote. "This is no longer a single social identity. Partisanship can now be thought of as a mega-identity, with all the psychological and behavioral magnifications that implies. . . . At a dinner party today, talking about politics is increasingly also talking about religion and race."[88] Partisanship has overflowed the boundaries of party—or party is simply the umbrella term under which a set of beliefs and attitudes gather.

Something she thought about a lot, Azari told me, "is how old the two parties are, and how stagnant," a view many young Americans would no doubt share. Yet partisanship is thriving and expanding, even when considering

CHART 120
The Increase in Partisan Uniformity in Politics

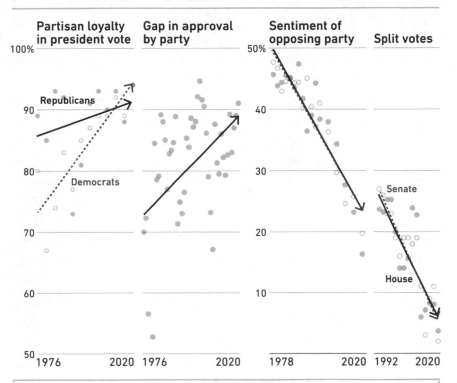

HOW TO READ THIS CHART A lot of data encapsulating a consistent trend. So let's deploy some bullet points. From left to right:

- The percentage of members of each party who voted for that party's presidential candidate, according to exit polling compiled by Edison Research.

- The difference in presidential approval by year between Democrats and Republicans, according to Gallup. As partisan views of presidential performance have concretized, the gap has grown.

- The average sentiment value from 0 (cold) to 100 (warm) members of one party assign to the other from the ANES. This excludes leaners. There are two arrows shown, but they overlap almost entirely.

- The percentage of Senate (outlined circles, dashed arrow) and House elections in which a district or state split its vote between a congressional candidate from one party and a president from the other. Data are from Polidata, *Daily Kos*, and Dave Leip's *Atlas of U.S. Elections*.

In each case, focus not on the dots but on the arrows, the trends.

only strictly political measures. Partisans are more likely to support their party's presidential candidate—when they vote—are less likely to approve of the other party's president, and are more likely to view the other party negatively. At the same time, there's been a consistent decrease in split-ticket voting; that is, districts that vote for a House member of one party nearly always support the presidential candidate of that same party, and the same holds true for Senate candidates.

That last data point is perhaps the most important. In part, it measures the nationalization of politics, the increasing overlap between what's happening and being discussed nationally with elections at the state and local level. The causes for this are myriad, including the erosion of local media outlets like newspapers.[89] (In 1990, about 62 million papers were delivered each weekday; by 2020, an estimated 24 million were in a country with 79 million more residents.)[90] This decline has been linked to lower local turnout and less competitive local elections,[91] but also necessarily means that political news and discussion will be centered on issues presented by regional or, usually, national outlets. State and local races are often driven to some extent by issues that are being discussed on MSNBC and Fox News. This is in part thanks to national organizations investing in local outcomes, but it's largely because people are more focused on the national left-versus-right debates.

This loops back to the Democratic Party's specific challenge in needing to overcome the disproportionate power of rural, largely White states while holding together a diverse coalition. Rachel Blum, a political scientist at the University of Oklahoma who focuses on political parties and institutions, suggested that the challenge was one of party identity. "The key thing here, I think, is the idea of parties as not as these unified wholes, but as coalitions that are trying desperately to hold together these warring interests," she told me when we spoke. "The more that they can hold these together, the more unified that brand is." That's easier with fewer, less different coalitions in the mix—though there is a broader downside, identified by Lilliana Mason: "When parties grow more socially homogeneous, their members are quicker to anger and tend toward intolerance."[92]

In the aftermath of the 2020 election, there was a robust debate within the Democratic Party about the response from left-wing activists to the killing of George Floyd, a Black man, by Officer Derek Chauvin in Minneapolis. Democrats from more rural and more moderate districts pointed to activists' mantra of "defund the police" as complicating their own electoral efforts. This is a complex discussion, one that necessarily includes consideration of how the party's efforts to define its national message is muddied by internal dissent and a robust right-wing media ecosystem that was often the point at which that mantra was amplified. But it is nonetheless a useful example of a challenge the big-tent political left faces that the political right can more easily sidestep.

As the Democratic data expert David Shor put it when we spoke, "Everything that you can do to make people think of Jon Tester in a way that's independent from national party politics is going to increase our ability to win in these biased maps." Tester is a relatively moderate Democrat who serves as senator from Montana, a state that Trump won by 16 points in 2020. Get Montanans to consider Tester's potential 2024 reelection bid on Montana-specific terms and Democrats are in better shape than if his candidacy is simply a reflection of national politics. The risk, of course, is that a local message specific to a mostly White, rural electorate then itself trickles up nationally, alienating other key voting blocs within the party like younger or Black voters.

One way in which the party is addressing this challenge is by owning up to its own limitations. "It's been a really, really, really long time since the Democratic Party, or any party structure or institution has been the anchor of any of these movements," Roger Lau, a senior official with the Democratic National Committee, told me when we spoke in 2021. "The power and the energy is going to come from communities and people who want to engage and want to see change," he said. "How they interact with the party is an interesting and powerful thing, because rather than us sitting there and dictating the terms of what it is that people should do, or instead of us convening these things and having people yell at us, we're part of this conversation now, an equal partner rather than this idea of a top-down party."

Let's assume for the moment that this is a choice the party is making and not one forced upon it. You can very quickly see how this approach encounters some significant challenges. The "defund the police" fight was a function of a robust constituency group helping establish rhetoric that, both organically and through enthusiastic efforts on the right's part, became interwoven with a party impotent to prevent it. While Lau expressed his intention to help empower local, demographically specific subsets of the party, the party's resources are not infinite. With what organizations does it become an equal partner? How is that choice made, particularly as those organizations are contesting with one another for money, attention, and engagement?

In the past, one of the ways in which these questions were negotiated was by having validators who could reliably speak for—and, importantly, organize—constituencies. The ward boss who could guarantee votes. The head of an activist group who could deliver a meaningful endorsement. But as Lau readily admitted, that's no longer really the case.

"We're used to a political world where various kinds of elite figures are held up as spokespeople for various mass constituencies," author David Hopkins told me. "The assumption is, well, if you get those elite figures on your side, then the mass constituencies sort of come with them, or that they can tell you how to appeal to this or that constituency that they're a member of. That's true some of the time—but not necessarily true."

There's an implied transactional element to both party politics and community validators that has weakened. In the days of New York City's Tammany Hall, loyalty to the party and party bosses earned you a government job or power. For elected officials, working with the party (or even across the aisle) could yield benefits for your district: funding for local projects that allowed you to show up and have your picture taken for the paper. But one politician's local earmark is another politician's pork, and, particularly in a nationalized political and media environment, it became harder to cut deals that quietly included local spending. That, in turn, made it harder to reward the community leaders who'd served as gatekeepers.

"Parties have lost the infrastructure of being able to offer their members benefits, to basically buy off coordination," Princeton's Corrine McConnaughy said. "This is Collective-Action Problems 101. Identifying with a group is not necessarily bad, but when it doesn't come hand in hand with tools for that group to do coordinating, in-group, *intra*party politics have become dysfunctional as well as *inter*party politics."

McConnaughy's expertise is specifically how institutional power overlaps with democracy in the United States. And what she spends a lot of time worrying about, she told me, was a question for which she didn't have an answer: Which organizations in civil society are poised to "help us smooth over the seams of living together"?

"What makes people interconnected to each other, and distant from others in meaningful, durable ways? What makes them see the connection between that groupness and what they make demands of the state, what they make demands of the economy for?" she wondered. "There's a background, broad sense that politics is this grand negotiation across groups but there's maybe not enough wrestling with what really makes groups, [or asking] where are the important group structures of today and what are going to be the important group structures of tomorrow?"

We've talked about the declines of these institutions. The percentage of American workers who belong to labor unions dropped from 20 percent in 1983 to just under 11 percent in 2020.[93] The percentage of Americans who had served in the military fell by more than half over the same period,[94] hollowing out groups like the Veterans of Foreign Wars. In March 2021, Gallup reported that less than half of Americans said they belonged to a church, synagogue, or other house of worship.[95] When Rachel Blum was describing the increase in polarization in politics, she framed the change in terms of this sort of diminished intermingling. It's no longer the norm that Republicans, for example, "go to the Rotary Club and they hang out with some Democrats on the weekend," she noted. Why join some social club when it's never been simpler to surround yourself with like-minded allies?

After all, it is easier than ever to organize people and for people to organize themselves. Roger Lau's example for how the Democratic Party— a nearly 200-year-old institution—was supporting the political efforts of other groups was the emergent anti-Trump effort that found its footing on the internet shortly after Trump won in 2016. It was almost trivial to build an organization online that brought together people for this emergent cause, and, as Lau noted, the Democratic Party subsequently injected itself into the effort. My favorite example of the power of the internet is that people who find personal enjoyment or sexual arousal from anthropomorphizing animals—so-called furries—learned that they were members of a community extensive enough to justify regular conventions focused on that niche interest. Putting together a group of people worried about Donald Trump's presidency was easier still.

The key difference is that these ad hoc organizations do not necessarily translate into lasting institutional power. What makes a political party or a labor union powerful is that it exists over time and aggregates power that it can leverage toward a particular end. That requires structure and an often tacit agreement among members that this is the intent. Bringing people together is step one and a form of power by itself. But it's easy for that power to quickly dissipate—particularly when the power isn't actually directed toward affecting concrete change.

"Online spaces can do this awesome thing of harnessing a moment," McConnaughy said. She used the example of the massive march involving hundreds of thousands of women that took place in Washington the day after Trump's inauguration. "You can't imagine the Women's March emerging on the quick timeline at the scale it did without this online space." In fact, she attended that march. But "it was just not at all clear what this was, what it was for, whether anybody understood why the people who had shown up did." There was some attempt to enroll attendees in a broader organization, she remembered, with signs encouraging people to text a particular number. "As far as I can tell," McConnaughy said, "texting whatever while I was there that day just results in funding requests and occasional outrage texts. That's not building citizens' capacity to do functional democratic accountability on a regular cycle."

Once, organizations tried to engage members. "Social media has flipped things around," she said. "You get people to mobilize and then you have to figure out how to organize them afterward without that preexisting structure." In the meantime, some of the effervescent power is lost.

It can now be perhaps too easy to aggregate anger or opinion, too easy to gin up outrage by exaggerating or overstating an issue, too easy to find enough people who will make a financial contribution or who will share a post or tweet that generates attention for an organization, media personality, or elected official. It becomes easy for corporate entities and brands to leverage political anger for commercial purposes. Organizations that vet concerns and deploy responses led by gatekeepers who can speak for a constituency have been edged aside by hazily bounded groups of angry citizens whose response to problems is often either displaying that anger or giving money to the voice that's shouting the loudest. What "I do my own research" was to the pandemic response or to conspiracy theorizing broadly, "I am undertaking my own activism" often is to politics.

McConnaughy referred to "institutionless politics," a different way of drawing Azari's weak-party/strong-partisanship distinction. Such a system erodes the understanding that solving problems is a process or even that problems can be addressed at all. What's needed, McConnaughy said, were institutions that could "solve problems in ways that people feel represented enough, they feel their voice heard enough. That they know that there is some way in which they can understand that losing today is not losing tomorrow." To understand, by extension, that not every fight is an existential one.

On both the left and right, there are those who believe both in the power of government to change Americans' lives and that such an outcome is generally preferable to having a tweet with a sweeping condemnation of the opposition go viral. But effecting such improvement, much less seeing political benefit from it, means overcoming inertia, the fact that doing nothing is always politically easier than doing something. It means being heard in a national conversation focused on any given day's furies, furies that are often presented as world ending. It means having the public understand that something was actually accomplished, which often doesn't happen. No wonder those most cynical about the utility of political parties are the young people who haven't seen political parties actually make significant change.

"People who haven't been part of the conversation need to become part of the conversation and have a meaningful role and exert political power," Azari said. Among those who often haven't been a loud part of the conversation, of course, are younger Americans: voting less, elected less, leading less even as they're increasingly organizing outside of electoral politics to be heard. But organizing without organizations is ephemeral.

One encouraging sign to that end comes from Melissa Deckman's research on Gen Z. She's seen young people, particularly young women, transitioning from online organizing to building organizations, securing funding, and establishing institutions. These organizations may themselves be transitory—or they may be a lasting foundation.

"Group organizations are what shape the structure of politics, and the health of democracy," Corrine McConnaughy told me. "That's the question going forward: Does our current society have and/or is it building the kind of group organization tools to maintain a healthy democracy?"

It is a question for which no answer can yet be determined.

TWO VIEWS OF THE PATH FORWARD

We began this discussion by considering two specific political actors. There was Alex Lee, the Democratic Socialist state legislator from California who lives with his parents and worked a gig-economy job to make ends meet while running for office. And there was Saurabh Sharma, the right-wing head of an organization centered on getting conservatives ready for public service. Each is unusually engaged in political institution building for their ages, with Lee seeking to use the power of the state government to make change and Sharma hoping to change how government works at the federal level.

I asked each to expound a bit on how they saw politics unfolding over the next few decades. Lee was optimistic, given the demographic patterns and the politics of his generation, that his tenure in politics would come to be seen not as leftist but landing somewhere in the middle.

"Two decades from now, a decade?" Lee said. "Knowing people in my age range or younger than my age and where their political beliefs are about all range of issues? . . . I will probably be seen as somewhere in the center—which is unfortunate, I think." He laughed. "Where I'm seen as an outsider today," he predicted, "will be the mainstream tomorrow."

Sharma's view was different. I'd asked him how he thought his side might convince skeptical younger voters to ally with him politically.

"I think that, largely as a by-product of the education system, a lot of younger people have a lot of left-wing priors and there are things that I would not want to give up as part of what it means to be on the right in order to account for that," Sharma began. In other words, his belief is that it's less the case that younger Americans are more progressive by nature and more that they lean left by nurture.

"However, my basic message would be something like: The neoliberal consensus in this country has told you exactly how they want you to live in thirty years. It goes something like, you will own nothing, and you will be happy," he continued. "At current trends, many of you are likely to never be married, to never have children, to never own real property, to basically be slaves to a gig economy where you will be paid little, have few benefits, and live in a country that you will not only not recognize from your childhood but you probably won't recognize decade over decade as the ruling class of this country tries to use ever-more-ridiculous levers to solve obvious problems. So if you'd like to stop living like Russian serfs, maybe give the right a try. What do you have to lose?"

That last appeal, you will recall, was the same one that Trump offered Black voters in both 2016 and 2020. It might have worked slightly better than observers expected.

10

Getting from Here to Wherever "There" Is

L et's begin our final consideration of what the future holds by looking once again at the past, to another cold January 6 where a political transition unfolded during a period of change. Republican Bob Martinez's guber-natorial inauguration in Tallahassee, Florida, on that day in 1987 was, hap-pily, marked not by violence and anger but by more mundane political impulses, like celebration and backbiting. Oh, and by furs.

"I saw a lot of dead animals hanging on people's arms and necks that I don't normally see in Democratic crowds," a (Democratic) county commis-sioner from farther south in the state sniffed.[1] I hesitated to use that hack-neyed verb here, but it's hard not to read that sentence without a near-audible sense of the disdain being offered. Sure, the dyed mink cowboy hat recorded by reporters was probably a bit over the top. But the observer's annoyance was also likely colored by the change in power that the person under the hat was there to celebrate: Martinez's win meant the governor's mansion would be controlled by a Republican for the first time in 15 years and only the second time since Reconstruction. "The time when Democrats ruled Tallahassee unchallenged are clearly gone," the *South Florida Sun-Sentinel*'s report on the inauguration began.

A new day was dawning in another sense as well. Bob Martinez was a native of Tampa, son of a restaurant worker and a seamstress. (Or so the campaign patter had it; Ida Martinez was also a supervisor at an athletic gear company.)[2] In addition to being one of the only Republican governors in the state's modern history at that point, he was also its first (and, of writing, still only) Hispanic chief executive. "¡Ole!" a headline in the English-language *Orlando Sentinel* welcomed him, in its way—"El tiempo de Martinez es aqui, you all."[3]

He took office at a remarkable moment. Florida was one of the fastest-growing states in the country, as he noted during his inaugural address. "Just last week, Florida became the fifth most populous state in the nation," he said, having passed Illinois. "Before the year is out," he continued, "we will move into fourth place, passing Pennsylvania."

Martinez mentioned this shift in status not to brag (or, not only to brag) but because of the implications it carried for the state and its government. "Eight hundred ninety-five new Floridians are arriving each day," Martinez said. "Each day, we need another 130,000 gallons of water. Each day, there's another 111,000 gallons of waste water and 4,200 more pounds of solid waste to dispose of, and each day we need two more miles of highway, three more jail beds, two more police officers, two more classrooms, and two more teachers to teach in those classrooms."

The state was undergoing a population boom. That litany of exponentially increasing demands probably sounds familiar—a bit like the assessment of those tasked with accommodating the nation's ballooning population of infants a quarter century before. More everything, and now.

"We are a growing, vibrant state on the cutting edge of national leadership," Martinez said at another point. This, clearly, was true, and Martinez—himself a descendent of immigrants from Spain—pointed to that population gain as the cause. "Our potential and our opportunities increase with the arrival of every new Floridian."

Martinez didn't get much of a chance to help bolster the state's fortunes. Four years later, he lost reelection handily, battered by low voter approval for various initiatives he undertook, including an effort to restrict access to abortion in the state, and a faltering national economy that pushed up unemployment rates. Then there were the intangibles. For example, there probably aren't many governors who are referenced in songs from popular artists, but in July 1990, a few months before his reelection, Martinez became one. Angered at his efforts to ban their music, the hip-hop act 2 Live Crew recorded and released the track "Fuck Martinez." A few months later, he was replaced by Democrat Lawton Chiles and a different set of befurred celebrants came to the capital.

On January 6, 1987, Bob Martinez's arrival represented multiple shifts in Florida's trajectory. The state's evolution since has come up a lot over the preceding pages, in part because no state serves as a better encapsulation of the baby boom generation. From the opening of Walt Disney World in Orlando in 1971, offering an East Coast destination for the boom's younger members, to the Potemkin Americana of the Villages, the state has been a mecca. That population boom occurring at the time of Martinez's election? Disproportionately a function of the arrival of baby boomers. In 1990, 4.9 percent of baby boomers lived in Florida. By 2020, more than 7 percent did, the biggest increase of any state.[4]

The question this book hopes to answer, though, is where we go next.

CHART 121
Where Baby Boomers Live

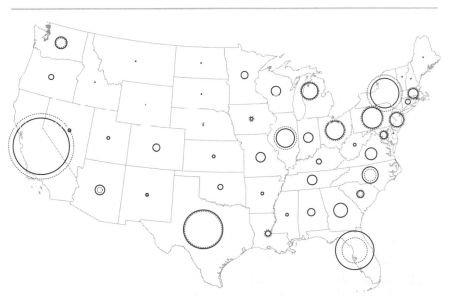

HOW TO READ THIS CHART Using single-year-of-age data from the Census Bureau, a look at the distribution of baby boomers by state in 1990 (dashed-line circles) and 2020 (solid line). Florida saw an increase in boomer density; the solid circle larger than the dashed one). Most states, particularly in the Northeast, saw a decline.

We've arrived at another point at which a new direction will emerge, but it's not clear what direction that will be. Perhaps the states offer some insights.

WHAT AMERICA'S LABORATORIES PRODUCE

One of the better summaries of the relationship between states and the country overall is downstream from a guy in Oklahoma who wanted to sell ice. In the late 1920s, refrigerators were uncommon,[5] so selling ice for iceboxes was a viable business venture. Unless, like Paul Liebmann, proprietor of Liebmann's Independent Ice Company, you lived in a state that granted monopolistic licenses to ice manufacturers. So when Liebmann opened up shop, the licensed provider, New State Ice Company, took him to court.

With Liebmann using the fight as a rallying cry for customers—"Your ice patronage and support will assist in the cause of individual operation against monopoly," one ad read[6]—the case in 1932 made its way to the Supreme Court. Liebmann won, in a 6 to 2 decision.

The case's broadest legacy, though, may come from the dissent offered by Justice Louis Brandeis. Brandeis objected to the court's interference in Oklahoma's process in part because he believed that the state was better positioned than he and his colleagues to determine its own needs. Moreover, allowing states to try things out was, he argued, one of the benefits of the form of government that the United States had enacted.

"There must be power in the States and the nation to remould, through experimentation, our economic practices and institutions to meet changing social and economic needs," Brandeis wrote. ". . . It is one of the happy incidents of the federal system that a single courageous State may, if its citizens choose, serve as a laboratory; and try novel social and economic experiments without risk to the rest of the country."[7]

Thus was born the idea that states serve as "laboratories for democracy," deploying bespoke systems of governance across 50 population centers that might survive Darwinistic competitions for effectiveness. The long-term manifestations of Brandeis's framing might not have been what he would have anticipated, as we'll see. But for Liebmann, the short-term effects of the decision were fruitful. He quickly opened a new ice plant in El Reno, Oklahoma, emblazoning the phrase "the firm that broke the monopoly ice law and made competition possible" on its side.[8] At the grand opening, he sold 100 pounds of ice for 40 cents.[9]

I'm going to leverage the decision in *New State Ice Co. v. Liebmann* somewhat differently. If we consider the states as offering previews of how legislation could evolve, we might similarly consider them as possibly offering previews of the country overall. Far from abstract, this is a matter of energetic jockeying at the moment as competing state-level experiments—often ones that have remained afloat in the sheltered harbors of unified single-party control—are presented as the country's inevitable or necessary future. If the United States' demographic, political, and economic changes progress as we might by now expect, what results likely won't look much like Vermont (heavily White, largely rural) or, say, Alaska. So what might it look like?

Perhaps California. As I spoke to people about how demography and politics were likely to evolve as the baby boom receded, several pointed to California as being a possible preview of that new United States. There's some irony to this; California was at one point seen as something of an epicenter of the boom itself, as Landon Jones documents in *Great Expectations*. But as the boom changed, so did the state.

Sociologist Richard Alba pointed to California as it was a place "where Whites are already a population minority." The state has already seen an "influx of people from new groups into the leadership," he continued, "but Whites are also still extremely important in the leadership of the state. At least in many parts of the country, there's going to be—you know, I use the word 'mainstream,' there'll be a mainstream. It'll be much more diverse than today but Whites will still be very important players in that mainstream. It's going to be a continuation of what we have today."

There are a few ways in which to read that pointed term "mainstream." Alba is saying that there is a central conduit for power in the state and that White Californians retain strong influence in that conduit. This isn't surprising, given what we've learned about the distinction between citizen and noncitizen residents[10] and the false presentation of non-Whites as forming a cohesive political bloc.[11] But it's fair to also understand Alba's term as an effort to rename a power and social structure that had been to some extent *predicated* on Whiteness.

This was a distinction drawn by demographer William Frey when we spoke. He also introduced a concept aimed at differentiating how power and importance might in the future be aggregated around something other than race. "It's true that, in the last century, people tended to integrate into the White communities and therefore take on White values and White norms," he said. "I think in this century, those people who are going to be taking on *American* norms aren't necessarily going to be White. In other words, the America of this century is not going to be a 'White America.' It will still be an America that has a mainstream, but that mainstream doesn't mean everyone has to identify with being White."

This is more true in California than in other states, including in the most literal manifestation of power. In 2020, the National Conference of State Legislatures estimated that only 55 percent of the state's legislators were White, the third-lowest percentage in the country.[12] Whites were still over-represented in elected leadership, mind you, as was the case in 47 of the 50 states.[13] But the political "mainstream" in California does reflect a demography that isn't entirely dependent on White Californians.

Historian David Roediger, whose past research has centered on White identity, pointed out that New Mexico's track record as a state in which power has been shared between racial groups is better established. There, he told me, "you have Hispanic people ruling the state politically, in a lot of cases, and have for a long time." His point was less that there was comity in power sharing but that Hispanic New Mexicans didn't need to fold into those White values and norms mentioned by Frey in order to hold that power. "They just rule in coalition with Whites," Roediger said. "The better question [for the country's future] might end up not being 'Will a White majority prevail?' but 'Will coalitions develop that challenge White supremacy as a result of these demographic changes?'" He's obviously not meaning "White supremacy" in the sense of overt neo-Nazism here but, rather, in the sense of power structures that explicitly or implicitly favor White Americans. And his question is not whether non-Whites can join with Whites in holding power but if, as they hold power, those structures will be deliberately dismantled or recentered, as in Frey's framing.

These are assessments of how leadership might evolve in a more diverse country that are optimistic, centered on an expansion of power among non-Whites and a reconciliation of what power looks like as a result. But there's also the pessimistic possibility that we considered in chapter 7, that White power systems will become more entrenched, particularly given the state-level backlash to Donald Trump's 2020 loss. In a 2021 book, former Ohio Democratic Party chairman David Pepper warned of states becoming "laboratories of autocracy."

The country has examples of that drift as well. Since Republicans "see very clearly that they cannot expect to keep dominating going forward if this country is a democracy," the historian Thomas Zimmer told me, "they are very blatantly and openly trying to restrict the electorate, restrict American democracy in a way that will result in a sort of a stable conservative minority rule. Something like Wisconsin, basically. Where you only get forty percent of the vote, but forty percent of the vote might be enough to stay in power."

Wisconsin is a useful example, with an assembly that is heavily lopsided to the benefit of Republicans. In 2016, Republicans won nearly two-thirds of the seats in the assembly—64 of 99—despite winning only 52 percent of the statewide vote. In 2018, Democrats won 53 percent of the vote. Republicans won 63 of the 99 seats. When Democrat Tony Evers won the governorship that year, Republican legislators quickly moved to constrict the powers of the office, a sudden change after eight years of Republican leadership.

In the wake of Trump's 2020 presidential election loss, a loss that depended in part on Wisconsin's flipping from supporting Trump in 2016 to supporting Joe Biden four years later, Wisconsin Republicans sought to expand their ability to direct voters' power. Senator Ron Johnson (R-Wisconsin) proposed that the legislature simply be allowed to assume control of federal elections.[14] Johnson had been filmed earlier in the year admitting that there was no evidence that the contest in his state had been marred by fraud,[15] but he nonetheless told *The New York Times* that his proposal was necessary because he and others "don't expect [Democrats] to follow the rules."[16]

Perhaps not the sort of state-level social experimentation that Brandeis, a fervent political progressive, had in mind.

There are various other examples of state legislators trying to undercut the results of democratic elections and, in particular, the election of Democrats. Often, as with Johnson's assertion, the predicate is some misinformation about or misinterpretation of the purported danger to the state or country. At other times, it's simply an undisguised response to losing an election, as when Georgia Republicans quickly moved to tighten election laws in that state after Biden's 2020 election win—a win that Republican officials were correctly insistent wasn't marred by significant problems.

When similar legislation restricting voter access was passed in Florida, Governor Ron DeSantis (R) held an unusual signing ceremony. He traveled to West Palm Beach, very near Trump's resort Mar-a-Lago, and invited supporters to join him for the event. The media was not allowed, though, save one outlet: Fox News, which covered the signing live during an interview on its morning program *Fox and Friends*.

And here we are, once again at Florida.

THE CASE FOR FLORIDA AS PARADIGM

As I was exploring what America's political future might look like, I took bookstore owner Sally Bradshaw's advice and called David Johnson. Johnson's an old hand in Florida politics, though his Tennessee accent betrays his roots. Politics pushed him to the Sunshine State with the Bush-Quayle election of 1988 and he's been there ever since.

Johnson was quick to point out that I might take his predictions with a grain of salt. After all, he and Bradshaw had worked together on the post-2012 assessment of how the Republican Party might move forward, an assessment that put an emphasis on reaching out to non-White voters in recognition of how the country was evolving. "And then Trump came and blew the whole thing apart in terms of, well, here's what you should do," Johnson said. Trump took a slightly modified approach: "Well, let's do exactly the opposite."

But, then, it also wasn't the case that increased diversity inexorably led to a decline in Republican fortunes, as passing elections in Florida itself made clear. "What's fascinating in Florida are the demographic changes and what we think we're going to see happen, oftentimes we don't," Johnson said. "We absolutely don't." The pool of registered voters in Florida has become significantly less White in the last few years, he noted—yet the state remains tightly competitive at both the national and state level.

In part, that's because the population continues to expand with the arrival of more retirees—often older Whites who vote regularly. In 2019, about 1,600 more people a day moved to the state than left.[17] "The boomer gener-

CHART 122

The Composition of the Registered Voter Pool in Volusia County

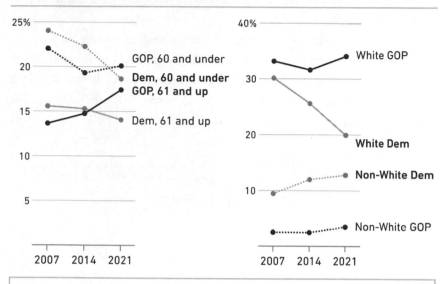

HOW TO READ THIS CHART A look at the composition of the voter pool in Florida's Volusia County, using county data. At left, the overlap of age and party; at right, race and party. Note the changes in the vertical axis between charts.

ation is moving into fuller retirement age now—we're seeing it. There's been a lot of money invested here in Florida in different areas trying to build retirement communities, much like the Villages or those type of model," Johnson said. "These are vast tracts of land, but they're in areas in the past where the Democrats have done well, like Volusia County."

Volusia County is home to Daytona Beach, just northeast of Orlando. In 2008, Barack Obama won it by about 6 points, slightly better than his national margin. In 2020, after an influx of older Republicans, Trump won it by 14 to 18 points better than his national performance. "It doesn't take much of a change in what's swimming in the swimming pool to really change the Florida landscape," Johnson said, offering a state-appropriate analogy.

Yet not all such changes necessarily affect the overall political landscape. Johnson's expectation in 2013 had been that the percentage of Whites in the electorate would drop a point or two in each cycle, he said. But "that has not been the case. That has not been the case at all." In part, that's because the number of Hispanics who vote has not grown at the same pace as the Hispanic population itself. In part, this is a function of citizenship: a fifth of the state's Hispanics weren't citizens in 2019.[18] We can expect a similar disparity nationally.[19]

Florida may offer a look at the future for another reason, as Johnson noted: climate change. A report from McKinsey released in April 2020 estimated that by 2030, tidal flooding due to higher sea levels would reduce the value of real estate in the state by 5 to 15 percent. By 2050, the decline was estimated at 15 to 35 percent—a total of $30 to $80 billion in lost real

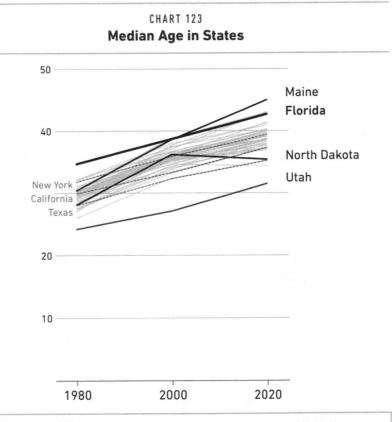

CHART 123
Median Age in States

HOW TO READ THIS CHART Median age in the states at each census. Florida is consistently higher than most states, though several New England states have recently supplanted it. Utah's high fertility rate consistently keeps its median age low. North Dakota is noted for its decline in the median age—largely a function of the boom in hydraulic fracturing that brought thousands of young workers to the state.[20]

estate value.[21] Not to mention more esoteric problems, like whether people can actually continue to live in places near the coast. "In ten years, if Miami Beach is not habitable, that's going to be a big deal," Johnson said, understating things a bit.

With its balance of disparate regions, from the deeply conservative Panhandle—essentially an extension of the Deep South—to the urban, Democratic region around Miami, the state includes an unusual geographic diversity. But there is a key way in which it's an outlier, one that certainly affects its politics and is obviously pertinent to this discussion: it is old.

Since older voters skew more Republican and more White, that suggests an influence on state politics that other places won't share. Though, of course, the America of the future will be similarly older and those older Americans still more densely White than younger generations. So is Florida an aberration, or is it a preview?

Johnson had some advice on this sort of speculation. "If we'd gone back forty years ago, if we go back to 1980 when I was a kid," he said, "in 1980, you could not dream of the internet economy. You could not fathom it. So what are we not fathoming that could happen within ten to fifteen years from now?"

In December 2019, we could not fathom what December 2020 would look like, much less December 2060. A useful reminder of our own shortsightedness. And one I'll immediately ask that you set aside.

LABORATORIES OF DEMOGRAPHY

When considering where the country may be headed, let's again fall back on what we can to some extent measure. We know what demographers expect the country to look like in 40 years' time and we know what the states look like now. Well, sort of. I've explained why projections of the proportion of Hispanics in the population should be considered with some skepticism. We've looked at the likelihood that political patterns are retained as people age, and if we try to look out a few decades—say, to 2060—describing our crystal ball as murky is akin to describing the Sun as merely warm.

But we press on. Figuring that the most salient characteristics of the population for comparison to the future were race and age, I took Census Bureau estimates for the demographics of each state and contrasted them with the projected 2060 figures for the United States overall.[22] If we compare the density of racial groups for those under 18 and those aged 65 and up in each state with those projections, there's a wide spread of how closely current demographics map where the country is going. West Virginia, heavily White

CHART 124

Comparing State Demography Now to U.S. Demography in 2060

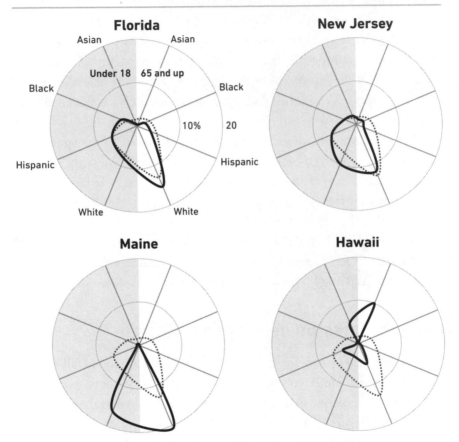

HOW TO READ THIS CHART These are radar graphs, contrasting current individual state demographics (solid line) with the projected composition of the country overall in 2060 (dashed line).[23] Eight data points are shown for both the state and the United States: the percentage of the population that's Asian, Black, Hispanic, or White both under the age of 18 and aged 65 or over. By plotting and overlaying all eight points, you can see which states largely mirror the country's likely future—Florida, followed by New Jersey—and two that very much don't.

and old, doesn't overlap with the future United States much at all. Nevada, more heavily Hispanic, aligns more closely.

The state that looks most like what we'd expect the United States to look like in 2060? Florida.

Where Florida's current population deviates the most from the America of the future is that, once again, it is older. That's even by the standard of the United States in 2060, when 23 percent of the population will be 65 and over, compared to about 17 percent in 2020. Florida's population now also has a lower density of Asian Americans than expected for the country in four decades.

This is a rough presentation of a rough calculus. If we look at the 10 states that land closest to the 2060 U.S. population on each of the eight measured values, you can see that Florida aligns more closely on some (percentage of Hispanic residents under 18) and deviates on others (older Whites).

You may also notice a pattern here: the ten states that most closely reflect the projected demography of the United States in 40 years, shown in Chart 125, are mostly ones that supported Joe Biden in 2020. These 10 states voted for Biden over Trump by a 4.6 million vote margin, 9.2 percentage points overall. They also constitute 30 percent of the population. The 10 states that *least* reflect that projected demography of the country in 2060 preferred Trump by 231,000 votes, a 2.9 point margin over Biden. Less than 5 percent of the population live in those states (though, of course, they have the same representation in the Senate as those 10 larger states). To put a fine point on it, the states that look most like how the United States is expected to look in the future are ones that right now vote more heavily Democratic. The ones that look least like that projection are ones that vote more heavily Republican.

And yet the state that appears to look *most* like 2060 was in 2020 governed by a Republican, Governor Ron DeSantis, who tied his fortune tightly to Donald Trump's. A governor who embraced right-wing culture-war fights, scaled back voting access, undercut an effort to allow convicted felons to vote, and touted his willingness to leverage state power against a corporation, Disney, that opposed his policies in part due to pressure from its young employees. Is this a better preview of the future?

This analysis is an attempt to construct one jigsaw puzzle out of 200 different boxes of pieces. Of course the country will look *something* like it does now, in the same way that the country looks now the way it did in 1980

CHART 125
How States Vary from the Future United States

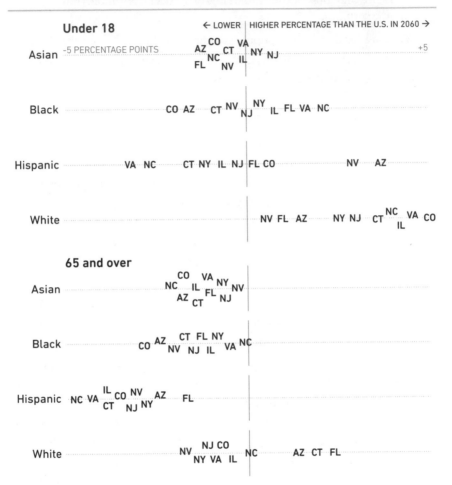

Under 18   ← LOWER | HIGHER PERCENTAGE THAN THE U.S. IN 2060 →

Asian   -5 PERCENTAGE POINTS   +5

Black

Hispanic

White

65 and over

Asian

Black

Hispanic

White

> **HOW TO READ THIS CHART** The graphs above are called beeswarm plots: the state markers swarm around their approximate values. States to the left of the vertical divider currently have lower percentages of the indicated demographic group than the United States is expected to have in 2060. States to the right have a higher percentage of that group (say, Asian residents under the age of 18, as in the first graph) than is projected for the United States. The closer to the line, the more that state currently looks like the projected future United States.

to at least some degree. Were I to tell someone in 1980 that a relatively un-known real estate developer from New York City had been president, they'd likely have been rather surprised, but if I told them that an ambitious young senator from Delaware named Joe Biden was, that might be less jarring.

One way in which 2060 will look something like now: there will still be baby boomers, nearly 2.5 million of them per the Census Bureau's pre-pandemic projections. Strom Thurmond was a senator until he was 100 years old; there will be nearly 2 million baby boomers younger than that in 2060, still eligible to serve. Biden was inaugurated at the age of 78, a reminder that the youngest boomers could be inaugurated in 2041 without surpassing Biden's record as oldest president upon taking office.

By then, there may also be other options.

"I remember somebody asking on social media who will be the first millennial president," Marquette University's Julia Azari told me, "and I was like, baby boomers are just going to holographically project themselves until the end of time."

This book makes no predictions about improvements in virtual reality technology or about the prospect of a digital singularity in which death is replaced with being uploaded. I will also not delve into any legal arguments over whether the constraints on presidential eligibility in the Constitution cover digital intelligences.[24] Suffice it to say, however, Azari's joke isn't as wild as you might expect.

OUR DESTINATION DEPENDS ON THE STEPS WE TAKE NOW

During his inaugural speech in 1987, Governor Bob Martinez celebrated Florida's growth and dynamism—but also identified the ways in which Florida's success could be hampered.

"Floridians, whether native or new, are a unique blend of ethnic, racial, and age groups. This diversity has produced a spirit of independence and enterprise—a can-do attitude—that is our greatest resource," Martinez said. The state's potential increased with every new migrant to the state, he added, before warning of the effects should that growth reverse. "The day they stop coming is the day we will find it more and more difficult to maintain the quality of life that has made Florida synonymous with the good life," he said.

It has consistently been migration, both domestic and international, that
has spurred Florida's population growth. While more Floridians were being
born each year than died when Martinez was governor, it was migration that
was pushing the population total up so quickly. (From 1985 to 1990, there
were about 5.5 new migrants to Florida from elsewhere in the United States
for every immigrant from another country.) Since then, however, natural
population change (that is, the number of births each year minus the number
of deaths) has gone negative, a trend exacerbated by the coronavirus pandemic but one that was otherwise projected by state data. The state's overall
population growth is now solely a function of migration. The recent period
when population growth was the smallest was when migration was lowest,
during the recession that began in 2007.

So what happens if significant parts of Florida become uninhabitable (or
even simply less habitable) due to climate change? What happens if changes

CHART 126
Contributors to Population Change in Florida

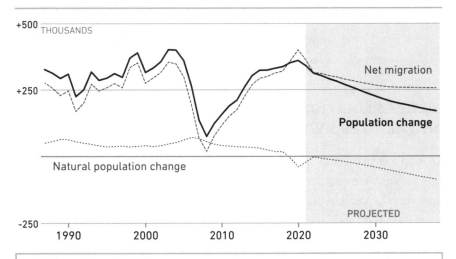

HOW TO READ THIS CHART Using data from the Florida Demographic Estimating
Conference,[25] the graph above shows population changes by fiscal year. The solid line
is the total change and represents the combination of the other two lines. The lower
dashed line is the natural population change, births minus deaths. The upper dashed
line is net migration, people arriving in the state minus those leaving.

in the state reduce the motivation for Americans or immigrants to move there? What if the federal government further constrains international migration?

Florida's future is dependent on decisions made in the present. What happens between now and 2060 depends on the choices we make and the policies we implement. The long term depends on the short term. With that in mind, here are five short-term things that might shape how America looks and how it sees itself.

Changing How We Describe a Changing America. A significant part of the political tension in the United States at the moment derives from concern about the status of White Americans. Often, this is a function of perceptions that consider those changes in stark terms—fewer Whites, more non-Whites—perceptions that likely don't accurately reflect how demography will evolve.

The reality of race is that racial identification is often murky and muddled. Given a choice to describe themselves with more complexity, many Americans will—and many Americans already *do*. There are millions of Americans who appear to be White who would describe themselves in more nuanced terms. As the 2020 census showed, America's increasing demographic diversity is in part a function of an increase in the complexity of how we allow people to describe themselves.

Appearance is salient, certainly, given the likelihood that prejudices based on skin color will continue. But it is not the case, as the far-right "great replacement theory" has it, that the status of White Americans will inexorably decline as they are intentionally overwhelmed by dark-skinned immigrants. That's no more likely than it was the case that White Anglo-Saxon Protestant Americans were subjugated or eradicated by Italian and eastern European immigrants. There were shifts in power, status, and identity, but ones that, in retrospect, seem minor.

What's more, the idea of a consistent, obviously non-White "Hispanic" identity is flawed. Those demographic projections depend on Hispanic families continuing to identify as Hispanic over time; the reaction depends on an ongoing bright line between "Hispanic" and "White." Neither of those assumptions is indisputable—or even more likely than not.

As the research of Dowell Myers and Morris Levy shows, how the changes in demography are presented shapes the response.[26] Describe the increasing complexity of racial identity as simply that, and most White Americans express hope or enthusiasm about the change. Describe it as being to the detriment of Whites, and those views become sharply negative.

That research was published in 2018. In the years since, Pew Research Center has conducted polling centered on how Americans perceive future demographic changes. Democrats have always been less likely to describe the prospect of a non-White majority as bad—but a decreasing share of Republicans have said the same thing in recent years.

Democrats and Democratic-leaning independents are also far more likely to say that the decline of a White majority would be good for the country. In part, this is for the same reason that Republicans are wary: the perception that this augurs a new dominance for the political left. But that, too, is a flawed assumption.[27] Just ask David Johnson how his expectations about Florida worked out.

The problem with prescribing changes in rhetoric is that there are often countervailing impulses. There's an element of schadenfreude that's compelling in a moment of deep partisanship; Democrats have come to see demographic trends as politically beneficial and therefore good. Republican officials and right-wing actors, meanwhile, have learned the power of amplifying these perceived changes as bad.

"The growing diversity of the United States is certainly making whites more conscious of their membership in an ethno-racial group that is just one part of the American population," Richard Alba wrote in his book *The Great Demographic Illusion*. "But their growing consciousness of whiteness may not have to become racially politicized in the way that was true in 2016. A less inflammatory alternative narrative may be possible."[28]

There's a reason that it was politicized in 2016, though—a useful one for Donald Trump. It may be more accurate to describe the evolution of American demographics as uncertain, nuanced, and in some ways misleading. It is probably better for the country if it is viewed that way. But over the short term, there's a lot more money and a lot more votes and viewers to be wrung from the more alarmist rhetoric.[29]

Understanding the Evolution of the Role of Immigration. The Census Bureau's projections for what the United States looks like depend on the number

CHART 127
Views of Increasing Diversity

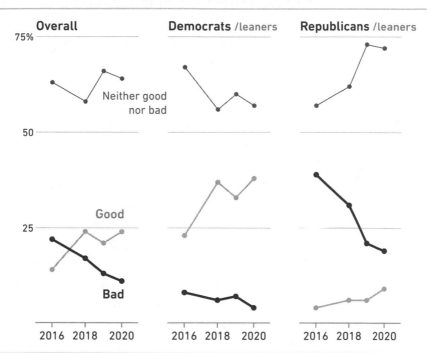

HOW TO READ THIS CHART   Pew Research Center has repeatedly asked Americans their view of the projection that "in the next 25 to 30 years, Black Americans, Latinos and Asian Americans will make up a majority of the population."[30] The decline in the percentage of Americans viewing this as bad for the country (graph at far left) is largely a function of the decline seen among Republicans and Republican-leaning independents (at far right).

of immigrants who come to the country. Lower immigration, a less diverse population. Specifically, 10 percent fewer Hispanic residents by 2060 and 21 percent fewer Asian. More important, the number of seniors per 100 working-age people (25 to 64) goes from 48 to 50.1. The imbalance between elderly Americans drawing on national resources and the working-age population contributing to that pool gets slightly larger.

Let's be blunt: as baby boomers retire and die, who's going to fill their jobs? In December 2011, about 40 percent of Americans in age groups that overlapped with the baby boom were out of the labor force. By December 2016, about 50 percent were. By December 2021, about 60 percent were.[31] This change occurred even as the overall labor participation rates among all adults increased.

To some extent, this decline in participation will be ameliorated by the same phenomenon we discussed when considering housing:[32] for every 100 baby boomers in the United States when the middle of that generation hit age 40, there will be 96 millennials when that generation reaches the same age. But there's still a gap. Some of the jobs held by boomers won't need to be filled, certainly, but most will be. What's more, there will be an increase in the need for particular kinds of employment, like elder care. With population growth slowing and the population aging, there's an irreconcilable tension—and that just to remain in place. As that 2016 report on immigration from the National Academies of Sciences, Engineering, and Medicine stated, "If the American economy grows and requires more workers both to replace those who retire and to create new firms and industries, the primary source of labor will be first and second generation immigrants. This basic fact will hold at all levels, from low-skilled service jobs to professionals with postgraduate degrees."[33]

You'll recall that Dowell Myers offered this as a point of opportunity, not challenge. There's long been a sense—one that's often exaggerated and exploited—that increased immigration necessarily increases competition for employment. But if there is instead pressure for *employees*, that rhetoric is inversed. As the economy began to rebound from the coronavirus pandemic, such pressure was already on display, overlapping with baby boomers increasingly withdrawing from the labor force.

"We actually need immigrants," Berkeley's Lisa García Bedolla told me. "We don't want to become like Japan, where we have economic stagnation because of how the population is distributed. Having a vehement anti-immigrant frame right now actually doesn't make any sense for the country."

Here again, though, the rhetoric in opposition to immigration is often more powerful, building on a long-standing set of assumptions that are at odds with the realities of the present.

Policy, Political Power, and Opportunity. Stephen Morgan, the Johns Hopkins professor who focuses on the transfer of wealth, articulated one of the unresolved questions about how the economy would evolve over the long term: how we choose to address the obvious issues. Would the country fix the immigration system to reduce the strains mentioned above, for example? How would policy decisions help to reduce the imbalance between the income generated by workers and that drawn down by retirees?

"It may be," he said, "that the political choices that boomer voters make will be more consequential [for the direction of the economy] than their own financial investment and consumption behavior."

While that is likely true, it also speaks to one of the central tensions at play. Younger Americans consistently and accurately see how America's political structure is weighted to a group, still heavily composed of baby boomers, that doesn't look like them or reflect their concerns. It's a system that gives primacy to homeowners and disproportionate weight to residents of rural areas. But it's also a system buffeted by class, where participation is easier for retirees and the wealthy and those voices are amplified. Deutsche Bank warned that the policy and economic gap seen between age groups was "simply unsustainable,"[34] but those are only two of a number of similar gaps.

One way in which these gaps can be reduced is by increasing representation from younger Americans. Run for Something's Amanda Litman described the engagement she saw from younger voters when their peers sought office; Melissa Deckman, the professor who focuses on Generation Z, detailed how younger, more diverse officeholders influenced political participation. But young elected officials are still a minority, often in multiple senses of the word, and the policy-making process still often has the effect of actively discouraging young people.

"If we are able to have the foresight to invest in our younger generation in terms of helping them get wealth and helping them get good jobs and helping them become part of the middle class, it'll put us in a much better place," Brookings's William Frey explained when we spoke. "It will also help them assimilate—not necessarily the way they identify their race, but certainly as far as being American." That welcoming approach to considering the needs of Americans has often been talked about in the context of immigration, but it also applies to younger Americans who might also feel excluded from the mainstream. But, of course, it still applies to immigrants, too. Jorge Masvidal identified the way in which Hispanics came to the United States with an eye toward personal success and to fulfill the American dream.[35]

That same motivation drives younger Americans, too—and the same need to ensure the possibility of achieving that dream also applies.

Consider the alternative, articulated by Michigan congressman Peter Meijer when we spoke: a feeling that the system, as structured, isn't meeting Americans' needs. A common feeling, he said, is that "our system is not redressing my grievances, and if I can't use the system to fix the system, then I'll go outside the system." That's a dangerous path—as we've frequently seen in recent years.

Defending and Preserving Democracy. The fissures in American democracy now appear nearly everywhere, even—at times especially—within the parties themselves.

"We go to people now to try to talk to them about running for office, and they say, 'Why would I want to do that?'" David Johnson, the Republican consultant from Florida, told me. He described the sentiment many potential candidates had: "I'm fine with the general election back-and-forth but I don't want to go to these Republican primaries and say things I don't believe in just to try to not make the Trump people mad at me." It's an outgrowth of a sentiment he'd seen for the past 10 years, and it's one that had "a debilitating effect on recruiting."

If politics are too toxic for Republicans to vie for the approval of Republicans, what hope do we have for bipartisanship?

The problem here is both acute and chronic. The acute problem is the efforts to decrease the connection between winning fairly conducted elections and holding power, efforts manifested in changes to voting laws or attempts to decouple presidential votes from electoral ones or in the ongoing imbalance of power between rural and nonrural states or in responding to an election loss by undermining the winner's power. This acute problem poses a short-term risk of undercutting the country's claim to being a liberal democracy.

It also stems from the chronic problem: the feeling that the system as constituted doesn't actually meet people's needs or that it fails to be responsive to what people want. This sense is often not wrong, but it can also be exaggerated by the perception that what one group wants overlaps with what the majority of Americans want. Donald Trump repeatedly claimed to speak for the American majority despite the results in both 2016 and 2020 suggesting a less robust mandate. He and his opponents also often framed political debates in apocalyptic language, making it worth reiterating Corrine Mc-Connaughy's quote from chapter 9: it's important in a democracy that people understand that "losing today is not losing tomorrow." It's important that people understand that not every political debate is an existential one or another slip down some dangerous slope. It's similarly important to disrupt the advantages given to those who exaggerate the stakes.

There's overlap here with the other challenges identified above. For example, George Washington University's Chris Warshaw pointed to that sense of an unstoppable trend away from White dominance as a challenge to political decision-making. "From a normative point of view, having it actually feel like things aren't inevitably Democratic in the future," he said, "would actually make both parties maybe behave more rationally in more and more pro-'small-d'-democratic ways." Decreasing the temperature in order to make it seem less necessary to break the political system in order to retain power. If possible.

"We've been in a radicalizing cycle since 1970," Ian Haney López said, "so we're at the fifty-year mark now of a radicalizing cycle. It's a cycle that begins with the adoption of racial demagoguery as an electoral strategy without fully recognizing the way in which racial demagoguery is a loaded gun: easy to pick up, but very hard to put down."

"We either change how we're talking about racial and more generally social solidarity in the United States," he insisted, "or we plummet off that cliff."

Changing the Conversation. You've no doubt noticed a theme by now: there are loud voices that are pushing things in a more dire direction.

"The public conversation is replete with teeth gnashing about the fracturing of American society and the growing instability and growing levels of partisanship and distrust. All true," Haney López said. "What is the main cause of that? The fact that we've grown meaner? No, the main cause of that is some of the most powerful people and some of the most sophisticated in their politics, and in their propaganda, have been promoting the disuniting of America." He pointed to figures like Stephen Bannon, the former head of Breitbart and former adviser to Donald Trump—someone who is explicit in his desire to reshape America. He might similarly have pointed at Trump himself or at the voices on Fox News's prime-time programming, for whom arguments about retention of power have often proven more important defenses of democratic elections. Of course, they would likely point at the far left as posing a different sort of risk to the United States, of a collapse into socialism cheered by Bernie Sanders or an embrace of violence and a policing of language that mirror strongman regimes in other parts of the world. Some would likely point to Haney López himself.

The short-term rewards of viewers or social-media followers or advertising revenue or campaign contributions or even votes are powerful incentives. Media figures who say what people want to hear will not be punished by their audiences; quite the opposite. Elected officials who encourage division and reactionary rhetoric often don't pay political costs in a system that benefits incumbents and, increasingly, partisanship.

How do you reshape the profit motive for Fox News? How do people like David Johnson prevent party primaries from descending into hyperpolarized contests in which unattainable promises are made? Perhaps recognition is a step to that end. Perhaps advocating for incremental shifts now will cumulatively affect where we are heading. Or perhaps we'll simply get lucky.

We are in a moment in politics and in culture that has never before existed. The most powerful country in the world is undergoing an enormous generational shift that overlaps with the invention of tools that allow for individuals to band together with and talk to anyone else. It's a moment of self-awareness: we see our national power being challenged and we see our internal divisions widening. But we also know that we've weathered unsteady moments before—even outright division, even violent conflicts over race and status. What we can say with the most certainty is that the America into which the baby boomers were born is long gone and that the America they built is crumbling. The uncertainty is whether that America is replaced by ashes or, once again, a phoenix.

THE FIRST BOOMER

After months of missed connections and pandemic-related hurdles, Kathleen Casey Kirschling and I met for the first time in person at a Starbucks near her home in southern New Jersey. A surge in coronavirus infections in the days before had made an indoor setting seem fraught for someone born in the first seconds of 1946—especially a Saturday one week before Christmas when our original planned meeting spot, a mall, was packed with people. So despite the fairly chilly weather and a bit of a drizzle, we opted for a sheltered table outside of the coffee shop instead.

Kirschling was prepared, she assured me, wearing warm boots and her red-checked coat. The face mask she dutifully carried was red, too, as was her sweater. Over its loose collar were visible two necklaces, one a medallion depicting Pope Francis and the other a Celtic cross she'd been given by her uncle, a Catholic priest. She'd arrived in her husband's tan pickup truck, prompting me to ask about his politics: he's a fairly conservative independent; she, a moderate Democrat. In keeping with the faith that's so central to her and her family, she's pro-life, but she insisted that wasn't the sole litmus test she used for politics. To her, pro-life was all-encompassing, meaning that she wanted politicians to address the availability of guns, too.

Shortly after we sat down, she told me a story about a recent "mini-reunion" of several of her classmates from Camden Catholic High School. They got together once a month, she said, "like we never left." On the most recent occasion, she found herself talking with two men.

Kirschling recounted part of the conversation: "'Kat, now let's face it, the whole issue is about racism.' And I said, 'You're right.'"

I asked which issue she was referring to.

"Meaning, they were talking about the issues of today, with what's happened," she replied. Later she explained that, while she agreed, she found it baffling that racism should be so pervasive, given that one of her generation's greatest achievements was its embrace of diversity.

I will admit that this seemed a bit too neat, particularly as the first story she told me upon my arrival. Kirschling has spent much of her adult life in spotlights of varying brightness and is used to the interrogations of journalists and writers. I'd written about race and generations for *The Washington Post*, so it was hard not to wonder whether she'd set that anecdote aside to share. But when I asked, she said she hadn't. It was just what she and her peers were talking about.

Another anecdote, though, was unquestionably spontaneous. She described being on a walk in the neighborhood near her Florida home and coming across a truck parked in the driveway of a house that had apparently just been sold. The back of the truck had a sticker indicating that it, like her, had come down from New Jersey. A man came out and she greeted him, learning that it was his brother-in-law who'd moved in.

"You know why he moved from New Jersey?" the man asked her. She told him she didn't. "Well, he's a boater," the man replied, "and a whole bunch of Italians moved around them."

"That's the mindset when I was growing up," Kirschling said. "They discriminated against us because we were Irish. And Italians. But, I mean, come on. We're beyond that. Am I wrong?" She marveled at "the weirdness of people."

It was an unexpected reminder of how progress can be impermanent and incomplete. There had been a gradual acceptance of people of Italian heritage as American and as White over the preceding century, but that didn't mean that there weren't still places or circumstances in which they were the target of hate—hate to the extent of selling one's house and moving to a new state, hate to the extent that you don't even hesitate to convey your hate to strangers. America is beyond broad discrimination against Italians, but it's by no means beyond being home to myriad small pockets of hostility. Maybe it's *not* all about racism, but a lot of it shares the same root structure.

Kirschling and I were speaking at the end of 2021, a tumultuous year in a chain of tumultuous years, a period in which there was no reason to assume that any unhappy thing wouldn't happen. She wondered what the immediate future held politically, from the 2022 midterms to the 2024 presidential election. She saw that overlapping with a broad unease and instability and anger that we both felt around us. She understood clearly that she and many in her generation had lived lives that were not only blessed, in her description, but perhaps irreplicable.

"That's my biggest worry, for our children or our grandchildren," Kirschling said over the generic holiday pop playing through Starbucks's speakers. "I mean, I've-lived-my-life kind of thing. But they haven't. They need a chance to be able to have all the wonderful things that this country has offered. Not that everything's perfect. It never has been."

"Never have I felt so upset about the future," she said at another point. Kirschling would later slot the riot at the Capitol just behind the Kennedy assassination as the darkest day in the country's history. She told me about a conversation she'd had with a neighbor of hers in Florida about politics and the advice she'd offered him: pray. "Well, that's about it," he replied. "That's all we have left."

We talked a bit more and then said our goodbyes, Kirschling climbing into her husband's truck. At one second after midnight about two weeks later—celebrating with friends after flying down to Florida—she would become the first baby boomer to turn 76 just as she'd been the first to turn every age prior.

Acknowledgments

The acknowledgments sections of books have always seemed to me somewhat self-aggrandizing. Writing a book is a long process but it isn't working in the salt mines; completing a book is an accomplishment but it isn't winning an Oscar for best actor. And then I wrote a book and I realized—no doubt too slowly—that the point is not self-congratulation but deep appreciation. A book is the pulling together of a million thoughts from yourself and from others and it's having the time and space to do so. The acknowledgments, then, are the recognition of all of those essential anchors.

In my case, that starts at home. My wife, China, managed two preschool-aged kids in the middle of a pandemic so that I could do this work. Without her grace and flexibility, you are looking at a blank page and wondering why you bought it. The extent to which our lives hinge on others is one of those realizations that can be infrequent until that dependence becomes a constant.

There is no book without Viking, certainly; without them, you're looking at nothing at all. My thanks to my editor, Wendy Wolf, for her guidance and assistance and to Amy Ryan for her keen-eyed copyedits. My thanks as well to Ryan Harbage, my agent, for letting me ping him every few years with ideas until it all finally came together. Enormous thanks also to *The Washington Post* and, in particular, Steven Ginsberg. The paper's willingness to both let me explore this project and give me the space to do so was generous in a way that seems necessarily exceptional for an employer. A number of my colleagues offered their own time in assistance, including Lenny Bronner, Emily Guskin, and Andrew Van Dam.

Scores of people I didn't know also provided me with their time as the project progressed. They got on Zoom or on the phone, often on short notice, to share their expertise or research or experiences. Many or most are identified in the text itself; hopefully my efforts to translate their thoughts into printed words were largely successful. I want to extend perhaps even more appreciation to those who *weren't* included in the book itself. Your assistance helped inform the direction and structure of what I wanted to convey even if your words themselves don't appear.

I'll start, once again, with Kathleen Casey Kirschling, who was generous with her time and her availability. A fitting representative of a complicated generation, if an accidental one. But I must also thank all of the following people, each of whom deserves more than a single mention of their name: Maria Abascal, Richard Alba, Julia Azari, Carlton Basmajian, Bill Bishop, Rachel Blum, Sally Bradshaw, Alison Bryant, D'Vera Cohn, Catherine Collinson, Melissa Deckman, Horace Dediu, Christopher DeSante, Tom DiPrete, G. William Domhoff, Katherine Levine Einstein, Ryan Enos, Ryan Erisman, David Faris, Andrew Feldman, William Frey, Lisa García Bedolla, Andrew Gelman, Megan Gerhardt, Tanya Golash-Boza, Donald Green, Ian Haney López, Katherine Hempstead, David Hopkins, Chayce Horton, David Johnson, Landon Jones, Robert Jones, Barbara Kahn, Benjamin Keys, Seoyoung Silvia Kim, Gray Kimbrough, James Knickman, Eric Knowles, Peter Kuli, Ann Larabee, Roger Lau, Alex Lee, Amanda Litman, Adam Looney, Taylor Lorenz, Hanno Lustig, Beth Mace, Robert Manduca, Douglas Massey, Corrine McConnaughy, Peter Meijer, Greg Mennis, Stephen Morgan, Monique Morrissey, Rich Moylan, Dowell Myers, Kim Parker, Fabian Pfeffer, Casey Rabin, Roger Rapoport, Sean Reardon, David Roediger, Patrick Ruffini, Saurabh Sharma, David Shor, Theda Skocpol, Michael Steele, Catherine Theroux, Shripad Tuljapurkar, Stephanie Valencia, Chris Warshaw, Thomas Zeitzoff, Jan Zilinsky, and Thomas Zimmer. Many other individuals are recognized through their work, identified in the book's footnotes.

Others offered more discrete assistance on a particular point or question. My thanks to Catherine Oseas Champion, assistant archivist at the Birmingham Public Library, for example. Also to several individuals who provided assistance over the internet, like Garson O'Toole, the pseudonymous writer of the site Quote Investigator, and like Craig Brownstein, who dug up a small piece of history that's included in chapter 4. And then there's r/Trucks, a Reddit forum that in short order identified the make of a pickup truck—the sort of thing that one doesn't expect to need but eventually does.

A number of individuals and organizations also provided data that helped me better understand and present the trends described in the book. Pew Research Center, truly an essential American institution, did so repeatedly. PRRI provided refined polling data, as did Gallup. I relied repeatedly on IPUMS's tools for accessing Census Bureau data and the University of California, Berkeley, Survey Documentation and Analysis tools for evaluating the General Social Survey and American National Election Studies. Anne Case and Angus Deaton provided the data behind graphs included in their own work so that I could recreate it, as did Yair Ghitza. Ryne Rohla shared his precinct-level vote data. These gestures of collegiality are much appreciated.

Too many other people provided assistance and encouragement to be able to identify comprehensively. I would, though, like to thank my friend Michael Elliott, who read the book as it progressed—useful feedback despite his constant insistence that each chapter begin with an inspirational quote.

Finally, I offer my appreciation to the two people to whom the book is dedicated, my sons Thomas and Henry. Both were too young as I wrote for them to have any future memory of my doing so; what's more, most of the book was written after they'd gone to sleep. They knew it was happening, of course. At one point, hearing that it was nearing completion, Thomas asked if that meant that I only had to add the pictures. But despite this detachment, they played a vital role in its creation: they were a reminder of the tangibility of the future and, of course, a constant source of joy and energy. Kids, man.

I hope that Thomas and Henry look back at this book in the decades to come as having been appropriately prescient. Or, barring that, that they at least look at it for the most distilled accomplishment it represents: something their father did to make their lives better and, however abstractly, to convey to them his love.

Notes

Introduction

1. U.S. Census Bureau, *Historical National Population Estimates: July 1, 1900 to July 1, 1999* (Washington, DC: 2000), https://bit.ly/36311pe.
2. Centers for Disease Control and Prevention, *Live Births, Birth Rates, and Fertility Rates, by Race of Child: United States, 1909–80* (Washington, DC: 1997), https://bit.ly/3MAVbcZ.
3. Centers for Disease Control and Prevention, *Provisional Data for 2020: Vital Statistics Rapid Release no. 12* (Hyattsville, MD: National Center for Health Statistics, 2021), https://bit.ly/3CuTcSN.
4. It's technically about 2.7 babies, but I hesitate to start the book by figuring out how to introduce seven-tenths of a baby to the population.
5. U.S. Department of Education, National Center for Education Statistics, "Enrollment in Public Elementary and Secondary Schools, by Level and Grade: Selected Years, Fall 1980 Through Fall 2029," *Digest of Education Statistics*, 2020, https://bit.ly/3tH5CTP.
6. Landon Y. Jones, *Great Expectations: America and the Baby Boom Generation* (New York: Coward, McCann & Geoghegan, 1980).
7. Jones, *Great Expectations*.
8. Ruth Igielnik, Scott Keeter, and Hannah Hartig, "Behind Biden's 2020 Victory," Pew Research Center, U.S. Politics & Policy, June 30, 2021, https://bit.ly/35M0KVt.

1. A Baby Tsunami

1. "More Babies in New York," *The New York Times*, December 14, 1946, https://bit.ly/3sXLcGT.
2. U.S. National Resources Committee, Committee on Population Problems, *The Problems of a Changing Population* (Washington, DC: 1938), https://bit.ly/3I0gfWW.
3. "World Populations," *Life*, September 3, 1945.
4. William Ogburn, "Who Will Be Who in 1980," *The New York Times*, May 30, 1948, https://nyti.ms/3KzBSie.
5. Data from the U.S. Census Bureau.
6. U.S. Census Bureau, *Forecasts of the Population of the United States* (Washington, DC: 1948), https://bit.ly/35GooTo.

7. The United Press, "War Gives 450% Boom to Baby-Buggy Business," *The New York Times*, February 8, 1949, https://bit.ly/3hXcze2.

8. New York Telephone Company, *Manhattan Telephone Directory* (New York, NY: 1940), https://bit.ly/3J19ghK.

9. New York Telephone Company, *Manhattan Telephone Directory* (New York, NY: 1946), https://bit.ly/3MPozMX.

10. "War Babies to Tax Schools This Fall," *The New York Times*, August 3, 1947, sec. Archives, https://bit.ly/3CCoAin.

11. U.S. Department of Education, Office of Educational Research and Improvement, *120 Years of American Education: A Statistical Portrait* (Washington, DC: 1993), https://bit.ly /3tNoX5N.

12. Author calculations from Centers for Disease Control and Prevention data.

13. These numbers should be considered in the context of the federal government having only begun collecting uniform birth data from states in the 1930s.

14. For the sake of comparison, the United States hasn't seen 4 million births in a year since 2010, despite more than double the 1946 population.

15. "Rocketing Births: Business Bonanza," *Life*, June 16, 1958, https://bit.ly/3pSTC0k.

16. Landon Y. Jones, *Great Expectations: America and the Baby Boom Generation* (New York: Coward, McCann & Geoghegan, 1980).

17. Los Angeles Unified School District, Educational Housing Branch, School Planning Division, *History of Schools* (Los Angeles: 1973), https://bit.ly/3sXVnLH.

18. Dwight Macdonald, "A Caste, a Culture, a Market," *The New Yorker*, November 22, 1958, https://bit.ly/365FREk.

19. U.S. Census Bureau, *Historical Statistics of the United States: Colonial Times to 1970* (Washington, DC: 1975), https://bit.ly/3KypH5y.

20. National Science Foundation, *Research on the Effects of Television Advertising on Children: A Review of the Literature and Recommendations for Future Research* (Washington, DC: 1977), https://bit.ly/3vQSSfR.

21. "Associated with Baby Boomers," *Wisconsin State Journal*, December 15, 1986, https://bit.ly /3hSGjZk.

22. Philip Bump, "Your Generational Identity Is a Lie," *The Washington Post*, April 1, 2015, https://bit.ly/3J09yp7.

23. Bruce Horovitz, "After Gen X, Millennials, What Should the Next Generation Be Called?," *USA Today*, May 4, 2012, https://bit.ly/3MzqaGx.

24. Neil Strauss and William Howe, "The New Generation Gap," *The Atlantic*, December 1992, https://bit.ly/3CuWkOE.

25. Alexander Abrams and David Lipsky, "The Boomlet Generation," *The New York Times*, January 4, 1993, https://bit.ly/3tRCjOy.

26. "The Echo Boomers," *60 Minutes*, CBS News, October 1, 2004, https://bit.ly/3qf9SJp.

27. Michael Dimock, "Defining Generations: Where Millennials End and Generation Z Begins," Pew Research Center, January 17, 2019, https://bit.ly/3sVHgqb.

28. Philip Bump, "Here Is When Each Generation Begins and Ends, According to Facts," *The Atlantic*, March 25, 2014, https://bit.ly/3I5JbwQ.

29. "What Would You Name Today's Youngest Generation of Americans?," Pew Research Center, March 12, 2014, https://bit.ly/376ntf5.

30. Annalisa Quinn, "Move Over Millennials, Here Comes 'iGen' . . . or Maybe Not," NPR, September 17, 2017, https://bit.ly/3vURFnP.

31. Philip Bump, "The White House Is Making Up Entire Generations Now," *The Washington Post*, October 9, 2014, https://bit.ly/3hSv971.

32. "MTV Wants to Call the Next Generation 'the Founders.' Sorry, but No," *The Washington Post*, December 3, 2015, https://bit.ly/3IV9Ayq.

33. As I began researching this book, this analogy struck me—only to discover it also appearing in Jones's book. *C'est la vie.*

34. Analysis of data compiled by the Migration Policy Institute. See: "Countries of Birth for

U.S. Immigrants, 1960–Present," Migration Policy Institute, November 5, 2013, https://bit
.ly/3CwtUnn.

35. Analysis of U.S. Census Bureau data compiled by IPUMS. Sarah Flood, Miriam King,
Renae Rodgers, et al., Integrated Public Use Microdata Series, Current Population Survey:
Version 9.0 (dataset) (Minneapolis, MN: IPUMS, 2021), https://bit.ly/3MAI5fV.

36. Dimock, "Defining Generations."

37. Conversation with author.

38. G. William Domhoff, *Who Rules America? Power, Politics, and Social Change*, 5th ed. (Boston:
McGraw-Hill, 2005).

39. Author calculations based on data from the @unitedstates project and *FiveThirtyEight*. See:
https://bit.ly/3MGa7qo; Nate Silver and Dhrumil Mehta, "Both Republicans and Democrats
Have an Age Problem," *FiveThirtyEight*, April 28, 2014, https://bit.ly/35PSeVg.

40. Silver and Mehta, "Both Republicans and Democrats Have an Age Problem."

41. "Claiborne, William Charles Cole," Office of the House Historian, *Biographical Directory of
the U.S. Congress,* https://bit.ly/3qfa8bl

42. U.S. Census Bureau, *P20-414: Voting and Registration in the Election of November 1986*
(Washington, DC), https://bit.ly/3sUtiVw.

43. Flood, King, Rodgers, et al., Integrated Public Use Microdata Series, Current Population
Survey: Version 9.0 (dataset).

44. U.S. Census Bureau and U.S. Department of Housing and Urban Development, "New
Privately-Owned Housing Units Started: Total Units," Federal Reserve Bank of St. Louis,
https://bit.ly/3KvQcIH.

45. U.S. Federal Housing Finance Agency, "All-Transactions House Price Index for the United
States," Federal Reserve Bank of St. Louis, https://bit.ly/3vUzxKY.

46. Here we're comparing net wealth (assets minus debts) with the asset value of real estate. See:
Board of Governors of the Federal Reserve System, "Table: Distribution of Household
Wealth in the U.S. Since 1989," https://bit.ly/3hWASss.

47. Board of Governors of the Federal Reserve System, "Table: Distribution of Household
Wealth in the U.S. Since 1989." Figures are for the third quarter in each year.

48. U.S. Census Bureau Current Population Survey microdata harmonized by the Economic
Policy Institute, https://bit.ly/3J2qsmV.

49. "Federal Student Loan Portfolio," U.S. Department of Education, Federal Student Aid,
https://bit.ly/3MzqlSd.

50. Board of Governors of the Federal Reserve System, "Table: Distribution of Household
Wealth in the U.S. Since 1989," https://bit.ly/3hWASss.

51. "The Generation Gap in American Politics," Pew Research Center, U.S. Politics & Policy,
March 1, 2018, https://bit.ly/3CtoeL1.

52. U.S. Census Bureau, "Voting and Registration in the Election of November 2020," Census
.gov, https://bit.ly/3tJvhv8.

53. U.S. Census Bureau, "Voting and Registration in the Election of November 2014," Census
.gov, https://bit.ly/3pTvmv4.

54. U.S. Census Bureau, "Voting and Registration in the Election of November 2020."

2. All Things Must Pass

1. Author calculations of *Life* magazine reporting. "Rocketing Births: Business Bonanza," *Life*,
June 6, 1958.

2. If you're not familiar with this episode of *I Love Lucy*, well, that sort of reinforces the
point.

3. Ryan Erisman, *Inside the Bubble: Ultimate Guide to the World's Largest Retirement Community*
(Florida: Ryan Erisman Inc., 2021).

4. U.S. Census Bureau, "Census—Table Results," Census.gov, https://bit.ly/34uYIIJ.

5. U.S. Census Bureau, "2020 Census Statistics Highlight Local Population Changes and Nation's Racial and Ethnic Diversity," Census.gov, https://bit.ly/3HSirQc.

6. Author calculations from National Institutes of Health data. See: "SEER Single Year of Age County Population Estimates—SEER Population Data," SEER, https://bit.ly/3Kyfxle.

7. Philip Bump, "Americans Are Moving West—but Also Toward Cities," *The Washington Post*, https://bit.ly/3vUAbbs.

8. Alex French, "Seven Days and Nights in the World's Largest, Rowdiest Retirement Community," *BuzzFeed*, https://bit.ly/3hUQFbb.

9. Julie Weed, "'Kind of Blingy': The Tricked-Out Golf Carts of the Villages, Fla.," *The New York Times*, July 3, 2019, sec. Business, https://bit.ly/3J5cu3J.

10. "QuickFacts: The Villages CDP, Florida," U.S. Census Bureau, https://bit.ly/3MFta3Q.

11. Chicago Tribune Service, "Negro Feared Victim of Florida Lynching," *Spokane Spokesman-Review*, October 29, 1956.

12. Chris Bodenner, "The Science Behind Florida's Sinkhole Epidemic," *Smithsonian*, https://bit.ly/3CvRcJZ.

13. "Hole Closes Southbound Lanes of U.S. 27/441," *The Villages Daily Sun*, November 27, 2018, https://bit.ly/3tOLoaR.

14. "Speech: Donald Trump Signs Executive Order on Medicare at the Villages, Florida," Factba.se, October 3, 2019, https://bit.ly/35M1dqH.

15. Victoria Knight, "In 10 Years, Half of Middle-Income Elders Won't Be Able to Afford Housing, Medical Care," *Kaiser Health News*, April 24, 2019, https://bit.ly/3sXLCNt.

16. Author analysis of U.S. Census Bureau population projections. See: U.S. Census Bureau, "Population Projections," Census.gov, https://bit.ly/3HYxNTj.

17. Lydia Saad, "Americans' Retirement Outlook Largely Intact," Gallup.com, April 28, 2020, https://bit.ly/3KtfAik.

18. Author analysis of Bureau of Labor Statistics data. "Continuing Care Retirement Communities and Assisted Living Facilities for the Elderly—May 2020 OEWS Industry-Specific Occupational Employment and Wage Estimates," Bureau of Labor Statistics, https://bit.ly/3vYJ4k3.

19. Centers for Disease Control and Prevention, National Center for Health Statistics, "Compressed Mortality Files 1968–2016," CDC WONDER Online Database, released June 2017, https://bit.ly/3hSg1GE.

20. "Buying a Casket," Funeralwise, https://bit.ly/3IZlMOB.

21. Walt Disney Company, Disney Meetings, *Your Story Told by Disney Meetings*, https://bit.ly/3ME1AnJ.

22. Bureau of Labor Statistics, "Table A-1. Employment Status of the Civilian Population by Sex and Age—2022 M01 Results," Bureau of Labor Statistics, https://bit.ly/3CvxmyG.

23. Wilbur Zelinsky, "Gathering Places for America's Dead: How Many, Where, and Why?," *The Professional Geographer* 46, no. 1 (1994): 29–38, https://bit.ly/3tNtF3k.

24. "History," Green-Wood Cemetery, https://bit.ly/3pRYNxC.

25. Cremation Association of North America, *CANA Annual Statistics Report 2021* (Wheeling, IL: 2021).

26. Cremation Association of North America, *CANA Annual Statistics Report 2021*.

27. "World's Oldest Person, Sarah Knauss, Dies at 119," *The Washington Post*, https://bit.ly/3sYH7lM.

28. U.S. Census Bureau, "Population Projections."

29. U.S. Census Bureau, "1890 Overview—History," Census.gov, https://bit.ly/3HYxVlL.

30. U.S. Census Bureau, "1930 Overview—History," Census.gov, https://bit.ly/3KyqLq4.

31. U.S. Census Bureau, "1930 Census Instructions to Enumerators," Census.gov, https://bit.ly/3vSFgAK.

32. E. Telles and T. Paschel, "Who Is Black, White, or Mixed Race? How Skin Color, Status, and Nation Shape Racial Classification in Latin America," *American Journal of Sociology* 120, no. 3 (2014): 864–907.

33. U.S. Census Bureau, "Research to Improve Data on Race and Ethnicity," Census.gov, https://bit.ly/3hTzs1J.

34. U.S. Census Bureau, "Research to Improve Data on Race and Ethnicity."

35. U.S. Census Bureau, "2020 Census Illuminates Racial and Ethnic Composition of the Country," Census.gov, https://bit.ly/3J5cBfF.
36. "FOIA Documents from Trump Administration on 2020 Census," Brennan Center for Justice, https://bit.ly/37k8v5p.
37. Mike Gonzalez, "A Census That Divides and 'Nudges,'" *The Wall Street Journal*, March 9, 2017, sec. Opinion, https://bit.ly/3CtybYN.
38. Under the U.S. Census Bureau's low-immigration forecast, for example, the point at which non-Hispanic Whites fall out of the majority occurs four years later.
39. https://bit.ly/3xFr7rF.
40. U.S. Department of Commerce, Bureau of the Census, *Projections of the Population of the United States, by Age, Sex, and Race: 1983 to 2080* (Washington, DC: U.S. GPO, 1986), https://bit.ly/3tNtNzQ.
41. U.S. Department of Commerce, Bureau of the Census, *Projections of the Hispanic Population: 1983 to 2080* (Washington, DC: U.S. GPO, 1986), https://bit.ly/35LFHSW.
42. U.S. Census Bureau, Population Division, *U.S. Census Bureau Measurement of Net International Migration to the United States: 1990 to 2000* (Washington, DC: U.S. GPO, 2001), https://bit.ly/34uZ2Hr.
43. ACTV Auburn, "Virtual Groundbreaking—Mary D. Stone," YouTube video, 2:16, August 3, 2020, https://bit.ly/3vTsYIt.
44. "Oak Street Senior Apartments," Sutton Real Estate, https://bit.ly/3HYBvwa.
45. "Retirement Residences of Glassport in Glassport, Pennsylvania," Affordable Housing Online, https://bit.ly/3KwiIKb.
46. "Action Plan: B-11-UN-26-0003," HUDExchange.info, https://bit.ly/3w1UvY6.
47. Cooper Fox, "Take a Sneak Peek at the Old Cony High School in Augusta," B98.5, https://bit.ly/34voAEd.
48. Gabrielle Banks, "From School Bells to Senior Bingo: Old Classroom Buildings Becoming Senior Centers," *Pittsburgh Post-Gazette*, https://bit.ly/3IZlZ4l.

3. How to Spot a Boomer

1. Taylor Lorenz, "'OK Boomer' Marks the End of Friendly Generational Relations," *The New York Times*, October 29, 2019, sec. Style, https://bit.ly/3MOtcXw.
2. "Google Trends," Google, https://bit.ly/365NMSn.
3. "Most Millennials Resist the 'Millennial' Label," Pew Research Center, September 3, 2015, https://bit.ly/3tH6FTL.
4. Amanda Barroso and Rachel Minkin, "Recent Protest Attendees Are More Racially and Ethnically Diverse, Younger Than Americans Overall," Pew Research Center, https://bit.ly/3pPjdaA.
5. Heather Krause, "Generation Activist Data," Orb Media, https://bit.ly/34xAvS6.
6. "National poll," *The Washington Post*–ABC News, September 21–24, 2020, https://bit.ly/3HTotzT.
7. "Who Uses TikTok, Nextdoor," Pew Research Center, Internet, Science & Technology, https://bit.ly/3KAMm19.
8. Michael Dimock, "Defining Generations: Where Millennials End and Generation Z Begins," Pew Research Center, https://bit.ly/3sVHgqb.
9. U.S. Census Bureau, "National Population by Characteristics: 2010–2020," Census.gov, https://bit.ly/3vVYbuM.
10. U.S. Census Bureau, "Population Projections," Census.gov, https://bit.ly/3HYxNTj.
11. Campbell Gibson and Kay Jung, "Historical Census Statistics on the Foreign-Born Population of the United States: 1850 to 2000," U.S. Census Bureau, February 2006, https://bit.ly/3J1JtWL.
12. Tom W. Smith, Michael Davern, Jeremy Freese, and Stephen Morgan, "General Social Surveys, 1972–2021 Cumulative File" (Chicago, IL: National Opinion Research Center), https://bit.ly/3MGsA5W.

13. Migration Policy Institute, "Legal Immigration to the United States, 1820–Present," Migration Policy Institute, August 13, 2013, https://bit.ly/3hYfWRT.

14. Gibson and Jung, "Historical Census Statistics on the Foreign-Born Population of the United States."

15. From chapter 1.

16. "Induction Statistics," Selective Service System, https://bit.ly/369eXM5.

17. U.S. Department of Education, National Center for Education Statistics, *Digest of Education Statistics, 2019*, https://bit.ly/3tKHDD9.

18. "Man of the Year: The Inheritor," *Time*, January 6, 1967, https://bit.ly/3pUC3Nj.

19. Leonard Buder, "Parents Warned on 'Right' School," *The New York Times*, September 25, 1962, https://bit.ly/3sZXXR6.

20. U.S. Department of Education, National Center for Education Statistics, *Digest of Education Statistics, 2020*, https://bit.ly/366TJy5.

21. In 1980, about 17 percent of adults over the age of 25 had completed four or more years of college. In 2020, about 38 percent had a bachelor's degree or higher. See: U.S. Census Bureau, *Years of School Completed by Persons 25 Years Old or Over, by Age and Sex* (Washington, DC: U.S. GPO, 1981), https://bit.ly/3KyfYvS; U.S. Census Bureau, "Educational Attainment in the United States: 2020," Census.gov, https://bit.ly/3vUAMtI.

22. Anthony Carnevale, Nicole Smith, and Jeff Strohl, "Recovery: Job Growth and Education Requirements Through 2020" (Washington, DC: Georgetown Public Policy Institute, Georgetown University, 2013), https://bit.ly/3hWisbm.

23. Using the symmetric property, naturally.

24. Eleanor Blau, "Guru's Followers Cheer 'Millennium' in Festivities at Astrodome," *The New York Times*, November 12, 1973, sec. Archives, https://bit.ly/3HYxpUR.

25. "Air Transport 1973" (Washington, DC: Air Transport Association of America, 1973), https://bit.ly/3KnWo5A.

26. Geoffrey C. Ward, *A First-Class Temperament: The Emergence of Franklin Roosevelt, 1905–1928* (New York: Vintage, 2014).

27. "The Future of World Religions: Population Growth Projections, 2010–2050," Pew Research Center, April 2, 2015, https://bit.ly/3CsMA7H.

28. Robert D. Putnam, *Bowling Alone: The Collapse and Revival of American Community*, anniversary ed., rev. and updated (New York: Simon & Schuster, 2001).

29. "Man of the Year: The Inheritor," *Time*.

30. Putnam, *Bowling Alone*.

31. Author analysis of GSS data.

32. "Household Data Series, Union Membership Tables," Bureau of Labor Statistics, https://bit.ly/3qfa1MX.

33. Philip Bump, "Like so Many Other Things, the Veteran Population Is Shrinking as America Ages," *The Washington Post*, November 11, 2021, https://bit.ly/3sZS0UE.

34. "In Changing U.S. Electorate, Race and Education Remain Stark Dividing Lines," Pew Research Center, U.S. Politics & Policy, June 2, 2020, https://bit.ly/3w1U7ZE.

35. County-level population data from the U.S. Census Bureau compared to CDC urban-rural designations.

36. Author analysis of U.S. Census Bureau housing data. U.S. Census Bureau, 2019 American Community Survey 1-Year Estimates, Table DP04.

37. U.S. Census Bureau, 2019 American Community Survey 1-Year Estimates, Table P2.

38. All citations in this paragraph are from the sources indicated earlier in the chapter.

39. Richard Fry, "Millennials Overtake Baby Boomers as America's Largest Generation," Pew Research Center, https://bit.ly/3J09AgJ.

4. The Politics of the New Generation Gap

1. Maddy Martin, "Politics and Personal Driving Preferences: Do Republicans and Democrats Drive Different Cars?," YourMechanic, February 12, 2016, https://bit.ly/3MOsUzU.

2. Experts at the Reddit forum r/Trucks identified Roseberry's truck when shown photos.

3. Video captured by *Heavy.com*. Jessica McBride, "Floyd Ray Roseberry: Facebook Live Video from Truck Near U.S. Capitol," *Heavy.com*, August 19, 2021, https://bit.ly/3tD91Ty.

4. *Heavy.com* video.

5. Josh Marshall, Twitter post, August 19, 2021, 2:40 p.m., https://bit.ly/3hUVUYr.

6. Tom Lynch, Twitter post, August 19, 2021, 2:01 p.m., https://bit.ly/3HYGg8Q.

7. Marshall, Twitter post.

8. Philip Bump, "For $7.75 Million, You Can Own What Donald Trump Never Did: Trump Island," *The Washington Post*, December 9, 2016, https://bit.ly/37cwjbf.

9. Philip Bump, "The Trumps Were Once One of Many Immigrant Families in the Working-Class Bronx," *The Washington Post*, April 5, 2019, https://bit.ly/3CumGQG.

10. George W. Bush, *Decision Points* (New York: Crown, 2010).

11. Bill Clinton, *My Life* (New York: Knopf Doubleday Publishing Group, 2004).

12. Clinton, *My Life*.

13. "How Groups Voted in 1992," Roper Center for Public Opinion Research, https://bit.ly/3qfadvF.

14. Author's analysis of exit poll data from the Roper Center for Public Opinion Research.

15. Births are disproportionately likely to occur in summer months in the United States. See: Remy Melina, "In Which Month Are the Most Babies Born?," Live Science, July 27, 2010, https://bit.ly/34xA4aq.

16. U.S. Census Bureau, "Population Projections," Census.gov, https://bit.ly/3HYxNTj.

17. Sara Rimer, "Experts Study the Habits of Genus Baby Boomer," *The New York Times*, April 21, 1986, sec. U.S., https://bit.ly/3w00T2p.

18. Neena Satjia, "Echoes of Biden's 1987 Plagiarism Scandal Continue to Reverberate," *The Washington Post*, https://bit.ly/3J2qoUd.

19. Exit polling compiled by the Roper Center.

20. "Republican Anger Bubbles Up at McCain Rally," Reuters, October 11, 2008, sec. Editor's Picks, https://bit.ly/37jKJ9G.

21. "Remarks by the President on the Mortgage Crisis," The White House, February 18, 2009, https://bit.ly/3tNp1T5.

22. U.S. Bureau of Labor Statistics, "All Employees, Total Nonfarm," Federal Reserve Bank of St. Louis, https://bit.ly/3hRbDrz.

23. U.S. Bureau of Labor Statistics, "Unemployment Rate," Federal Reserve Bank of St. Louis, https://bit.ly/3HYxGHn.

24. Theda Skocpol and Vanessa Williamson, *The Tea Party and the Remaking of Republican Conservatism*, ill. ed. (New York: Oxford University Press, 2016).

25. U.S. Census Bureau, *The Size, Place of Birth, and Geographic Distribution of the Foreign-Born Population in the United States: 1960 to 2010* (Washington, DC: U.S. GPO, 2012), https://bit.ly/3KxS0Ro.

26. If not, please reread chapter 3.

27. TaMaryn Waters, "Sally Bradshaw Turns the Page with Midtown Reader Bookstore," *Tallahassee Democrat*, https://bit.ly/3CxpOeB.

28. "How Groups Voted in 2008," Roper Center for Public Opinion Research, https://bit.ly/3F1fUn6.

29. "How Groups Voted in 2008," Roper Center for Public Opinion Research, https://ropercenter.cornell.edu/how-groups-voted-2008, https://bit.ly/3Kfa6r7.

30. "ICYMI: Hannity Hails Rubio's Immigration Proposal as 'Most Thoughtful' Yet," U.S. Senator Marco Rubio (website), https://bit.ly/35J08zT.

31. Ryan Lizza, "Getting to Maybe," *The New Yorker*, June 24, 2013, https://bit.ly/3sXKKbG.

32. Tal Kopan, "Coulter Waits for 'Rubio-Free' Senate," *Politico*, https://bit.ly/3vURRU5.

33. Garrett Quinn, "Ann Coulter Blasts Chris Christie, Says He's 'Off My List' for 2016 in Fiery CPAC Speech," *Mediaite*, March 16, 2013, https://bit.ly/3J0KDlg.

34. "Dennis Michael Lynch Talks 'They Come to America II,'" Fox News, https://bit.ly/3ME37dy.

35. Gary Langer, "Policy Divisions Challenge Obama, but GOP Battles Its Own Discontent," Langer Research Associates, July 23, 2013, https://bit.ly/3tJljtE.

36. Sean Trende, "The Case of the Missing White Voters, Revisited," RealClearPolitics, June 21, 2013, https://bit.ly/3hSG5Bl.
37. Thomas B. Edsall, "Atwater Is Elected Chief of RNC, Outlines Goals," *The Washington Post*, January 19, 1989, https://wapo.st/3I0v2Rc.
38. Art Levy, "Former Political Consultant Sally Bradshaw," Florida Trend, https://bit.ly /3KwdeiB.
39. Philip Bump, "The Day the Ku Klux Klan Took Over Pennsylvania Avenue," *The Washington Post*, May 6, 2016, https://bit.ly/3Cs8Z4Z.
40. Bump, "The Day the Ku Klux Klan Took Over Pennsylvania Avenue."
41. Ken Ringle, "Klan's 1925 Rally: A 'Great Parade,'" *The Washington Post*, November 29, 1982, https://bit.ly/3qfaoHl.
42. Ringle, "Klan's 1925 Rally."
43. "Propaganda Handbills Flood Autos and Houses," *The Washington Post*, August 9, 1925.
44. Sabrina Tavernise, "Why the Announcement of a Looming White Minority Makes Demographers Nervous," *The New York Times*, November 22, 2018, sec. U.S., https://bit.ly/3sX5ksA.
45. "Rush Baby Asks Advice on Battling the Stereotyping of Conservatives," *The Rush Limbaugh Show*, June 4, 2009, https://bit.ly/35DHvxr.
46. Mackenzie Weinger, "Bill O'Reilly: 'The White Establishment Is Now the Minority,'" *Politico*, https://bit.ly/3IYKS0g.
47. Campbell Gibson and Kay Jung, "Historical Census Statistics on the Foreign-Born Population of the United States: 1850 to 2000," U.S. Census Bureau, February 2006, https://bit.ly /3J1JtWL.
48. "Racial and Ethnic Diversity in the United States: 2010 Census and 2020 Census," Census .gov, https://bit.ly/3MOt76a.
49. "Times Have Changed?," *Southern Courier*, May 14, 1967.
50. "Nomination of Walter J. Bamberg for Department of Justice," U.S. Congress, February 5, 1990, 101st Congress (1989–1990), https://bit.ly/3tJvDSu.
51. Corey Mitchell, "Data: The Schools Named After Confederate Figures," *Education Week*, June 17, 2020, https://bit.ly/3hYfrHv.
52. Tom W. Smith, Michael Davern, Jeremy Freese, and Stephen Morgan, "General Social Surveys, 1972–2021 Cumulative File" (Chicago, IL: National Opinion Research Center), https://bit .ly/3MGsA5W.
53. Ethan Zell and Tara Lesick, "Ignorance of History and Political Differences in Perception of Racism in the United States," *Social Psychological and Personality Science*, November 15, 2021, https://bit.ly/3I0v9MC.
54. "American Voters Are Pro-Immigrant, Anti-Wall, Quinnipiac University National Poll Finds, Voters Concerned About Immigrants' Values," Quinnipiac University Poll, September 16, 2016, https://bit.ly/3Kto9cU.
55. "The Economist/YouGov Poll," YouGov, January 27, 2019, https://bit.ly/365j8si.
56. Data provided to author by PRRI.
57. Max Ehrenfreund and Scott Clement, "Economic and Racial Anxiety: Two Separate Forces Driving Support for Donald Trump," *The Washington Post*, March 22, 2016, https://bit.ly /3pSTYEc.
58. Michael Miller, "'The War of Races': How a Hateful Ideology Echoes Through American History," *The Washington Post*, December 27, 2019, https://bit.ly/3sXVMhb.
59. Philip Bump, "Nearly Half of Republicans Agree with 'Great Replacement Theory,'" *The Washington Post*, May 9, 2022, https://bit.ly/3wdTMD9.
60. Gallup, "Most Important Problem," October 12, 2007, https://bit.ly/3vUzIpC.
61. Gallup, "Most Important Problem."
62. Rick Perlstein, "Exclusive: Lee Atwater's Infamous 1981 Interview on the Southern Strategy," *The Nation*, November 13, 2012, https://bit.ly/3IZHCBP.
63. Jane Mayer, "The Secret Papers of Lee Atwater, Who Invented the Scurrilous Tactics That Trump Normalized," *The New Yorker*, May 6, 2021, https://bit.ly/3MA21iW.
64. Philip Bump, "The 'Southern Strategy' Goes South," *The Washington Post*, February 10, 2022, https://bit.ly/3tDzv7e.

65. Cleve Wootson, "Trump and Allies Try to Redefine Racism by Casting White Men as Victims," *The Washington Post*, https://bit.ly/3hSgfxu.
66. Chris Stewart, "What Will Trump Loyalists' Sensed Powerlessness Mean for Politics?," Democracy Corps, March 26, 2021, https://bit.ly/3HY7kVO.
67. Robert W. Terry, "The Negative Impact on White Values," in *Impacts of Racism on White Americans*, ed. Benjamin Bowser and Raymond Hunt, Sage Focus Edition (Thousand Oaks, CA: Sage Publications, 1981).
68. Mike Pearl, "All the Evidence We Could Find About Fred Trump's Alleged Involvement with the KKK," *Vice*, March 10, 2016, https://bit.ly/3Ky2u3u.
69. "Warren Criticizes 'Class' Parades: Police Head Declares Neither Fascisti nor Klan Had Any Place in Memorial March," *The New York Times*, June 1, 1927.
70. "In Changing U.S. Electorate, Race and Education Remain Stark Dividing Lines," Pew Research Center, U.S. Politics & Policy, June 2, 2020, https://bit.ly/3w1U7ZE.
71. Igielnik, Keeter, and Hartig, "Behind Biden's 2020 Victory."
72. "In Changing U.S. Electorate, Race and Education Remain Stark Dividing Lines."
73. Philip Bump, "Independent Leaners Hate the Other Party More Than They Like the One They Vote For," *The Washington Post*, https://bit.ly/368aKZ2.
74. U.S. Census Bureau data, as in chapter 3.
75. "In Changing U.S. Electorate, Race and Education Remain Stark Dividing Lines."
76. "In Changing U.S. Electorate, Race and Education Remain Stark Dividing Lines."
77. U.S. Census Bureau, "National Population by Characteristics: 2010–2020," Census.gov, https://bit.ly/3vVYbuM.
78. "In Changing U.S. Electorate, Race and Education Remain Stark Dividing Lines."
79. Igielnik, Keeter, and Hartig, "Behind Biden's 2020 Victory."
80. Igielnik, Keeter, and Hartig, "Behind Biden's 2020 Victory."
81. *Jimmy Kimmel Live*, ABC, August 12, 2021.
82. Chapter 2.
83. "2020 Census Redistricting Data Files Press Kit," Census.gov, https://bit.ly/35Jx8YM.
84. Rachel Marks, "Improvements to the 2020 Census Race and Hispanic Origin Question Designs, Data Processing, and Coding Procedures," U.S. Census Bureau, August 3, 2021, https://bit.ly/34zVRyg.
85. Richard Alba, *The Great Demographic Illusion: Majority, Minority, and the Expanding American Mainstream* (Princeton: Princeton University Press, 2020).
86. Dowell Myers and Morris Levy, "Racial Population Projections and Reactions to Alternative News Accounts of Growing Diversity," *The Annals of the American Academy of Political and Social Science* 677, no. 1 (May 2018): 215–28, https://bit.ly/3vQJq5p.
87. Tavernise, "Why the Announcement of a Looming White Minority Makes Demographers Nervous."
88. "Ideological Gap Widens Between More, Less Educated Adults," Pew Research Center, U.S. Politics & Policy, April 26, 2016, https://bit.ly/3IZHL8l.
89. Jeffrey Jones, "Non-College Whites Had Affinity for GOP Before Trump," Gallup, April 12, 2019, https://bit.ly/3MDNp2c.
90. Kim Parker, "The Growing Partisan Divide in Views of Higher Education," Pew Research Center, August 19, 2019, https://bit.ly/3tNunxp.
91. Philip Bump, "90 Minutes in Iowa with Donald Trump," *The Washington Post*, August 15, 2015, https://bit.ly/3hUWi9l.
92. Stoyan Zaimov, "Donald Trump Declines to Name His Favorite Bible Verse: 'That's Very Personal' (Video)," *The Christian Post*, August 27, 2015, https://bit.ly/3HSFevj.
93. Philip Bump, "The Evangelical Vote? The Conservative Vote? The GOP Race Isn't Breaking Down so Neatly," *The Washington Post*, September 25, 2015, https://bit.ly/3KzCzYS.
94. Igielnik, Keeter, and Hartig, "Behind Biden's 2020 Victory."
95. Robert Jones and Daniel Cox, "Backing Trump, White Evangelicals Flip Flop on Importance of Candidate Character: PRRI/Brookings Survey," PRRI, https://bit.ly/368aSru.
96. "Religion in America: U.S. Religious Data, Demographics and Statistics," Pew Research Center, https://bit.ly/35LFUWe.

97. Elizabeth Dias, "'Christianity Will Have Power,'" *The New York Times*, August 9, 2020, sec. U.S., https://bit.ly/3sXfYj0.
98. "History Timeline," Corporation for Public Broadcasting, October 31, 2014, https://bit.ly /35Gp3US.
99. The population of New York City was nearly 9 million in 2020. By 1990, the population living on farms had already dropped below 4 million.
100. Richard Hofstadter, "The Paranoid Style in American Politics," *Harper's Magazine*, November 1, 1964, https://bit.ly/3IVa2wC.
101. Miles Parks, "Fact Check: Trump Repeats Voter Fraud Claim About California," NPR, April 5, 2018, https://bit.ly/3MGsuv6.
102. She didn't really say this. See: James Wolcott, "The Fraudulent Factoid That Refuses to Die," *Vanity Fair,* https://bit.ly/3tNpkxd.
103. Amina Dunn, "Few Trump or Biden Supporters Have Close Friends Who Back the Opposing Candidate," Pew Research Center, https://bit.ly/3hSvSFh.
104. Two-thirds of Republicans say they don't trust national news organizations. See: Jeffrey Gottfried and Jacob Liedke, "Partisan Divides in Media Trust Widen, Driven by a Decline Among Republicans," Pew Research Center, August 30, 2021, https://bit.ly/367YPtZ.
105. Rohla provided the data for this analysis.
106. Jane Mayer, "The Big Money Behind the Big Lie," *The New Yorker*, August 2, 2021, https:// bit.ly/3KBiS3b.
107. Theda Skocpol, Caroline Tervo, and Kirsten Walters, "Citizen Organizing and Partisan Polarization from the Tea Party to the Anti-Trump Resistance," in *Democratic Resilience: Can the United States Withstand Rising Polarization?*, ed. Kenneth M. Roberts, Robert C. Lieberman, and Suzanne Mettler (Cambridge: Cambridge University Press, 2021), 369–400, https://bit.ly/3Ct22QY.
108. Leah E. Gose and T. Skocpol, "Resist, Persist, and Transform: The Emergence and Impact of Grassroots Resistance Groups Opposing the Trump Presidency*," *Mobilization: An International Quarterly* 24, no. 3 (2019): 293–317, https://bit.ly/3pU1UF5.
109. Author analysis of ANES data compiled by the Survey Documentation and Analysis project at the University of California Berkeley.
110. "In Changing U.S. Electorate, Race and Education Remain Stark Dividing Lines."

5. The Post-Boomer Cultural Era Has Arrived

1. Camden Catholic High School, *Vista* (Cherry Hill, NJ: 1964), Classmates.com, https://bit .ly/3sVI3r9.
2. John Jackson, *American Bandstand: Dick Clark and the Making of a Rock "n" Roll Empire*, 1st ed. (New York: Oxford University Press, 1999).
3. Andy Baio, "The Whitburn Project: 120 Years of Music Chart History," *Waxy.org* (blog), May 15, 2008, https://bit.ly/3vVTHnM.
4. These data are all from the Whitburn Project.
5. Jeff Greenfield, *No Peace, No Place: Excavations Along the Generational Fault*, 1st ed. (Garden City, NY: Doubleday, 1973).
6. Landon Y. Jones, *Great Expectations: America and the Baby Boom Generation* (New York: Coward, McCann & Geoghegan, 1980).
7. Hugh McIntyre, "Half a Century Later, the Beatles Are Still Scoring New Hits on the Billboard Charts," *Forbes,* https://bit.ly/3JclXGk.
8. Paul Taylor and Rich Morin, "Forty Years After Woodstock, a Gentler Generation Gap," Pew Research Center, August 12, 2009, https://bit.ly/3MxkZH3.
9. Pamela Klaffke, *Spree: A Cultural History of Shopping*, ill. ed. (Vancouver, BC: Arsenal Pulp Press, 2003).
10. Jones, *Great Expectations*.
11. "Employed Persons by Detailed Industry and Age," Bureau of Labor Statistics, https://bit .ly/3hUQGvW.

12. "Regency Model TR-1 Transistor Radio," National Museum of American History, https://bit.ly/3HZGJaM.

13. Justin Berkowitz, "The History of Car Radios," *Car and Driver,* October 25, 2010, https://bit.ly/37cwVxz.

14. "Demographics of Internet and Home Broadband Usage in the United States," Pew Research Center, 2021, https://bit.ly/3CuX2eM.

15. Andrew Perrin and Sara Atske, "About Three-in-Ten U.S. Adults Say They Are 'Almost Constantly' Online," Pew Research Center, https://bit.ly/3pOXtLF.

16. Brooke Auxier and Monica Anderson, "Social Media Use in 2021," Pew Research Center, Internet, Science & Technology, April 7, 2021, https://bit.ly/3sZSN84.

17. From chapter 4.

18. Glenn C. Altschuler, *All Shook Up: How Rock "n" Roll Changed America* (New York: Oxford University Press, 2003).

19. As you might have guessed, this happened. See: Luke Winkie, "Meet the 19-Year-Old from Kazakhstan Who Remixed 'Roses' into a Hit," *The New York Times,* July 15, 2020, sec. Arts, https://bit.ly/3vUv4I0.

20. "Saint Jhn," *Billboard,* https://bit.ly/361rIIq.

21. Cache McClay, "Why Black TikTok Creators Have Gone on Strike," BBC News, July 15, 2021, sec. U.S. & Canada, https://bit.ly/3MDmWlf.

22. J. Clara Chan, "Black TikTok Creators Grapple with How Far to Take Strike: 'Why Should We Have to Leave?,'" *The Hollywood Reporter,* July 28, 2021, https://bit.ly/3tRD4XU.

23. The Ringer, "Dua Lipa's Grammy Performance," Facebook, 2021, https://bit.ly/34vp2lT.

24. "Levitating by Dua Lipa," Tokboard, October 1, 2021, https://bit.ly/3HZH3Gw.

25. Gary Trust and Keith Caulfield, "The Year in Charts 2021: Dua Lipa's 'Levitating' Is the No. 1 Billboard Hot 100 Song of the Year," *Billboard,* December 2, 2021, https://bit.ly/377QW8q.

26. Howell Davies, "Dua Lipa Made £1.9m a MONTH Last Year—and Doubled Her Wealth to Almost £50m," *The Sun,* December 8, 2021, https://bit.ly/365O0ZJ.

27. According to Dediu's data.

28. "American News Pathways: Explore the Data," Pew Research Center, https://bit.ly/3qfb9QH.

29. Sarah Fiorini, "Skeptics or Cynics? Age Determines How Americans View the News Media," Knight Foundation, September 21, 2021, https://bit.ly/3sYHi0A.

30. "American News Pathways: Explore the Data."

31. Andrew Guess, Jonathan Nagler, and Joshua Tucker, "Less Than You Think: Prevalence and Predictors of Fake News Dissemination on Facebook," *Science Advances* 5, no. 1 (n.d.): eaau4586, https://bit.ly/3vYJxCP.

32. Michael Hiltzik, "The Tucker Carlson Mystery: How Does His Show Survive Without Major Advertisers?," *Los Angeles Times,* April 30, 2021, https://bit.ly/3IYAhSJ.

33. "The Right's Grifter Problem," *National Review,* June 3, 2019, https://bit.ly/3MCadPM.

34. Brendan Brown, "Search on Trump Twitter Archive," https://bit.ly/3tDa5qw.

35. "*Meet the Press*—March 13, 2016," NBC News, https://bit.ly/3hVOpQU.

36. Ashley Parker, "Kellyanne Conway to Leave the White House at the End of the Month, Citing the Need to Focus on Her Family," *The Washington Post,* https://bit.ly/367Yd7F.

37. Stuart Elliott, "As Pepsi Regroups, It Strikes a Generational Note Once Again," *The New York Times,* January 21, 1997, sec. Business, https://bit.ly/3IZukFt.

38. "James Bond Franchise Box Office History," The Numbers, https://bit.ly/3Mxks81.

39. "List of All James Bond Girls," 007James, https://bit.ly/3Cs8PKV.

40. Donn Devine, "How Long Is a Generation? Science Provides an Answer," ISOGG, https://bit.ly/3hVxu0R.

41. Stephanie Convery, "Toy Story 2 Casting Couch 'Blooper' Deleted by Disney After #MeToo Movement," *The Guardian,* July 3, 2019, sec. Film, https://bit.ly/3pPiKVS.

42. Google Ngrams data, reviewing use of terms in books, shows an increase in use of the term beginning in about 1988. See: "Google Books Ngram Viewer," https://bit.ly/3Kz2EY0.

43. Christopher P. Andersen, *The Baby Boomer's Name Game* (New York: Putnam, 1987).
44. Clark Spencer, "Game Is Up for Trivial Pursuit," *Orlando Sentinel*, May 15, 1987, https://www.orlandosentinel.com/news/os-xpm-1987-05-15-0130090085-story.html.
45. First spotted by Colgate's Sam Rosenfeld but also picked out of my own personal set of cards.
46. Copyright Office, author's research. See: "Search Copyright Records: Copyright Public Records Portal," U.S. Copyright Office, https://www.copyright.gov/public-records/.
47. Hasbro, "Monopoly for Millennials Board Game," https://shop.hasbro.com/en-ca/product/monopoly-for-millennials-board-game:441D164A-4E09-477A-892C-F6A5CE9202A4.
48. Christina Maxouris and Nadeem Muaddi, "Monopoly for Millennials Is Not About Real Estate Because 'You Can't Afford It Anyway,' Hasbro Says," CNN, November 16, 2018, https://www.cnn.com/2018/11/16/us/monopoly-for-millennials-trnd/index.html.
49. "New 'Monopoly: Baby Boomer Edition' Has a Free House on Every Square," July 31, 2019, https://www.thedailymash.co.uk/news/society/new-monopoly-baby-boomer-edition-has-a-free-house-on-every-square-20190731187853.

6. Who Will Inherit the Economic Boom?

1. Sylvanus Griswold Morley, *An Introduction to the Study of the Maya Hieroglyphs* (Washington, DC: Government Printing Office, 1915), https://bit.ly/3MA1I7M.
2. "S2504: Physical Housing Characteristics for Occupied Housing Units," U.S. Census Bureau, 2019, https://bit.ly/3Cvx0rQ.
3. Board of Governors of the Federal Reserve System, "Distribution of Household Wealth in the U.S. Since 1989," https://bit.ly/3hWE0o1.
4. "Quarterly Residential Vacancies and Homeownership, Fourth Quarter 2021," U.S. Census Bureau, February 2, 2022, https://bit.ly/35M0R3h.
5. Richard Fry, Jeffrey S. Passel, and D'Vera Cohn, "A Majority of Young Adults in the U.S. Live with Their Parents for the First Time Since the Great Depression," Pew Research Center, https://bit.ly/3sXKLwg.
6. "Country Financial Security Index," Country Financial, June 20, 2018, https://bit.ly/3KALSYT.
7. Jiaquan Xu et al., "Mortality in the United States, 2015," National Center for Health Statistics, December 2016, https://bit.ly/3tM9Ppi.
8. National Center for Health Statistics (U.S.), "Life Expectancy at Birth, Age 65, and Age 75, by Sex, Race, and Hispanic Origin: United States, Selected Years 1900–2018," text, National Center for Biotechnology Information, National Center for Health Statistics (U.S.), 2021, https://bit.ly/3vURNnj.
9. Figures for 1992 are averaged from 1991 and 1993.
10. T. J. Mathews and Brady Hamilton, "Mean Age of Mother, 1970–2000," CDC, National Vital Statistics Reports, December 11, 2002, https://bit.ly/367YszB.
11. National Center for Health Statistics (U.S.), "Life Expectancy at Birth, Age 65, and Age 75."
12. Federal Reserve System, Board of Governors of the Federal Reserve System "Table: Distribution of Household Wealth in the U.S. Since 1989."
13. Author's calculations of U.S. Census Bureau data.
14. Eric Levitz, "Will 'the Great Wealth Transfer' Trigger a Millennial Civil War?," *Intelligencer, New York,* July 18, 2021, https://bit.ly/3IZHhPz.
15. Megan Brenan, "U.S. Retirees' Experience Differs from Nonretirees' Outlook," Gallup, May 18, 2021, https://bit.ly/3MDCULZ.
16. Gallup polling provided to the author.
17. "Increase in Retirement Age," Social Security Administration, https://bit.ly/3Csk464.
18. Alicia Munnell and Matthew Rutledge, "The Effects of the Great Recession on the Retirement Security of Older Workers," *The Annals of the American Academy of Political and Social Science* 650 (November 1, 2013): 124–42, https://bit.ly/3hUQkp6.

19. Munnell and Rutledge, "The Effects of the Great Recession."

20. Megan Brenan, "U.S. Retirees' Experience Differs from Nonretirees' Outlook," Gallup, May 18, 2021, https://bit.ly/3MDCULZ.

21. "Actuarial Status of the Social Security Trust Funds," Social Security Administration Research, Statistics, and Policy Analysis, https://bit.ly/3pUYr9w.

22. George Johnson, "Leon Lederman, 96, Explorer (and Explainer) of the Subatomic World, Dies," *The New York Times*, October 3, 2018, sec. Science, https://bit.ly/3sVHBZZ.

23. James R. Knickman and Emily K. Snell, "The 2030 Problem: Caring for Aging Baby Boomers," *Health Services Research* 37, no. 4 (August 2002): 849–84, https://bit.ly/376nG1R.

24. Nisha Kurani et al., "How Has U.S. Spending on Healthcare Changed over Time?," Peterson-KFF Health System Tracker, https://bit.ly/3tK9mnB.

25. David Lassman et al., "US Health Spending Trends by Age and Gender: Selected Years 2002–10," *Health Affairs* 33, no. 5 (May 2014): 815–22, https://bit.ly/35GoOJs.

26. Board of Governors of the Federal Reserve System. "Table: Distribution of Household Wealth in the U.S. Since 1989."

27. Interview with Alison Bryant, AARP.

28. Sarah Flood, Miriam King, Renae Rodgers, et al., Integrated Public Use Microdata Series, Current Population Survey: Version 9.0 (dataset) (Minneapolis, MN: IPUMS, 2021), https://bit.ly/3I0Y03z.

29. Flood, King, Rodgers, et al., Integrated Public Use Microdata Series, Current Population Survey: Version 9.0.

30. Raj Chetty, David Grusky, Maximilian Hell, et al., "The Fading American Dream: Trends in Absolute Income Mobility Since 1940," *Science* (2017): 398–406.

31. Daniel L. Greenwald et al., "Financial and Total Wealth Inequality with Declining Interest Rates," Working Paper Series, National Bureau of Economic Research, March 2021, https://bit.ly/365qdJc.

32. Department of Education, "Federal Student Loan Portfolio, https://bit.ly/3y5gH4L.

33. Department of Education data on college costs measured against annual federal minimum wage, as indicated by the Department of Labor. See: "History of Federal Minimum Wage Rates Under the Fair Labor Standards Act, 1938–2009," U.S. Department of Labor, https://bit.ly/3MwOI2G.

34. U.S. Department of Education, National Center for Education Statistics, *Digest of Education Statistics, 2019,* https://bit.ly/3CuWCoI.

35. Tawnell Hobbs and Andrea Fuller, "How Baylor Steered Lower-Income Parents to Debt They Couldn't Afford," *The Wall Street Journal*, October 13, 2021, sec. U.S., https://bit.ly/3hUQCw1.

36. "Household Debt Among Older Americans, 1989–2016," Congressional Research Service, September 11, 2019, https://bit.ly/3pOWRWn.

37. This indexed data, which comes from the Federal Reserve, sets national home prices in January 2000 as the index value of 100. A value of 200 in a month, then, indicates that home prices were twice as high that month as they were in January 2000. See: S&P Dow Jones Indices LLC, "S&P/Case-Shiller U.S. National Home Price Index," Federal Reserve Bank of St. Louis, https://bit.ly/3sZScmQ.

38. CPS data via IPUMS.

39. Alvaro Mezza, Daniel Ringo, and Kamila Sommer, "Can Student Loan Debt Explain Low Homeownership Rates for Young Adults?," Board of Governors of the Federal Reserve System, January 2019, https://bit.ly/3Kyfu92.

40. That's true both because homeowners have structural reasons for voting more (not having to update registrations, etc.) and because more boomers are homeowners and there are still a lot of baby boomers. Again: the generation's scale is part of the calculus.

41. Andrew B. Hall and Jesse Yoder, "Does Homeownership Influence Political Behavior? Evidence from Administrative Data," *The Journal of Politics* 84, no. 1 (January 2022): 351–66, https://bit.ly/35M3x0H.

42. Alicia Munnell, Anqi Chen, and Robert Siliciano, "The National Retirement Risk Index: An

Update from the 2019 SCF," Center for Retirement Research at Boston College, January 2021, https://bit.ly/3vU33QN.

43. Ryan Dezember, "If You Sell a House These Days, the Buyer Might Be a Pension Fund," *The Wall Street Journal*, April 4, 2021, sec. Markets, https://bit.ly/367YEyP.

44. In 1995, there were about 77.6 million boomers. In 2029 there are projected to be 74.7 million millennials.

45. Author calculations based on U.S. Census Bureau projections.

46. Dave Leip, "2012 Presidential General Election Results—Miami-Dade County, FL," *Atlas of U.S. Presidential Elections*, 2019, https://bit.ly/3J5cCAf.

47. "Miami-Dade School District Bond Measure (November 2012)," Ballotpedia, https://bit.ly/3MAIlvp.

48. James Button and Walter Rosenbaum, "Seeing Gray: School Bond Issues and the Aging in Florida," *Research on Aging* 11 (July 1, 1989): 158–73, https://bit.ly/3Cun0Po.

49. Corporate Center-Research IT, "Intergenerational Conflict: The Next Dividing Line," Deutsche Bank Research, https://bit.ly/34t5m1Y.

50. National Academies of Sciences, Engineering, and Medicine, *The Economic and Fiscal Consequences of Immigration*, ed. Francine D. Blau and Christopher Mackie (Washington, DC: The National Academies Press, 2017), https://bit.ly/3pR2Tpu.

51. Julia Preston, "Immigrants Aren't Taking Americans' Jobs, New Study Finds," *The New York Times*, September 21, 2016, sec. U.S., https://bit.ly/3sZSjig.

52. From 1995 to 2005, the country was averaging 14.2 births per 1,000 residents with the figure never dropping below 14. In 2009, it did. By 2019, the figure was only 11.4.

53. "Job Openings and Labor Turnover Survey," Bureau of Labor Statistics Data, https://bit.ly/3KxBIrP.

54. "SOI Tax Stats—All Top Wealthholders by Size of Net Worth," Internal Revenue Service, https://bit.ly/3tK9xzh.

55. Mark Baldassare et al., "Proposition 13: 40 Years Later," Public Policy Institute of California, https://bit.ly/3w014uB.

56. Adam Looney, "Who Owes the Most Student Debt?," Brookings, June 28, 2019, https://bit.ly/365BRng

57. Philip Bump, "The Economy Is Feeling the Effects of the Fading Baby Boom," *The Washington Post*, January 7, 2022, https://bit.ly/3IZuRXZ.

7. The Importance of What We Don't Know

1. "Keeper of the Flame," *Birmingham News*, June 21, 1950.

2. "See the Stars Through UA's New Telescope," *University of Alabama News*, February 2005, https://bit.ly/3MFtlfw.

3. "Freedom and Fire!: A Civil War Story," University of Alabama News Center, November 2016, https://bit.ly/3CvxvCe.

4. "Keeper of the Flame," *Birmingham News*.

5. "Birmingham AL City Hall Time Capsule," Waymarking, https://bit.ly/3hZzXas.

6. Frederick Othman, "Machines Don't Have Wars, but Only Humans Have Fun," *Tampa Bay Times*, June 7, 1950, https://bit.ly/35M1idV.

7. "Shiny, New, Red Riot Car Will Grace the Basement," *Birmingham News*, August 2, 1950, sec. Special Section.

8. Birmingham Public Library, Hill Ferguson Records, Cornerstone Box Birmingham City Hall, August 3, 1950, File 56.2.10.40.

9. "Our History," Interpol, https://bit.ly/3t0dYXA.

10. It can be seen in images from Getty. See: https://bit.ly/3Kw3cya.

11. "He Likes Our Jail," *Birmingham News*, August 5, 1950.

12. Thomas Fuller, "Before the Pandemic, Many States Had Anti-Mask Laws on the Books. Repealing Them Could Be a Challenge," *The New York Times*, June 5, 2021, sec. U.S., https://bit.ly/3tJ5pzh.

13. In chapter 6.

14. Frank Hobbs and Bonnie Damon, "65+ in the United States," U.S. Census Bureau, 1996, https://bit.ly/3vVTtgq.

15. Author calculations based on age data published by the CDC, November 2021. See: CDC, "COVID Data Tracker," Centers for Disease Control and Prevention, https://bit.ly/3I3dHXY.

16. Julie Bosman, Amy Harmon, and Albert Sun, "As U.S. Nears 800,000 Virus Deaths, 1 of Every 100 Older Americans Has Perished," *The New York Times*, December 13, 2021, sec. U.S., https://bit.ly/3J1Jmuj.

17. Anne Case and Angus Deaton, *Deaths of Despair and the Future of Capitalism* (Princeton: Princeton University Press, 2021).

18. Case and Deaton, *Deaths of Despair and the Future of Capitalism*.

19. Janet Adamy, "Life Expectancy in U.S. Declined 1.8 Years in 2020, CDC Says," *The Wall Street Journal*, December 22, 2021, sec. U.S., https://bit.ly/3MwOR6e.

20. Dan Keating and Lenny Bernstein, "100,000 Americans Died of Drug Overdoses in 12 Months During the Pandemic," *The Washington Post*, November 17, 2021, https://bit.ly/3CwuEZH.

21. Figures are adjusted to 2000 population.

22. Roger Harrabin, "Climate Change: Science Failed to Predict Flood and Heat Intensity," BBC News, July 16, 2021, sec. Science & Environment, https://bit.ly/34txAd0.

23. Each of these metrics has its own sourcing, per ProPublica's report: "Chi Xu, School of Life Sciences, Nanjing University (global human climate niche), Rhodium Group/Climate Impact Lab (economic damages), John Abatzoglou, University of California, Merced (very large fires)." See: Al Shaw, Abrahm Lustgarten, and Jeremy W. Goldsmith, "New Climate Maps Show a Transformed United States," ProPublica, September 15, 2020, https://bit.ly/3pRS6M3.

24. The CDC has guidance on this. See: https://bit.ly/3sYHqgq.

25. Jason Schachter and Antonio Bruce, "Revising Methods to Better Reflect the Impact of Disaster," Census.gov, August 19, 2020, https://bit.ly/3KwdEWd.

26. Brian Glassman, "A Third of Movers from Puerto Rico to the Mainland United States Relocated to Florida in 2018," Census.gov, September 26, 2019, https://bit.ly/3tLUaGh.

27. Ben Lefebvre, "How 'Climate Migrants' Are Roiling American Politics," *Politico*, https://bit.ly/3w01scx.

28. Jeffrey A. Groen and Anne E. Polivka, "Going Home After Hurricane Katrina: Determinants of Return Migration and Changes in Affected Areas," *Demography* 47, no. 4 (November 2010): 821–44.

29. Doyle S. Rice, "Report: Climate Change Behind Rise in Weather Disasters," *USA Today*, https://bit.ly/3HYy6NX.

30. Andrew and Peters, "The Global Carbon Project's Fossil CO_2 Emissions Dataset."

31. This estimate looks only at emissions of CO_2 from oxidation of fossil fuels and decomposition of fossil carbonates, according to the Global Carbon Project's definition. It is primarily a tally of emissions from burning fossil fuels (largely for transportation and electricity generation), venting gases, and cement production. See: Robbie M. Andrew and Glen P. Peters, "The Global Carbon Project's Fossil CO_2 Emissions Dataset," Zenodo, October 14, 2021, https://bit.ly/3J1MPsO.

32. Brad Plumer, "U.S. Greenhouse Gas Emissions Bounced Back Sharply in 2021," *The New York Times*, January 10, 2022, sec. Climate, https://bit.ly/3MxkYCZ.

33. "Inaugural Address by President Joseph R. Biden, Jr.," The White House, January 20, 2021, https://bit.ly/368b0qY.

34. Larry M. Bartels, "Ethnic Antagonism Erodes Republicans' Commitment to Democracy," *Proceedings of the National Academy of Sciences* 117, no. 37 (September 15, 2020): 22752–59, https://bit.ly/3hUQFbm.

35. Anna Lührmann et al., "V–Dem Party Coding Units v1," Varieties of Democracy (V–Dem) Project, https://bit.ly/3qfb2Vh.

36. Elena Samuels and Alex Mejia, "Has Your State Made It Harder to Vote?," FiveThirtyEight, June 16, 2022, https://bit.ly/3NIW6gI.

37. Despite repeated efforts to prove that rampant fraud had occurred, only two dozen arrests for

possible fraud had been made by May 2021. See: Philip Bump, "Despite GOP Rhetoric, There Have Been Fewer Than Two Dozen Charged Cases of Voter Fraud Since the Election," *The Washington Post*, May 4, 2021, https://bit.ly/3Krovk8.

38. Michael Wines, "Some Republicans Acknowledge Leveraging Voter ID Laws for Political Gain," *The New York Times*, September 16, 2016, sec. U.S., https://bit.ly/3tD9THO.

39. Aaron Blake, "The GOP's Increasingly Blunt Argument: It Needs Voting Restrictions to Win," *The Washington Post*, June 14, 2021, https://bit.ly/3vToRMx.

40. Philip Bump, "After Seven Months of Debunking, the False Belief That Biden Won Because of Fraud Hasn't Budged," *The Washington Post*, June 21, 2021, https://bit.ly/3HV1g0h.

41. The most notable was in Arizona, a state that flipped from Trump to Biden. See: Howard Fischer Capitol Media Services, "Proposed Law Would Allow Arizona Legislature to Overturn Presidential Election Results," *Arizona Daily Star*, https://bit.ly/3J22aJF.

42. J. Michael Luttig, "The Republican Blueprint to Steal the 2024 Election," CNN, April 27, 2022, https://bit.ly/3koPeDc.

43. David Shor, Twitter post, January 10, 2021, 11:26 a.m., https://bit.ly/3ME3C7q.

44. Stephen Wolf, "How Minority Rule Plagues Senate: Republicans Last Won More Support Than Democrats Two Decades Ago," *Daily Kos*, February 23, 2021, https://bit.ly/3Cx2bmo.

45. Mike Lee, Twitter post, October 7, 2020, 9:34 p.m., https://bit.ly/34txhij.

46. Mike Lee, Twitter post, October 8, 2020, 2:24 a.m., https://bit.ly/3pUCZRM.

47. Mariana Alfaro, "Lee Worked Hard to Overturn Election, Keep Trump in Power, Texts Show," *The Washington Post*, April 15, 2022, https://bit.ly/3y0gL5T.

48. George Thomas, "'America Is a Republic, Not a Democracy' Is a Dangerous—and Wrong—Argument," *The Atlantic*, November 2, 2020, https://bit.ly/3sZYfYc.

49. *1910 Census*, vol. 1, *Population, General Report and Analysis* (Washington, DC: U.S. Census Bureau, 1910), https://bit.ly/37609B9.

50. Steven Levitsky and Daniel Ziblatt, *How Democracies Die* (New York: Crown, 2018).

51. Philip Bump, "Approval of the Jan. 6 Capitol Riot Is More Deeply Embedded Than You Might Think," *The Washington Post*, July 21, 2021, https://bit.ly/3tNufhw.

52. Philip Bump, "Most Republicans See Democrats Not as Political Opponents but as Enemies," *The Washington Post*, February 10, 2021, https://bit.ly/3vUvqOQ.

53. Philip Bump, "After the Political Violence and the Threats Come the Rationalizations," *The Washington Post*, November 2, 2021, https://bit.ly/3HXlDtW.

54. Barton Gellman, "Trump's Next Coup Has Already Begun," *The Atlantic*, December 6, 2021, https://bit.ly/3Jcm1WA.

55. As we touched on at the beginning of chapter 3.

56. U.S. District Court for the District of Columbia, Criminal Complaint, Case 1:21-cr-00633, August, 12, 2021, https://bit.ly/3kvSOvj.

57. Philip Bump, "The Americans Who See Democracy Most at Risk? Republicans," *The Washington Post*, October 20, 2021, https://bit.ly/3MDDAkv.

58. Philip Bump, "What Did John Eastman Really Want to Have Happen?," *The Washington Post*, November 1, 2021, https://bit.ly/365O1Nh.

59. Paul Bedard, "Exclusive: Trump Urges State Legislators to Reject Electoral Votes, 'You Are the Real Power,'" *Washington Examiner*, January 3, 2021, https://bit.ly/3hUR0e8.

60. Emma Green, "The Conservatives Dreading—and Preparing for—Civil War," *The Atlantic*, October 1, 2021, https://bit.ly/35J0xlT.

61. Ben Rhodes, "The Path to Autocracy," *The Atlantic*, June 15, 2020, https://bit.ly/3t0emW2.

62. Gareth Browne, "Orbán Is the Original Trump, Says Bannon in Budapest," *The National*, May 24, 2018, https://bit.ly/3KA264y.

63. Philip Bump, "The Actual Threat Posed by a Political 'Cult' in America," *The Washington Post*, May 10, 2022, https://bit.ly/3Ngbz20.

64. Sarah Churchwell, "American Fascism: It Has Happened Here," *The New York Review of Books*, https://bit.ly/3tLUvc1.

65. "Dr. James Waterman Wise Warns Audience Against Incipient American Fasicm [*sic*]," *Central New Jersey Home News*, February 20, 1936, https://bit.ly/35EkdaF.

66. Eugene Scott, "'Racists Think He's a Racist': Gillum on White Supremacists' Support for DeSantis," *The Washington Post*, October 25, 2018, https://bit.ly/3IbNK8V.
67. Michael Greenberger, "Undoing Reconstruction: Racial Threat and the Process of Redemption, 1870–1920," *Social Science Quarterly* (May 4, 2022), https://bit.ly/3Nk3FVD.
68. As in chapter 4.
69. "Jurisdictions Previously Covered by Section 5," Department of Justice, August 6, 2015, https://bit.ly/362TB2L.
70. U.S. Census Bureau voting data.
71. "Black Firsts in Birmingham," Birmingham Public Library, December 21, 2020, https://bit.ly/3tJl6Xo.
72. "Here's Every Word from the Fourth Jan. 6 Committee Hearing on Its Investigation," NPR, June 21, 2022, https://bit.ly/3NoXcI.

8. The Importance of What We Don't Know About Ourselves

1. U.S. Census Bureau, "Table I: Population of the United States" (Washington, DC: 1870), https://bit.ly/3vUswd9.
2. "1870—History—U.S. Census Bureau," U.S. Census Bureau, https://bit.ly/3sWjiuJ.
3. Karen Humes and Howard Hogan, "Measurement of Race and Ethnicity in a Changing, Multicultural America," *Race and Social Problems* 1 (September 1, 2009): 111–31, https://bit.ly/3KuFuSO.
4. U.S. Census Bureau records.
5. "Supreme Court to Rule on Color Line," *Durham Morning Herald*, August 17, 1922, https://bit.ly/3MDgvyz.
6. "*Ozawa v. United States*, 260 U.S. 178 (1922)," Justia Law, https://bit.ly/3CtobPl.
7. "*In Re Halladjian*, 174 F. 834 (1909)," Caselaw Access Project, https://bit.ly/3hSGrIi.
8. "Citizenship for Armenians; Circuit Court Declines to Bar Them on Government's Plea," *The New York Times*, December 25, 1909, sec. Archives, https://bit.ly/3pS3reQ.
9. "*United States v. Bhagat Singh Thind*, 261 U.S. 204 (1923)," Justia Law, https://bit.ly/3HZ9bcX.
10. Author calculations from Pew Research Center and U.S. Census Bureau data. See: "Hispanic Population Growth and Dispersion Across U.S. Counties, 1980–2020," Pew Research Center, Hispanic Trends Project, https://bit.ly/3J5cd0H.
11. Mark Hugo Lopez, Ana Gonzalez-Barrera, and Gustavo Lopez, "Latino Identity Declines Across Generations as Immigrant Ties Weaken," Pew Research Center, Hispanic Trends Project, December 20, 2017, https://bit.ly/37nvRqZ.
12. Ana Gonzalez-Barrera, "The Ways Hispanics Describe Their Identity Vary Across Immigrant Generations," Pew Research Center, September 24, 2020, https://bit.ly/3vYJtmy.
13. Heather Silber Mohamed, *The New Americans?: Immigration, Protest, and the Politics of Latino Identity* (Lawrence, KS: University Press of Kansas, 2017).
14. From chapter 4.
15. Remember that the bureau separates race from ethnicity; that is, Hispanic identity.
16. Mark Hugo Lopez, Jens Manuel Krogstad, and Jeffrey S. Passel, "Who Is Hispanic?," Pew Research Center, September 23, 2021, https://bit.ly/3sWn4Er.
17. Richard Alba, *The Great Demographic Illusion: Majority, Minority, and the Expanding American Mainstream* (Princeton: Princeton University Press, 2020).
18. Chapter 4.
19. The bureau conducts an annual survey, the American Community Survey, that provides intercensal data including about race.
20. As explained in chapter 2.
21. "Bump" used to be "Boumpasse," or so our family understands.
22. "Web Event: The Great Demographic Illusion," American Enterprise Institute, 2021, https://bit.ly/3KtnVm4.
23. "Google Books Ngram Viewer," Google, https://bit.ly/3MOsUjo.

24. Tanya Golash-Boza, "Dropping the Hyphen? Becoming Latino(a)-American Through Racialized Assimilation," *Social Forces* 85, no. 1 (2006): 27–55.
25. Tanya Golash-Boza and William Darity, "Latino Racial Choices: The Effects of Skin Colour and Discrimination on Latinos' and Latinas' Racial Self-Identifications," *Ethnic and Racial Studies* 31, no. 5 (2008): 899–934.
26. Charles W. Mills, *The Racial Contract*, 1st ed. (Ithaca, NY: Cornell University Press, 1999).
27. Jennifer Lee and Frank D. Bean, *The Diversity Paradox: Immigration and the Color Line in Twenty-First Century America* (New York: Russell Sage Foundation, 2010).
28. This was the boundary offered for pornography by Justice Potter Stewart in the 1964 case *Jacobellis v. Ohio*. See: Peter Lattman, "The Origins of Justice Stewart's 'I Know It When I See It,'" *The Wall Street Journal*, September 27, 2007, sec. Law, https://bit.ly/3Cto9XJ.
29. Wendy Roth, "The Multiple Dimensions of Race," *Ethnic and Racial Studies* 39 (March 21, 2016): 1–29, https://bit.ly/3hXd1ZM.
30. Maria Abascal, "Contraction as a Response to Group Threat: Demographic Decline and Whites' Classification of People Who Are Ambiguously White," *American Sociological Review* 85, no. 2 (April 1, 2020): 298–322, https://bit.ly/3pOJINa.
31. Again, per Dowell Myers's research.
32. Sonya R. Porter, Carolyn A. Liebler, and James M. Noon, "An Outside View: What Observers Say About Others' Races and Hispanic Origins," *American Behavioral Scientist* 60, no. 4 (April 1, 2016): 465–97, https://bit.ly/3I0XVgh.
33. Cybelle Fox and Thomas A. Guglielmo, "Defining America's Racial Boundaries: Blacks, Mexicans, and European Immigrants, 1890–1945," *American Journal of Sociology* 118, no. 2 (September 2012): 327–79, https://bit.ly/3J1NqdM.
34. David R. Roediger, *Colored White: Transcending the Racial Past*, 1st ed. (Berkeley: University of California Press, 2002).
35. Fox and Guglielmo, "Defining America's Racial Boundaries."
36. Roediger, *Colored White*.
37. Eduardo Bonilla-Silva, "From Bi-Racial to Tri-Racial: Towards a New System of Racial Stratification in the USA," *Ethnic and Racial Studies* 27, no. 6 (November 1, 2004): 931–50, https://bit.ly/3tKEoeV.
38. By 1950, there were already more baby boomers than non-White Americans. By 2000 that was no longer true.
39. AEI event.

9. A New American Politics

1. As explained by Michigan State's Ann Larabee in chapter 1.
2. Thom File, "Young-Adult Voting: An Analysis of Presidential Elections, 1964–2012," U.S. Census Bureau, April 2014, https://bit.ly/3vTot0x.
3. Ruth Igielnik, Scott Keeter, and Hannah Hartig, "Behind Biden's 2020 Victory," Pew Research Center, U.S. Politics & Policy, June 30, 2021, https://bit.ly/35M0KVt.
4. David Faris, "Republicans' Problems with Young Voters Go Far Deeper Than Trump," *The Washington Post*, September 15, 2020, https://bit.ly/34v9qPt.
5. Author calculation based on adjusted U.S. Census Bureau turnout data compiled by Michael McDonald. See: Michael McDonald, "Voter Turnout Demographics," United States Elections Project, https://bit.ly/377QuqK.
6. Author's ANES analysis.
7. U.S. Census Bureau.
8. Rob Griffin, William Frey, and Ruy Teixeira, "America's Electoral Future," Center for American Progress, October 19, 2020, https://bit.ly/37jKOKw.
9. "In Changing U.S. Electorate, Race and Education Remain Stark Dividing Lines," Pew Research Center, U.S. Politics & Policy, June 2, 2020, https://bit.ly/3w1U7ZE.
10. Yair Ghitza, A. Gelman, and Jonathan Auerbach, "The Great Society, Reagan's Revolution, and Generations of Presidential Voting," Semantic Scholar, 2014, https://bit.ly/3CxpPiF.

11. Philip Bump, "Why Has Biden's Approval Plunged with Young People?," *The Washington Post*, April 14, 2022, https://bit.ly/3vX0cVE.
12. If anyone is looking for a good label for Generation Z or later, here you go.
13. "Turning Point USA Inc—Form 990," ProPublica Nonprofit Explorer, June 2020, https://bit.ly/3hUW5TB.
14. Theodore Schleifer, "First on CNN: Koch Operative Leaves Group amid Tumult," CNN, September 1, 2015, https://bit.ly/3pV9pvH.
15. "Crenshaw Youth Summit—Houston, TX, September 12," Crenshaw for Congress, October 22, 2021, https://bit.ly/3I3NyIp.
16. Author calculations from U.S. Census Bureau data.
17. "Political Advertising on Google," Google Transparency Report, https://bit.ly/3J4croQ.
18. Rebecca Heilweil, "Why the Trump Campaign Is Going All-in on YouTube," *Vox*, November 3, 2020, https://bit.ly/3tHtQxi.
19. *The Washington Post*'s polling average in mid-September 2020 had Biden up more than 30 in Arizona but only a bit over 10 in Florida. See: Philip Bump, "Why the Hispanic Vote in Florida Is Particularly Worrisome to Biden's Campaign," *The Washington Post*, September 14, 2020, https://bit.ly/3vS1x1N.
20. Igielnik, Keeter, and Hartig, "Behind Biden's 2020 Victory."
21. "In Changing U.S. Electorate, Race and Education Remain Stark Dividing Lines."
22. Monte Poole, "Equality Movement Leaves Some Latinos Feeling Marginalized," NBC Sports, October 2, 2020, https://bit.ly/3A9PoY1.
23. Michael McDonald's corrected values for U.S. Census Bureau turnout estimates.
24. "Election Statistics: 1920 to Present," U.S. House of Representatives, History, Art & Archives, https://bit.ly/3sYGVD4.
25. Author analysis of 2020 U.S. Census Bureau data for the population overall and 2019 single-year data for adult citizens.
26. Dave Leip, *Atlas of U.S. Presidential Elections*, "2020 Presidential General Election Data—National," https://bit.ly/37138Z6.
27. As discussed in chapter 4.
28. EquisLabs uses the "Latinx" descriptor.
29. Carlos Odio and Rachel Stein, "2020 Post-Mortem (Part Two): The American Dream Voter," Equis Research, December 14, 2021, https://bit.ly/3KOtU5l.
30. Amanda Seitz and Will Weissert, "Inside the 'Big Wave' of Misinformation Targeted at Latinos," AP News, November 29, 2021, https://bit.ly/3MA1Wf8.
31. "How Facebook Can Flatten the Curve of the Coronavirus Infodemic," Avaaz, April 15, 2020, https://bit.ly/3CuWCVK.
32. Elizabeth Dwoskin, Tory Newmyer, and Shibani Mahtani, "The Case Against Mark Zuckerberg: Insiders Say Facebook's CEO Chose Growth over Safety," *The Washington Post*, October 25, 2021, https://bit.ly/3hX7tOG.
33. From the researchers: "EquisLabs/Logistic regression model predicting 'more concerned about socialism on the left' vs. 'more concerned about fascism on the right.' Controls for gender, age, education, language, generation, national origin, region, party ID and ideology, using data from Equis national post-mortem survey."
34. Jack Herrera, "Why Democrats Are Losing Texas Latinos," *Texas Monthly*, September 13, 2021, https://bit.ly/3pVUMIn.
35. You'll remember this point from chapter 8.
36. In contrast to the group identity among non-Whites perceived by Whites, as in the research discussed in chapter 4.
37. Philip Bump, "A Reporter Pressed the White House for Data. That's When Things Got Tense," *The Washington Post*, August 2, 2017, https://bit.ly/365BTeS.
38. National Academies of Sciences, Engineering, and Medicine, *The Economic and Fiscal Consequences of Immigration*, ed. Francine D. Blau and Christopher Mackie (Washington, DC: The National Academies Press, 2017), https://bit.ly/3pR2Tpu.
39. See chapter 6.

NOTES

40. Ian Haney López, "Trump Exploited Status Anxiety Within the Latino Community," *The Washington Post*, November 6, 2020, https://bit.ly/3JclrrS.

41. William H. Frey, *Diversity Explosion: How New Racial Demographics Are Remaking America* (Washington, DC: Brookings Institution Press, 2018).

42. The distribution of support is an estimate combining the composition of the electorate with levels of support by race. Given the margins of error with exit polling, these numbers should be taken with large grains of salt. Exit polls are from the *Los Angeles Times*, population data from the U.S. Census Bureau. See: "State Propositions: A Snapshot of Voters," *Los Angeles Times*, November 7, 1996, https://bit.ly/3tMa1Vy.

43. Ruy Teixeira, "Demography Is Not Destiny," *Persuasion*, July 16, 2020, https://bit.ly/3vUYUfp.

44. Ruy Teixeira, "The Return of Class," Substack newsletter, *The Liberal Patriot* (blog), May 27, 2021, https://bit.ly/34xKqqM.

45. Ronald Kessler, "Donald Trump: Mean-Spirited GOP Won't Win Elections," Newsmax, November 26, 2012, https://bit.ly/3Krr1aa.

46. As described in chapter 4.

47. Conducted by NORC for Fox News and the Associated Press. See: "Voter Analysis: Elections 2020," Fox News, https://bit.ly/3ME3kNS.

48. Amory Gethin, Clara Martínez-Toledano, and Thomas Piketty, "Brahmin Left Versus Merchant Right: Changing Political Cleavages in 21 Western Democracies, 1948–2020," *The Quarterly Journal of Economics* 137, no. 1 (February 2022): 1–48, https://bit.ly/3CCp7Rp.

49. Refer to chapter 4.

50. Jonathan Swan and Alayna Treene, "McConnell: No Legislative Agenda for 2022 Midterms," Axios, December 3, 2021, https://bit.ly/3hUWa9R.

51. Gethin, Martinez-Toledano, and Piketty, "Brahmin Left Versus Merchant Right."

52. GDELT analysis of closed-captioning data collected by the Internet Archive. See: https://bit.ly/3pS3QxS.

53. Igielnik, Ketter, and Hartig, "Behind Biden's 2020 Victory."

54. See chapter 4 if you don't.

55. Pia Deshpande, Zachary Hertz, and Brian Schaffner, "Many College Republicans Didn't Vote for Trump in 2020. His Racist Rhetoric May Be Why," *The Washington Post*, January 20, 2022, https://bit.ly/3HYBuIC.

56. David Shor, Twitter post, February 9, 2022, 10:40 a.m., https://bit.ly/3J6OSfi.

57. Kristin Kobes Du Mez, *Jesus and John Wayne: How White Evangelicals Corrupted a Faith and Fractured a Nation* (New York: Liveright, 2020).

58. While it can admittedly be fraught to ascribe particular violent acts solely to a broad, intangible sense of disempowerment, it's clear that incidents like the spree killing in Isla Vista, California, in 2014 or the murders of Asian women at spas in Atlanta in 2021 were at least motivated in part by misogyny, if not personal impotence.

59. Derek Robertson, "How Republicans Became the 'Barstool' Party," *Politico*, June 20, 2021, https://bit.ly/3kkaEkJ.

60. Douglas Belkin, "A Generation of American Men Give Up on College: 'I Just Feel Lost,'" *The Wall Street Journal*, September 6, 2021, sec. U.S., https://bit.ly/3tIj2il.

61. Using U.S. Census Bureau data from 2020. The vote-total figures in this section use the two-party vote.

62. If you're curious, which you should be: Los Angeles, Houston, Miami, Chicago, Phoenix, Riverside County, San Antonio, San Bernardino County, and San Diego. Each was home to at least a million Hispanic residents in 2020.

63. Philip Bump, "Most Trump Voters Live in States Won by Biden," *The Washington Post*, December 9, 2020, https://bit.ly/3vUAmn8.

64. U.S. Joint Economic Committee, "Losing Our Minds: Brain Drain Across the United States," https://bit.ly/3Lx8GcO.

65. Take away Arizona, Georgia, and Wisconsin, the states where he won most narrowly, and the Electoral College result was a 269 to 269 vote tie.

66. Jacob R. Brown and Ryan D. Enos, "The Measurement of Partisan Sorting for 180 Million Voters," *Nature Human Behaviour* 5, no. 8 (August 2021): 998–1008, https://bit.ly/3t0gey1.

67. A reference, of course, to research we discussed in chapter 4.

68. Brown and Enos, "The Measurement of Partisan Sorting for 180 Million Voters."

69. Seventy years ago, about 1 in 5 Americans moved in a given year. By 2010, the figure was about 1 in 9. See: Cheryl Russell, "Demo Memo: Geographic Mobility Again Falls to All-Time Low," *Demo Memo* (blog), November 18, 2021, https://bit.ly/3KwiJ0H.

70. In 1950, Bull Connor was a Democrat.

71. Zachary Hertz, Lucas Pyle, and Brian Schaffner, "Virginia's Upcoming Election Pits Rural Voters Against Urban Ones. Why Is There Such a Divide?," *The Washington Post*, September 22, 2021, https://bit.ly/3MDNgfa.

72. David A. Hopkins, "As New Census Numbers Show, the Biggest Divide Isn't North v. South Anymore—It's Metro v. Rural," *Honest Graft* (blog), https://bit.ly/3CuhIDC.

73. Though there was no significant fraud. See: "Missouri, 2000," Brennan Center for Justice, November 10, 2007, https://bit.ly/34twUUX.

74. Though there was no significant fraud. See: Cassie Owens, "Internet: Philly Rigged the 2012 Presidential Election. Experts: Still No," Politifact, August 12, 2016, https://bit.ly/3pUYAtA.

75. Though there was no significant fraud. See: Philip Bump, "Guess What? There (Still) Wasn't Any Significant Fraud in the 2020 Presidential Election," *The Washington Post*, December 14, 2021, https://bit.ly/367YJm7.

76. Clara Hendrickson, "GOP Members Reverse Course, Vote to Certify Wayne County Election Results," *Detroit Free Press*, November 17, 2020, https://bit.ly/363lyHK.

77. Using University of Wisconsin Population Health Institute categories.

78. Molly Beck, "A Blue Wave Hit Statewide Races, but Did Wisconsin GOP Gerrymandering Limit Dem Legislative Inroads?," *Milwaukee Journal Sentinel*, November 8, 2018, https://bit.ly/3tJvJJQ.

79. In fact, the fraud theories were thoroughly debunked by a conservative group. See: Patrick Marley, "Conservative Group Finds No Signs of Widespread Voter Fraud in Wisconsin but Urges Changes to Election Processes," *Milwaukee Journal Sentinel*, December 7, 2021, https://bit.ly/3vVTwJ8.

80. Some of these examples are drawn from 2017 research conducted by Pew Research Center. See: "Political Typology: Financial Well-Being, Personal Characteristics and Lifestyles," Pew Research Center, October 24, 2017, https://bit.ly/34uZiGp.

81. Lilliana Mason, *Uncivil Agreement: How Politics Became Our Identity*, ill. ed. (Chicago: University of Chicago Press, 2018).

82. Mason, *Uncivil Agreement*.

83. "How Groups Voted in 1980," Roper Center for Public Opinion Research, https://bit.ly/3KxSjf0.

84. "Partisans Differ Widely in Views of Police Officers, College Professors," Pew Research Center, U.S. Politics & Policy, September 13, 2017, https://bit.ly/3MDDglN.

85. "Many Latino Americans Believe the Democratic and Republican Parties Take Them for Granted," Ipsos, December 21, 2021, https://bit.ly/36bdwgc.

86. Julia Azari, "Weak Parties and Strong Partisanship Are a Bad Combination," *Vox*, November 3, 2016, https://bit.ly/34t5A9k.

87. Vianney Gómez and Andrew Daniller, "Younger U.S. Adults Less Likely to See Big Differences Between the Parties or to Feel Well Represented by Them," Pew Research Center, December 7, 2021, https://bit.ly/3pNUu6r.

88. Mason, *Uncivil Agreement*.

89. My day-to-day job is as a correspondent for *The Washington Post*, so recognize that some bias may be at play here.

90. "Trends and Facts on Newspapers: State of the News Media," Pew Research Center, June 29, 2021, https://bit.ly/3HYGX1W.

91. Meghan E. Rubado and Jay T. Jennings, "Political Consequences of the Endangered Local

Watchdog: Newspaper Decline and Mayoral Elections in the United States," *Urban Affairs Review* 56, no. 5 (September 1, 2020): 1327–56, https://bit.ly/3J19RA0.

92. Mason, *Uncivil Agreement*.
93. Bureau of Labor Statistics, "Household Data Series, Union Membership Tables," https://bit.ly/3Km1z5p.
94. Jonathan Vespa, "Those Who Served: America's Veterans from World War II to the War on Terror," U.S. Census Bureau, June 2020, https://bit.ly/3tFxK9M.
95. Jeffrey Jones, "U.S. Church Membership Falls Below Majority for First Time," Gallup, March 29, 2021, https://bit.ly/35FCVyH.

10. Getting from Here to Wherever "There" Is

1. Diane Hirth, "Plenty of Fun, Furs as GOP Crowd Gathers," *South Florida Sun-Sentinel*, January 7, 1987.
2. Grace Agostin, "Ida Martinez, First Fan of Former Governor, Dies at 86," *Tampa Bay Times*, July 9, 2004, https://bit.ly/3sYHv3I.
3. Maya Bell, "¡Ole!—El Tiempo de Martinez Es Aqui, You All," *Orlando Sentinel*, January 7, 1987, https://bit.ly/3KzCFQe.
4. My estimate, based on single-year-of-age data for Florida from 1985 to 1986 is that just under half of the increase in the state's non-infant and non-elderly population was attributable to baby boomers.
5. As you may recall from chapter 5.
6. *The Blue Valley Farmer*, August 20, 1931.
7. "*New State Ice Co. v. Liebmann*," LII/Legal Information Institute, https://bit.ly/37jLkbq.
8. "Beautiful New Liebmann Ice Plant Formally Opens Saturday," *El Reno Daily Tribune*, June 9, 1932.
9. "Beautiful New Liebmann Ice Plant Formally Opens Saturday."
10. As discussed in chapter 9.
11. As discussed in chapter 4.
12. "State Legislator Demographics," National Conference of State Legislatures, 2020, https://bit.ly/3CyEl9Z.
13. Philip Bump, "In 47 of 50 States, Non-Whites Are Underrepresented in State Legislatures," *The Washington Post*, December 10, 2021, https://bit.ly/3hSF3W7.
14. Patrick Marley and Bill Glauber, "Ron Johnson Calls for Having Republican Lawmakers Take Over Federal Elections in Wisconsin," *Milwaukee Journal Sentinel*, November 10, 2021, https://bit.ly/3pUD0VQ.
15. Philip Bump, "The Use of Unfounded Fraud Claims to Limit Voting Access Is More Obvious Than Ever," *The Washington Post*, September 1, 2021, https://bit.ly/3I0qQRJ.
16. Reid J. Epstein, "Wisconsin Republicans Push to Take Over the State's Elections," *The New York Times*, November 19, 2021, sec. U.S., https://bit.ly/3J1MUg6.
17. U.S. Census Bureau, "State-to-State Migration Flows," Census.gov, October 8, 2021, https://bit.ly/37nwukl.
18. Interestingly, Cuban-born Hispanics in Florida are more likely than other foreign-born Hispanics to be naturalized.
19. As discussed in chapter 9.
20. Lindsey Bever, "America's Getting Older, Except in the Energy Rush States in the Plains," *The Washington Post*, June 26, 2014, https://bit.ly/3sU6CVj.
21. Steven A. McAlpine and Jeremy R. Porter, "Estimating Recent Local Impacts of Sea-Level Rise on Current Real-Estate Losses: A Housing Market Case Study in Miami-Dade, Florida," *Population Research and Policy Review* 37, no. 6 (December 2018): 871–95, https://bit.ly/3vVTEIC.
22. Using vintage 2019 estimates.
23. Both are U.S. Census Bureau data. The current demographics are 2019 vintage one-year estimates.
24. If you're curious, though, I have written about this in the past. See: Philip Bump, "You're

Worried About Trump? In 100 Years, Robots Might Be Running for President," *The Washington Post*, December 10, 2015, https://bit.ly/37cwYJL.

25. As of December 2021. See: https://bit.ly/37iO60B.
26. Chapter 4.
27. See chapter 9.
28. Richard Alba, *The Great Demographic Illusion: Majority, Minority, and the Expanding American Mainstream* (Princeton: Princeton University Press, 2020).
29. See: Carlson, Tucker.
30. Abby Budiman, "Americans Are More Positive About the Long-Term Rise in U.S. Racial and Ethnic Diversity Than in 2016," Pew Research Center, https://bit.ly/3CxqLDH.
31. Author analysis of Bureau of Labor Statistics data.
32. See chapter 6.
33. National Academies of Sciences, Engineering, and Medicine.
34. See chapter 6.
35. As described in chapter 9.

Index